Turkey and the EU: Accession and Reform

Turkish accession to the European Union is an important but controversial item on the agenda of the European Union. By focusing on the various domestic sources that drive Turkish politics, this comprehensive study of both classic and new topics supported by fresh, new insights fills a void in the current literature on Turkey–EU relations.

This volume is a comprehensive, state of the art study of domestic politics and policies and their role in Turkey's EU accession. Contributions are obtained from established scholars, acknowledged for their expertise in their respective fields. The content is structured along issues, dynamics, actors and policies that drive Turkish politics and it provides an integrated assessment of the dynamics in Turkey–EU relations to general readers, students and specialists in EU Enlargement and Turkish politics alike.

Original contributions to 'classic' topics such as the customs union, human rights, military, civil society, public and elite opinion, political parties and the Kurdish issue are made by assessing the domestic sources of recent developments during the negotiations period. In addition, 'new' topics are included that previously have not been covered or analysed in volumes on Turkish–EU relations such as the Alevi issue, European Turks, corruption in Turkey, and Turkish parliamentary elite opinion on Turkey and the EU.

This book was published as double special issue of *South European Society and Politics*.

Gamze Avcı is a Lecturer at University College Utrecht at Utrecht University in the Netherlands. She received her MA, PhD, at the University of Georgia in the US and her MSc from the London School of Economics. Her areas of research are primarily Turkey's relationship with the European Union and Turkish immigration to Western Europe.

Ali Çarkoğlu is a Professor of Political Science at the College of Administrative Sciences and Economics at Koç University, Istanbul, Turkey. He received his PhD at State University of New York-Binghamton in 1994. His areas of research interest are comparative politics, voting behaviour, public opinion and party politics in Turkey.

Turkey and the EU: Accession and Reform

Edited by
Gamze Avcı and Ali Çarkoğlu

LONDON AND NEW YORK

First published 2013
by Routledge
2 Park Square, Milton Park, Abingdon, Oxfordshire OX14 4RN

Simultaneously published in the USA and Canada
by Routledge
711 Third Avenue, New York, NY 10017

First issued in paperback 2014

Routledge is an imprint of the Taylor and Francis Group, an informa business

© 2013 Taylor & Francis

This book is a reproduction of *South European Society and Politics*, vol. 16, issues 2 and 3. The Publisher requests to those authors who may be citing this book to state, also, the bibliographical details of the special issue on which the book was based.

All rights reserved. No part of this book may be reprinted or reproduced or utilised in any form or by any electronic, mechanical, or other means, now known or hereafter invented, including photocopying and recording, or in any information storage or retrieval system, without permission in writing from the publishers.

Trademark notice: Product or corporate names may be trademarks or registered trademarks, and are used only for identification and explanation without intent to infringe.

British Library Cataloguing in Publication Data
A catalogue record for this book is available from the British Library

ISBN13: 978-0-415-61532-7 (hbk)
ISBN13: 978-0-415-75476-7 (pbk)

Typeset in Times New Roman
by Taylor & Francis Books

Publisher's Note
The publisher would like to make readers aware that the chapters in this book may be referred to as articles as they are identical to the articles published in the special issue. The publisher accepts responsibility for any inconsistencies that may have arisen in the course of preparing this volume for print.

Contents

Part I: Historical Perspectives

1. Introduction: Taking Stock of the Dynamics that Shape EU Reforms
   in Turkey
   Gamze Avcı and *Ali Çarkoğlu*   1

2. Speeding up or Slowing down? Lessons from the Last Enlargement
   on the Dynamics of Enlargement-Driven Reform
   Antoaneta L. Dimitrova   13

3. The EU–Turkey Customs Union Fifteen Years Later: Better, Yet not
   the Best Alternative
   Kamil Yılmaz   27

4. Challenges of Triangular Relations: The US, the EU, and Turkish Accession
   Sabri Sayarı   43

Part II: Political Change through EU Reforms

5. The Turkish–EU Odyssey and Political Regime Change in Turkey
   Ersin Kalaycıoğlu   57

6. Turkish Foreign Policy, its Domestic Determinants and the Role of the
   European Union
   Meltem Müftüler-Baç   71

7. The Impact of EU-Driven Reforms on the Political Autonomy of the
   Turkish Military
   Yaprak Gürsoy   85

8. Is Corruption a Drawback to Turkey's Accession to the European Union?
   Fikret Adaman   101

CONTENTS

Part III: Human Rights and Minorities

9. Human Rights and Turkey's EU Accession Process: Internal and
   External Dynamics, 2005–10
   William Hale — 115

10. The Kurdish Issue in Turkey: Limits of European Union Reform
    Kemal Kirişci — 127

11. A Precarious Relationship: The Alevi Minority, the Turkish State
    and the EU
    Ali Çarkoğlu and *Nazlı Çağın Bilgili* — 143

Part IV: Mass Public Opinion, Elites and Civil Society

12. Diagnosing Trends and Determinants in Public Support for Turkey's
    EU Membership
    Ali Çarkoğlu and *Çiğdem Kentmen* — 157

13. Interacting Actors: The EU and Civil Society in Turkey
    Ahmet İçduygu — 173

14. The Turkish Parliamentary Elite and the EU: Mapping Attitudes towards
    the European Union
    Sait Akşit, Özgehan Şenyuva and *Işık Gürleyen* — 187

Part V: Political Parties

15. The Justice and Development Party and the EU: Political Pragmatism in
    a Changing Environment
    Gamze Avcı — 201

16. The Republican People's Party and Turkey's EU Membership
    Ödül Celep — 215

17. The Nationalist Movement Party's Euroscepticism: Party Ideology
    Meets Strategy
    Gamze Avcı — 227

Part VI: The European Response

18. Between Reason and Emotion: Popular Discourses on Turkey's Membership
    of the EU
    Bernard Steunenberg, Simay Petek and *Christiane Rüth* — 241

19. Turkish Accession and Defining the Boundaries of Nationalism and
    Supranationalism: Discourses in the European Commission
    Senem Aydın Düzgit and *Semin Suvarierol* — 261

20. Turcoscepticism and Threat Perception: European Public and Elite Opinion
    on Turkey's Protracted EU Membership
    Ebru Ş. Canan-Sokullu — 275

CONTENTS

21. Euro-Turks as a Force in EU–Turkey Relations
Ayhan Kaya   291

Index   305

INTRODUCTION

Taking Stock of the Dynamics that Shape EU Reforms in Turkey

Gamze Avcı and Ali Çarkoğlu

The aim of this introductory article is to present the objectives, contents and main findings of the special issue on 'transformative power' of the European Union (EU) in Turkey. We discuss how this publication differs in its approach to Turkish–EU relations. Finally, we examine and connect the key findings of the individual articles, with the purpose of illustrating the logic and pace of (EU-related) domestic reforms in Turkey.

Reform has been on the political agenda of modern Turkey since the concluding phase of the Ottoman Empire (Davison 1963; Hanioğlu 2008; Moreau 2010). Similarly, throughout its Republican history, Turkey consistently looked towards the West, and in particular Europe, in search of political and economic models. One might expect that this European orientation would result in a smooth accession to the European Union (EU). But the relationship with the EU, which started formally as early as the 1963 Ankara Agreement, has had various ups and downs (Müftüler-Baç 1997; Öniş 2000; Uğur 1999).

Turkey's pursuit of EU membership took a major turn in December 1999, when the Helsinki Council recognised Turkey as an EU candidate country. This belated development gained pace in 2001 when the then outgoing three-party coalition led by Prime Minister Bülent Ecevit of the Democratic Left Party (Demokratik Sol Parti, DSP) pushed through wide-ranging reforms. The Justice and Development Party (Adalet ve Kalkınma Partisi, AKP), a conservative party with religious roots, replaced the broad-based coalition in 2002, and as of early 2011, moving towards its third general election in June 2011, remains, at least on paper, committed to EU membership and the necessary reforms. At the same time, it appears that the reforms are not complete and that there are particular problems in many areas of reform and their implementation.

Today, more than a decade after the decision to recognise Turkey as a candidate, the conditions for accession together with pressures for further adaptation and policy convergence prompt s to study what the impact of the EU and required reforms has been on domestic change in Turkey.[1] Therefore, the central question we raise in this special issue is: 'What is the "transformative power" of the EU in Turkey?'[2] Related to this, we inquire, 'How and why do differences remain between the two sides?' Furthermore, we investigate what explains the limitations or the absence of EU influence. Hence, the contributions to this volume discuss and question the impact— or lack thereof—of the EU in various issue areas by providing empirical perspectives on domestic politics and institutions, government and administration, public policies, political actors and interest groups, as well as the relevant international and global context. We isolate and distinguish the domestic bases of reform, rather than focusing exclusively on the impact of foreign policy developments and/or presenting a compilation of developments in political, security and socio-economic realms as has been typically done in recent EU–Turkey studies (Arıkan 2006; Arvanitopoulos 2009; Çakır 2010; Joseph 2007; LaGro & Jorgensen 2007; Lake 2005).

The Turkish case is a critical one for researchers in EU studies. Although it exhibits similarities with other EU member states, it also presents unique challenges for the EU accession process. As a rule, the latter has numerous 'mechanisms' such as financial aid and technical advice that effect change and transformation in candidate countries. By and large, there are also intervening variables in the transformation process, such as the asymmetry of the relationship with the EU and the uncertainty of the accession process (see Dimitrova in this volume). However, in the Turkish case there are added factors that limit the EU's role. First of all, on the Turkish side, there is a perceived weakness of EU commitment towards Turkey's membership. Second, and linked to the EU's lack of commitment, which is based on weak popular support within the EU for Turkish membership, Turkish public support for EU membership is declining (McLaren 2007; Çarkoğlu & Kentmen in this volume). As a consequence of both, the EU's leverage and conditionality mechanisms are not working to their full potential. Third, there is little congruence between broad party ideologies and EU-related positions (see Avcı & Celep in this volume). Fourth and finally, there are historical forces that work against a smooth EU candidacy (Deringil 2007). Altogether, these constraints make the EU a more complex political resource than it has been with other candidate countries.

Objectives

Our aim in this volume is to describe, analyse and explain the larger social, economic and political dynamics that shape the incentives and preferences of relevant domestic actors and groups that either support or oppose the EU accession process. For that reason, the argumentation, activities and support bases of these various groups and actors are mapped out. An important consideration in the articles is why, in different issue areas, we see different levels of success in meeting required EU standards, in surpassing thresholds of policy harmonisation and in plainly cooperating with European counterparts. In those cases where there is more of a mixed picture, where success and failure alternate, the articles investigate which domestic actors have been more influential. In which specific sectors are domestic players more successful or influential in the adjustment to EU standards? How do we account for differences across specific sectors and policy areas and how do they differ in terms of the relevant political actors?

By doing this, we aim to provide an in-depth analysis of the role of the EU and other actors in the changes that have taken place in Turkey in the last decade. The literature on candidate country Europeanisation—i.e. the impact of the EU on domestic politics and policies—has developed primarily in the context of the EU's eastern enlargement (for a discussion of Europeanisation in new member and candidate states, see Sedelmeier 2006). We believe that our comprehensive analysis of domestic actors, issues and dynamics in Turkey–EU relations is not only of relevance for scholars of Turkish politics but also for scholars working on Europeanisation and comparative aspects of European integration. Ultimately, however, we hope that this study will provide impetus for more in-depth studies on Turkey and the EU.

Structure

Following a broader political and economic contextualisation of EU–Turkish relations, the articles are grouped into six areas: (1) introduction, (2) political change through EU reform, (3) the case of human rights and minorities, (4) mass public opinion, elites and civil society, (5) political parties and (6) the European response.

The introductory section of the volume covers a broad contextualisation of EU–Turkey relations. For that reason, the Turkish case is first positioned within the larger EU enlargement experience. Next, an economic evaluation of Turkey's customs union agreement with the EU is presented, which is followed by an evaluation of the United States (US) 'anchor' as a supporting factor in shaping EU–Turkey relations. The ensuing analyses in the subsequent section primarily focus on the phenomenon of 'change' in Turkish politics at large which is attributable to EU reforms. Therefore, authors in this section focus on political regime change via constitutional amendments and on corruption as an impediment to further reform in especially the economic arena. Furthermore, attention is paid to the control of the military by civilian authorities and to domestic sources of foreign policy shifts that lead to a divergence or convergence between Turkish and European foreign policy trends. In the third section of the special issue, a closer look is then directed towards developments and change in the human rights area in general as well as more specifically in ethnic and sectarian minority issues.

Then, authors in the fourth section focus on foundations of support and resistance to change associated with EU reforms. Following a closer inspection of mass public opinion trends in support of EU membership for Turkey, the nature of civil society is explored and the approach of parliamentary elites towards EU–Turkey relations are investigated. Subsequently, in the fifth section, detailed analyses are presented of major political parties as key actors that shape Turkey's relations with the EU.

The final section focuses on European responses to developments on the Turkish side and in relations between the EU and Turkey. It begins with a closer inspection of the rhetoric adopted in the European media towards Turkey's EU membership and continues with an article focusing on the bureaucratic elites of the European Commission. The section continues with a broader examination of European public and elite opinion on Turkey's protracted bid for membership, and concludes with an analysis of the case of Euro-Turks as a source of support or reluctance in Europe towards Turkish membership.

Contexts and Challenges

Although the Turkish candidacy is, among the remaining candidates, the oldest case, one may draw on other enlargement experiences such as that of the Central and Eastern European countries (CEECs). Therefore, the volume starts with an article by Antoaneta Dimitrova which discusses post-communist processes of transformation and Europeanisation of the CEECs. Dimitrova's discussion establishes a valuable framework for comparison on the basis of the CEEC enlargement experience and concludes with a discussion of parallels with and differences from Turkey's accession negotiations. She highlights the mechanisms that have driven reform in other candidate countries and investigates whether the same conditions and mechanisms work for Turkey. Furthermore, Dimitrova provides a framework of analysis by drawing attention to the role of key concepts of 'credibility of conditionality' and 'asymmetry in relations' between the EU and candidate countries. As for the CEECs, both of these concepts emerge as being critical to the Turkish case.

In the economic realm, where integration with the EU started much earlier when Turkey entered into the Customs Union (CU) on 1 January 1996, the question is whether this has benefited Turkey. Kamil Yılmaz's contribution focuses on and evaluates the CU experiences and how it affects further integration with the EU. Yılmaz points to the mixed results in the different fields of manufacturing, competition policy and trade, and argues that, especially given the EU's 2006 change of trade strategy in favour of free trade agreements (FTAs), it would have been better for Turkey to have signed an FTA with the EU.

Sabri Sayarı tackles the rather peculiar transatlantic connection in Turkey–EU relations. The author argues that since Turkey gained formal membership status in 1999 and Ankara began negotiations with Brussels in 2005 the tension between the US and its European allies over Turkish membership has somewhat lessened. Nevertheless, he observes that the differences between the US and European perspectives on Turkey's European integration have continued to pose a challenge to strengthening cooperation and solidarity in transatlantic ties.

Domestic Politics and Uneven Patterns in EU Reforms

EU accession dynamics and enlargement policy are considered effective (albeit limited) tools for democratisation in candidate countries (Pridham 2005). Ersin Kalaycıoğlu describes the established roots and characteristics of the current democratic regime in Turkey and analyses whether and how the EU has impacted on the democratisation of the political regime in Turkey. His study draws attention to the power struggles between the ruling AKP and other political actors in the post-2002 period, and how these have influenced the discussion around reform in different periods. Critical in Kalaycıoğlu's argument is that constitutional reforms in Turkey have a long-term domestic agenda that is independent of the push and pull factors emanating from the EU.

Turkey's foreign policy presents a paradox for Turkey's relations with the EU. As Turkey continues to negotiate accession to the EU, the country's foreign policy orientation—in particular its proactive engagement in the neighbouring region—is being increasingly questioned. In this context, Meltem Müftüler Baç investigates whether and how Turkish foreign policy has changed in recent years, specifically relating it to the EU accession process and uncovering the main dynamics behind these changes. Her main finding is that the domestic changes in Turkey have led to a reshuffling of foreign policy objectives and placed a renewed emphasis on improving relations with the country's non-EU neighbours. In other words, what emerges is that EU reforms and 'Europeanisation' have possibly contributed to more versatile and independent foreign policy choices in Turkey.

One of the key areas of democratisation reform in Turkey concerns the role and mission of the military. Although the military has traditionally looked 'west', the EU has been keen on reducing the military's role in Turkey. Yaprak Gürsoy looks at how EU-related reforms have impacted on the balance of civil–military relations and the role of the military in politics. She concludes that the reforms have affected the political autonomy of the military but appear to be insufficient to reduce it to a secondary player in Turkish politics, subordinate to civilian control, especially in the areas of coordination of the defence sector and intelligence.

The final article in this section elaborates on the question of whether or not the current level of corruption in Turkey constitutes a major drawback for EU membership. Fikret Adaman argues that a full-scale anti-corruption strategy should include not only policing-type regulations and improved institutional structures, but also systemic reforms to deal with patron–client networking and informality.

EU Credibility and Reforms in Human Rights

Turkey's human rights record, in particular in the field of minorities, has been highly politicised in the Turkey–EU debate. Against this background, William Hale attempts to explain the relative strength of external and internal factors in aiding or impeding the extension of civil liberties in Turkey. His analysis of the historical record of Turkish–EU relations since 2001 shows that, although the Copenhagen criteria provided a powerful boost, it is difficult to establish a 'neat' linkage between the Turkey–EU relationship and human rights improvements in Turkey. Hale also underlines that the moment the credibility of the EU commitment to Turkey's full membership declined, the human rights improvements appeared to stop. The recent move by the AKP government for further democratisation in the field of ethnic and sectarian minority rights appears to be primarily motivated by domestic policy concerns rather than EU pressures.

William Hale's findings are further strengthened by the articles on the Kurdish question and the Alevi issue. Kemal Kirişçi questions why the reforms induced by the EU have failed to resolve the Kurdish question in Turkey. He argues that the EU's decision to grant Turkey a prospect of membership helped to empower the liberal approach to the Kurdish question. Yet, he also finds that the EU, at least partly, bears responsibility for the failure of the Kurdish 'opening' and the resolution of the Kurdish problem in Turkey. Ali Çarkoğlu and Nazlı Çağın Bilgili's analysis of the Alevi minority similarly demonstrates that the EU integration process at some point may have been supportive of further advancing the Alevi community's conditions. However, as the political will and credibility of the EU slowly disappeared, the reform initiatives in Turkey began to obtain their energy from primarily domestic sources and in many instances lost their earlier momentum.

Who Is Afraid of the EU?

Public opinion has come to play a crucial role in European integration. This is valid for EU member states but also for public opinion in candidate countries and European enlargement in particular (Gabel 1998; Grabbe & Hughes 1999). Thus, Ali Çarkoğlu and Çiğdem Kentmen have analysed levels of and variations in Turkish public opinion support for the EU. Using extensive survey data, the authors first of all diagnose declining support in Turkey for EU membership and test whether economic considerations, support for democracy, attachment to national identity and religiosity affect Turkish individuals' attitudes toward Turkey's EU membership. They find that perceived national economic conditions and national identity have a negative impact on attitudes. Contrary to their expectation, religion exerts no statistically significant influence over attitudes while it is confirmed that satisfaction with democracy is positively linked to Turkish public support for EU membership. The authors conclude by underlining the need to further evaluate the rising nationalist fervour and reactionary rhetoric in the country in response to recent reforms concerning the ethnic and sectarian minorities and which underlie the declining support for EU membership.

The EU considers a strong civil society to be an important criterion in European enlargement (see COM [Communication from the Commission] 2005). In this context, civil society is often assumed to be naturally pro-EU. Ahmet İçduygu addresses this issue and shows that the civil society discourse in Turkey remains primarily pro-EU. However, he argues that, unlike in earlier times, civil society organisations in Turkey no longer prefer to use the EU as a framework on every issue.

The author underlines that the involvement of civil society organisations in the EU setting is crucial and symbiotic, and that both stand to gain from collaborating on issues of European integration. In this context, he claims that a failure to fully empower civil society in Turkey as a key player could become a concern for the future.

Sait Akşit, Özgehan Şenyuva and Işık Gürleyen map out the opinions and attitudes of the Turkish parliamentary elite regarding their general evaluations of the EU and Turkish membership in particular. Their findings indicate that the support of Turkish parliamentarians from both government and opposition parties for Turkey's EU membership is strong. Similarly, the EU has a rather positive image in the eyes of the member of parliament (MPs) and they believe that Turkey would benefit from being an EU member. However, the MPs appear to have a low level of trust in the EU and its institutions, and their national identity and attachment to Turkish nationality are very strong whereas their European identity and European attachments are much lower.

Has the EU Become a Non-issue in Turkish Politics?

Political parties are central and critical to the functioning of representative democracies. They also play a key role in conditioning domestic attitudes towards European integration. This is no different in Turkey. Gamze Avcı evaluates the claim that the governing AKP has reversed its EU course since the beginning of negotiations in 2005. Her conclusion is that the AKP's basic long-term EU commitment has not fundamentally changed, but that the AKP has reverted to a 'passive activism' due to the dynamics and nature of EU negotiations and changes in domestic and European politics. Ödül Celep discusses the Euroscepticism of the official opposition, the CHP (Cumhuriyet Halk Partisi—Republican People's Party), the traditionally pro-Western founding party of Turkey. Celep argues that the CHP's controversial stance in the last decade is explained by domestic political power struggles, i.e. the CHP being in opposition and fighting electorally and politically with the ruling AKP. The analysis of the ultra-nationalist MHP (Milliyetçi Hareket Partisi—Nationalist Movement Party) by Gamze Avcı describes how this party has consistently rejected Turkey's EU membership, and what conditions or specific issues have led to shifts in its position. Avcı argues that, without doubt, ideology matters for the MHP, but that shifts in degrees of Euroscepticism can be explained by strategic political considerations.

Overall, the three articles focusing on the three major political parties in Turkish politics diagnose no major ideologically motivated opposition to Turkey's EU membership. The debate around the issue of EU membership and its reforms appears to be shaped primarily by domestic electoral incentives. At the same time, the authors observe and confirm that Turkish party politics is being reshaped as a consequence of the rising electoral appeal of the ruling AKP. The opposition seems to be suffering from weakening electoral support and is opting to oppose the EU goal and EU-related reforms for the sake of opposing the AKP and with the aim of mobilising more votes for themselves from the more nationalist component of the electorate.

The European View

On the European side, there are influential players and critical issues that can impact on Turkish–EU relations. A very active player is the media. Therefore, Bernard Steunenberg, Simay Petek and Christiane Rüth analyse and compare the existing domestic discourses in Germany and Turkey on the relationship between Turkey and the EU. They explore how Turkey's EU membership is discussed and understood. They argue that domestic discourses have an impact on the accession process. If a discourse is opposed to, or even incompatible with, Turkish accession to the EU, political leaders in the EU or Turkey may have to address these concerns in order to maintain their popular support. The authors claim that these statements affect the accession negotiations, in which credibility plays an important role. The authors find that – in both Germany and Turkey – the discourses are incompatible with Turkish accession and form a serious challenge for Turkey's EU membership.

Typically, the European Commission is considered the most supranational institution of the EU and the one most 'sympathetic' towards candidate countries. Senem Aydın-Düzgit and Semin Süvarierol concentrate on assessing the boundaries of the supranationalist discourse in the European Commission. Their findings challenge the image of the Commission as a supranational actor. The authors argue that when it comes to strategic reflections on Turkey's membership the discourses of Commission officials become what in this article are termed 'Euro-nationalistic'.

The issues of religion and migration potential to Europe have long haunted Turkey's EU application. It is in that context that Ebru Canan-Sokullu focuses on the particular issue of fear of Islamic fundamentalism and the fear of immigration into Europe. Using polling data, she investigates how Islamophobic and anti-immigrationist concerns over Turkish membership reflect themselves in the form of threat-driven Turcoscepticism and how perceived threats affect public and elite attitudes towards Turkey's application for EU membership. Her analysis reveals that Islamophobia and anti-immigrationist fears contribute to Turcosceptic anxiety in Europe at the mass but not the elite level.

Is the Turkish diaspora in Europe a natural ally or an obstacle to Turkish EU accession? Ayhan Kaya concentrates on the role of Turkish migrants residing in Europe and their views on Turkey–EU relations. Kaya claims that these so-called 'Euro-Turks' have constructed various hyphenated identities in a way that successfully incorporates them into the multiple identities of Europeanness and that Euro-Turks constitute a bridge between Turkey and the EU.

Conclusions

In this special issue we have provided a case study of Turkey and the EU during the negotiations period. Turkey can also be regarded as a critical case and as such it allows us to obtain country-specific and more general findings. During the negotiations period we would expect positive effects of the EU on human rights records, democratic attitudes among citizens, and the level of democratic governance. In our studies, we observe that the EU matters for reform in Turkish politics but, more importantly, that domestic bases indeed respond to EU actors, incentives and mechanisms. However, as the EU connection weakens and the credibility of EU rewards declines, domestic politics prevails and at times constrains further reform opportunities. This is most apparent in the field of democratisation reforms and in the area of ethnic and sectarian minority rights. Our study also points to the lack of convincing transformative discourses and instead shows discourses that are incompatible with or even opposed to Turkey's EU accession, both in Turkey and in Europe. Although domestic motivation remains high among actors such as civil society (but mixed among Turkish parliamentarians and political parties), the domestic perception of the credibility of the EU's conditionality mechanism has dampened the enthusiasm for the EU among the Turkish public. Domestic themes govern the domestic agenda. Arguably, this means that the EU can act as a limited channel but not as the main driver for reform. Nevertheless, no matter who initiates reforms and how reforms are pursued, the rather unexpected outcome of the process is that Turkey is moving closer to the EU despite the EU's increasingly lukewarm attitude.

Acknowledgements

We have been working on this edited volume for more than two years. After contacting more than fifty potential authors and discussing their potential contributions, we organised a two-day workshop in Istanbul in January 2010 attended by our selected contributors, all experts in their fields. Twenty empirical case studies emerged, which focused on specific aspects of whether, how, where and through which mechanisms the EU had an impact on Turkey. We included additional articles to complement the existing case studies, and the combined effort constitutes the current volume.

Several individuals and institutions have been very helpful and instrumental in shaping this volume. First, the Netherlands Institute for Advanced Study in the Humanities and Social Sciences (NIAS)—where Ali Çarkoğlu had the opportunity to spend a sabbatical during 2008–09—gave us time and space to develop the framework of the project. Susannah Verney, the editor of *South European Society and Politics* responsible for our special issue, helped us to remain within meaningful boundaries and presented reliable advice throughout the process of bringing so many different pieces together. Mehmet Baç, the Dean of the Faculty of Arts and Social Sciences at Sabancı University, provided valuable funds for our workshop in Istanbul. We also used the Jean Monnet course module funds granted to Ali Çarkoğlu's 'Analytical Approaches to the EU' course. We would like to thank all our article reviewers for very constructive and critical comments. Finally, we would like to thank Brian Rodrigues for his thorough and careful language editing. We are grateful for all the support we were given and sincerely hope that this edited volume will lead to new insights for the study of Europeanisation and inspire further research on Turkey and the EU.

Notes

[1] For a similar approach see Çarkoğlu and Rubin (2003) and Aydın Düzgit and Çarkoğlu (2008).
[2] For a detailed analysis of the EU's transformative power, see Grabbe (2006).

References

Aydın Düzgit, S. & Çarkoğlu, A. (2008) 'Turkey: reforms for a consolidated democracy', in *International Actors, Democratisation and the Rule of Law: Anchoring Democracy?* eds L. Morlino & A. Magen, Routledge, London, pp. 120–155.

Arıkan, H. (2006) *Turkey and the EU: An Awkward Candidate for EU Membership?*, Ashgate, Aldershot.

Arvanitopoulos, C. (ed.) (2009) *Turkey's Accession to the European Union: An Unusual Candidacy*, Springer-Verlag, Berlin.

Çakır, A. E. (2010) *Fifty Years of EU–Turkey Relations: A Sisyphean Story*, Routledge, London.

COM (2005) 290 'Communication from the Commission to the Council, the European Parliament, the European Economic and Social Committee and the Committee of the Regions, civil society dialogue between the EU and candidate countries', Brussels.

Çarkoğlu, A. & Rubin, B. (eds) (2003) *Turkey and the European Union: Domestic Politics, Economic Integration, and International Dynamics*, Frank Cass, London.

Davison, R. H. (1963) *Reform in the Ottoman Empire 1856–1876*, Princeton University Press, Princeton, NJ.

Deringil, S. (2007) 'The Turks and Europe: the argument from history', *Middle Eastern Studies*, vol. 43, no. 5, pp. 709–723.

Gabel, M. (1998) 'Public opinion and European integration: an empirical test of five Theories', *Journal of Politics*, vol. 60, pp. 333–354.

Grabbe, H. (2006) *The EU's Transformative Power. Europeanisation through Conditionality in Central and Eastern Europe*, Palgrave Macmillan, New York.

Grabbe, H. & Hughes, K. (1999) 'Central and East European views on EU enlargement: political debates and public opinion', in *Back to Europe: Central and Eastern Europe and the European Union*, ed. K. Henderson, UCL Press, London, pp. 185–202.

Hanioğlu, Ş. (2008) *A Brief History of the Late Ottoman Empire*, Princeton University Press, Princeton, NJ.

Joseph, S. J. (2007) *Turkey and the European Union: Internal Dynamics and External Challenges*, Palgrave Macmillan, New York.

LaGro, E. & Jorgensen, K. E. (2007) *Turkey and the European Union: Prospects for a Difficult Encounter*, Palgrave Macmillan, New York.

Lake, M. (ed.) (2005) *The EU & Turkey: A Glittering Prize or a Millstone?* I.B. Tauris, London.

McLaren, L. (2007) 'Explaining opposition to Turkish membership of the EU', *European Union Politics*, vol. 8, no. 2, pp. 251–278.

Moreau, O. (2010) *Reformlar Çağında Osmanlı İmparatorluğu. Askeri Yeni Düzen'in İnsanları ve Fikirleri 1826–1914* [The Ottoman Empire in the Age of Reform. Men and Ideas of the Military New Order 1826–1914], İstanbul Bilgi University, Istanbul.

Müftüler-Baç, M. (1997) *Turkey's Relations with a Changing Europe*, Manchester University Press, Manchester.

Öniş, Z. (2000) 'Luxembourg, Helsinki and beyond: Turkey–EU relations', *Government and Opposition*, vol. 35, no. 4, pp. 463–483.

Pridham, G. (2005) *Designing Democracy: EU Enlargement and Regime Change in Post-Communist Europe*, Palgrave Macmillan, New York.

Sedelmeier, U. (2006) 'Europeanisation in new member and candidate states', *Living Reviews in European Governance*, vol. 1, no. 3, available online at: http://europeangovernance.livingre views.org/Articles/lreg-2011-1/.

Uğur, M. (1999) *The European Union and Turkey: An Anchor/Credibility Dilemma*, Ashgate, Aldershot.

Gamze Avcı (PhD University of Georgia) is currently a lecturer at University College of Utrecht University. Between 1997 and 2002, she worked as assistant professor in the Department of Political Science and International Relations at Boğaziçi University, Istanbul. Her research is primarily on Turkey's relationship with the EU and on Turkish immigration into Western Europe. Her work has appeared in journals such as *European Foreign Affairs Review, European Journal of Political Research, European Journal of Migration and Law* and *International Migration.*

Ali Çarkoğlu (PhD State University of New York—Binghamton) is a professor of political science at Koç University, Istanbul. His research interests are in comparative politics, voting behaviour, public opinion and party politics in Turkey. His publications have appeared in the *European Journal of Political Research, Electoral Studies, Turkish Studies, New Perspectives on Turkey, South European Society and Politics, Middle Eastern Studies, Political Studies* and in many edited volumes. His most recent book is *The Rising Tide of Conservatism in Turkey* (Palgrave Macmillan 2009, co-authored with E. Kalaycıoğlu).

Speeding up or Slowing down? Lessons from the Last Enlargement on the Dynamics of Enlargement-Driven Reform

Antoaneta L. Dimitrova

This article highlights the lessons from the European Union's (EU's) eastern enlargement relevant for Turkey. The EU's approach to candidates, developed during the last enlargement, was founded on asymmetry, objectivity and conditionality, with the latter evolving as the key policy tool. Clearly, some of the tools and rules of the previous enlargement cannot work as well with Turkey. The article examines the mechanisms underlying the success of conditionality and sketches some of the scope conditions needed for it to work in Turkey's case. Ultimately, the success of conditionality will depend on EU credibility and the preferences of domestic actors, which are more heterogeneous than in Central and Eastern European states.

The last enlargement[1] of the European Union (EU), including the post-communist states from Central and Eastern Europe (CEE) and Cyprus and Malta, was both a huge challenge for the EU and a success. The reasons why it was a challenge are well known: the large number of applicant states, their economic weakness and the need for fundamental transformations of their states and societies after communism, as well as the huge gap between their policies and the *acquis* of the EU. The reasons why enlargement was a success have emerged gradually as the process of preparation imposed its rhythm and requirements on the candidates' transformations. Ultimately, the post-communist states reformed so profoundly that the EU can look back on enlargement as its most successful foreign policy tool.[2] This is because the EU has extended stability beyond its existing borders as well as managing, to a considerable extent, to project its norms and rules to the candidate states.

The closer a candidate state is to joining the EU, the more its policies and institutions are harmonised with the EU's *acquis*. This is, however, far from an automatic process. The relative success of the eastern enlargement should not obscure the fact that, although the CEE candidates adapted to the EU's rules, other countries are not so responsive to the EU's pressure for change.[3] The current enlargement research agenda should, therefore, pay attention to the factors that make the EU a successful agent for change in candidate states, but also investigate the scope conditions that limit the working of mechanisms underpinning successful EU rule transfer through conditionality.

A first and obvious condition for EU demands for reform to work is that political parties need to be united on the goal of membership—a consensus that was so stable in CEE[4] that the EU tends to take it for granted. This may not be the case for other candidates. Furthermore, the demands of accession preparation and negotiation often overshadow the debate on why a country wants to become a member of the EU. Such a discussion, rooted in the specific domestic context and historical circumstances of a country, is a necessary prerequisite for starting to work towards accession. The assumptions underlying the reasoning of enlargement proponents should be explicated, and the main discourses in this debate should be analysed, as these play an important role in shaping domestic preferences on accession.

When the majority of domestic actors subscribe, at least symbolically, to the benefits of becoming 'European', domestic adaptation to the EU's requirements can begin. An official application to join the EU represents only the first step. Nowadays, the EU requires such a profound and broad adaptation to its rules and principles that nothing short of a country-wide mobilisation for reform is sufficient for the successful completion of the accession negotiations.

Comparative research into the adaptation of the last group of candidate states to the EU's accession requirements (Dimitrova 2004; Schimmelfennig & Sedelmeier 2005; Vachudova 2005) shows that it is the interplay between domestic factors and external pressure that creates the dynamics of reform. This paper sets out to discuss what we have learned from the last enlargement about these dynamics. The reforms made by candidates to comply with EU accession criteria have been analysed as a form of Europeanisation: 'Europeanisation East' (Schimmelfennig & Sedelmeier 2005; Héritier 2005). The most important feature of Europeanisation East is the considerable impact the EU has had on polity and policy in the candidate states even before accession. Thus, this article aims to address one of the most important puzzles surrounding EU enlargement, namely, under what conditions is the EU able to stimulate candidate states to reform?

The EU itself changed profoundly with the last enlargement; it went through a decade of institutional and policy change to prepare for the accession of CEE states. As these adjustments are covered by a rich body of literature on enlargement and institutional change, they will not be examined here. Rather, the goal of this article is to focus on the lessons of enlargement for candidate states that may want to use enlargement as a driving force for modernisation. What have we learned about the dynamics between domestic actors and the EU that produce change, and can the most important lessons of the last enlargement be applied to Turkey? Turkey is, after all, a very different country from the small and medium-sized states acceding in the last enlargement. In order to say something meaningful about Turkey's accession, we should not make automatic comparisons between CEE states and Turkey, but should carefully distinguish mechanisms that have driven reform in the candidates and investigate whether the conditions are present in Turkey for these mechanisms to work again. This paper will mostly focus on the first part of this task and proceed as follows. In the next section, I will outline the most important characteristics of the post-communist processes of transformation and Europeanisation in order to form a basis for comparison with Turkey's transformation. In the second part, I will discuss the EU's main accession rules and tools affecting Europeanisation East, with a special emphasis on conditionality. Last, I will reflect on some parallels with and differences from Turkey's accession negotiations as a way of opening the discussion about the EU and reform in Turkey which is the subject of the other articles in this special issue.

Post-communist Transformations and EU Accession: Separate but Mutually Reinforcing

The post-communist transformations of CEE states started in 1989, well before the EU accepted these countries as candidates for accession.[5] The changes in policies and polity that we now define as 'Europeanisation East' took place even later, after 1997, when the Commission's Agenda 2000 presented the candidates with a comprehensive blueprint for change.[6]

It is important for both empirical and analytical clarity to separate the processes of Europeanisation and post-communist transformation (Dimitrova 2004). Post-communist transformations comprised multiple transitions of planned to market economies, of authoritarianism to democracy, in some cases along with redefining of national identities, statehood and borders. Claus Offe's perceptive early analysis predicted that democratisation and the transformation of property rights and the economy would create mutual obstruction effects. Elites were faced with the problem of making simultaneous choices over privatisation and democratisation which made the successful completion of both more difficult (Offe 1991). As accession became a realistic option, the EU played the role of an external power that guided the choices of elites. In this sense, and with a time lag of approximately eight to ten years, Europeanisation overlapped with the multiple post-communist transformations.

It was mostly after early 1998, when negotiations actually started with the first group of candidates,[7] that processes of Europeanisation began. Initially, the main challenge was preparing to deal with EU requirements for adopting the *acquis*, divided into negotiating chapters. It must be noted that the negotiations on the *acquis* did not have much to do with democratisation, as there was little basis for it in the founding treaties (EU 2010). The EU focused, as in all enlargements, on adoption of its *acquis*, which had become much larger and more complicated after the coming into force of the internal market. As Mayhew (2000, p. 5) observed, for the CEE states, 'the internal market acquis added another large layer of new legislation to that occasioned by their own systemic reform'.

Thus, the EU's conditions and its impact were first seen, as was only fit for an economic community, in the area of the economy and the market. Stark and Bruszt (1998) have shown the importance of the EU for the emerging markets and regulatory regimes in the post-communist states. That the EU has left its mark is obvious when compared with the very different economic and regulatory models adopted, for example, by a country like Georgia in its transition to a market economy.

In contrast to the post-communist states, however, Turkey is a market economy. What is more relevant for Turkey is to establish the impact of the EU on polity, on democratisation. The reason for this is that questions of democratic transformation are at the centre of Turkey's negotiations with the EU, much more so than they were in the last enlargement. The second reason to dwell on the EU's impact on democratisation is that the approach developed by the EU in the late 1990s has served as a template for handling the negotiations with Turkey and evaluating Turkey's progress in democratisation.

To understand how the EU developed into an actor that was able to support the latter stages of democratisation in the CEE candidates, we need to examine several aspects of its influence. Having specified the channels of EU influence, we can then look at whether similar opportunities exist for the EU to influence Turkey.

The EU's impact on democracy was initially modest, but it evolved considerably over the pre-accession period. As stated above, the CEE states had already taken the most important steps to establish the basic institutions of democracy: they had free elections, they established multiparty systems, freedom of speech was being restored, parliaments and courts were learning to operate according to new rules. I argue here that the EU influence on democratisation can be seen as increasing over the time span of enlargement and evolving from passive to active leverage (see also Vachudova 2005). In the early stages of enlargement, the main aspects of the EU influence can be defined as the three Ps: presence, perception and promises.

The EU itself did not initially have the tools to influence democratisation, so, as a first step, it included clauses making the operation of the association or 'Europe' agreements (governing relations between the EU and the candidates) conditional on respect for human rights and democratic principles. The European Parliament developed a democracy initiative, but its influence in negotiations was modest in the early stages.

Arguably, it was the EU's presence as an example of successful integration of states that were both democratic and prosperous that played a role in promoting CEE democratisation in the early 1990s. When the possibility of accession arose, the EU's geographical proximity and prosperity became a source of passive leverage (Vachudova 2005). In addition, the deep crisis that followed the fall of communism made post-communist countries especially keen to look to the EU for guidance. European-Union-led reforms were accepted more easily by policymakers as the economic, political and societal crisis that accompanied the end of communism created a window of opportunity for policy change. Arguably, Turkey's successful economic development in recent years does not present a similar window of opportunity.

The second aspect of early EU influence was linked to perception. Although the EU assumed, somewhat reluctantly, the role of mentor of CEE democratisation, the connection between democratisation and joining the EU was very much present in the perceptions of CEE elites. Political leaders from Prague and Warsaw to Sofia and Bucharest committed their countries to joining the EU because they saw the EU as a guarantor of the irreversibility of democratic transitions and market reforms. As Schimmelfennig's insightful study (2001) has shown, rhetorical commitments to supporting democratisation and the unification of Europe made by Western European leaders ensured that CEE states ultimately joined the EU even when enlargement proved to be costly for the latter. These rhetorical commitments shaped the expectations of the public in CEE as well. Thus the promises of EU leaders also played a role in supporting democratisation.

The turning point that marked the evolution of the CEE applicants into candidates was the formulation of three main criteria for membership by the Copenhagen European Council in 1993, together with the acknowledgement that candidates could accede when they had fulfilled them. These well-known criteria comprised democracy, human rights and the rule of law; the existence of competitive market economies; and the ability to adopt the *acquis* of the EU. While taking on board the *acquis* had been part of every previous enlargement, the focus on markets and democracy was new. It was a response to the need to accommodate countries in transition, in the specific historical circumstances at the end of the Cold War. That a country should be a democracy to join had been considered self-evident, as all countries that had joined the EU up to that point had already been democracies.[8]

As the *acquis* could not serve as a basis for evaluating democratisation, the EU and especially the European Commission had to interpret the democracy criterion from Copenhagen at the start of the negotiations. Already in 1997, in Agenda 2000, the Commission based its recommendations for candidates ready to start negotiations partly on this criterion. Slovakia, in particular, was considered not ready to start negotiations owing to its inability to fulfil the first Copenhagen criterion on democracy. The principle that a country should fulfil the political criterion before starting negotiations was established with this precedent and later applied to Turkey.

The necessity to define democracy for the candidates forced the EU to develop its own vision and legal basis as part of 'a political struggle to set the rules by which the community would respond to applications for membership' (Thomas 2006, p. 1191). As part of the negotiations of pre-enlargement institutional reform for the Treaty of Amsterdam, the EU adopted a treaty article specifying that member states should respect democracy and the rule of law. Article 6 (former F) of the Amsterdam Treaty made the EU's commitment to fundamental democratic principles and human rights explicit and created a procedure to deal with potential violations by a EU member state. Some important analyses have claimed that, by struggling to define democracy for the candidates and for its own legislative framework, the EU was pushed towards constitutionalisation (Rittberger & Schimmelfennig 2006; Thomas 2006).

By offering the Copenhagen criteria as a template to follow, the EU limited the choices of CEE elites in the last phase of their multiple transformations, playing the role envisaged by Offe (1991) of an external stabilising power. Formulating, and later interpreting, the Copenhagen criteria also became the basis for the development of the EU's most powerful tool—detailed conditionality. Specific conditions and demands for democratic reform, which had hitherto been based on the suspension clause of the association agreements mentioned above, could now be based on the interpretation of the first Copenhagen criterion.

By formulating concrete requirements for democratic change in every regular progress report, the EU gradually altered the domestic opportunities structure in the post-communist states, empowered reformers and offered incentives even to illiberal elites to fulfil EU requirements (Vachudova 2005).

The Commission, the key actor interpreting conditions and progress, quickly learned and gathered the expertise to follow closely the process of democratic consolidation. Compensating for the lack of specific instruments, the EU used the expertise of other international actors such as the Council of Europe and the Organisation for Security and C-operation in Europe (OSCE). The Commission also gained insights into democratisation processes by drawing on advice from non-governmental actors and experts in the post-communist states themselves.

Using this expertise, the EU ensured that its pre-accession instruments, such as for example the Accession Partnerships and the Regular Progress reports, created a sort of roadmap for further democratic consolidation and monitored human and minority rights. Even though some observers have argued that the EU's position in areas such as minority rights has been inconsistent and has weakened after accession (Schwellnus 2005), following these aspects of democratisation helped new democracies, especially fragile regimes in Slovakia, Bulgaria and Romania, to avoid sliding back into authoritarianism.

It must be noted, however, that the process of accession did not bring only positive influences for democracy. It is widely accepted that the structure of the accession negotiations privileges executives over parliaments (Grabbe 2001, pp. 1016–1017). It is also clear that the pressures of pre-accession adaptation and conditionality led to speedy adoption of many new policies and institutional rules without serious political and societal debate in CEE (Dimitrova 2004; 2010). Despite this imbalance, and based on the arguments listed above, one has to agree with analysts who have noted that the countries where democratisation, however imperfect, has endured are the ones that have attained EU membership (Ekiert 2008).

Linking this discussion with the findings of the Europeanisation literature[9] provides an interesting contrast with the effects of the EU on its older member states. Starting from the widely used conceptualisation of Europeanisation as a process whereby the EU's rules affect policies, polity and politics, it is clear that the EU has affected polity and politics in candidate states much more than in the older member states (Grabbe 2001; Héritier 2005; p. 208; Vachudova 2005). Besides the channels for influencing polity and politics outlined above, Europeanisation East was affected most by the tools and rules that the EU developed in the process of negotiations. Before examining these in more detail, the question needs to be addressed of whether Turkey is in a similar state of transformation, allowing the EU to play the role it played in Eastern Europe.

Given that aspects of Turkey's transformation are the subject of a number of articles in this issue, here I will only sketch the obvious parallels and differences between CEE countries and Turkey as candidates for EU accession. The main similarity is that Turkey's political system has been in flux for many decades and can be defined as undergoing a protracted and uncertain process of democratisation. The scope of Turkey's transformation is, however, less extensive than that of the post-communist states—for example, as already mentioned above, Turkey is already a market economy that has customs union links with the EU.

Another obvious and crucial difference is linked to Turkey's size, location and historical legacies, which all differ dramatically from those of CEE states. Turkey is a large country in terms of both population and territory. Apart from its size, its geographical location is such that it can easily play the role of a regional power without being an EU member. Compared with Central European states, Turkey's size, geopolitical importance and economic situation make it much less susceptible to the EU's passive leverage. Grabbe's (2001, p. 1015) observation that Poland was the only CEE state able to bargain hard with the EU, because it was seen as impossible to exclude because of its size and geopolitical importance, is relevant to Turkey's case. At the same time, perceptions of Turkey's 'otherness' featuring in the discourses found by Steunenberg, Petek and Ruth (in this issue) may mean that Turkey's size may be interpreted as a factor against it.

The puzzle remains as to whether the choice of Turkish elites to engage in the process of accession leaves the country open to Europeanising influences and especially conditionality, the EU's main tool of inducing reform. Before addressing this, I will first look at the rules and tools developed in the course of the last enlargement and the mechanisms underlying the main EU tool, conditionality.

The Rules and Tools of EU Enlargement

The preparation for enlargement on the side of the EU was driven by a set of enlargement rules that can be described as enlargement governance. It is a hierarchical mode of governance and its main features are asymmetry, complexity and conditionality (Dimitrova 2002; Maniokas 2005). Another major feature emerging in the last enlargement is the Commission's gatekeeping role, linked to the framing of negotiations as an objective and technical exercise. I will briefly discuss these features of enlargement governance in turn.

Asymmetry

Similar to past enlargements, the EU's approach to accession negotiations has been that they are only about adoption of the *acquis*, 'taking on board the rules of the club' (Avery & Cameron 1998). In the words of the former director of the European Commission's Enlargement Directorate, E. Landaburu (2007, p. 10), 'enlargement implies de facto that there are candidate countries which are willing to assimilate to the existing centre by integrating its model'. This meant that negotiations were not open to bargaining or compromises between equals. Furthermore, the last enlargement witnessed increased asymmetry between candidates and the EU, evident for example in the change from bilateral enlargement instruments such as the association agreements to unilateral ones such as the Accession Partnerships (APs) (Maniokas 2005, p. 42).

'Objectivity'

If negotiations are about how candidates are adapting to the *acquis*, a crucial place is reserved for the actor that has the task of judging their progress. This actor has been the European Commission. In the last enlargement, the Commission's role went beyond the technical, and it became an important political actor in the process of enlargement (Christoffersen 2007, p. 36). Because of its task of interpreting the *acquis* and judging candidates' progress, the Commission became a gatekeeper of the process of enlargement and is likely to keep this role in the future.

An important consequence of the Commission's central role in interpreting the accession criteria was the definition of negotiations as technical and objective. Aware of the enormous political sensitivity of selecting the first countries to start accession negotiations, the Commission framed the issue in terms of objective evaluation of readiness to adopt the *acquis*. 'It was necessary', as former Commission officials Avery and Cameron testify about the initial Agenda 2000 Opinions, 'to ensure scrupulous equality of treatment in the analysis, and a secure basis of comparison for the conclusions' (1998, p. 37). Faced with various political arguments, the Commission decided on 'an objective approach instead of a political one' (Christoffersen 2007, p. 31; Friis 1998). Subsequent monitoring through Regular Reports and the differentiation of candidates' progress were more acceptable because of the frame of objectivity (Grabbe 2003). The use of the objectivity frame, however, has created an inflated perception of the measurability of progress, which may be justified for economic data but is difficult to substantiate for democratic reforms, which remain the main focus of negotiations with Turkey.

Besides the underlying rules of the process, new institutional tools were created during the last enlargement that will remain as features of the EU's approach to future candidates. The most important institutional tools that the EU developed for the first time in the eastern enlargement were the APs and the Regular Reports. These and all other EU instruments such, as financial support, were underpinned by ever-increasing conditionality.

Institutional Tools and Conditionality

The APs were adopted as Council Regulations and set short-, medium- and long-term reform priorities for reform in the candidate states more or less unilaterally. Candidates were expected to respond to the APs by adopting National Programmes for the Adoption of the Acquis (NPAAs) strategy documents that more or less replicated the order of priorities of the APs. The APs have been criticised for their one-sided approach, embodying the asymmetry of the negotiations.

Turkey's response to the adoption of the revised AP in 2006 is an interesting illustration of the country's different reaction to tools that worked well in the case of CEE. The Council of the EU adopted Turkey's AP in 2001 and revised versions in May 2003 and January 2006. Turkey responded by adopting the first version of its NPAA in 2001 and the second in 2003. The last version was only adopted by the Turkish parliament in 2009, after almost three years' delay. The delay, coupled with the delayed appointment of a new independent chief negotiator, indicates that Turkish politicians may have started using a selective approach to the EU's instruments. The possible reasons for this will be discussed in the next section dealing with the mechanisms underpinning the effectiveness of EU conditionality.

The Regular Progress Reports presented yearly by the Commission from 1997 onwards are a tool that has been crucial in the application of the EU's most important policy instrument, conditionality. Conditionality has been the subject of numerous analyses that have applied different theoretical perspectives to discover the mechanisms that made it such a successful policy tool. Before exploring these mechanisms, it must be pointed out that conditionality remains the most favoured EU policy tool, both in enlargement negotiations and in other areas such as the European Neighbourhood Policy (ENP). The mechanism underlying conditionality, however, is based on the interplay between external incentives and domestic preferences. Domestic preferences and the configuration of domestic actors differ in every enlargement, for every candidate and also over time. So even though conditionality remains a key EU tool, whether it works depends on the actual combination of credibility of external incentives and domestic actors' preferences.

Mechanisms Underlying Conditionality

Conditionality is the main enlargement policy tool of the EU credited with successfully driving candidate countries to change. Recent analyses suggest the effect of conditionality is based on a rational mechanism whereby domestic actors take into account external incentives and choose the best course of action. The cost–benefit calculations of key domestic actors lead to their responses to EU demands for change (Schimmelfennig & Sedelmeier 2005; Vachudova 2005; Steunenberg & Dimitrova 2007).

In such a framework, the effectiveness of conditionality depends on supply and demand factors. In terms of the supply side of EU conditionality, research focusing on the EU's rewards and punishments shows that, regardless of domestic responses, if the credibility of accession is diminished, compliance with EU demands is negatively affected. It is clear that if the moment of accession is too far away or too close, domestic elites slow down their reform efforts (Steunenberg & Dimitrova 2007).

Research focusing on the demand side of conditionality shows that there are certain configurations of preferences of key domestic political actors on two sets of issues, namely for liberal democracy and for EU accession, that make elites respond to conditionality with reform. According to Vachudova, the different regimes in transition in CEE, liberal and illiberal democracies, responded differently to EU democratic reform demands (2005, pp. 25–61). In liberal regimes such as the Czech Republic or Hungary, EU conditionality reinforced domestic strategies of reform (2005, p. 81). For illiberal regimes, EU conditionality played an even more important role, by helping to change the domestic balance of power in favour of reformers and making the political system more competitive (2005, pp. 139–179).

What this model explains less well is why illiberal political parties also ultimately contributed to the fulfilment of EU demands and took the steps required for accession. I argue here that the most important scope condition for EU conditionality to work was a general commitment by all political parties, including nationalists and former communists, to EU accession. With the exception of a few marginal political parties, no major party opposed EU membership, even though some political actors played with Euroscepticism.

The mechanism underlying conditionality, however, would fail if a mainstream political party stood against accession on principle, or if major political and societal forces subscribed to a different ideological project than the EU's free market and liberal democracy. Based on this discussion, we can assume that there is a range of domestic preferences, in terms of public opinion, outside which it is not worthwhile for political leaders to persevere on the path to the EU. If, for example, leaders are elected on a nationalist platform, it is likely that being an advocate for EU accession will not be a winning electoral strategy. In addition to domestic preferences, domestic political institutions mediate external influences. For example, the electoral costs for complying with EU demands may be too high for leaders elected via a preference aggregation rule that gathers the ethnic vote of a particular group. Furthermore, we can expect that when EU demands affect the power base of key veto players, the costs of compliance for such actors will be too high.

In Conclusion: Domestic Preferences on EU Accession Remain Key

Based on the analysis above, in conclusion I offer a few final comments on whether the enlargement rules and tools defined in the last enlargement represent a problem for Turkey.

As discussed above, Turkey is a large country, with significant economic and demographic potential and, in the last decade, strong economic growth. This means that the asymmetric character of enlargement negotiations is particularly problematic for Turkey. There are tensions on both the EU and Turkish sides. On the one hand, Turkey, like any large state engaged in international negotiations, is aware of its importance in the international arena, which makes it less inclined to follow EU demands. On the other hand, the EU has applied its usual asymmetric approach in the negotiations with Turkey, treating it as any other applicant state expected to follow EU positions unilaterally.

Turkish politicians, clearly, also have problems with the EU's interpretation of the democracy criterion in the context of the enlargement's objectivity frame. When new aspects of democracy, procedural or substantive, become the subject of discussion between the EU and a candidate, this clashes with the assumption underlying the objectivity frame that conditions are fixed. Turkish politicians often react by complaining that the EU is moving the goalposts or creating new conditions.

Besides Turkey's reaction to the EU's tools, there are two major questions that should be considered in further discussion. Following from the discussion above, the first question is whether, regardless of domestic dynamics, reforms will slow because the credibility of conditionality is low due to the EU's enlargement fatigue. Such a slowing down could also be triggered by statements and discourses, in large EU member states, that are sceptical of Turkey's accession (see Steunenberg et al in this issue).

The second important question concerns domestic political cleavages and especially the cleavage between secularists and the new pro-Islamic Justice and Freedom Party (AKP). Domestic dynamics in Turkey have always been complex, but this complexity seems to have increased since the rise of the AKP and especially since this party's second electoral victory.

Research into the preferences of major parties coupled with public opinion and electoral support should give us an indication whether the conditions for effectiveness of conditionality identified above are present in Turkey, namely, whether the main actors still feel that compliance with EU demands will bring them more benefits than costs. Several of the articles in this issue shed light on this and ultimately address the question of whether key domestic actors are sufficiently committed to the goal of accession to remain on track even if reforms undermine their power base.

Notes

[1] The term 'last enlargement' is used here consistently with EU official policy according to which the accessions in 2004 and 2007 were part of the same enlargement (Verheugen 2007, p. 4). The reason for this is that the post-communist countries from CEE applied to join the EU at roughly the same time, and the rules and stages of their accession were similar almost to the end. Therefore, we speak of the accession of Estonia, the Czech Republic, Hungary, Latvia, Lithuania, Poland, Slovakia, Slovenia, Cyprus and Malta in 2004 and Bulgaria and Romania in 2007 as one round of enlargement.

[2] See for example former EU Commissioner for enlargement Verheugen (2007, pp. 4–5) for the argument why the EU considers enlargement a success.

[3] An example of a state that has a membership perspective but resists EU demands for reform is the Federation of Bosnia and Herzegovina.

[4] For the CEE candidates, the EU was a symbol of both prosperity and geopolitical security as well as of a certain kind of modernisation often described simply as being 'European'.

[5] CEE states applied for accession in the early 1990s. In June 1993, the EU recognised them as candidates when the Copenhagen European Council agreed to the CEE accession in principle, provided the candidates fulfilled a set of criteria that the Council defined.

[6] The Commission's White Paper on the internal market presented the first guidelines for change, but candidates did not start adapting to the EU's requirements until after the Agenda 2000 document came out in 1997.

[7] Estonia, the Czech Republic, Hungary, Poland and Slovenia—the so-called Luxembourg group of candidates deemed ready to start negotiations. Bulgaria, Latvia, Lithuania, Slovakia and Romania were considered not ready based on various aspects of the Copenhagen criteria and could only start negotiations in 2000 following the decisions of the Helsinki European Council in December 1999.

[8] Greece, Spain and Portugal had undergone democratic transitions relatively recently before accession, but their democratic transitions were regarded as completed and the EU was cited as a positive influence in democratic consolidation.

[9] Even though this literature is too vast to be summarised here, I am relying on its basic assumption that the EU exerts an influence on the polity, politics and policies of its member states.

References

Avery, G. & Cameron, F. (1998) *The Enlargement of the European Union*, Sheffield Academic Press, Sheffield.

Christoffersen, P. S. (2007) 'Organization of the process and beginning of negotiations', in *The Accession Story: The EU from 15 to 25*, ed. G. Vassiliou, Oxford University Press, Oxford, pp. 34–51.

Dimitrova, A. L. (2002) 'Enlargement, institution building and the EU's administrative capacity requirement', *West European Politics*, vol. 25, no. 4, pp. 171–190.

Dimitrova, A. L. (2004) 'Enlargement driven change and post communist transformations: a new perspective', in *Driven to Change: The European Union's Enlargement Viewed from the East*, ed. A. L. Dimitrova, Manchester University Press, Manchester, pp. 1–17.

Dimitrova, A. L. (2010) 'The new member states of the EU in the attermath of enlargement: do new European rules remain empty shells?' *Journal of European Public Policy*, vol. 17, no. 1, pp. 137–148.

Ekiert, G. (2008) 'Dilemmas of Europeanization: Eastern and Central Europe after the EU enlargement', *Acta Slavica Japonika*, vol. 25, pp. 1–28.

EU. (2010) 'The Amsterdam Treaty: a comprehensive guide', European Union Factsheet, available online at: http://europa.eu/legislation_summaries/institutional_affairs/treaties/amsterdam_treaty/index_en.htm

Friis, L. (1998) 'The end of the beginning of eastern enlargement—Luxembourg Summit and agenda-setting', *European Integration Online Papers*, vol. 2, no. 7, available online at: http://eiop.or.at/eiop/texte/1998-007a.htm

Grabbe, H. (2001) 'How does Europeanization affect CEE governance? Conditionality, diffusion and diversity', *Journal of European Public Policy*, vol. 8, no. 6, pp. 1013–1031.

Grabbe, H. (2003) 'Europeanization goes east: power and uncertainty in the EU accession process', in *The Politics of Europeanization*, eds K. Featherstone & C. Radaelli, Oxford University Press, Oxford, pp. 303–331.

Héritier, A. (2005) 'Europeanization research east and west: a comparative assessment', in *The Europeanization of Central and Eastern Europe*, eds F. Schimmelfennig & U. Sedelmeier, Cornell University Press, Ithaca, NY, pp. 199–210.

Landaburu, E. (2007) 'The need for enlargement and differences from previous accessions', in *The Accession Story: The EU from 15 to 25*, ed. G. Vassiliou, Oxford University Press, Oxford, pp. 9–24.

Maniokas, K. (2005) 'Road to negotiations: enlargement instruments and the development of Lithuania's status', in *Lithuania's Road to the European Union: Unification of Europe and Lithuania's EU Accession Negotiation*, eds K. Maniokas, R. Vilpišauskas & D. Žeruolis, Eugrimas, Vilnius, pp. 19–59.

Mayhew, A. (2000) 'Enlargement of the European Union: an analysis of the negotiations with the Central and Eastern European candidate countries', SEI Working Paper No. 39, Sussex European Institute, Brighton.

Offe, C. (1991) 'Capitalism by democratic design? Democratic theory facing the triple transition in East Central Europe', *Social Research*, vol. 58, no. 4, pp. 865–892.

Rittberger, B. & Schimmelfennig, F. (2006) 'Explaining the constitutionalization of the European Union', *Journal of European Public Policy*, vol. 13, no. 8, pp. 1148–1167.

Schimmelfennig, F. (2001) 'The community trap: liberal norms, rhetorical action and the eastern enlargement of the European Union', *International Organization*, vol. 55, no. 1, pp. 47–80.

Schimmelfennig, F. & Sedelmeier, U. (2005) 'Conclusions: the impact of the EU on the accession countries', in *The Europeanization of Central and Eastern Europe*, eds F. Schimmelfennig & U. Sedelmeier, Cornell University Press, Ithaca, NY, pp. 210–229.

Schwellnus, G. (2005) 'The adoption of nondiscrimination and minority protection rules in Romania, Hungary and Poland', in *The Europeanization of Central and Eastern Europe*, eds F. Schimmelfennig & U. Sedelmeier, Cornell University Press, Ithaca, NY, pp. 51–71.

Stark, D. & Bruszt, L. (1998) *Postsocialist Pathways: Transforming Politics and Property in East Central Europe*, Cambridge University Press, Cambridge.

Steunenberg, B. & Dimitrova, A. (2007) 'Compliance in the EU enlargement process: the limits of conditionality', *European Integration Online Papers*, vol. 11, no. 5, available online at: http://eiop.or.at/eiop/texte/2007-005a.htm

Thomas, C. D. (2006) 'Constitutionalization through enlargement: the contested origins of the EU's democratic identity', *Journal of European Public Policy*, vol. 13, no. 8, pp. 1190–1210.

Vachudová, M. A. (2005) *Europe Undivided: Democracy, Leverage and Integration After Communism*, Oxford University Press, Oxford.

Verheugen, G. (2007) 'Introduction: challenges and opportunities of the enlargement of the European Union', in *The Accession Story: The EU from 15 to 25*, ed. G. Vassiliou, Oxford University Press, Oxford, pp. 1–6.

Antoaneta L. Dimitrova (PhD University of Limerick) is an Associate Professor at the Institute of Public Administration, Leiden University, the Netherlands. Among her research interests are the democratic transformations of the post-communist states of CEE and the role of the EU. Her research has been published in journals such as *European Union Politics*, *West European Politics*, *Journal of European Public Policy* and *Democratization*.

The EU–Turkey Customs Union Fifteen Years Later: Better, Yet not the Best Alternative

Kamil Yılmaz

Overall, the Customs Union (CU) has had a positive impact on Turkish economy. Through an increase in import penetration, the CU increased the competitive pressure on Turkish manufacturing industry, forcing it to improve productivity in the long-run. It also contributed to the transformation of the Turkish economy through the implementation of a competition policy. With increased productivity and competitiveness, the manufacturing industry was able to weather the storm during the 2001 economic crisis and in the wake of China's entry into world export markets. However, following the successful initial adaptation phase and the significant changes in the European Union's trade policy framework towards preferential trade agreements, the CU has recently started to generate some strains on Turkish trade.

The 1990s were a lost decade for Turkey. The macroeconomic environment that could not be fully stabilised in the 1980s deteriorated further, leading to the economic crisis of 1994. With some quick fixes and external financial support, the economy went back to 'normal' within a year. However, as is always the case, quick solutions produced no lasting improvements: macroeconomic conditions deteriorated further over time, sowing the seeds of the 2001 crisis that brought the country to the brink of collapse.

Aside from increased political and economic uncertainty, the 1990s also witnessed the formation of the Customs Union (CU) between Turkey and the European Union (EU) in 1996, an important milestone in Turkey's integration with the EU. Turkey was the first country to sign a CU agreement with the EU without being a full member and with very little financial support from the EU. Turkish elites chose to go ahead with the CU because they wanted to successfully conclude the final phase of the Ankara

Agreement that was signed between Turkey and the EU in 1963.They opted for the CU because it gave them the opportunity to pursue economic integration with the EU without undertaking serious political and institutional reforms, viewed as a precondition for full membership (Öniş 2003, p. 33).

This article provides a thorough analysis of the impact of the CU on the Turkish economy. The paper also aims at linking the impacts of the CU on different industries and segments of the society and, hence, contributes to the identification of the sources of support as well as resistance within Turkey to further integration with the EU. In the next section, I provide a review of the CU decision and discuss its major elements. In the third section, I analyse the effect of the CU on tax revenues, on Turkish trade flows, on sectoral and aggregate production and productivity, on overall welfare and on the welfare of different segments of the society. The fourth section concludes the paper.

The CU Decision

The agreement to form a CU between Turkey and the EU was signed in March 1995, but its history goes back to September 1963, when the institutions of the EU–Turkey Association Council were established by the Association Agreement signed in Ankara (also called the 'Ankara Agreement'). Being the final phase of this process, the CU agreement involved critical trade policy actions from the Turkish side, as the EU had already eliminated tariffs on Turkish imports in the first two phases.

By signing the CU agreement, Turkey agreed to impose the common external tariffs of the EU against third countries. The EU, in turn, agreed to eliminate quotas facing Turkish exporters of textiles and clothing. The CU has more serious implications for Turkey compared with other forms of associations such as free trade agreements (FTAs) or preferential trade agreements (PTAs). As Turkey's EU membership process continues, it is expected to include service sectors as well as public procurement and agriculture. As such, the CU also entailed harmonisation of Turkish competition policies with those of the EU. The CU agreement required Turkey to adopt EU competition rules before the agreement went into effect in 1996. As part of the efforts to prepare for the CU, the Turkish parliament passed the competition law in 1994, which also established the Competition Authority.

Following the implementation of the CU, Turkish tariff rates on imports from the EU declined from 10.2 per cent in 1994 to 1.34 per cent in 2001. The tariff rates on imports from FTA partners of the EU declined even more dramatically, from 22 per cent to 1.34 per cent (Togan 2000). As a result of these cuts, the tariff rates applied by Turkey on industrial imports from members of the World Trade Organisation (WTO) were the lowest among countries at the same level of development as Turkey. Interestingly, Turkey's weighted and simple average tariff rates on industrial imports are substantially lower than tariffs in countries that joined the EU after the CU (Kaminski & Ng 2007).

Before the CU went into effect there was some visible and less visible opposition in Turkey to its implementation. There was visible opposition from the labour unions, which claimed that, as a result of the increased competition from imports, the CU would lead to job losses in many sectors. In addition, there were some industries, notably the automotive industry, which lobbied behind closed doors against the CU. As a result, the automotive industry was able to persuade the authorities to declare it a sensitive industry, which enabled Turkey to implement tariffs on auto imports from third countries above the EU rates until 2001. Moreover, with the help of another clause included in the CU agreement, Turkey was able to restrict imports of used motor vehicles from the EU for 10 years.[1]

The sharp depreciation of the Turkish lira (TL) during the 1994 economic crisis was quite instrumental in keeping the increase in imports under control as the CU went into effect in 1996. As of the end of 1995, the real exchange rate was 18 per cent below its level as of the end of 1993. As a result, even though it would appear that the tariff cuts on products from the EU could lead to an increased demand for imports, an undervalued TL curtailed this increase.

As emphasised by Kaminski and Ng (2007), the CU changed the Turkish trade policy framework completely by bringing in predictability, transparency and stability as well as liberalising market access for both preferential and most favoured nation (MFN) suppliers. As a result of the CU, contestability in the Turkish markets for industrial and agricultural goods increased substantially. The increased contestability and competition, in turn, forced domestic producers to be better prepared to undertake productivity-enhancing investment.

The Impact of the CU Decision on the Turkish Economy

Even though it has been classified as an emerging market economy, with the CU Turkey adopted the trade policy regime of a group of industrial countries. EU member states can afford to apply low tariff rates on imports of goods in labour-intensive industries. As production in these economies is tilted overwhelmingly towards skilled-labour-, capital- and technology-intensive industries, they tend to import products of unskilled-labour-intensive sectors. However, it is difficult to conclude the same for Turkey, which has an abundant supply of unskilled labour. As a result, Turkey, over time, had to learn how to effectively use non-tariff barriers (NTBs) to keep imports from low-cost developing countries under control. A commonly used category of the NTBs that have been frequently used by industrial countries is anti-dumping duties. With 137 cases, Turkey is ranked tenth among WTO members in terms of the number of anti-dumping investigations initiated between 1996 and 2008.[2] The majority of these investigations (102 of them) were initiated between 2002 and 2008.

In this section, we analyse the impact of the CU on the Turkish economy from several perspectives.

Tax Revenue

Perhaps, the most immediate effect of the CU was the tariff revenue loss for the government. There was a decline in import tax revenues as Turkey lowered tariffs on imports from the EU. Import tariff revenues fell from 2.8 per cent of total tax revenues in 1995 to an average of 1.1 per cent over the period 2001–05 (Taymaz & Yılmaz 2007). The short-run negative impact on tariff revenue cannot be used as an argument against the CU. As the tariff revenue losses from the CU were not large, they cannot be a major factor contributing to the chronic budget deficits of the 1990s which eventually led to the 2001 economic crisis.

Trade Flows and Increased Competition from Imports

In the literature, it is a well-established fact that North–South trade agreements, irrespective of whether they be CUs or FTAs, are more beneficial for Southern countries than South–South trade agreements. Because of differences in technology and factor abundance, the sectors in which Southern and Northern countries have comparative advantage tend to be different. Once lower-income Southern countries gain free access to markets in their richer Northern trade partners, they are expected to export labour-intensive goods in which they have a comparative advantage. In return, they import capital- and human-capital-intensive goods in which Northern countries have a comparative advantage. The outcome of increased trade based on comparative advantage is definitely more beneficial for Southern countries (see Harrison et al. 2003).

As the tariff rates on imports were brought down substantially, imports from the EU and total imports were expected to increase, and this was actually what happened in the first couple of years. Imports increased from $35.7 billion in 1995 to $54.5 billion in 2000. Over the same period. imports from the EU increased from US$23.7 billion to $28.5 billion. The increase in total imports translated into an increase in the import penetration (IP) rate (the ratio of imports to total sales in the domestic market) from 22.2 per cent in 1995 to 27.8 per cent in 1996 and almost 29.6 per cent in 2000.[3] The increase in the overall IP rate within five years was mostly a result of the CU.

The EU had been Turkey's most important trade partner before 1996 and it stayed so for some time after. However, its share in Turkish imports has declined over time and especially since China became a WTO member in 2001 and entered as a major player the world export markets. The share of imports from the EU has followed a secular downward trend since 1995, from 66 per cent to 52 per cent in 2000 and further to 39 per cent in 2010 (Figure 1). Turkish imports from China and the other East Asian countries increased rapidly in the 2000s. From 2.2 per cent in 2001, the Chinese share in Turkish imports had risen to 9.2 per cent by 2010.

The CU agreement with the EU did not have much impact on Turkish exports in the first five years. The compounded annual growth rate of exports between 1996 and 2001 was 6.2 per cent compared with a 14.3 per cent growth rate between 1980 and 1995. One of the reasons was that the EU had already removed tariffs on Turkish goods before the CU. In addition, despite the CU, the EU continued to reserve the right to impose anti-dumping duties on Turkish exports to the EU as well as keeping technical (regulation) barriers (Togan et al. 2005). This being coupled with the appreciation of

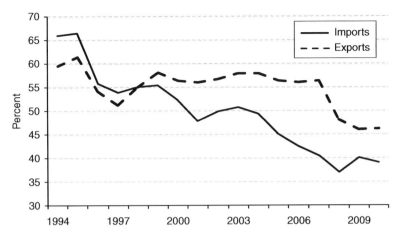

Figure 1 Turkey's Trade with the EU (per cent of total)
Source: TurkStat.

the TL, it is not surprising that Turkish exports to the EU did not experience a serious surge immediately.

The positive impact of the CU on Turkish exports was realised after a long delay, and only after the 2001 crisis. The depreciation of the TL and the contraction in domestic demand that followed the economic crisis of February 2001 forced domestic producers to search for export markets. Export revenues increased 12.6 per cent in 2001. Exports grew faster in 2002 and 2003 even though domestic demand resumed growth.[4] Better than expected export performance in 2002 and 2003 was achieved despite a 25 per cent real appreciation of the TL during this period, in part thanks to the appreciation of the euro against the US dollar.

Sectoral and Economy-wide Effects on Production and Productivity

The CU helped further open up the Turkish economy to international competition, and trade figures show the changes in the structure of Turkey's foreign trade after the CU. The track record of the Turkish manufacturing industry in response to the CU has been better than initially expected, especially when one considers that Turkey received very little financial support from the EU to help ease the adjustment burden; in fact, from 1996 to 2000 Turkish industry proved that it had the capacity to cope with competitive pressure from imports. Since 2001, it has become apparent that the transformation of Turkish industry following the CU helped it prepare itself for even more formidable competitors such as China and other East Asian countries.

The increased competition from imports could have been quite harmful for Turkish economy if it were to take place in a short period of time; resulting in factory shutdowns and job losses, and hampering the growth prospects of the manufacturing industry. The official statistics show that this was not the case. Turkish industrial production increased by 10.2 and 15.3 per cent in 1996 and 1997, respectively. This was perhaps due to the fact that the export–output ratio increased from 21 per cent in 1995 to close to 25 per cent in the next three years.

The increased competition from imports led to important changes in the behaviour of domestic producers of manufactured goods. Despite the import liberalisation process that had started in 1984, prior to the CU, some sectors, such as the automotive industry, durable home appliances, electrical machinery and basic metals, had continued to receive protection behind high tariff barriers. However, productivity growth in these and other import-competing sectors was higher than in export-oriented and non-traded goods sectors (see Özler & Yılmaz 2009). Taymaz and Yılmaz (2007) have also shown that the total factor productivity in manufacturing industry did not increase much between 1996 and 2000, but increased substantially in those sectors that experienced significant increases in IP rates after the CU. This effect was statistically significant even after other variables such as the real exchange rate, the export–output ratio and time variables (time trend or time dummies) were included as explanatory variables for plant-level total factor productivity.

While the export revenue growth rate in the first four years after the CU was not very high, exports grew rapidly after the 2001 economic crisis. This was in part due to the disciplining effect of the CU. Also there were differences across sectors in terms of export performance. Especially after China joined the WTO in 2001, there has been a secular decline in the export share of textiles and wearing apparel sectors. Together, the two sectors accounted for 45 per cent of total exports in the first half of the 1990s, which declined slightly to 41.7 per cent in the second half (see Figure 2). The decline in their relative export performance gained momentum in the 2000s because China had become a dominant player in export markets. In 2010, the two sectors together accounted for only 20 per cent of total exports from Turkey. Food and beverages and chemical products industries were also among the industries that experienced a

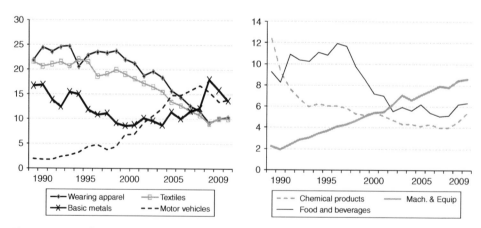

Figure 2 Manufacturing Exports Share for Selected Industries (per cent)
Source: TurkStat.

decline of export shares from close to 12 per cent in 1996 to around six per cent in 2010.

The export share of the automotive industry (including parts and components) increased from two per cent in 1990 to five per cent in 1996 (Figure 2). Although it was expected to be among the most adversely affected sectors, the automotive industry benefited enormously from the CU. After stalling for a couple of years after the CU, automotive exports started to increase at a rapid pace (45 per cent per year) after the 2001 crisis. As a result, the export share of the industry reached 17 per cent in 2007 (Figure 2). Another sector that has increased its export share over time is the machinery and equipment industry. Its export share increased steadily from a low of two per cent in 1990 to reach eight per cent in 2009. Finally, consumer electronics exports grew at a rate of 28 per cent per annum from 2001 to 2005.

The increases in production and exports in the automotive and consumer electronics industries were fuelled by rapid improvements in productivity. Total factor productivity growth in consumer electronics (and especially in the production of colour TV sets) increased by almost two-thirds from 1995 to 2001. Total factor productivity growth in the automotive industry was slow (less than 15 per cent from 1995 to 2000), but improved further after the 2001 crisis by close to 30 per cent (Taymaz & Yılmaz 2008).

While both industries were successful in riding the CU tide, differences in the characteristics of the two industries have led to a divergence in their performances since 2005. The automotive industry has been dominated by multinational corporations, had a strong domestic supplier base and seized the opportunities opened up by the CU by investing in new product and process technology and learning. The consumer electronics industry, on the other hand, has been dominated by a few large domestic firms and relied heavily on imported technology and intermediate inputs. The industry became competitive in the European market thanks to its geographical proximity, productive domestic labour, and focus on a protected and technologically mature segment of the market, which also helps explain the recent decline in the industry's fortunes. The fortunes of the consumer electronics industry were worsened by the fact that it was losing market share not only in the EU market but also in the domestic market due to the rapid switch from tube TV receivers to plasma and liquid crystal display (LCD) TV receivers. As a result, from 2005 to 2008 the production of the consumer electronics industry declined by 55 per cent, whereas that of the automotive industry increased by 26 per cent.

Focusing back on the trends in the manufacturing industry as a whole, the CU drove the transformation of Turkish industry towards higher productivity much faster than it would have otherwise experienced. Most of the productivity gains due to increased competition from the EU were realised until the early 2000s. After 2003, the EU's share in Turkish imports has been decreasing steadily, while the share of the East Asian countries has been on the rise. The productivity gains that have accrued since 2003 are mainly due to increased labour productivity in those sectors that faced increased competition from China.

Turkish manufacturing industry achieved higher productivity growth through increased reliance on intermediate input imports from East Asian countries and especially from China (Yükseler & Türkan 2006). While Turkey conducts approximately 50 per cent of its export transactions with the euro, the euro's share in import transactions is less than 35 per cent. The appreciation of the euro against the dollar after 2002 enabled Turkish exporters to rely more and more on imported inputs from China and other Asian economies in their quest to keep their production costs under control.

Problems Caused by the Asymmetric Nature of the CU Arrangement

After this detailed analysis of the impact of the CU on Turkish industry, we can now turn our attention to the problems caused by the asymmetric nature of the CU agreement. As discussed above, Turkey wanted to use the CU agreement as a strong signal that it was committed to the objective of full EU membership. As a result, Turkey accepted the EU's trade regime as it was, and was not able to persuade the EU to include a clause that would force the EU to consult with Turkey before signing FTAs with third countries. The EU negotiated and signed FTAs with third countries without any involvement of Turkey and without taking Turkey's interest into account, something that could potentially lead to unfair trade competition for Turkey. Turkey was supposed to sign FTAs of its own with these countries, but it has proven rather difficult for Turkey to obtain concessions as lucrative as the EU has. Nevertheless, Turkey has signed FTAs with 26 countries or country groups since 1996. As ten of these countries later became EU members, the FTAs with these countries were all cancelled. Finally, FTAs that have been signed with four other countries (Montenegro, Serbia, Chile and Jordan) are awaiting parliamentary approval.

As part of its 'Growth and Jobs Strategy' in 2006, the EU adopted a new trade policy framework that aims to enhance competitiveness and increase the market share of EU exports around the world. The EU Commission explicitly declared that it would pursue FTAs with Asian and Latin American countries, and the expected FTAs with India, South Korea and Association of South East Asian Nations (ASEAN) countries could potentially be quite problematic for Turkey. If Turkey cannot sign FTAs with these countries when the EU concludes negotiations with them, sectors such as textiles, electronics and motor vehicles will face serious competitive pressures.

At the moment the CU agreement with the EU prohibits Turkey from negotiating FTAs with its other major trade partners independent of the EU. This is another welfare-constraining impact of the CU, which would not have been in effect had Turkey signed a FTA rather than forming a CU with the EU in 1996.[5]

Welfare Effects

The welfare effects of the CU on the Turkish economy have been analysed by several studies, all based on computable general equilibrium (CGE) models of the Turkish economy.[6] Harrison and colleagues (1997) showed that, depending on the implementation of complementary policies, the CU will lead to an increase in Turkish welfare by an amount equal to 1.0–1.5 per cent of gross domestic product (GDP) on an annual basis.[7] This will happen despite a loss of tariff revenue equivalent to 1.4 per cent of GDP. Their counterfactual simulations showed that the tariff revenue loss could be compensated by a uniform application of value added tax (VAT) to all products and services.

CGE simulation results reported by Bayar and colleagues (2000) showed that the short-run impact of the CU on Turkish welfare was negligible (equivalent to 0.12 per cent of GDP). The most significant welfare impact took place under the long-run scenario, which assumed that the CU would lead to a decline in the country risk and to a significant increase in foreign direct investment (FDI) inflows, and would enable Turkish producers to increase the speed of technological change. Under this scenario, the CU led to a welfare increase equivalent to 2.5–4.55 per cent of GDP in 1995. The welfare impact of this scenario was rather big compared with that of Harrison and colleagues (1997) because some of the assumptions of this scenario reflected more than the CU agreement entailed.

De Santis (2001) developed a similar CGE model of Turkey and showed that the CU did not have trade diversion effects and the welfare losses associated with them.[8] This finding is consistent with the fact that Turkish imports from low-cost third countries have partially substituted the imports from higher-cost EU countries over time.

In order to undertake a complete welfare analysis of the CU, one should go beyond trade policy measures. Aside from trade-related implications, the CU agreement foresaw changes in commercial policy and its legislation that would imply 'deeper integration' of the two economies. These 'deep integration elements' include the harmonisation of Turkey's competition policy legislation with that of the EU, the adoption of the EU's commercial policy towards third countries (the FTAs with all the EU's preferential partners which worked against Turkey) and the adoption of the EU *Acquis* regarding the standardisation of industrial products and consumer rights (Zahariadis 2002; Togan et al. 2005).

The efforts towards deeper integration of the Turkish economy with that of the EU, however, have not prevented the EU from imposing anti-dumping and anti-subsidy duties on some Turkish exports. In addition, the EU's safeguard instruments on a limited number of products also imply restrictions on Turkish exports to the EU. Since the beginning of the CU, the EU has opened 18 anti-dumping and subsidy investigations against Turkish imports.[9] In some cases anti-dumping duties lasted years. Overall, the use of anti-dumping measures against partners is against the spirit of the CU, and it is encouraging that the EU's use of anti-dumping and anti-subsidy measures has declined substantially in recent years.

Zahariadis (2002) looked at the welfare effects of deep integration following the completion of the EU–Turkey CU, by focusing on technical barriers to trade (standards harmonisation), as well as barriers emerging from border formalities and related procedures, and found that gains from deep integration were smaller than tariff-related ones.

Even though the assumptions about the relevant scenarios are of critical importance, all four studies briefly summarised above showed that the net effect of the CU on Turkish welfare is positive. Based on these studies, it would not be wrong to conclude that the Turkish economy has performed well under the CU. Turkey has withstood the competitive pressure from the EU and elsewhere while it has continued to increase its exports in a renewed product mix as well as taking steps towards deeper integration with the EU.

Experience with the CU so far demonstrates the resiliency and adaptability of Turkish manufacturing industries to rapidly changing conditions during a period with almost no net FDI flows. In fact, there was no increase in FDI flows into Turkey immediately after the CU (especially those from Europe) and this was a major disappointment with the CU for many.

The CU did not lead to an increase in FDI flows because the consequences of the economic and political uncertainty surrounding Turkey in the 1990s were so grave that foreign investors decided to stay away even after the CU. The importance of political and economic stability for attracting FDI inflows was proven again after the 2001 economic crisis. Turkey started to implement monetary and fiscal reforms immediately after the crisis, and the Justice and Development Party (AKP) government that came into power after the November 2002 elections pursued the economic reforms further. In addition, the AKP government prioritised political and democratic reforms that were crucial for the future EU membership of Turkey. Both political and economic reforms were critical in convincing the EU to open accession talks with Turkey. Unlike the CU, the EU's decision at the end of 2004 to start accession talks with Turkey, together with economic and political stability, had played a critical role in attracting FDI because it invigorated expectations for a rapid and consistent implementation of the rules and regulations that ensure a level playing field for all companies, domestic and foreign alike.

Thanks to the bold reform agenda adopted, and the EU decision to start membership negotiations with Turkey at the end of 2004, the improvements in the business environment increased Turkey's attractiveness as a destination for foreign capital. The benign external conditions helped Turkey change the composition of the financing of its current account deficit towards long-term capital inflows.

A few years after the CU went into effect, many questioned its usefulness as an anchor for Turkey. Uğur (2000), for example, argued that the CU did not deliver what it was expected to: Turkey was not able to attract large sums of FDI, was unable to gain easy access to the EU and third country markets, and deep integration with the EU did not take place. As a result, he and others argued that the CU could not be considered an anchor for Turkey (Eder 2003). However, the performance of the Turkish economy after the 2001 crisis, and especially after the EU's December 2004 decision to open accession talks with Turkey, changed the perceptions of many in terms of the anchor role of the CU and EU membership for the Turkish economy.

Identifying Winners and Losers

So far, we have seen that the CU has favourably affected the Turkish economy as well as the overall welfare of Turkish society. However, I am also aware that showing that the impact is favourable does not imply that all social groups and sectors are affected equally. Overall, the analysis does not really respond to the concerns of many analysts, as well as the person on the street, who believed that certain segments of society as well as certain sectors would be worse off as a result of the CU.

When one reads through what the Turkish press had to say before the CU went into effect, job losses and bankruptcies among small and medium enterprises (SMEs) were regarded as the most important expected impact of the CU.[10] For this reason, it is important to have a closer look at the data. According to the productivity growth rates reported by Taymaz and colleagues (2010), SMEs performed better than expected. Between 1995 and 2000, the average annual labour productivity growth in the manufacturing industry was 2.6 per cent. SMEs attained a productivity growth rate of 2.5 per cent while productivity growth in large-scale enterprises (LSEs) was only 1.7 per cent.[11] The bulk of productivity growth among the SMEs was due to within variation, which indicates that individual SMEs increased their labour productivity between 1995 and 2000. The second most important contribution to productivity growth during the period was the intra-industry between-effect, which implies that there was a reallocation of output from less productive to more productive SMEs within each industry. These findings show that SMEs did not perform as badly as some news analysts had predicted before 1996.

Bayar and colleagues (2000) analysed the sectoral impact of the CU within the CGE model under the long-run scenario with lower risk, increased FDI inflows and technological change elements. They showed that in the short run the CU had a positive impact on the agricultural products, textiles and wearing apparel, leather products and mineral products. The short-run production impact of the CU on the machinery and equipment, automotive, and consumer electronics industries, on the other hand, was negative. In the long run, all sectors made necessary adjustments and increased their production; however, those sectors that suffered in the short run turned out to experience the largest gains in production in the long run. The numerical estimates of Bayer and colleagues (2000) at the sectoral level are consistent with the qualitative results we have seen in my discussion of the sectoral impact of the CU.

A complete analysis of distributional effects is rather difficult to find. While some researchers use the CGE framework to undertake this analysis, what they end up analysing as a result is rather the distributional effects implied by the particular structure of the CGE model and the available data as well as the CU itself. Keeping this caveat in mind, we can look at the distributional impact analysis by De Santis (2001) and Harrison and colleagues (2003). De Santis (2001) showed that the CU led to a decline in the welfare of urban households (equivalent to 0.5 per cent of their income), along with an improvement in the welfare of the rural households (equivalent to 2.3 per cent of their income). The rural households' welfare gains and the urban households' welfare losses were mainly due to the expansion of the traditional agricultural and industrial sectors at the expense of services sectors after the CU. Overall, income inequality declined by between 1.1 and 1.7 per cent, due to the rise in both agricultural capital income and farmers' earnings, which has brought about a substantial decline in inequality between these groups.

Harrison and colleagues (2003) also showed that the CU had distributional effects. According to their simulation results, after the CU the wage rate of production labour declined by 2.9 per cent, the greatest percentage decline among all factors of production. This was as expected. Before the CU, manufacturing industry received more trade protection than other sectors, but as the CU went into effect the prices of manufactured goods declined, which in turn implied that the wage rate of production labour, which was used more intensively in manufacturing industry, had to decline. Unskilled production labour happened to be the factor that was most important for the four poorest urban household groups and thus it appears that the principal reason that these household groups lost out was that the wages of unskilled production labour declined. At the same time, these results also showed that the two richest urban household groups also suffered welfare losses, mostly because the return on their capital decreased after the CU. Overall, when measured by the Gini coefficient, income distribution slightly improved, a result similar to that obtained by De Santis (2001).

Conclusions

Until 2004, EU–Turkey relations had greatest influence in the economic rather than the political sphere. The CU has been an important milestone in the process of integration of the Turkish economy with that of the EU. In this study I have undertaken an overview of research on the overall and sectoral impact of the CU on the Turkish economy. The evidence put together by many researchers suggests that overall the CU has been beneficial for Turkey, especially in the long run through improved productivity in manufacturing industries. With increased productivity and competitiveness, manufacturing industries were able to weather the storm of the 2001 economic crisis and in the wake of China's entry into world export markets. Furthermore, the CU also involved the deep integration of the Turkish economy with that of the EU, through the convergence of Turkish commercial policy and related institutions towards those of the EU.

There are some major shortcomings of the CU agreement for Turkey which should have been pre-empted at the outset. With the benefit of hindsight and especially after the EU's 2006 change of trade strategy in favour of FTAs, one can now claim that it would have been better for Turkey to have signed an FTA with the EU. This would have given Turkey more flexibility in pursuing more effective trade policy with third countries. With the membership objective alive, Turkey has so far refrained from questioning the logic of the CU and renegotiating an FTA instead of the CU. However, since 2005 the EU's political will to accept Turkey as a member at some future date has been fading away. With the current economic troubles of its members, the EU will be in no position for another wave of accession in the near future. In such an atmosphere, Turkey's membership seems to be postponed to the indefinite future. This is obviously a major cause for concern for Turkey. As EU membership becomes a very distant possibility, the Turkish government will have no choice but to ask for a revision of the original CU agreement, which will in effect convert it into an FTA.

Acknowledgements

The author thanks the editors of this issue, Gamze Avcı and Ali Çarkoğlu, and two anonymous referees for very helpful comments, Metin Uyanık for research assistance and Brian Rodrigues for editorial assistance.

Notes

[1] In August 2008, Turkey extended the implementation period of the import restrictions on used cars indefinitely until Turkey's full EU membership goes into effect.
[2] During this period only 44 anti-dumping investigations were initiated against Turkish exporters.
[3] The IP rate defined for the imports from the EU increased from 16.5 per cent in 1995 to 22.3 per cent in 1996 and 23.6 per cent in 2000 (Taymaz & Yılmaz 2007).
[4] Exports grew by 15 per cent in 2002, by 31 and 34 per cent in 2003 and 2004, respectively, and by 16 per cent in both 2005 and 2006 (source: Turkstat).
[5] See Harrison and colleagues' (2002) study on Chile.
[6] CGE models are a class of economic models composed of numerous equations describing major economic decisions, including production, consumption, employment, investment, trade and government finance decisions. In addition, CGE models include equations describing the equilibrium conditions in the markets for goods and factors of production. These models are built using detailed input–output matrix data for the country of interest. They are used to study how an economy might react to changes in external factors in the long run. Most importantly they are used to evaluate the long-run impact of permanent policy changes. They are important tools of policy analysis because they enable the researcher to consider economy-wide effects of a change in any part of the economy. Over the last 40 years they have been extensively used to study trade policy changes around the world, but most importantly in developing countries. In order to parameterise CGE models one needs to use a plethora of information that is not consistently available in developing countries. For that reason, one has to be very careful in reaching any sweeping policy conclusions based on the CGE analysis.
[7] Harrison and colleagues (1997) note that, by design, their model could not measure the productivity gains from trade liberalisation, so the gains from the CU were likely to be bigger than their estimates
[8] The welfare analyses of the CU or other forms of preferential arrangements focus on two effects on trade flows. These arrangements are beneficial to the extent that they create more trade (*trade creation*). Trade is created if those goods that used to be produced and consumed domestically are imported from more efficient partner country producers after the CU goes into effect. To the extent that the CU diverts imports from a low-cost third country to a higher-cost partner country it leads to *trade diversion*. While trade creation is a welfare-improving effect of the CU, trade diversion will have the opposite welfare effect. Whether the CU or an FTA is beneficial in a static sense will depend on the net outcome of the two effects.

[9] Textiles (cotton fabrics, polyester fibres and yarn), steel (hot-rolled coils, hollow sections, steel ropes and cables, steel wire rod, welded tubes and pipes, etc.), pharmaceuticals (paracetamol and pentaerythritol), consumer electronics (colour TVs) are the Turkish sectors affected by the investigations (Based on statistics provided by the EU Commission, http://trade.ec.europa.eu/doclib/html/113191.htm). Sixteen out of 18 investigations resulted in the imposition of anti-dumping or anti-subsidy duties on Turkish exports to the EU.

[10] See, for example, Cumhuriyet, 8 March and 15 December 1995.

[11] Taymaz and colleagues (2010) define SMEs (LSEs) as domestic firms employing less (more) than 150 employees. 'Foreign firms' are defined as those joint ventures in which foreign ownership is ten per cent or more. Foreign firms are not classified by size because most of them are large.

References

Bayar, A., Nuray, H. & Reçberoğlu, S. (2000) *Gümrük Birliği'nin Türkiye Ekonomisine Etkileri* [Effects of the Customs Union on Turkish Economy], Economic Development Foundation Publications, Istanbul.

De Santis, R. (2001) 'The 1990 trade liberalisation policy of Turkey: an applied general equilibrium assessment', *International Economic Journal*, vol. 15, no. 2, pp. 115–132.

Eder, M. (2003) 'Implementing the economic criteria of EU membership: how difficult is it for Turkey?', *Turkish Studies*, vol. 4, no. 1, pp. 219–244.

Harrison, G. W., Rutherford, T. F. & Tarr, D. G. (1997) 'Economic implications for Turkey of a Customs Union with the European Union', *European Economic Review*, vol. 41, no. 3–5, pp. 861–870.

Harrison, G. W., Rutherford, T. F. & Tarr, D. G. (2002) 'Trade policy options for Chile: the importance of market access', *World Bank Economic Review*, vol. 16, no. 1, pp. 49–79.

Harrison, G. W., Rutherford, T. F. & Tarr, D. G. (2003) 'Trade liberalisation, poverty and efficient equity', *Journal of Development Economics*, vol. 71, no. 1, pp. 97–128.

Kaminski, B. & Ng, F. (2007) 'Turkey's evolving trade integration into pan-European markets', *Journal of International Trade and Diplomacy*, vol. 1, no. 2, pp. 35–103.

Öniş, Z. (2003) 'Domestic politics, international norms and challenges to the state: Turkey–EU relations in the post-Helsinki era', *Turkish Studies*, vol. 4, no. 1, pp. 9–34.

Özler, S. & Yılmaz, K. (2009) 'Productivity response to reduction in trade barriers: evidence from Turkish manufacturing plants', *Review of World Economics*, vol. 37, no. 2, pp. 479–488.

Taymaz, E. & Yılmaz, K. (2007) 'Productivity and trade orientation: Turkish manufacturing industry before and after the Customs Union', *Journal of International Trade and Diplomacy*, vol. 1, no. 1, pp. 127–154.

Taymaz, E. & Yılmaz, K. (2008) 'Integration with the global economy: the case of Turkish automobile and consumer electronics industries', World Bank, Commission on Growth and Development, Working Paper No. 37.

Taymaz, E., Voyvoda, E. & Yılmaz, K. (2010) 'Global links and local bonds: the role of ownership and size in productivity growth', mimeo, Koç University.

Togan, S. (1997) 'Opening up the Turkish economy in the context of the Customs Union with EU', *Journal of Economic Integration*, vol. 12, no. 2, pp. 157–179.

Togan, S. (2000) 'Effects of Turkey-European Union Customs Union and prospects for the future', *Russian and East European Finance and Trade*, vol. 36, no. 4, pp. 5–25.

Togan, S., Nebioğlu, H. & Doğan, S. (2005) 'Integration and the manufacturing industry', in *Turkey: Economic Reform and Accession to the European Union*, eds B. Hoekman & S. Togan, Oxford University Press, Oxford, pp. 87–121.

Uğur, M. (2000) 'Europeanisation and convergence via incomplete contracts? The case of Turkey', *South European Society and Politics*, vol. 5, no. 2, pp. 217–242.

Yükseler, Z. & Türkan, E. (2006) 'Türkiye'nin Üretim ve Dış Ticaret Yapısında Dönüşüm: Küresel Yönelmeler ve Yansımalar' [The transformation of Turkey's production and foreign trade structure: global trends and reflections], TÜSİAD-Koç University Economic Research Forum Research Report.

Zahariadis, Y. (2002) 'Deep integration in the EU–Turkey Customs Union: a preliminary analysis based on the GTAP model', paper presented at the DESG Annual Conference in Development Economics, University of Nottingham, 18–20 April.

Kamil Yılmaz is Professor of Economics at Koç University. In 2003, he received the Encouragement Award in the Social Sciences and Humanities given by the Turkish Academy of Sciences. Between 2007 and 2009, he served as the Director of TUSIAD-Koç University Economic Research Forum. He is currently on sabbatical leave, visiting the Department of Economics at the University of Pennsylvania. His recent publications include "Productivity Response to Reduction in Trade Barriers: Evidence from Turkish Manufacturing Plants", *Review of World Economics*, 2009 (with S. Özler); "History Matters for the Export Decision: Evidence from Turkish Manufacturing Industry", *World Development*, 2009 (with S. Özler and E. Taymaz); and "Measuring Financial Asset Return and Volatility Spillovers, with Application to Global Equity Markets", *The Economic Journal*, 2009 (with F. X. Diebold). Mailing address: Koç University, Rumelifeneri Yolu, Sariyer 34450, Istanbul, Turkey.

Challenges of Triangular Relations: The US, the EU, and Turkish Accession

Sabri Sayarı

The US government became deeply involved in European Union (EU)–Turkey relations from the mid-1990s and has provided extensive diplomatic support for full Turkish membership in the EU since then. Washington's strategic considerations have been paramount in the US government's approach to Turkey's full integration into the EU. The US policy on this issue has played a constructive role in Turkish–US relations. However, it has also created strains in transatlantic ties, since the pressure the US has put on the EU has angered many European officials, who resent what they view as interference in the EU's internal affairs. The US has become more sensitive to the complaints voiced by European leaders and EU officials, and it has adopted a more subtle approach to the issue of Turkish membership. While Washington continues to support Turkey's European integration, it has also recognised that the accession process is likely to be lengthy.

Turkey's quest for membership in the European Union (EU) has an important transatlantic dimension. The United States (US) has been a strong supporter of Turkey's full integration into the EU and it has been actively involved in EU–Turkey relations since the mid-1990s. Beginning with the Customs Union agreement between Ankara and Brussels in 1995, the firm backing given by the US to Turkey's European integration has continued until the present under Republican as well as Democratic administrations. US policy has played a constructive role in bilateral relations between Washington and Ankara. However, it has also been a source of strain in transatlantic relations, since it has angered many Europeans who have increasingly viewed the US policy as unwarranted American interference in the internal affairs of the EU. Since Brussels opened accession negotiations with Ankara, the tensions between the US and its European allies over the Turkish membership issue have somewhat lessened. Nevertheless, the differences between the US and European perspectives on Turkey's

European integration have continued to pose a challenge to cooperation in transatlantic ties.

Explaining US Policy on EU–Turkey Relations

Unlike French President Nicholas Sarkozy, who has argued that 'Turkey is not a European country' and that Turkey's entry into the EU would 'kill the very idea of European integration' (Gordon & Taspinar 2008, p. 48), US presidents have repeatedly asserted that Turkey is part of Europe and that it can make a significant contribution to European integration. For example, in his address to the Turkish parliament in November 1999, President Clinton declared,

> the future that we want to build together will require foresight on the part of our other allies in Europe—the foresight to see that our vision of a Europe that is undivided, democratic, and at peace for the first time in all of history will never be complete unless and until it embraces Turkey. (White House 1999)

A decade later, President Obama expressed similar sentiments in his address to the Turkish parliamentarians in April 2009 when he stated,

> Turkey is bound to Europe by more than bridges over the Bosporus. Centuries of shared history, culture, and commerce bring you together. Europe gains by diversity and ethnicity, tradition and faith—it is not diminished by it. And Turkish membership would broaden and strengthen Europe's foundation once more. (White House 2009)

The views expressed by Presidents Clinton and Obama are notable for the emphasis they give to the idea that Turkey belongs to Europe and that the goal of creating a united Europe cannot be achieved without Turkey's participation in the EU. President Obama's statement is also noteworthy for highlighting his conviction about the benefits that Europe would gain through greater cultural diversity and ethnicity—a remark that is clearly aimed at those Europeans who oppose Turkish membership of the EU because of Turkey's Islamic identity and cultural traditions.

There are several reasons for the strong US support for Turkish membership in the EU. Clearly, the most important concerns the long history of close bilateral and multilateral ties between the two countries and Turkey's geopolitical importance for US foreign policy interests. Washington's policy has been based on its expectation that support for Turkey's European aspirations would strengthen bilateral ties. Moreover, the US has been concerned about the consequences of Turkey's exclusion from the EU for US and Western security interests. US policy-makers have frequently emphasised the importance of 'anchoring Turkey' to the West through membership in the EU, which would significantly improve the prospects for strategic cooperation between Turkey, the US, and Europe (Khalilzad 2000, p. 93).

The Turkish–US military and political alliance came into existence at the outset of the Cold War, when Turkey was confronted with Moscow's demand for territory in eastern Anatolia and a base for the joint defence of the Turkish Straits (Kuniholm

1994). For Ankara, the US–Turkish alliance meant, first and foremost, military aid to meet the country's security and defence requirements against the perceived Soviet threat. In addition, Turkish officials supported an alliance with the US because it promised to provide Turkey with much-needed economic aid. The US viewed Turkey as an important strategic asset in its containment strategy against the Soviet Union.

Both countries achieved their principal objectives from their growing military and security cooperation. Turkey became one of the main pillars of US containment policy. During the height of the Cold War in the 1950s, the large US military presence in Turkey included nearly 30,000 US servicemen, who were stationed in more than two dozen bases around the country. For its part, Turkey found a credible deterrent against the Soviet Union through its alliance with the US and membership in the North Atlantic Treaty Organisation (NATO). In addition to the assistance it received from the US for the modernisation of its armed forces, Turkey also became the third-largest recipient of US economic aid in the world, after Israel and Egypt (Sayari 2003, pp. 27–28).

The bilateral and multilateral security cooperation between Turkey and the US remained strong throughout the Cold War period. Turkey, along with Greece and Italy, became one of the main pillars of NATO's southern flank. The US–Turkish alliance weathered several crises during the 1960s and 1970s over the Cyprus conflict; in particular, the imposition of an arms embargo on Turkey by the US Congress following the landing of Turkish troops on the island in 1974 caused serious tensions between Ankara and Washington. However, the Turkish–US alliance was put back on track with renewed strength during the 1980s, following the Soviet invasion of Afghanistan in 1979 and the Islamic Revolution in Iran later in the same year. Both of these developments reasserted Turkey's strategic importance for the US (Sayari 2006). Although the end of the Cold War and the disintegration of the Soviet Union led to a major transformation of the international system, Ankara and Washington continued their cooperation on a number of important regional security issues in the Middle East, the Balkans, and the Caucasus during the 1990s. In particular, Turkey's prestige in Washington soared as a result of the Turkish government's decision to depart from its established policy of non-interference in regional conflicts involving its neighbours, and to support the Allied Coalition led by the US during the 1990–91 Gulf War (Sayari 2004).

In the 1990s, when the US began to champion Turkish entry into the EU through active diplomatic involvement, close military and political ties between the two countries had been in existence for more than four decades. The US remained Turkey's most important ally in world politics. And Turkey continued to maintain its strategic importance for US foreign policy interests in the Middle East, the Balkans, and the Caucasus. While strong bilateral ties provided the broader context for the deep involvement of the US in EU–Turkey relations, two developments in the mid-1990s played a more immediate and direct role in Washington's decision to pursue active diplomacy on behalf of Turkey's European integration (Makovsky 2000, pp. 223–225). First, the US became concerned about Russia's increased political activism in the

Caucasus and reassertion of its influence in its 'near abroad' in the post-Cold-War era. The emergence of the Caspian region as a major new potential source of petroleum and natural gas and Russia's efforts to maintain its monopoly on the transport of energy to Western markets added to US concerns. Secondly, two individuals who believed strongly in Turkey's strategic importance for the US were appointed to key positions in the formulation of US policy towards Turkey in 1994. Richard Holbrooke, who became assistant secretary of state for European affairs, and Mark Grossman, who was appointed ambassador to Ankara, worked hard to strengthen the bilateral relationship. Their advocacy of new policy initiatives was designed to 'enhance Washington's standing in Turkish eyes' and to promote 'the notion of the United States as "Turkey's best friend" in the international arena' (Makovsky 2000, p. 223).

In addition to strategic considerations, the US government has promoted Turkish membership for its wider ramifications in the Islamic world. The view that the EU can send a powerful positive message to the millions of Muslims around the world by accepting a predominantly Muslim country into its ranks has found wide acceptance in the Washington policy-making community. Conversely, the EU's refusal to grant full membership to Turkey, which has long sought to become part of the European community of nations, would send a 'wrong message' because it would contribute to the growing strength of anti-American and anti-Western sentiments in the Islamic world (Islam 2008, pp. 21–22).

It is also worth noting that US support for Turkey on the EU membership issue has been relatively cost-free for Washington. If and when Turkey becomes a member of the EU, the US will not face the challenges and problems that worry European officials, such as the feared influx of new waves of migrants from Turkey into Europe in search of jobs or the costs of integrating a large country like Turkey into the EU. While Turkey's bid for EU membership has become a hotly debated domestic political issue in many EU member states, in the US it has not figured prominently in domestic politics and has had virtually no impact on the electoral preferences of US voters. As Morton Abramowitz, a former US ambassador to Turkey puts it, the only cost of this policy for Washington is a 'certain European annoyance, and perhaps anger at times at American pressure' (Abramowitz 2000, p.180).

Some observers, especially those who oppose Turkey's European integration, have argued that the main reason for Washington's support for Turkey's quest for full EU membership is essentially based on its expectation that Turkey will faithfully support US foreign policy objectives when it enters the EU. The so-called 'American Trojan Horse' argument rests on the assumption that Turkey would, in fact, be 'a Trojan Horse for US interests in Europe' (Grant 2005), However, this explanation for the US's motive in supporting Turkey's inclusion in the EU overlooks several facts. First, the EU already includes countries that have been strong supporters of US foreign policy; in particular, the British government has traditionally sided with the US on various issues over the years. The most recent example of the cooperation between London and Washington on a major international conflict was the war in Iraq, where the British government supported the US despite strong opposition from France and Germany.

Other EU members, including Spain and Italy, also supported US policy and sent troops to Iraq. Some of the newer EU members from Eastern Europe have also displayed a favourable attitude towards Washington and sought closer alignment with US foreign policy interests and objectives. Second, the 2003 Iraq War has also underscored the fact that on an issue of major strategic importance for the US, namely, the deployment of US troops through Turkey at the outset of the war, Ankara refused to cooperate with Washington. Similarly, despite strong pressure from the US concerning Iran's nuclear programme, Ankara has, so far, refused to follow Washington's suggestion that Turkey endorse stronger sanctions against the Iranian regime.

Although the US has been a strong supporter of Turkey's European integration, US officials have not urged the EU to change the rules of the game for membership in order to accommodate Turkey. Washington has also refrained from asking its European allies to make a special case for Turkish membership. In their endorsement of Turkey's European aspirations, US officials have repeatedly stated that the EU has the right to apply the rules for admittance to all applicant countries, including Turkey. The US policy on EU–Turkey relations has been based on the following considerations. First, Turkey should be treated on an equal basis with all the other applicants, and Turkish membership should not be judged as a special case. Second, the EU should refrain from using religion or culture as the basis for membership, and Brussels should evaluate Turkey's application strictly according to the Copenhagen criteria. Third, in the late 1990s, the US position was that the EU should leave the door open for eventual membership by formally recognising Turkey's candidacy and by setting a firm date for the beginning of the accession process. Fourth, Turkey should, under no circumstances, be denied entry into the EU when it meets all the formal criteria for membership (Makovsky 2001).

The approach of the US to the Turkish membership issue, therefore, has rested on the recognition of the fact that membership is an internal matter for the EU and that Turkey's progress towards full integration depends on Ankara's ability to undertake the reform measures needed to comply with the Copenhagen criteria. Washington's main concern, until the Turkish candidacy was formally recognised by Brussels in 1999, was that the EU would decide officially to terminate the discussions for eventual membership. Therefore, the US concentrated its diplomatic efforts among key EU member states on keeping the door open for Turkey and avoiding sending messages to Ankara that gave the impression that Turkey would be denied membership even if it met all the requirements for joining the EU.

Differences between US and European Perspectives on EU–Turkey Relations

The sharp difference between the US support for Turkish membership and the opposition to it by some major EU countries stems from several sources, including the issue of Turkey's 'Europeanness', the role of strategic considerations in EU accession, and the pressures of domestic politics. The US views Turkey as belonging to Europe.

The official US perspective on Turkey's European identity is also reflected in the US State Department's administrative organisation, where Turkey is included in the Bureau of European and Eurasian Affairs. Although Turkey has been a member of several important European-based organisations for nearly half a century, its European identity continues to be questioned by those European officials and observers who oppose Turkish entry into the EU (Yesilada 2002, pp. 101–102). French President Sarkozy's outright rejection of Turkey's Europeanness or the European Christian Democratic Union's declaration that 'the EU is in the process of building a civilisation in which Turkey has no place' (Gordon & Taspinar 2008, p. 41) represent the views of those who categorically refuse Turkey's European identity and vocation. While they may not entirely support these views, many other Europeans do not seem to share Washington's whole-hearted endorsement of Turkey's European identity.

A second major reason for the divergence between the two approaches is that while the US policy is based mainly on strategic considerations, Europeans tend to focus on Turkey's political, economic, and cultural attributes (Khalilzad 2000, p. 93). For US policy-makers, Turkey's strategic importance increased in the post-Cold-War period as a result of the political crises and conflicts in countries near Turkey's borders in the Middle East, the Balkans, the Caucasus, and Central Asia (Kuniholm 2001, p. 37). This broad, global strategic perspective has been largely missing from the EU's outlook on world affairs, which has 'never developed a strategic place for Turkey within political conceptions about, for instance, the Middle East, Central Asia, or the Caucasus' (Kramer 2000, p. 233). Moreover, some European observers have argued that Turkey's inclusion in the EU could, in fact, be a strategic liability, since it would extend the EU's borders to the dangerous neighbourhood of Iran, Syria, and Iraq (Larrabee 1997, pp. 160–161). The chaos and violence that seized Iraq following the Coalition occupation have lent greater credibility to their views (Barkey 2008). For the US, however, Turkey's strategic importance drives precisely from its proximity to these countries which have become major concerns for US foreign and security policy. While US policy-makers emphasise Turkey's strategic importance in their advocacy of Turkish membership, their European counterparts tend to focus on the shortcomings of Turkish democracy, the country's level of economic development, Turkey's ethnic and religious identity, and the problem of integrating a country of 73 million people into the EU (Schauble 2004).

US Involvement in EU–Turkey Relations

From 1995 to 1999, the US government invested a great deal of its diplomatic capital and energy in the signing of a customs union agreement between Brussels and Ankara, and the formal recognition of Turkey's candidacy for membership. In the early 2000s, the US diplomatic campaign in Europe aimed at getting Ankara a specific date for the beginning of the EU accession process. Since 2004, Washington has directed its efforts at speeding up the accession talks between the EU and Turkey, and frequently reminding its European allies of the importance of Turkey's full integration into the EU for greater cooperation in the triangular relations between the US, EU, and Turkey.

The Customs Union Agreement (1995)

When the issue of signing a customs union agreement with Turkey first came up for discussion in the European Parliament, it met with considerable opposition and criticism. In particular, there was strong opposition from the Greek government, which endeavoured to link the customs union agreement with the opening of accession negotiations with Cyprus (Kuniholm 2001, p. 28). The Clinton administration used various diplomatic channels, including phone calls by the President himself to several European leaders, to press for the ratification of the customs union agreement. The US efforts on behalf of Turkey also received the support of many European Social Democrats. The EU's decision to begin accession talks with Cyprus finally broke the deadlock between Brussels and Ankara. But US pressure and lobbying played an equally important role in the final approval of a customs union treaty in December 1995 (Larrabee & Lesser 2003, p. 174).

Verification of the Turkish Candidacy: The Helsinki Summit (1999)

The European Council's decision at its Luxembourg meeting in December 1997 not to include Turkey on the list of candidate states was a setback to Turkey's European aspirations. Ankara's shock at what most Turks perceived as a 'rejection' by the EU was shared by Washington. The Clinton administration expressed its disappointment at the outcome of the Luxembourg summit and urged the EU to adopt a more favourable policy towards Turkey. During their visits to Washington, 'European officials were lectured at length by the Americans on the injudiciousness of denying Turkey a chance to join the EU' (Barkey 2003, p. 215). Prior to the 1999 EU summit in Helsinki, US officials, working jointly with their British counterparts, lobbied extensively for the formal recognition of Turkey's candidacy. President Clinton again personally called European leaders and asked them for their support (Gordon & Taspinar 2008, pp. 42–43). In addition to the favourable view adopted by the German and Greek governments, Washington's assertive diplomacy was critical in the European Council's decision to affirm Turkey's candidacy for EU membership at the Helsinki summit in December 1999 (Larrabee & Lesser 2003, p. 174).

Date for the Start of the Accession Talks: The Copenhagen Summit (2002)

The policy of the US government concerning EU–Turkey relations did not change following the election of George Bush as president in 2000. As had been the case on the eve of the EU summits in 1997 and 1999, the meeting of the EU leaders in Copenhagen in December 2002 witnessed growing US pressures on Europe. Joined by the British government, the US pressed for the earliest possible date to start EU accession talks with Turkey (Daniel 2002). The British–US lobbying on Turkey's behalf came amidst Washington's efforts to seek Ankara's support for the impending war in Iraq (*New York Times* 2002). In particular, the US government wanted to reach an agreement with Turkey for the passage of approximately 60,000 US troops through Turkish territory. In return for agreeing with its request, the US offered a generous economic aid package and promised an important military role for Turkey in northern Iraq, following the occupation of the country. To ensure Turkey's cooperation, Washington intensified its campaign in Europe for Turkish membership in the EU. President Bush called several European leaders, including Danish Prime Minister Anders Forgh Rasmussen, the host of the EU summit, and urged the EU to set a firm date for the start of accession talks with Turkey. The strong pressure by the US leadership led to a similarly strong response from Rasmussen, who declared that he would listen carefully to the advice offered by others but that 'the choice was entirely in EU leaders' hands' (UPI 2002). However, Turkish officials discounted European reactions to US strategy. As the Turkish Ambassador in Washington, Faruk Logoglu, put it, 'We hear from time to time that the Europeans [don't like] so much pressure and persuasion, but in the end we think the US attitude is making a positive contribution' (Daniel 2002). The decision of the EU leadership meeting in Copenhagen failed to fulfil the expectations of Ankara and Washington. The EU Council declared that the opening of accession negotiations in 2004 would be conditional on Turkey fully meeting the Copenhagen criteria, particularly with respect to improving its human rights record and reducing the military's influence in politics (*New York Times* 2002). In this instance, Washington's pressure on the EU seemed to have backfired (Onis & Yilmaz 2005, p. 273).

The failure of the US to get a specific date for the start of the EU–Turkey accession talks underscored the declining effectiveness of US pressure on Europe. By refusing to comply with Washington's requests at the Copenhagen summit, the EU clearly showed its displeasure at the Bush administration's intensive lobbying activities. In fact, many EU officials indicated that the US efforts to influence the EU's decision were counterproductive. As the French Industry Minister, Nicole Fontaine, put it, 'It's certainly not up to the President of the United States to interfere in something so important and which mainly concerns the Europeans' (*New York Times* 2002).

The outcome of the Copenhagen summit was instructive for US policy-makers. Although the highest-ranking US officials, including Presidents Bush and Obama, continued to express their support for Turkey's European integration, the US approach to the Turkish membership issue became more discreet and low-key in the 2000s in comparison with the period from 1995 to 2002. This change stems partly from the fact that the US has accomplished two of its major policy objectives, namely, the formal recognition of Turkey's candidacy and the start of accession talks between Brussels and Ankara in 2004. While Washington favours Turkey's full membership in the EU, it has also recognised that the accession process is likely to be lengthy. The shift from intense diplomatic engagement to a more subtle approach reflects Washington's view that further pressure on France or Germany on the issue of Turkish membership issue is not likely to change the policies of these countries (Atlantic Council 2004,

p. 20). Moreover, the US has become more sensitive to the complaints voiced by European leaders and EU officials about what they consider to be unwarranted US interference in the internal affairs of the EU.

The Consequences of US Support for Turkey's EU Membership

Washington's active engagement in EU–Turkey relations has had several important consequences. First and foremost, the firm and vocal support the US gave to Turkey's European aspirations has played a critical role in Turkey's progress towards integration with the EU. Washington's persistent and enthusiastic backing of Turkey provided Ankara with an important asset in its efforts to sign a customs union agreement with Brussels in 1995 and to obtain formal candidacy for membership in 1999. Had it not been for Washington's decision to engage fully in EU–Turkey relations at the highest levels and provide its support to Ankara on one of the most important objectives of Turkish foreign policy, Turkey would probably have faced far greater difficulty in making progress towards joining the EU. However, Washington's advocacy of Turkey's inclusion in the EU has not been without its drawbacks. Most importantly, the pressure the US put on the EU increasingly led to anger and frustration among European officials, who resented what they perceived to be the 'heavy-handedness' of US officials and reacted strongly against what they viewed as interference in the internal affairs of the EU (Daniel 2002).

Washington's policy on Turkish membership in the EU has also had a significant impact on Turkey's domestic politics and foreign policy. To strengthen the case for Turkey's entry into the EU, the US has urged Turkey to push through political reforms and democratisation measures to fulfil the Copenhagen criteria and work towards a peaceful resolution of the Cyprus conflict. Since the early 1990s, the US government has developed a strong interest in Turkey's human rights record and the Kurdish issue. Utilising both public diplomacy and informal channels, Washington has frequently urged the Turkish government to improve its human rights performance. The US Congress adopted several measures during the 1990s to restrict arms sales to Turkey, on the grounds that some weapons systems were used against civilians in the Turkish government's counterterrorism campaign against the Kurdistan Workers' Party (PKK) (Makovsky 2000, p. 253). US policy-makers have also emphasised that while the US supports Turkey's efforts to fight the PKK's campaign of terrorism and political violence, they would like Turkey to implement policies to end human rights violations and to adopt measures that would lead to a political solution of the Kurdish problem. The annual human rights reports prepared by the US State Department have provided detailed information about the Turkish government's approach to human rights issues and practices. Over the years, the issues concerning democratisation, political reforms, and human rights in Turkey have become an important part of the bilateral agenda in the official meetings held in Ankara and Washington (Sayari 2004, pp. 102–103). US officials have joined their EU counterparts in stressing the need for political reforms and democratisation measures in Turkey. The combined impact of the US and

European pressures on Turkey has been important in the progress made since the late 1990s regarding human rights problems, especially those related to the Kurdish issue.

Another important consequence of the US support for Turkey's EU membership concerns the Cyprus conflict. The US has been deeply involved in the Cyprus problem since the early 1960s (Guney 2004). Initially, Washington's main objective was to prevent the escalation of the Greek–Turkish conflict over Cyprus into an armed confrontation between its two NATO allies. To this end, the US pressured both Athens and Ankara to refrain from increasing tensions on the island during the 1960s. Following the landing of Turkish troops on Cyprus in 1974, Washington launched a series of diplomatic initiatives, including sending nearly a dozen 'special envoys' to the island to broker a peace deal between the Greek and Turkish communities. After the US began to be actively involved in EU–Turkey relations, Washington's pressure on Ankara over the Cyprus problem increased significantly. Although a peaceful settlement of the Cyprus problem is not part of the Copenhagen criteria, the political stalemate on the island has nevertheless been an important obstacle to progress in EU–Turkey relations, especially after Cyprus joined the EU and succeeded in linking Turkey's membership prospects to the resolution of the conflict (Suvarierol 2003). Washington supported the EU's criticisms of the Turkish Cypriot leadership for the lack of progress in the negotiations between the two communities on the island. Additionally, the US urged Turkey to use its influence on the Turkish Cypriot leaders to reach an accommodation with their Greek Cypriot counterparts in order to lessen Greek–Turkish tensions and advance Turkey's accession to the EU. The US also played an important role in the negotiations among the principal parties involved in the Cyprus conflict which led to the formulation of a new plan by the United Nations (UN) Secretary General, Kofi Annan, in 2004 (Weston 2005). Washington's efforts, together with the pressures from Brussels, were instrumental in Turkey's support for the Annan Plan. The US was disappointed that the Greek Cypriot side chose not to support the Annan Plan in the referendum held on the island. Although the US would like to see a negotiated settlement, Washington, for the time being, seems to have chosen to play a less active role and leave the search for a solution to the Cyprus problem to the EU (Lesser 2008, p. 49).

Conclusion

The US government became deeply involved in EU–Turkey relations from the mid-1990s and has provided extensive diplomatic support for full Turkish membership in the EU since then. Washington's policy was formulated at a time when the US and Turkey had strong military and political ties. US support for Turkey's European integration was based largely on strategic considerations and Washington's wish to have Turkey firmly anchored to the West. To this end, US policy-makers sought to influence their European counterparts through personal diplomacy behind closed doors in addition to well-publicised public statements. US efforts on behalf of Turkey have played an important role in the progress in EU–Turkey relations, especially from

1995 to 2002. However, Washington's ability to influence the EU on the Turkish membership issue has declined since the early 2000s, as it also has over a number of other critical issues in transatlantic relations.

It is important to note that the Turkish–US alliance has experienced serious strains in recent years. The Turkish government's refusal to permit the passage of US troops through Turkey at the onset of the Iraq War in March 2003 led to a major crisis in US–Turkish relations. Moreover, since it came to power in 2002, the Justice and Development Party (AKP) has sought to reorient Turkish foreign policy through greater emphasis on closer ties with Iran, Syria, and radical Islamic groups such as Hamas. Turkey's vote in the UN Security Council against a new round of economic sanctions against Iran for its nuclear development programme and the escalation of tensions in Israeli–Turkish relations over the deadly confrontation in the Mediterranean between Israeli commandos and Turkish citizens sailing towards Gaza have led to growing feelings in the Washington policy community that Turkey is 'drifting away' from the West (Stokes 2010). Although the strains in bilateral ties have not, so far, led to a discernible change in Washington's support for Turkey's entry into the EU, the US stand on this issue is likely to be affected if Turkish–US relations continue to experience major problems in the near future. It is also possible that, given the declining popularity of the EU in Turkey and the growing opposition to Turkish membership in Europe, Washington may decide to work towards 'continued Turkish convergence with European norms, rather than the issue of membership per se' (Lesser 2010).

US support for Turkish accession does not represent an anomaly in Washington's approach to the enlargement of the EU. Since the beginning of European integration, the US has favoured a strong and unified Europe. US policy was largely based on strategic considerations, in which the security of Europe depended on economic stability and prosperity through the creation of a large market. Over the years, the US government has been involved, with varying degrees of diplomatic activity, in the expansion of the EU. For example, during the discussions concerning the large eastern enlargement in 2004, Washington played an important role in the EU's decision to extend membership to eight former communist countries in Eastern and Central Europe, along with Cyprus and Malta (Morningstar 2010). However, it is safe to conclude that on no other EU enlargement issue has Washington spent as much diplomatic capital and energy as it has on the protracted and complex process of Turley's accession to the EU.

Acknowledgement

The author would like to thank the anonymous reviewers of this article for their valuable comments and suggestions.

References

Abramowitz, M. (2000) 'The complexities of American policy-making on Turkey', in *Turkey's Transformation and American Policy*, ed. M. Abramowitz, Century Foundation Press, New York, pp. 153–184.

Atlantic Council of the US (2004) *Turkey on the Threshold: Europe's Decision and US Interests*, Washington.

Barkey, H. J. (2003) 'The endless pursuit: improving US–Turkish relations', in *The United States and Turkey: Allies in Need*, ed. M. Abramowitz, Century Foundation Press, New York, pp. 207–250.

Barkey, H. J. (2008) 'The effect of US policy in the Middle East on EU–Turkey Relations', *International Spectator*, vol. 43, no. 4, pp. 31–44.

Daniel, C. (2002) 'Bush and Powell press EU to take Turkey as member', *Financial Times*, 28 November, available online at: http://news.ft.com/servelet...toryFT&cid=1037872384631&p=1012571727291

Gordon, P. H. & Taspinar, O. (2008) *Winning Turkey: How America, Europe, and Turkey Can Revive a Fading Partnership*, Brookings Institution Press, Washington.

Grant, C. (2005) 'Turkey offers EU more punch', Centre for European Reform Comment and Analysis, available online at: http://www.cer.org.uk/articles/grant_europeanvoice_sep05.html

Guney, A. (2004) 'The USA's role in mediating the Cyprus conflict: a story of success or failure', *Security Dialogue*, vol. 35, no. 1, pp. 27–42.

Islam, R. D. (2008) *The Accession of Turkey to the European Union: Security Implications for Transatlantic Relations*, Dusseldorfer Institut für Aussen- und Sicherheitspolitik (DIAS), Dusseldorf.

Khalilzad, Z. (2000) 'A strategic plan for Western–Turkish relations', in the *Future of Turkish–Western Relations: Toward a Strategic Plan*, eds Z. Khalilzad, I. O. Lesser & F. S. Larrabee, RAND, Santa Monica, CA.

Kuniholm, B. (1994) *The Origins of Cold War in Near East: Great Power Conflict and Diplomacy in Iran, Turkey, and Greece*, 2nd edn. Princeton University Press, Princeton, NJ.

Kuniholm, B. (2001) 'Turkey's accession to the European Union: differences in European and US attitudes, and challenges for Turkey', *Turkish Studies*, vol. 2, no. 1, pp. 25–53.

Kramer, H. (2000) *A Changing Turkey: The Challenge to Europe and the United States*, Brookings Institution Press, Washington.

Larrabee, S. F. (1997) 'US and European Policy toward Turkey and the Caspian Basin', in *Allies Divided: Transatlantic Policies for the Greater Middle East*, eds R. D. Blackwill & M. Stürmer, MIT Press, Cambridge, MA, pp. 143–173.

Larrabee, S. F. & Lesser, I. O. (2003) *Turkish Foreign Policy in an Age of Uncertainty*, RAND, Santa Monica, CA.

Lesser, I. O. (2008) *Beyond Suspicion: Rethinking US–Turkish Relations*, Southeast Europe Project, Woodrow Wilson Center for Scholars, Washington.

Lesser, I. O. (2010) 'Rethinking Turkish–Western relations: a journey without maps', in *On Turkey: Analysis*, German Marshall Fund, Washington.

Makovsky, A. (2000) 'US Policy toward Turkey: progress and problems', in *Turkey's Transformation and American Policy*, ed. M. Abramowitz, Century Foundation Press, New York, pp. 219–266.

Makovsky, A. (2001) 'The US stake in Turkey's relations with Europe', paper presented at the Conference on 'Turkey in European and American Policy', CERI, Paris, 10–11 December.

Morningstar, R. L (2010) 'European Union enlargement: in the US interest', US Mission to the EU, available online at: http://useu.usmission.gov/About_The_Ambassador/Morningstar/May 1000_BAAA.asp

New York Times (2002) 'US is pressing Turkey to play an important role in any campaign against Iraq', 28 November, p. A1.

Onis, Z & Yilmaz, S. (2005) 'Turkey–EU–US triangle in perspective: transformation or continuity?', *Middle East Journal*, vol. 59, no. 2, pp. 265–284.

Sayarı, S. (2003) 'Turkey and the United States: changing dynamics of an enduring alliance', in *Turkey's Foreign Policy in the 21st Century: A Changing Role in World Politics*, eds T. Y. Ismael & M. Aydin, Ashgate, Farnham, pp. 27–39.

Sayarı, S. (2004) 'Turkish–American relations in the Post-Cold War era: issues of convergence and divergence', in *Turkish–American Relations: Past, Present, and Future*, eds M. Aydin & C. Erhan, Routledge, London, pp. 92–105.

Sayarı, S. (2006) 'Regional security issues and U.S.–Turkish relations in the 1980s', paper presented at the International Conference on the History of American Turkish Relations 1833–1989, Bogazici University, Istanbul, 5–6 June.

Schauble, W. (2004) 'A still-European Union', *Foreign Affairs*, vol. 83, no. 6, pp. 134–136.

Stokes, B. (2010) 'Turkey drifts away', *National Journal* (18 September) pp. 56–57.

Suvarierol, S. (2003) 'The Cyprus obstacle on Turkey's road to membership in the European Union', *Turkish Studies*, vol. 4, no. 1, pp. 55–78.

UPI (United Press International) (2002) 'EU raps Bush for Talking Turkey', available online at: http://www.Upi.com/view.cfm?StoryID=20021212-014508-4503r

White House, Office of the Press Secretary (1999) 'Remarks by the President in address to the Turkish Grand National Assembly', 15 November, available online at: http://www.whitehouse.gov/WH/New/html/19991115.html

White House, Office of the Press Secretary (2009) 'Remarks of President Obama address to Turkish Parliament, Ankara, Turkey', 6 April, available online at: http://www.whitehouse.gov/the_press_office/Remarks-By-President-Obama-To-The-Turkish-Parliament/

Weston, T. G. (2005) 'Next steps on Cyprus', in *Greek–Turkish Relations: A Key to Stability in the Eastern Mediterranean*, ed. MarisoR Lino, Libreria Bonomo, Bologna, pp. 117–132.

Yesilada, B. A. (2002) 'Turkey's candidacy for EU membership', *Middle East Journal*, vol. 56, no. 1, pp. 94–11.

Sabri Sayarı (PhD Columbia University) is Professor of Political Science at Sabanci University in Istanbul. Between 1994 and 2005, he served as the director of the Institute of Turkish Studies at Georgetown University in Washington, DC. His research interests include democratisation issues, political parties and party systems, and foreign policy analysis, with special focus on US–Turkish relations. He has published extensively on Turkish domestic politics and foreign policy. Most recently he published in *Terrorism and Violence* (2010) and co-edited (with M. Heper) *Türkiye'de Siyasi Liderler ve Demokrasi* Kitap, Istanbul, 2008).

The Turkish–EU Odyssey and Political Regime Change in Turkey

Ersin Kalaycıoğlu

Turkish–EU relations have occupied the Turkish political agenda since 1959. However, it was only after the Cold War that relations gained momentum and began to have a deep running impact on Turkish socio-political developments. One such area of impact has been the political regime of Turkey. In an effort to accommodate the standards of Turkish democracy with the Copenhagen Criteria, Turkish governments have initiated several constitutional amendments. This paper analyses the context and the nature of constitutional amendments made in the last three decades, and examines the role that EU–Turkish relations played in the modification of the Turkish political regime.

It is not unwarranted to argue that relations between Turkey and the EU seem to be a protracted and meandering process replete with various imperfections, though it is also fair to argue at the same time that Turkey's relations with the EU have correlated with the country's democratic reform process. Nevertheless, the credibility of full membership for Turkey in the EU has come under doubt in Turkey; opinion polls suggest that only about half the population are in favour of EU membership (Çarkoğlu & Kalaycıoğlu 2009).[1] In addition, recent research also indicates that attitudes towards EU membership have made a small but noticeable impact on the outcome of national elections in Turkey (Kalaycıoğlu 2009). Therefore, it seems that EU–Turkish relations matter, and Turkish governments seem to be taking steps to upgrade Turkish democracy to meet the Copenhagen Criteria. The central focus of this paper is to examine this process of the democratisation of the political regime in Turkey vis-à-vis the role played by the EU perspective of Turkish political elites.

The first part of this paper will examine the main characteristics of the 1982 Constitution and the related political laws that constitute the essence of the current democratic regime, and discuss the political context in which that regime has been functioning since the early 1980s. In the second part of the paper, the record of constitutional amendments that have been adopted since the 1980s will be documented, and the characteristics of those changes in the constitutional characteristics of the democratic regime will be examined. In the third and final section of the paper, the overall findings, conclusions, and difficulties that lie ahead of the democratisation of the regime in Turkey are discussed.

The Turkish Political Regime: The 1982 Constitution and More

Our main objective here is not to discuss the 1982 constitution per se; however, providing a short list of major constitutional amendments in its framework would still be necessary to appraise the impact of the EU membership process on the democratisation process in Turkey.

Starting in the 1980s and continuing ever since, there have been many attempts at amending the 1982 Constitution. The record of constitutional amendments has been relatively mixed. The political party system in Turkey, which is highly fragmented and polarised due to a long history of sharp, deep, and wide socio-cultural divisions along mainly confessional (secular versus pious), sectarian (Alevi versus Sunni), and ethnic nationalist (Kurdish versus Turkish) lines, operates in an environment of multiple political tensions, stresses, and conflicts. The electoral system with its ten per cent national threshold tends to deform the picture of the party system that emerges in the Turkish Grand National Assembly (TBMM), and often simplifies the extra-parliamentary picture as an image of the extra-parliamentary kulturkampf.[2] Such a milieu of deep and wide cultural cleavages among the legislative elite renders parliamentary politics difficult to manage, as it is often filled with reciprocal suspicion, distrust, and even enmity among the parliamentary parties and their deputies.[3] Such perceptions do not need much political stress to degenerate into relations between friends and foes, where little cooperation remains between the parliamentary parties in the TBMM.

Such a picture is not only specific to the TBMM, but also tends to permeate all branches of government. The Turkish public bureaucracy and the different agencies of the state experience similar divisions and expressions of the same kulturkampf. The sharpest contrasts have emerged between the civilian and military bureaucracies of the executive branch of the government, and also between the party or parties in government and the Constitutional Court (Anayasa Mahkemesi, CC), Supreme Court (Yargıtay, SC), and Council of State (Danıştay, CS). The images of a good society presented by the conservative government parties, the armed forces, non-conservative parties, and the judiciary have differed sharply and provided fertile ground for political conflict. In a recent book, Osman Can examines the sharp divide in the legal community in Turkey and enquires into the ideological roots of the continuing divide between the high courts and the lower-ranked members of the judiciary (Can 2010). The academic, business, trade union, media, and press circles of the country have also been deeply divided over the role of religion in the public space and over contrasting images of a good society. The declarations of TÜSİAD (Turkish Industrialists and

Businessmen's Association), KESK (The Confederation of State Employees' Union), DISK (Revolutionary Trade Union Confederation), and other business and labour unions in the campaign for the 12 September 2010 referendum, and their clashes over their support or lack of it for a 'Yes' vote with the leader of the Justice and Development Party (AKP) and the Prime Minister (PM), Erdogan, provide the most clear evidence of that divide among the interest groups of Turkey.[4]

Under these circumstances, it looks as if Turkey lacks a common ground on which any major national compromise over the basics of a constitutional regime that would serve as the core of a democratic regime can emerge with ease. It is this highly fragmented political culture with its multi-polar confrontations that renders the smooth operation of democracy difficult in the country. Such a cultural background has also made it very difficult for political movements and parties to come to terms with each other on the fundamentals of a democratic political regime that could be encapsulated in a written constitution. Small scale, urgent, and pressing alterations in the 1982 Constitution have been made by the Turkish political elite. In fact, up to the end of 2009 the 1982 Constitution was amended 15 times, changing the preamble and almost half of the articles, though a full-scale substitution of the text with a new document has not yet been attempted. The AKP government was able to push through a major amendment in the status of the President of the Republic through a referendum that took place on 21 October 2007, which introduced a popularly elected president into the country's formerly semi-parliamentary regime. Therefore, the relations between the Office of the President and the Council of Ministers and the PM and also with the TBMM and the judiciary need to be redesigned before the election of such a president in the next few years. Finally, the fact that the country has been involved in full accession negotiations with the European Union (EU) since 2005 makes it imperative that more changes be made. A closer examination of relations between Turkey and the EU will shed more light on why such a need persists in Turkish politics, and on how Turkey may pursue a course of constitutional reform in the near future.

Kulturkampf meets *Acquis*

When the Cold War came to an end in 1989, Turkish–EU relations became more complicated. However, Turkey continued to insist on the application of the 1963 Ankara Treaty and campaigned for closer ties with the EU. In 1995 a Customs Union Agreement between the EU and Turkey was signed; it came into operation on 1 January 1996.[5] It seemed as if the EU and Turkish markets were on the way to becoming integrated. In practice, the Customs Union Agreement enabled less restricted movement of goods and some services, though new visa practices imposed by EU member countries upon Turkish citizens kept the whole of the labour market out of the integration process. In spite of all its limitations, in practice the Customs Union seemed to motivate Turkish governments to seek full membership with added zeal in 1997. Although the government was severely rebuffed in 1997 (Hamilton 1997), and put all political contacts with the EU on hold, two years later in Helsinki the EU decided that Turkey was eligible for full membership in the EU (Müftüler-Baç 2002). The negotiations that started after this decision in 1999 were again less than smooth. It took a full five years for the EU to accept Turkey as a candidate for full membership, with some caveats, and to start the accession negotiations in 2005. Although the process of accession negotiations is moving with difficulty, neither side yet appears to see any merit in terminating them. Many issues continue to complicate the negotiations, which we recognise here but do not consider within the scope of this paper.[6]

The 1982 Constitution has gone through several amendments, which gained in relative frequency and scope between 1995, when the Customs Union negotiations started, and 2005, when the accession talks for Turkey's full membership began. Table 1 provides a summary of the data concerning constitutional amendments, and Figure 1 presents the trajectory of the constitutional amendments over time.

When Figure 1 and Table 1 are closely examined, one observes that a large number of the constitutional amendments were made between 1995 and 2001. When we consider the fact that the AKP was established on 14 August 2001, it is obvious that two-thirds of the constitutional amendments took place before the AKP was even established, let alone before it rose to power in 2002. In fact, the greatest incidence of constitutional amendments occurred in 2001, followed by 1995 and 2004 (see Figure 1).

On examining the contents of the constitutional amendments, one cannot detect any major difference in the three instances in 1995, 2001, and 2004 when major attempts to overhaul a large number of articles of the 1982 Constitution were made, by coalition governments in the first two instances, and by the AKP in the last. All of these amendments were primarily directed at lifting several restrictions pertaining to political, social, and cultural liberties, on the one hand, and providing for equality, on the other. All of the major constitutional amendments of 1995, 2001, and 2004 represent different examples of the promotion of civil liberties.[7] Most of the other amendments dealt primarily with procedural matters concerning elections, political parties, and the TBMM. Although these centre more on the procedures of the institutions of representation, they are important for the fair, smooth, and effective operation of representative democracy in Turkey and, as such, should be considered to be measures promoting democracy. Of these, the 2007 amendments constitute an attempt at introducing sweeping changes in the procedures of the TBMM and the election of the President of the Republic, which is nothing less than changing the character of the political regime of the country from a semi-parliamentary to a semi-presidential regime. However, such a shift in regime character has more to do with the power struggle between the AKP and the opposition than with the quality of representative democracy in Turkey. The major amendments of 1995, 2001, and 2004 have coincided with the junctures in Turkish–EU relations. C. Brewin (2002, pp. 10–11) argues that at the Helsinki Summit of 1999 it was agreed that

> it was up to Turkey as a sovereign state to reform itself in line with the conditions demanded of all candidates for membership ... Mr. Bülent Ecevit's letter to

TURKEY AND THE EU: ACCESSION AND REFORM

Table 1 The Odyssey of the Constitutional Amendments in Turkey (1983–2010)

Years	Amendments	%	Type of government	Total (%)	The subject matter of the amendments
1983	0	0			
1984	0	0			
1985	0	0			
1986	0	0			
1987	4	3.8	Party		Election regulations
1988	0	0			
1989	0	0			
1990	0	0			
1991	0	0			
1992	0	0			
1993	1	0.9	Coalition		Privatisation of the TRT (Turkish Radio and Television) + news agencies
1994	0	0			
1995	14	13,6	Coalition		Liberties + legislative procedure + status of local administrations + procedures for political parties + procedures for the CC
1996	0	0			
1997	0	0			
1998	0	0			
1999	3	2.9	Coalition		Privatisation + judicial review + Council of State
2000	0	0			
2001	29	28.2	Coalition	49.5	Liberties + protection of the family + right to organise labour unions + Turkish citizenship + right to vote + legislative procedure + National Security Council + trial procedures + Provisional Article 15
2002	2	1.9	Party		Eligibility to be a deputy + deferment of elections to the TBMM, and by-elections
2003	0	0			
2004	10	9.7	Party		Equality + liberties + suspension of rights and freedoms + protection of printing facilities + general provisions of legislature + ratification of international treaties + higher education + state security courts + audit court
2005	7	6.8	Party		Institutions of higher education + TRT administrations and state-financed news agencies + audit court + budget + principles governing budgetary amendments
2006	1	0.9	Party		Eligibility to be a deputy

(continued)

Table 1 – *Continued*

Years	Amendments	%	Type of government	Total (%)	The subject matter of the amendments
2007	6	5.8	Party		21 October 2007 referendum: tenure of TBMM + administration and supervision of elections + quorum of TBMM + impartiality in elections + election of the President of the Republic + Provisional Article 17
2008	0	0			
2009	0	0			
2010	26	25.2	Party	50.5	12 September 2010 referendum: composition of the CC, Higher Council of Prosecutors and Judges + Military Tribunals + Human Rights + Ombudsman + Right to Strike of Public Employees
Total	103	100		100	

Source: http://www.tbmm.gov.tr/anayasa.htm.
Note: The total number of amended articles is 94, though some articles are amended several times; since I counted each time an article was amended, with multiple counts the total amended articles add up to 103.

Chancellor Schröder of May 26, 1999 had agreed that Turkey must first fulfill the general accession criteria set down in 1993 in the Copenhagen EU summit and meet the obligations in the Amsterdam Treaty of 1997 before negotiations can begin.

From 1993 onwards Turkish governments have made various depositions of commitment to adapt the political regime of the country to the Copenhagen and

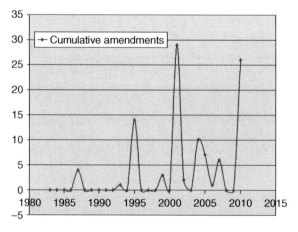

Figure 1 Amendments of the 1982 Constitution (1987–2010)
Source: http://www.tbmm.gov.tr/anayasa.htm.

Maastricht political and economic criteria before starting accession negotiations (Steinbach 2000). The effects of these commitments are visible in the incidence and frequency of constitutional amendments carried out since 1993 (see Figure 1 and Table 1).

The Customs Union Agreement (1995) provided a new incentive for the Turkish government to undertake new political and economic reforms, and a spate of constitutional amendments were motioned and successfully carried through in 1995. Ergun Özbudun, who analysed the 1995 constitutional amendments at length, argued that the main opposition to the amendments came from the ranks of the political Islamist Welfare Party (RP), whereas all the other small parties in the TBMM were positively disposed towards the amendments motioned by a coalition government of two parties, the True Path Party (DYP) and the Social Democratic People's Party (SHP), and also supported by the Motherland Party (ANAP), which was the main opposition party at that time. The 1995 amendments, according to Özbudun's account, were the most comprehensive overhaul of the 1982 Constitution yet and were carried out by a coalition government amidst a highly fragmented parliamentary party system. This seems to have taken place at the time of the Customs Union negotiations, when the major parties across the secular and conservative divide were in a coalition government in the TBMM. It was only the radical parties of the right such as the RP that opposed the amendments at the time, and their opposition could be surmounted through a coalition of centre-left and centre-right parties (Özbudun 2000). After Turkish eligibility for EU membership was recognised at the Helsinki Summit of 1999, the Turkish government renewed its pledge to make several changes in the legal system of the country to meet the Copenhagen Criteria that year (Brewin 2002), which precipitated new motions by the coalition government of the time not only to amend the constitution in 1999 but also eventually to carry through a more comprehensive set of constitutional amendments in 2001. In fact, to date, no new set of constitutional amendments has surpassed the incidence of amendments carried through in 2001. Özbudun and Gençkaya (2010), who analysed the 2001 amendments at length, came to the conclusion that they were the most comprehensive amendments to date, and remarkable for a political system that is notorious for its political elites' lack of ability to cooperate. It was indeed striking that a coalition government of three political parties could form a large enough coalition to get the amendments through a highly fragmented parliament in 2001 in the midst of a severe financial crisis that was deeply influencing the political system. It is also interesting to note that the former RP had been banned and the current AKP and the Felicity Party (SP) had emerged as its successors and both had resisted the amendments of several articles. However, their resistance was not comprehensive and they seem to have supported some amendments, such as decreasing the length of custody in terror cases to four days without a judge's decision, which enabled the amendments to be adopted by the TBMM.

What is more remarkable about the constitutional amendments of the 1990s and of 2001 is that they were motioned by coalition governments and were adopted by large majorities in the TBMM of a highly fragmented and polarised legislature. During the 1995 constitutional amendments, the DYP and the SHP were in government and they had to persuade the opposition to adopt their motion for constitutional amendments. In 1999, and later in 2001, it was the Democratic Left Party (DSP), the ANAP, and the Nationalist Action Party (MHP) coalition government, with an ailing and elderly PM, Bülent Ecevit, which carried through the constitutional amendments. Therefore, it is plausible to conclude that there has been relatively large-scale support among Turkish political elites of almost all ideological backgrounds for the deepening of relations between Turkey and the EU. Full membership in the EU is a project that transcends partisan politics and carries multi-party consensus. I would like, though, to caution the reader that these constitutional amendments were not made with ease. Many proposed amendments failed to go through in this period. However, in a political milieu of high discord and deep cultural divides, to be able to carry through any meaningful amendment is a major accomplishment (Özbudun 2000).

The procedural content of the constitutional amendments that materialised after the coming into power of the AKP differed markedly from the earlier ones. In 2002, the AKP was able to capture more than two-thirds of the seats in the National Assembly with a mere 34 per cent of the vote. It was the idiosyncrasy of the Turkish electoral laws, which resemble a proportional representation formula though functioning as a majoritarian one in converting votes into legislative seats, that enabled the AKP to control a huge majority of the seats in the National Assembly with about one-third of the national vote. This strategic position of the AKP in the TBMM enabled it to motion constitutional amendments without any serious negotiations with the major opposition parties between 2002 and 2007, when it gained many more votes at the national elections but lost some seats and its two-thirds majority in the TBMM. Hence, when the AKP developed a predilection for unilateral action in 2007 it precipitated political tension and conflict along the cultural divides in the country. It did not take long before a no-holds-barred war among the major political parties and movements of the country resurfaced. The AKP presenting itself as the representative of the people, values of the nation, democracy and the like, versus the CHP and others as the representatives of the secular–modernist elite emerged in no time. There is no evidence that such a style of legislative politics leaves much room for contacts-seeking, negotiations, and compromise between the government and the opposition parliamentary parties in the TBMM. There is no evidence that such a majoritarian legislative posture, married with political tension and conflict outside the TBMM, has hurt the AKP or the CHP in national elections.

When the AKP made a determined move to start accession negotiations for full EU membership in 2004, there were hardly any hurdles for it to clear to motion the constitutional amendments it saw fit. In that atmosphere, the 2004 constitutional amendments, which also coincided with the EU's decision to start accession negotiations with Turkey the next year, were carried through smoothly. A series of other laws and regulations were also altered, among them the criminal code (*ceza kanunu*), the code on criminal adjudications (*ceza muhakemeleri kanunu*), the associations act (*dernekler kanunu*), and the charitable endowments act (*vakıflar kanunu*), which went through drastic changes that have improved the standards of governance in the country. We should hasten to add that these changes not only coincided with the rapprochement between Turkey and the EU, but were also a continuation of the process that had started earlier. For example, another major legal reform took place during the term of the coalition government of PM Ecevit when the civil code of the country was completely reformulated. It was with the new civil code that large-scale changes in the social and economic status of women could be introduced. It is uncertain whether such progressive changes in the status of women could have taken place under the reign of conservative AKP, with its front bench of leaders with solid careers in the Islamist movement, which has produced a predilection for misogynist decisions in government. The Islamist character of the AKP surfaces at critical times. For example, when the criminal code was voted on, a group of AKP deputies moved an amendment in the criminal code to define adultery as a criminal offence, punishable with a stiff sentence for women. The uproar from feminist organisations, and among them female lawyers, triggered strong reactions from the EU and the Council of Europe, which seem to have led to the eventual defeat of the amendment on the floor of the TBMM (İnce 2004). Such changes gained pace as Turkey courted the EU, yet we should emphasise that the political reform process through Turkish-EU interface has been a process, and not a discrete phenomenon that started only after the AKP came to power in 2002.

The seven articles of the 1982 Constitution on several procedural matters concerning the executive branch of the government and the budgetary procedure were amended, as was another article concerning the eligibility requirements for membership in the TBMM in 2005 in such an environment. However, these amendments were mostly unrelated to the EU or the quality of governance and democracy in the country. The AKP motioned another set of procedural changes in the operation of the TBMM and the election of the president in 2007. They seem to have emerged all of a sudden, without any previous planning, and were carried through at the height of a confrontation between the AKP and the opposition in 2007.

Eventually, the AKP seemed to gain enough self-confidence to exploit its position of legislative hegemony to sharply confront and even slight the opposition. Such a stance triggered a similarly abrasive and confrontational response from the main opposition parties in the TBMM. Heightened political conflict, culminating in the questioning of the allegiance of the government party to the republican regime and of the main opposition parties to democracy, precipitated a deepening legitimacy crisis as Turkey headed towards a presidential election in the spring of 2007, a general election in the summer of 2007, and a referendum in the autumn of 2007.

The opposition became increasingly abrasive, anti-AKP, and anti-EU, and started to present an image of the AKP as an unconstrained hegemon ready to compromise any values and any interests of Turkey to promote its goals, constituted around a set of Islamist, anti-Republican values. The opposition also began to portray the AKP as a hostile force ready to undermine the secular characteristics of the Republic and accept almost any EU proposal to consolidate its power and undermine the national interests of Turkey. In their eyes, the AKP had become the enemy. The country headed once again towards a no-holds-barred war between alternative images of a good society. When AKP spokespersons began to voice criticism of the secular record of the Republic and suggested ways of amending the constitution to modernise secularism, or make it look less like French and more like American standards of secularism, the opposition declared that the AKP was about to launch a counter-revolution. It seems as if all chances of establishing any accord over a new set of constitutional amendments had been squandered by 2005, let alone the adoption of a whole new constitution.

In spite of all the hype about the 2007 constitutional amendments, they were totally unrelated to the improvement of the quality of democracy. In the last few months of 2007 and early 2008 the country was also occupied with the amendment of two articles of the 1982 Constitution dealing with the *türban*-donning practices of religious-conservative women and Islamist activists in educational institutions and state agencies, this amendment being struck down by the CC. It is hard to categorise that initiative of the conservative democrat AKP, ethnic Turkish nationalist conservative MHP, and ethnic Kurdish nationalist Democratic Society Party (DTP) as a move of adaptation to the EU *acquis* either. What that move has managed to do is to fan the fears of the secular opposition that the CHP seems to represent—that the AKP has revealed its zeal for tinkering with the secular regime of the Republic.

Under the circumstances, it seems that the Turkish government and the TBMM stopped promoting an EU agenda soon after Turkey began accession negotiations with the EU in 2005. The focus of the government moved inwards and towards consolidating its power by establishing full-scale control of all the autonomous agencies of the state, from the Central Bank, Radio and Television Supreme Council (RTÜK) to the Council of Higher Education (YÖK) and the rectors of the public universities. The AKP also moved to establish as Islamic revivalist an image as possible in such high political offices of the land as that of the Presidency of the Republic, the Speakership of the TBMM, and the PM. From 2007 onwards, all of those positions were occupied by members of the AKP frontbench who had had solid careers in Islamic revivalism. It appears as if the AKP and its conservative–Islamic revivalist sympathisers decided to confront and challenge the secularists head on by scaling up the conflict to the highest positions of the Turkish state. This seemed to coincide with the move of the Chief Prosecutor of the Supreme Court (Yargıtay Başsavcısı) to indict the AKP as constituting a focal point of activities against the secular principles of the Republic as stated in the article 2 of the 1982 Constitution. Coincidentally, the CC concurred with the Chief Prosecutor's argument, as ten judges, including a staunchly conservative judge, voted to uphold and only one conservative judge voted against the indictment. It seems as if the challenge by the AKP to the secular practices and standards of the Republic precipitated a kulturkampf between the secularist and the Islamic revivalist blocs of the country.

From 2007 onwards, the country showed signs of having lost its focus on EU-related policy efforts in its domestic as well as foreign policies. In fact, from 2005 to January 2009 the government refrained from appointing a chief negotiator whose job would solely consist of the management of the EU portfolio of the country. The state minister in charge of the economy and later the minister of foreign affairs, Ali Babacan, held the position of chief negotiator as a part-time job for four years, until Egemen Bağış was finally appointed as the chief negotiator in the post of a state minister on 11 January 2009. It was this appointment that moved the EU agenda back into the limelight of politics. Although the general secretariat in charge of EU affairs (ABGS) had its authority and role augmented for the first time and Minister Bağış was able to acquire more than 300 cadres for his bureaucracy in 2009, by the end of 2009 these developments had not led to any major attempts to push for the democratising amendments to the 1982 Constitution demanded by the EU.

There is no tangible evidence that either the local elections campaign of early 2009 or the overture directed at the Kurds, Alevis, and Roma in Turkey which started in the summer of 2009 were legitimised as part of the EU accession process. The overtures were eventually presented as new rights for the relatively marginalised ethnic and religious communities of the country, with only sporadic reference to democratisation in the process.

At last, new constitutional amendments were motioned in March 2010. These were mainly focused on changing the composition of the CC and the High Council of Judges and Prosecutors, and the political party closure clauses, and appear to have more to do with a potential closure case against the AKP before the national elections of 2011. The rest of the constitutional amendment package included several articles introduced to enhance the quality of constitutional democracy in Turkey, but generally considered by the opposition parties and the non-governmental media in Turkey to be sweeteners to make people vote affirmatively in a referendum. The motion was carried in the TBMM in May 2010 by the AKP votes, as all of the opposition parties resisted, though not all of the opposition parties shared the same perspective on the substance of the amendments. These amendments were approved by the President, though the CHP and other opposition party members appealed to the CC that they breached the constitution. The CC decided that there were only minor problems with two articles of the amendments, which were altered by the High Election Commission. With those final alterations, the amendments were motioned for a referendum, for the 1982 Constitution made it mandatory for any amendment that receives more than 60 per cent approval in the TBMM but less than two-thirds to be automatically submitted to popular vote for final approval. On 12 September 2010 the referendum received 58 per cent of popular support at the polls and the amendments were thus legally adopted. These amendments changed the composition of the CC and also extended its role in the judiciary. Similarly, the Higher Council of Prosecutors and Judges now have new members elected by all prosecutors and judges in the country. Military tribunals also have new standards. With the participation of new and probably more conservative judges on the bench, the banning of political parties, which seems to have been a worry of the governing AKP, has become much more difficult to vote on in the CC.[8] Such changes have been generally accepted as further democratisation of Turkey, though it is certainly not clear whether such democratising moves have taken place with the EU in mind or not.

Conclusion: Plus ça change, plus c'est la même chose!

The effect of the EU on the democratisation of the Turkish political regime seems to have gone through two different periods. In the earlier process, the calibration of Turkish democratic practices according to the Copenhagen Criteria seemed to be a multi-partisan or national project shared by all political parties. From 1993 to 2002 all major parties jointly negotiated, deliberated, and eventually established pro-amendment coalitions of compromise in the TBMM. All of the constitutional amendments that promoted political liberties and rights between 1993 and 2002 were the acts of several political parties coalescing to secure more than a two-thirds majority in the TBMM to alter articles of the 1982 Constitution. A second period seems to have started in 2002, in which constitutional amendments were presented as the partisan accomplishment of the AKP, which moved to promote liberties and rights while the other political parties resisted democratisation and the EU perspective of the AKP. Although this perspective is popular among pro-AKP government media, Turkey experienced a major shift of style in the conducting of legislative business after 2002. A two-party format in the intra-parliamentary party system in Turkey led to a non-conciliatory style of operation for the majority AKP group in the TBMM, which was in very sharp contrast with the earlier conciliatory style of constitutional amendments in the TBMM. With the two-thirds majority the AKP obtained after the 2002 elections, that party obtained the strategic size to motion constitutional amendments as a single party. The peculiarities of the electoral system in Turkey accorded the front-running AKP a huge exaggeration of its mandate in the TBMM. The election results created huge disproportionalities of seat distribution in the national legislature in favour of the AKP, which relieved that party of any need to seek compromise with other parliamentary groups to move constitutional amendments. Thus, the AKP won the potential to act alone in projecting its own priorities and vision into the amended articles of the 1982 Constitution.

This situation also enabled the AKP to project an image of itself as the only party that should be given credit for creating higher standards of liberties, rights, and democracy in Turkey. Cooperation and coordination were sidelined in the conduct of business in the TBMM, and instead confrontation and conflict between the governing AKP and the opposition parties became the norm in the two-party parliament of 2002–07 and also in the post-2007 multi-party parliament with the AKP as hegemon. The AKP thus developed the habit of ignoring all opposition to its legislative initiatives, which further contributed to a style of politics that cast all opposition as foe, on the one hand, and, on the other, projected an image of the AKP as the only party for democracy and the EU while the other parties were deemed to have dubious democratic and Europeanising credentials. What is amazing is that this rather simple and fallacious image could be effectively propagated to the Turkish voters and to the Eurocrats and other foreign allies of Turkey. Such a posture in EU circles further poisoned Turkish domestic politics. The EU seemed to be taking sides in the domestic power struggles in Turkey, as it appeared to be extending support to the AKP, which the Eurocrats perceived as the only pro-EU party in Turkish politics. However, the kulturkampf in Turkey simply places the AKP on one side of a deep-running cultural cleavage and therefore, by supporting the AKP, the Eurocrats became allies of the AKP and thus the enemy in the eyes of those on the other side of the cleavage. As earlier analysed in this paper, the current kulturkampf in Turkey depicts the AKP, in the eyes of its opponents, as the new and most sophisticated political organisation of the Islamist movement in Turkey, not so much a party of and for democracy, but a force of the Islamist movement in democratic garb. The AKP's opponents perceive the EU as colluding with Islamic revivalists to transform the secular republic, not necessarily in the direction of a liberal representative democracy. The overall impact of the EU in Turkish politics after 2002, by contributing to the deepening of the kulturkampf in Turkish politics, has been to widen and deepen the conflict between the AKP and its opponents. If this strategy succeeds in consolidating liberal democracy in the country, Turkey will emerge as the first example in Europe, and probably the world, of the consolidation of liberal democracy through elite divergence.

Notes

[1] Figure 7.1 on page 122 of their book shows the trend of popular support for EU membership in Turkey.

[2] The definition of the socio-cultural cleavages causing political confrontation and clash as 'kulturkampf' belongs to Yalman (1973).

[3] Depicting the intra-elite political interactions in the 1950s and the 1960s, Frey referred to them as 'no-holds-barred-war' (see Frey 1975, p. 65).

[4] *Hurriyet*, 2–10 September.

[5] http://europa.eu/abc/history/1990-1999/1996/index_en.htm

[6] http://www.hurriyet.com.tr/dunya/12688838.asp, http://www.abhaber.com/haber.php?id=32649

[7] One of the most important authorities on constitutional law in Turkey, Ergun Özbudun (2002), in a report on the 2001 amendments, argued that they constituted important democratising reforms: 'The overall conclusions [reached by experts] on the constitutional amendments carried out in 2001 were that even though most of the amendments were on the details of legal procedures ... the shortening of the time one is kept under custody, abolishing of the death penalty, rendering the banning of the political parties more difficult, and the lifting of the limitations on the legal control over the decisions of the regime of the National Security Council [military government of 1980–83] have been important democratizing political reforms.'

[8] There is not yet much academic analysis of the topic; however one may refer to the papers by Turan (2010) and Kalaycıoğlu (2010a) on the pre- and post-referendum politics of Turkey in 2010.

References

Brewin, C. (2002) *Turkey and Europe after the Nice Summit*, TESEV, Istanbul.

Can, O. (2010) *Darbe Yargısının Sonu: Karargâh Yargısından Halkın Yargısına* [The End of the Judiciary of the Coup: From the Judiciary of the Military Headquarters to the Judiciary of the People], Timaş Yayınları, Istanbul.

TURKEY AND THE EU: ACCESSION AND REFORM

Çarkoğlu, A. & Kalaycıoğlu, E. (2009) *The Rising Tide of Turkish Conservatism*, Palgrave Macmillan, New York.

Frey, F. W. (1975) 'Patterns of Elite Politics in Turkey', in *Political Elites in the Middle East*, ed. George Lenczowski, American Enterprise Institute for Public Policy Research, Washington.

Hamilton, D. (1997) 'Tension over Turkey at EU summit talks', 13 December, available online at: diaspora@disapora-net.org; see also *Turkish Daily News*, 14–15 December 1997.

İnce, Ö. (2004) 'Şenlik Başladı', [The festival has started], available online at: http://hurarsiv.hurriyet.com.tr/goster/haber.aspx? id=259842&yazarid=72

Kalaycıoğlu, E. (2009) 'Public choice and foreign policy: democracy and international relations in Turkey', *New Perspectives on Turkey*, no. 40, pp. 57–81.

Kalaycıoğlu, E. (2010) 'Turkish referendum: divided we stand', GMF's, *On Turkey* series, 17 September, available online at: http://www.gmfus.org/onturkey

Müftüler-Baç, M. (2002) *Enlarging the European Union: Where Does Turkey Stand?* TESEV, Istanbul.

Özbudun, E. (2000) *Contemporary Turkish Democracy*, Lynne Rienner, Boulder, CO.

Özbudun, E. (2002) *2001 Anyasa Değişiklikleri ve Siyasal Reform Önerileri*, TESEV, Istanbul.

Özbudun, E. & Gençkaya, Ö. F. (2010) *Türkiye'de Demokratikleşme ve Anayasa Yapım Politikası* [Democratization in Turkey and the Politics of Constitution-Making], Doğan Kitap, Istanbul.

Steinbach, U. (2000) 'Pro: provider of stability', in Peter Scholl-Latour & Udo Steinbach, 'EU Membership for Turkey', *Internationale Politik* (Transatlantic Edition), no. 2.

Turan, İ. (2010) 'A background to the constitutional referendum: reinforcing the politics of polarization', GMF's *On Turkey* series, 30 August 2010, available online at: www.gmfus.org/onturkey

Yalman, N. (1973) 'Some observations on secularism in Islam: the cultural revolution in Turkey', *Daedalus*, vol. 102, pp. 139–167.

Ersin Kalaycıoğlu (PhD University of Iowa) is a professor of political science at Sabancı University Faculty of Arts and Social Sciences, Istanbul. He previously served as a full-time faculty member at Istanbul and Boğaziçi Universities, Istanbul, and in the capacity of rector at Işık University, Istanbul, and has been a visiting scholar at the Universities of Iowa, Minnesota, and Oxford. He has published extensively on Turkish politics, and his most recent book is entitled *The Rising Tide of Conservatism* (Palgrave-Macmillan, 2009, co-authored with A. Çarkoğlu).

Turkish Foreign Policy, its Domestic Determinants and the Role of the European Union

Meltem Müftüler-Baç

This paper investigates whether Turkish foreign policy has changed in recent years, specifically in line with the EU accession process, and tries to uncover the main dynamics behind these changes. The main proposition in the paper is that domestic changes in Turkey have led to a reshuffling of foreign policy objectives with a renewed emphasis on improving relations with the country's neighbours. The paper investigates whether such a policy change is complementary to the Turkish goal of inclusion in the EU, and further proposes that the changes in Turkish foreign policy since 2002 involve an increased activism partly in line with the EU accession process and as a result of the changes in domestic politics.

On 17 May 2010, the Turkish government signed an agreement for a uranium swap with Iran and Brazil in order to find a peaceful solution to the question of a nuclear Iran and avert an international crisis. This initiative taken by the Turkish government on the Iranian question demonstrated a more visible, confident and daring Turkey in international politics. It is now becoming commonplace to argue that Turkey has become an active, visible player in world politics, a 'benign power' in its region, as well as a regional economic power. There are a number of related questions here. Does this activism constitute a rupture in Turkish foreign policy, or is it merely the continuation of post-Cold-War activism? If indeed Turkey is becoming more active, then what kind of factors account for this new activism? Are they domestically driven or internationally stimulated? Finally, what role does the European Union (EU) play in shaping Turkish foreign policy, if any? There is an ongoing debate in the existing literature on Turkish foreign policy as to whether there has been continuity in Turkish foreign policy since 1989 (Aydın 2000), whether there is a newly found activism that presents a rupture from earlier positions (Aras & Fidan 2009) and whether domestic politics or international changes play the most important role in shaping Turkey's foreign policy (Altunışık 2009; Keyman 2009). Accordingly, this paper addresses the question of what has made Turkish foreign policy more effective in recent years, if at all, and whether the EU accession process has had a role in this.

The purpose of this paper is to investigate Turkish foreign policy from the angle of its accession process to the EU. There are two main points here. First, the EU accession process provides an effective mechanism to stimulate political changes in Turkey; consequently, as Turkey becomes more democratic, groups previously excluded from foreign-policy-making become more vocal, leading to more activism as well as the formulation of new objectives. This does not, of course, imply that there were no internal mechanisms that led to a change in domestic politics, although the EU may have enhanced their power and visibility. Second, the uncertainties surrounding the accession process have led Turkey to look for new avenues to increase its power, partly to enhance its material benefits for the EU. The interplay of these two factors, the domestic political transformation partly in response to EU political conditionality and systemic factors such as the EU accession process, have been critical in shaping Turkish foreign policy.

The opening of accession negotiations between Turkey and the EU on 3 October 2005 constituted an important breakthrough for Turkey's foreign relations. The accession negotiations stimulated a Europeanisation process in Turkey in many aspects, one of which of course was foreign policy (Zucconi 2009; Müftüler-Baç & Gürsoy 2010). This process, however, has been ridden with many complexities because, as Turkey adjusted to the EU norms in foreign policy (Rumelili 2003), it found itself confronted with its complex past (Öniş & Yılmaz 2009). At the same time, there have been substantial changes in Turkish foreign policy. These changes are visible in such developments as the 2010 agreement with Iran on a uranium swap, the multi-million dollar energy deal with Iran in November 2009, the military cooperation scheme with Syria, cancellations of military exercises with Israel, the protocol signed with Armenia in 2009, and even the invitation of Sudan's President, Bashir Al-Omar, in 2008 for a visit while he was under investigation by the International Criminal Court for war crimes. There have been, of course, other periods in Turkish history when a similar activism could be observed, such as the 1950s or the end of the Cold War; however, since 2002, there seems to have been a new dimension in Turkish foreign policy which needs close scholarly analysis. Even though there are clear lines of continuity such as the relations with European countries (Müftüler-Baç 2008), a rupture in the policy towards Armenia and Syria as well as a different foreign policy making style, including increased economic tools and enhanced diplomatic initiatives, can be observed.

This paper proposes that the changes in Turkish foreign policy since 2002 could be investigated in line with the changes in domestic preferences: more specifically, one could argue that the new foreign policy dimensions adopted by the —Justice and Development Party (AKP) government are largely shaped by the process of democratisation, partly motivated by the EU accession process, and this could be seen as an indirect impact of the EU on Turkish foreign policy. In addition, Turkey seems to have experienced a Europeanisation of foreign policy with an increased emphasis on diplomatic tools, economics measures and increased public debate on foreign policy. Consequently, this paper analyses Turkish foreign policy by focusing on the role of domestic preferences and the impact of the EU accession process on the shaping of these domestic preferences. This does not mean that the shifts in the international distribution of power, or United States (US) policy in the Middle East, or the internal dynamics in Turkey between different political actors are unimportant, but they are beyond the purposes of this paper. First, the paper focuses on the changes in Turkish foreign policy, and then proceeds to an analysis of these changes by investigating domestic determinants in the light of the democratisation process. The findings of the paper will contribute to the literature on Turkish foreign policy and the EU's normative power.

The Changing Turkish Foreign Policy

With the opening of accession negotiations between Turkey and the EU in 2005, one could witness a Europeanisation of Turkish foreign policy (Müftüler-Baç & Gürsoy 2010). Turkish foreign policy demonstrated an adjustment to the EU's practice of diplomatic and economic measures, rather than the implicit use of force. These civilian tools involve seeking international legitimacy, collaborating with others in the region and looking for solutions in multilateral settings and international or regional institutions (Zielonka 1998). There are two main dimensions here: first, as foreign–policy-making adjusts to the EU norms, there seems to be an increased reliance on soft power rather than hard power tools. Second, there is an increased emphasis on removing all sources of tension with Turkey's neighbours. In addition, Turkey's economic strength as the sixteenth largest economy in the world has enhanced its power and visibility in international politics. The interplay of these three factors has led to a more effective Turkish foreign policy with an increased resonance. Consequently, Turkey, on the one hand, has developed a more active line in its foreign policy towards its neighbours and, on the other, it has adopted an EU-inspired foreign policy style of increased reliance on soft power tools. These are profound changes in Turkish foreign policy, setting it apart from other periods of activism, and these differences can be seen both in rhetoric and in action.

To turn to the rhetoric first, the declarations and speeches of Turkish foreign-policy-makers since 2002 reflect a more confident, conciliatory and cooperative mood, with one notable exception—towards Israel. On 4 May 2009, the Turkish Minister of Foreign Affairs, Ahmet Davutoğlu, declared, 'Turkish foreign policy has changed away from crisis-oriented to being based instead on "vision"', allowing Turkish policy-makers to identify potential crises before they erupt and devise appropriate policies to tackle them' (Aras 2009). This is in line with his main vision—the concept of 'strategic depth' (Davutoğlu 2008, p. 80; 2001)—that is determined by Turkey's geo-strategic position and history. Accordingly, 'the strategic depth theory maintains that Turkey can emerge as a regional power only if it establishes good ties with all these basins and hence all its neighbors' (Çağatay 2007, p.14). This has led to the adoption of new tools and instruments for protecting Turkish national interests with its neighbours in the Middle East, Caucasus and Central Asia, most importantly by eliminating all sources of hostilities.

In terms of action, one has to mention Turkey's foreign policy changes towards Iraq, Syria and Armenia, as well as its position in international institutions, as empirical proof of the changes in Turkish foreign policy. A case in point is the rapprochement with Armenia. When Turkish President Abdullah Gül visited Armenia in 2008, this was a breakthrough development constituting a rupture with previous policies.

In 2009, Turkey signed a protocol with Armenia to open the borders between the two countries, which constituted an important step in normalising Turkey's relations with Armenia in line with its aim of zero problems with neighbours. Turkey also began to rely increasingly on economic tools in its foreign policy, and, as it became the largest trading partner for Azerbaijan, Georgia and Iraq as well as one of the largest investors in these countries, its power became enhanced. For example, the prevalence of Turkish soft power over Iraq since 2005 can be witnessed in increased Turkish economic activities—trade and foreign investment—in the country. Turkish companies have invested extensively in Iraq and engaged in important projects: more than 80 Turkish companies have invested in US$1.5 billion worth of initiatives in the country.[1] As of 2009, there were 400 Turkish companies doing business in various parts of Iraq. The economic interactions between Turkey and Iraq have reached such proportions that Iraq is now the fifth-largest partner for Turkish exports, but, more importantly, Turkey has become Iraq's largest trading partner: the trade volume with Turkey in 2008 was $7 billion with a projected rise to $20 billion by 2011. On his visit to Iraq in 2009, the Turkish Foreign Minister, Ahmet Davutoğlu, stated that 'the aim of the meeting is not only cooperation but an integration of the two countries and the establishment of the scope of security issues' (Açıkalın 2008). Turkey's reliance on economic measures, such as trade and capital flows, and diplomatic measures for the resolution of conflicts between Turkey and Iraq fits well with the EU's foreign policy tools. This is why it is also possible to argue that there has been a Europeanisation of Turkish foreign policy in Iraq and Syria, mainly due to the increased reliance on diplomatic tools and economic measures rather than the use of force (Müftüler-Baç & Gürsoy 2010).

In addition to the increased use of diplomatic and economic tools, changes in Turkey's foreign policy are also visible in increased multilateralism in its policy formulations. Since 2003, Turkey's foreign policy has become very active in international organizations, as illustrated through its presence in the Organisation of the Islamic Conference (OIC),[2] its United Nations Security Council membership and the summits it has hosted since 2003. In 2004, a Turkish professor, Ekmeddin Ihsanoğlu, was elected secretary general of the OIC in its first elections, and this indicated Turkey's leadership role in the Muslim world. Turkey became a member of the G20, the main institutional mechanism for developing countries in the world, when it was established on 20 August 2003. In 2004, Turkey developed a project entitled 'Alliance of Civilisations' in order to advance intercultural dialogue in the world, which was then adopted by the UN in 2005; the second major forum of the Alliance was held in Istanbul in April 2009. The Alliance's main aim is to defuse possible conflicts and misunderstandings between the Western and Islamic worlds, and its evolution as an initiative attests to the increased importance of Turkey as a critical player in this field (Aydın & Açıkmeşe 2008).

Turkey expanded this active role in international organisations by pursuing membership in the Security Council of the United Nations. In the 2008 elections for the Security Council's rotating membership, Turkey was able to secure 151 votes—more than its main contenders, Austria and Iceland—and consequently was elected to the Security Council for the 2009–2011 period. This was a major success and a source of prestige for Turkey, as the last time it held this position was in 1961. The Turkish government held the rotating presidency of the Security Council in June 2009, and made the situations in Afghanistan, Pakistan and Gaza its top priority. In addition, in 2010, it brokered a deal with Iran to find a peaceful resolution to the nuclear question. Turkey's role in pushing for a UN resolution on the Israeli intervention on the Gaza aid flotilla in June 2010 was also noteworthy, demonstrating a more vocal and active Turkish foreign policy on the Israeli–Palestinian issue, a clear departure from earlier policies.

Turkey's role as a regional player expanded over multiple initiatives and through multiple platforms. In 2004, Turkey hosted the North Atlantic Treaty Organisation (NATO) summit in Istanbul with a new set of proposals for the NATO mission in Afghanistan and Iraq; in 2006, Turkey hosted the World Economic Forum, and in 2008, it hosted the African summit; in 2009, Turkey hosted the Alliance of Civilisations forum in April, the International Monetary Fund/World Bank summit in October and the OIC in November. In all of these summits, Turkey's active role as a regional leader was visible. In 2008, Turkey initiated the Caucasus Stability and Cooperation Platform following the war between Georgia and Russia. It has taken over command of the NATO force in Afghanistan three times since 2004 and it participated in the UN force in Lebanon (UNIFIL) in 2006, contributing significantly in all cases. Turkey has acted as a mediator between the US and Iran repeatedly since 2005, and between Syria and Israel before the 2010 crisis with Israel.[3] These developments also demonstrate Turkey's increased international prestige in international politics.

Turkey's increased visibility in international politics results partly from these initiatives within the auspices of the UN, OIC and G20. It is also the friendly relations the AKP government has with the Islamic world that lends credibility to these endeavours. These steps are in line with the above-mentioned strategic depth doctrine, and what Davutoğlu describes as 'rhythmic diplomacy', which means pursuing Turkey's key national interests through multilateralism and by relying on the institutional power of international organisations.

In short, its OIC leadership, Security Council membership, accession negotiations with the EU and the initiatives it undertakes in regional conflicts all indicate Turkey's increased activism in foreign policy. The increased emphasis on diplomatic tools, international organisations, and multilateralism and the pronounced policy of zero problems with neighbours are indicators of a new shift in Turkish foreign policy. According to Davutoğlu, this active policy is in line with the EU accession goal.

> Our integration to the EU is a strategic, historical choice of the Turkish nation, and it will continue. Our active involvement in other regions is an asset to our relations with the EU, rather than an alternative to the EU. (*Turkish Weekly* 2010b)

Thus, it seems that Turkish foreign policy has become more effective and more visible through such developments and endeavours. If so, how can one explain these changes? The next section looks at the domestic determinants of foreign policy in Turkey as influenced by the EU accession process.

The Impact of Domestic Politics on Turkish Foreign Policy

In the international relations literature, the influence of domestic preferences and the process of democratisation are increasingly taken as critical variables shaping foreign policy choices. This, however, does not mean that the domestic politics perspective is the only framework that can be used to analyse these changes. The systemic impacts on foreign policy formulations are not investigated in this paper, even though systemic factors play a role in shaping the domestic actors' preferences. This is because the international distribution of power as the most important systemic-level determinant would have a linkage to the domestic players' preferences. For example, during the Cold War years, the balance of power between the US and the Unions of Soviet Socialist Republics (USSR) and the US policy of containment against communism were diffused into the Turkish political scene as a tendency to view any political movement with socialist tendencies as a Soviet plot, greatly diminishing the potential role that socialist movements could have played in Turkish politics. Turkey's inclusion in the Western alliance, as motivated by the systemic balances at the time, also impacted on the domestic balances between political actors. A similar development was seen at the end of the Cold War, with changes in Turkish foreign policy to adjust to the resultant uncertainty.

Turkish foreign policy since 1989 has become more active in the Middle East, Caucasus and Central Asia. A task at hand is to find out how the post-2002 developments differ, if at all, from the post-Cold-War activism. It is an interesting question whether the EU accession process has played a similar role. One possible answer lies in the impact of the EU in increasing the power of political reformers at home. As the EU accession process stimulated democratisation and strengthened the hands of the political reformers, new politically powerful actors, such as the AKP, were able to shape Turkish foreign policy significantly. The role of democratisation in changing Turkish foreign policy is evident in President Gül's declaration that

> Its democracy should be strong, undoubtedly. Its democracy, in its broad meaning soft power, should be open ... Turkey makes significant progress towards these

matters. Under these circumstances, the economy would certainly be strengthened. Democratic reforms and legal reforms are the major causes behind Turkey's gradually growing economy. (USAK [Uluslararasi Stratejiik Arastirmalar Kurumu] 2009)

Inclusion in the European order and being accepted as a European state have always been the main goals of Turkey's foreign policy (Müftüler-Baç 1997). Although there were economic and security-related material benefits that could be reaped from being included in Europe, the main reason behind this goal has always been the desire to be part of Europe (Öniş 2000). As a result, Turkey's foreign policy in the post-1945 period and the post-Cold-War period has been relatively consistent and in accordance with its place in the Western alliance. In other words, even the post-Cold-War activism in Turkish foreign policy was geared to getting the country's Europeanness recognised to some degree (Müftüler-Baç 1996). Turkey's position in the Western alliance and its inclusion in 'Europe' contributed to the adjustment of Turkish foreign policy to European interests. Thus, despite some fluctuations and various ups and downs over these four decades from 1945 to 1989, Turkish foreign policy has been, to a large extent, pro-Western and pro-European. One could judge this to be the main line of continuity in Turkish foreign policy.

At the end of the Cold War, parallel with the changes in the international security environment, a process of democratisation that Turkey went through in the 1990s and early 2000s led to shifting power balances in the domestic scene. In the post-Cold-War period, Turkey still followed a pro-Western policy and aligned its position with the US and Europe despite its activism. However, increasingly after 2002, this began to change. It is the contention of this paper that the factors that account for these changes since 2002 may be found in the domestic political changes stimulated by the post-2002 process of democratisation, partly with respect to the increased pressure coming from the EU. Thus, in order to understand the changes in Turkish foreign policy, one needs to look at the changes in domestic politics after 2002.

With the EU candidacy in 1999, Turkey was presented with a rare opportunity for democratic transformation. Political reforms had already begun under the coalition government of the Motherland Party (ANAP), Democratic Left Party (DSP) and Nationalist Action Party (MHP), which adopted the August 2002 political reform package that lifted the death penalty. However, the most important domestic changes came with the election of the Justice and Development Party (AKP) in 2002 and its re-election in 2007, this time with 47 per cent of the national vote. As the political balances in Turkey shifted towards the AKP in terms of voting power, the preferences of the AKP became important in shaping Turkey's foreign policy choices. Interestingly, one of the main goals of the AKP government in 2002 was to adjust Turkish politics to the EU accession criteria in order to begin negotiations. The AKP's position on Turkish accession to the EU was illustrated by Recep Tayyip Erdoğan, the leader of the AKP and the prime minister who declared in 2002, 'We aim for EU accession in order to increase the living standards of our people and to enhance democracy in Turkey' (EU General Secretariat 2002). This position has been reflected in the policies and decisions made by the AKP since 2002 with the emphasis on the EU's role as a stimulus to democratisation. Turkey's goal of EU membership has enabled Turkey to adopt a series of political reforms, at an increasing pace since 2002 (Özbudun 2007, pp.193–194; Cizre 2008, pp. 132–171; Michaud-Emin 2007). With the political reforms adopted since 2002 in line with the EU's accession criteria, the Turkish government's power balances began to change.

The main foreign policy actors during the Cold War period were the foreign affairs ministry and the military—the secular state establishment—whose preferences were largely shaped by Cold War dynamics and their own ideology. In that period, since Turkey was not yet a full fledged democracy, the role of the public was largely absent in foreign policy discourse, and so, surprisingly, were the elected politicians. Cold War dynamics greatly contributed to the state elite's control of foreign policy. Cold War balances and institutions, the perceived Soviet threat and the relative lack of involvement of domestic actors as a result of low levels of democratisation provided the unique interplay of international determinants with domestic forces which shaped Turkish foreign policy. Turkey's process of accession to the EU began to change the domestic balances.

The democratisation process in Turkey was crucial for meeting the political aspects of the Copenhagen criteria, which led to significant political reforms in civil–military relations[4] and a change in the hold of the secularist state establishment on policy-making. At the same time, the democratisation process underway since 2002 enabled the increased visibility of various social groups (Fisher-Onar & Müftüler-Baç 2009). Since 2002, the public preferences and the increased role of domestic factors in Turkish foreign policy is largely due to the domestic changes in Turkey, where the main actors in foreign-policy-making of the previous period—the military and the state establishment—witnessed a decrease in their power. This changing power configuration resulted largely from the democratisation process that began in 2002 in order to fulfil the EU's accession criteria. This is a very interesting and unexpected development of the EU's political conditionality. Even though this is not to say the AKP's rise to power was an outcome of the EU accession process, there was a convergence between the new political actors and the EU in restructuring the Turkish political scene. The rise of the AKP has been the most important and most visible factor in increasing the role of domestic preferences in Turkish foreign policy.

It must be said that it was not only the AKP government that set the EU accession goal for Turkey's foreign policy; however, the policies they adopted made it more credible. The AKP was clearly pro-EU whereas other political parties were less so. For example, Deniz Baykal, the former leader of the CHP, declared, 'We approach the Turkish EU membership with skepticism and we have given direction to our economy for years in line with the EU, but the EU is looking for an alternative to membership for Turkey' (Yılmaz 2007). Since democratisation has enabled the rise of the AKP in Turkish politics, and since the EU is an important promoter of democratisation, then it makes sense that the AKP will be in favour of the EU and work towards Turkey's accession to the EU. Conversely, among political actors who have been losing their position of power with the rise of the AKP, if the EU is a tool for the AKP's rise, support for the EU will decline.

This is, of course, a very interesting and paradoxical crossroads in Turkish politics, with a shift in the relative power and positions of political actors. The Islamic roots of the AKP also enabled the realisation of a diversification of foreign policy. When the secularists gave direction to Turkish foreign policy, for example during the Cold War years, there was a greater reluctance to improve relations with Middle Eastern neighbours because of the Islamic threat. Relations with Iran, for example, were sour after the 1979 Islamic revolution, owing to fear of the diffusion of revolutionary zeal. However, the new political elite under the AKP does not share these fears. As a result, the foreign policy stance towards such Middle Eastern countries has changed dramatically. This also fits well with this paper's proposition that the domestic determinants of foreign policy in Turkey need to be taken into account to understand the foreign policy formulations in Turkey since 2002. The Turkish role in the Iranian swap agreement in 2010 and the signing of the 2009 protocol with Armenia are clear empirical illustrations of the changes in Turkish foreign policy.

The shifting power balances in domestic politics and the relative power of different political groups in Turkey as a result of the Turkish democratisation process have created new bases for foreign-policy-making. Similarly, the democratisation process has also created a public space for Turkish citizens to become involved in foreign policy formulations, which they lacked in the Cold War years. Therefore, an analysis of domestic determinants of foreign policy would be incomplete without a look at the role of the public at large.

In democracies, the public's attitude towards certain countries acts provides boundaries for the government actions. The public does not play the most determining role in foreign policy choices, but if there are increased public sensitivities on certain issues, then these sensitivities will determine the size of the win-set for governments, in line with Putnam's two-level games logic (Putnam 1988). Conversely, the domestic audience costs of an action that the public is against will be very high for governments (Fearon 1994). For example, if the public is totally against the use of force, let's say against Syria, it would be very risky and costly for the government to push for that action. Thus, the public acts as a boundary setter for the government's foreign policy choices, and the public's support of or opposition to certain countries restricts the available policy alternatives the government may choose from. This is, of course, a consequence of the democratisation process and was less of a problem in the Cold War years, as the public preferences then were not reflected in government policy choices. Even though the public is not the key player in foreign-policy-making, the preferences of the public can no longer be ignored where there is no permissive consensus.

Similarly, since the AKP has significant public support, if the public preferred establishing closer ties with Middle Eastern neighbours, then AKP foreign policy choices would reflect this public preference. In short, the relative power changes between the political actors in domestic politics and the changes in the role of the public was effective in the Turkish foreign policy formulations. As the social groups that were previously excluded from political dynamics increased their power, the preferences of these actors were reflected in foreign policy choices. The EU's impact on the democratisation process has been the most effective tool in bringing about this transformation. A perfect illustration of the role of domestic preferences in shaping Turkish foreign policy choices is the Turkish stance towards Israel. Turkish–Israeli relations came to breaking point in Davos in January 2009, when Prime Minister Erdoğan openly disagreed with the Israeli President, Shimon Peres, over Gaza, and a diplomatic crisis erupted between Turkey and Israel. This incident is important to illustrate the role of the public's increased relevance in Turkish foreign policy. Erdoğan declared that his action in Davos, in protest against Peres for the Gaza war, was a response to public demand in Turkey, as summarised in his declaration, 'Anyone who exercises political power has to take account of public opinion ... I can't just put the calls from the public to one side; it's a question of sincerity' (Watan 2009). Turkish foreign policy towards Israel was thus formulated in line with domestic preferences. According to Erdoğan, the most important factor behind the rising Turkish power is the internal process of democratisation.

> We most willingly believe that if we had not performed the biggest reforms in the area of democratisation in the past seven years, we would not be at the same point that we have reached today in economic terms or in foreign policy. (*Turkish Weekly* 2010a)

This is in line with this paper's main argument that the process of democratisation as motivated by the EU accession process has led to the formulation of a more effective and active foreign policy.

Conclusion

Since 2002, it has been possible to witness a more active Turkish foreign policy, relying on tools such as increased diplomatic initiatives, economic packages and becoming more visible in international organisations. These changes in Turkey's foreign policy can be explained by analysing domestic factors: domestic procedures as well as the Turkish public's preferences. The democratisation process in Turkey with increased attempts to fulfil the EU's accession criteria has led to the strengthening of the new players in Turkish politics. The AKP, for example, greatly benefited from the political reforms which shifted power balances in Turkish politics. Thus, a change in Turkey's foreign policy became visible with respect to a new activism towards the country's Middle Eastern neighbours.

An important reason behind these foreign policy changes in Turkey is the shifting power balances in domestic politics; as the status quo upholders, namely the secularists, lose some of their hold on power, and as the political Islamists rise in power, the dominant social preferences in the country change. What remains to be seen is whether these changes are taking Turkey away from its goal of inclusion in the EU, or not. The increased multilateralism in Turkish foreign policy and the increased reliance on soft power tools, such as economic measures and diplomatic instruments, all indicate a Europeanisation of Turkish foreign policy. It is possible to see the endeavours in Turkish foreign policy as contributing to the Turkish goal of EU accession. This is why Davutoğlu claimed, 'We should work together to render Turkey and the EU as primary actors of the global economic–political and legal system, in which Turkey will add value to the EU, rather than be a burden' (Şimşek 2009). As Turkey's process of accession the EU unfolds, it will be possible to see more changes in Turkish foreign policy, and new dynamics, in both the domestic and the foreign policy spheres, will likely emerge.

Acknowledgements

This paper emanates from RECON (Reconstituting Democracy in Europe), an integrated project supported by the European Commission's Sixth Framework Programme (contract no. CIT4-CT-2006-028698).

Notes

[1] Unofficial estimates are three times as much.
[2] The OIC is an international organization composed of 57 Muslim members representing 1.5 billion Muslims in the world. Turkey became an active player in OIC after 2004.
[3] On 31 May 2010, Turkish–Israeli relations came to breaking point with the Israeli raid on the aid flotilla to Gaza.
[4] See Yaprak Gürsoy's paper in this volume.

References

Açıkalın, S. (2008) 'Turkish–Iraqi relations in the light of Ahmet Davutoğlu's visit', USAK, 21 August, available online at: http://www.usak.org.tr/EN/makale.asp?id=1029

Altunışık, M. (2009) 'Worldviews and Turkish foreign policy in the Middle East', *New Perspectives on Turkey*, vol. 40, pp. 169–192.

Aras, B. (2009) 'Davutoğlu era in Turkish foreign policy', *Today's Zaman*, 30 June, available online at: http://www.todayszaman.com/tz-web/news-179504-159-davutoglu-era-in-turkish-foreign-policy.html

Aras, B. & Fidan, H. (2009) 'Turkey and Eurasia: frontiers of a new geographic imagination', *New Perspectives on Turkey*, vol. 40, pp. 193–215.

Aydın, M. (2000) 'Determinants of Turkish foreign policy: changing patterns and conjuctures during the Cold War', *Middle Eastern Studies*, vol. 36, no. 1, pp. 103–139.

Aydın, M. & Açıkmeşe, S. (2008) 'Identity-based security threats in a globalized world: focus on Islam', *Uluslararası İlişkiler* [International Relations], vol. 5, no. 18, pp. 197–214.

Çagatay, S. (2007) *Secularism and Foreign Policy in Turkey*, Washington Institute, Washington.

Cizre, Ü. (ed.) (2008) *Secular and Islamic Politics in Turkey: The Making of the Justice and Development Party*, Routledge, London.

Davutoğlu, A. (2001) *Stratejik Derinlik: Türkiye'nin Uluslararası Konumu* [Strategic Depth: Turkey's International Position], Küre Yayınları, Istanbul.

Davutoğlu, A. (2008) 'Turkey's foreign policy vision: an assessment of 2007', *Insight Turkey*, vol. 10, no. 1, pp. 77–96.

EU General Secretariat. (2002), Press release, 20 November, available online at: http://www.euturkey. org.tr/index.php?p=23357&l = 1

Fearon, J. (1994) 'Domestic political audiences and the escalation of international disputes', *American Political Science Review*, vol. 88, no. 3, pp. 577–592.

Fisher-Onar, N. F. & Müftüler-Baç, M. (2009) 'Cosmopolitan Europe: oxymoron or aspiration? Views from Turkey', Recon Working Paper, available online at: www.reconproject.eu

Keyman, F. (2009) 'Globalization, modernity and democracy: in search of a viable domestic polity for a sustainable Turkish foreign policy', *New Perspectives on Turkey*, vol. 40, pp. 7–27.

Michaud-Emin, L. (2007) 'The restructuring of the military high command in the seventh harmonization package and its ramifications for civil–military relations in Turkey', *Turkish Studies*, vol. 8, no. 1, pp. 25–42.

Müftüler-Baç, M. (1996) 'Turkey's predicament in the post-Cold War era', *Futures*, vol. 28, no. 3, pp. 255–268.

Müftüler-Baç, M. (1997) *Turkey's Relations with a Changing Europe*, Manchester University Press, Manchester.

Müftüler-Baç, M. (2008) 'Turkey's accession to the European Union: the EU's internal dynamics', *International Studies Perspectives*, vol. 9, no. 2, pp. 208–226.

Müftüler-Baç, M. & Gürsoy, Y. (2010) 'Is there a Europeanization of Turkish foreign policy? An addendum to the literature on candidate countries', *Turkish Studies*, vol. 11, no. 3, pp. 405–427.

Öniş, Z. (2000) 'Luxemburg, Helsinki and beyond', *Government and Opposition*, vol. 35, no. 4, pp. 463–483.

Öniş, Z. & Yılmaz, S. (2009) 'Between Europeanization and Euro-Asianism: foreign policy activism in Turkey during the AKP era', *Turkish Studies*, vol. 10, no. 1, pp. 7–24.

Özbudun, E. (2007) 'Democratization reforms in Turkey, 1993–2004', *Turkish Studies*, vol. 8, no. 2, pp. 179–196.

Putnam, R. (1988) 'Diplomacy and domestic politics, the logic of two-level games', *International Organization*, vol. 42, no. 3, pp. 427–660.

Rumelili, B. (2003) 'Liminality and perpetuation of conflicts: Turkish–Greek relations in the context of community building by the EU', *European Journal of International Relations*, vol. 9, no. 2, pp. 213–248.

Şimşek, A. (2009) 'The changes and challenges of Turkey's foreign policy', *SoutheastEuropean Times*, 10 June, available online at: http://www.setimes.com/cocoon/setimes/xhtml/en_GB/features/setimes/features/009/06/10/feature-03

Turkish Weekly. (2010a) 'The changing balances and the rising importance of Turkey', 10 February, available online at: http://www.turkishweekly.net/news/97459/full-text-of-prime-minister-erdogan-39-s-speech-at-usak-39-the-changing-balances-and-the-rising-importance-of-turkey-39-.html

Turkish Weekly. (2010b) 'Turkey must have a very active diplomacy', 12 March, available online at: http://www.turkishweekly.net/news/99310/turkish-fm-turkey-must-have-a-very-active-diplomacy-for-global-peace.html

USAK. (2009), President Gül's speech at USAK, November 4, available online at: http://www.usak. org.tr/EN/makale.asp?id=1272

Watan. (2009) 'Turkey airs a series on Israel's massacres in Gaza', 18 October, available online at: http://www.watan.com/en/feaute/671-2009-10-19-06-19-19.html

Yılmaz, Ö. (2007) 'Almayacaksanız Açıkça söyleyin', [If you are not going to accept, say it openly], *Milliyet*, 16 February, available online at: http://www.milliyet.com.tr/-almayacaksaniz-acikca-soyleyin-/siyaset/haberdetayarsiv/16.02.2007/189466/default.htm

Zielonka, J. (1998) *The Paradoxes of European Foreign policy*, Kluwer Law International, The Hague.

Zucconi, M. (2009) 'The impact of the EU connection on Turkey's domestic and foreign policy', *Turkish Studies*, vol. 10, no. 1, pp. 25–36.

Meltem Müftüler-Baç (PhD Temple University) is a professor of international relations at Sabancı University, Istanbul. She was awarded the Jean Monnet Professorship *ad personam* in 2004. Her publications include *Turkey's Relations with a Changing Europe* (Manchester University Press, 1997) and *Turkey and the European Union* (co-edited with Y. Stivachtis (Lexington Books, 2008), as well as articles in journals such as *Journal of European Public Policy, Middle Eastern Studies, International Journal, Journal of European Integration, South East European Politics and Society, Security Dialogue* and *Turkish Studies*.

The Impact of EU-Driven Reforms on the Political Autonomy of the Turkish Military

Yaprak Gürsoy

Turkish civil–military relations entered a new phase starting with the first European-Union-induced reforms in 1999, and have gained a new momentum since 2007. This article first introduces the amendments to Turkish civil–military relations, then asks how much the constitutional and legal amendments have affected the political autonomy of the military. The article takes the indicators of military autonomy into consideration as a whole and argues that legal amendments have not introduced any changes to one-third of the military prerogatives. In those areas where some adjustments have been made, either more reforms must follow or democratic practices must endure the test of time.

Democratic reforms have been introduced in Turkey since 1999 as a result of the European Union (EU) accession process, and these amendments have also included changes in the area of civil–military relations. The Turkish military has had political autonomy since the establishment of the Turkish Republic in 1923, and with each military coup after 1960 the privileges of the armed forces were further increased. In contrast with previous Turkish political history, the reforms that have been carried out in accordance with the Copenhagen criteria of the EU appear to have challenged the prerogatives of the military. However, in reality, how much influence have the EU reforms had on the powers and autonomy of the Turkish military? This paper will argue that even though the reforms are positive steps in the right direction, they have not altered the political autonomy of the military in important respects. Despite the reforms, the armed forces have retained important privileges and spheres of autonomy.

In the first section of this article, developments in civil–military relations since 1999 will be examined in two different phases. The first period will cover the EU reform process and the legal amendments to the autonomy of the military until 2007. The following section will examine the changing balance of power in civil–military relations after 2007, and reforms that have taken place in practice and in terms of laws that have been enacted. The third section will elucidate the main arguments of the paper and address the following questions: Has the Turkish military come under civilian control as a consequence of the reforms that have been carried out since 1999? What are the remaining areas where the military retains autonomy? The article will attempt to respond to these questions by employing the indicators of military prerogatives that Stepan (1988), Pion-Berlin (1992) and others have used for Latin American cases and which Cizre-Sakallıoğlu (1997) first adapted to the Turkish case (see also Gürsoy 2009). Methodologically, this section focuses on the outcomes of the reforms, and not on the process of enacting these amendments or the reasons for their shortcomings. This is a worthwhile endeavour because such an outcome-oriented analysis can determine the areas that need further amendments in civil–military relations. The political autonomy of the military historically provided the legal right to the Turkish armed forces to veto policies and restrict the areas in which democratically elected civilian governments could make decisions. 'Political autonomy' refers to the military 'act[ing] as if it were above and beyond the constitutional authority of the government' (Pion Berlin 1992, pp. 85). Highly autonomous militaries defy the civilian government's control and authority over the armed forces, and in some cases even have more decision-making powers than the civilian government (Pion Berlin 1992, pp. 84–85). Thus, the question of how much political autonomy, prerogative and privilege[1] the military has so far retained in Turkey is an important question for Turkish democracy in general, and civil–military relations in particular.

In order to assess the outcomes of the reforms, the analysis implicitly uses comparative tools. It contrasts the legal framework that was established after 1999 with the institutional structure of the previous era, founded during the 1980 coup. This type of analysis results in the conclusion that positive steps have been taken in the right direction as a result of the EU reform process. The article also intrinsically compares Turkish civil–military relations with ideal-type democracies, where all the indicators of military prerogatives are low, and this second comparison leads to the conclusion that the EU-induced reforms must continue, since there are remaining spheres of autonomy that have not been amended by the reform process. When the indicators of military autonomy are taken into consideration as a whole, it becomes clear that legal amendments have not introduced any changes to one-third of the military prerogatives. In those areas where some adjustments have been made, either more reforms must follow or democratic practices must endure the test of time. Thus, the reforms that have been introduced since 1999 are still short of elevating Turkish civil–military relations to the level of ideal-type democracies. However, if the pace of reforms continues and the civilian supervision of the military increases in practice in the coming years, there is room for optimism that Turkey will bring to completion the democratic control of the armed forces.

The First Phase of Changing Civil–Military Relations (1999–2007)

The political system and the constitution that were created in Turkey after the 12 September 1980 coup provided important spheres of political autonomy to the military. However, the fact that the Turkish Armed Forces have enjoyed prerogatives does not fit with the preconditions of EU accession. As a result, the first impetus for reforms in the area of civil–military relations came after the 1999 Helsinki summit of the EU, which recognised Turkey as a candidate country. During the reform period induced by the EU's Copenhagen criteria, some of the powers of the Turkish military were reduced by parliament.

Most of the amendments focused on the National Security Council (NSC), which was first established after the 1960 coup and which functioned as an institution that facilitated communication between the chief of the General Staff, commanders of the armed forces and cabinet ministers. In the 1961 constitution, the NSC was envisioned as an advisory body, but after the 1980 coup the powers of the NSC vis-à-vis the government were increased, and with the 1982 constitution the cabinet was required to give precedence to the NSC's decisions. Until the early 2000s, the armed forces functioned almost as a second pillar of the executive through the NSC, especially in matters of external and internal security (Cizre-Sakallıoğlu 1997, p. 158).

The EU-induced reform process has changed the powers, functions and composition of the NSC. In 2001, an amendment was made to Article 118 of the constitution, increasing the number of civilians participating in the NSC meetings. The seventh harmonisation package, which was enacted in July 2003, changed the function of the NSC and, similarly to the 1961 constitution, turned it into a body that only advises the cabinet (Michaud-Emin 2007). The new law of the NSC stipulates that the meetings of the NSC will take place once every two months, rather than once every month as used to be the case. The secretary general of the council is now selected by the prime minister and approved by the president. As a result, it has become possible to appoint civilians to the position, and the first civilian secretary general started in his post in 2004 (Cizre 2008, p. 137; Özcan 2006, pp. 39–40).

Some of the powers of the general secretariat were abolished, such as requesting information from civilian institutions, running national security inspections and supervising the implementation of NSC decisions by the government. Other specific duties of the NSC secretariat were also terminated by closing down the relevant departments in the secretariat: for instance, the community relations presidency was abolished, eradicating the legal authority to conduct 'psychological operations' (Cizre 2008, p. 138; Özcan 2006, pp. 47–50). The clause in the NSC law which stated that appointments to the secretariat shall not be disclosed to the public was removed, and, as a result, members of the military are not predominantly represented in the secretariat any more (Jenkins 2007, pp. 346–347). The increasing number of civilians, in turn, has led to their ascendancy in preparing the briefing documents and a decrease in the military's control over the agenda.

In May 2004, the eighth harmonisation package was approved in parliament, and this new package brought increased civilian supervision of defence expenditures by expanding the right of the Court of Auditors to oversee the budget, including what was previously considered confidential property. The same package also removed the remaining seats of the military on civilian boards. In 2003, the seat of the NSC on the Board of Inspection of Cinema, Video and Musical Works was abolished, and in 2004 the representation of the military in the Radio and Television Supreme Council, the Council of Higher Education and the Supreme Communication Board was eliminated (Ünlü Bilgiç 2009, pp. 805-806).

Various reform packages also restricted the role of the military in the judiciary. In 1999, the seats of the military judges were removed from the state security courts and in 2004 the courts were abolished altogether. Whereas, in the past, military courts could hear cases against civilians, several amendments 'gradually restricted the military courts' jurisdiction, and in 2006, finally ended the trials of civilians by these courts during peacetime' (Ünlü Bilgiç 2009, p. 806).

These amendments were significant turning points in Turkish civil–military relations as the events of 2007 highlighted. When President Ahmet Necdet Sezer's term in office was about to end, a fierce discussion among the public started over who should be his successor. Since the Justice and Development Party (AKP) controlled the majority of the seats in parliament, it was expected that the party would elect its chairman, Prime Minister Tayyip Erdoğan, to the presidency. Some of the military officers perceived the possibility of the AKP controlling both the parliament and the presidency as a threat to secularism in Turkey. After considerable pressure from both civilian and military circles, the AKP partially backed down and nominated Foreign Minister Abdullah Gül to the presidency. However, before the parliamentary session that would vote for the new president, the General Staff issued an announcement on its website. The declaration stated that the Turkish Armed Forces had 'observed the situation with anxiety' and that they were 'taking part in these disputes' as 'the certain defenders of secularism', who would also 'openly and clearly put forward their attitudes and behaviour when necessary' (Hürriyet 2007). Shortly thereafter, the Constitutional Court decided that the presidential elections were null and void because the parliamentary session had failed to reach the necessary quorum of deputies. In response, the AKP called for a new general election to resolve the impasse, and, after renewing its mandate in parliament, the party elected Gül to the presidency (Kaya 2009, pp. 391–392).

The 2007 website declaration of the General Staff is significant because it displays the existence of a degree of continuity between the period before and after the first reforms. The announcement was a clear indication that legal amendments of the NSC or institutional reforms alone were not enough to reduce the generals' willingness to influence Turkish politics (Aydın-Düzgit & Çarkoğlu 2009, p. 141). Despite this continuity, however, the 2007 declaration is also important for starting the second phase of reforms in civil–military relations. The declaration was made on the General Staff's website and it did not succeed, partly because the military had lost the NSC as an important instrument of intervention in politics due to the EU reforms. The EU provided a positive context in which civilian actors in Turkey felt empowered. Because the civilians increased their powers vis-à-vis the military, the armed forces could not prevent the AKP government—strengthened by a victory at the ballot box—from electing its candidate to the presidency. This marked the failure of the General Staff's attempt to apply pressure on the AKP, and hence resulted in the military's further loss of power relative to the government.

The Second Phase of Changing Civil–Military Relations in Turkey (2007 onwards)

Even though the pace of legal amendments in the area of civil–military relations somewhat declined after 2005, it picked up again after 2010. Apart from the failed 2007 website declaration, two other interrelated developments preceded this new wave of reforms. The first important factor was the split among members of the armed forces on the role of the military in Turkish politics and on the strategies that needed to be followed when dealing with civilians (Aydınlı 2009; Demirel 2010). When the AKP came to power in 2002, some groups among the public and factions within the military regarded a cabinet with Islamist roots as a threat. The electoral success of the AKP and the difference of opinion on whether this was a threat to the secular Republic contributed to the disunity of the armed forces. Moreover, the constitutional changes and the legal amendments in accordance with the EU's Copenhagen criteria were perceived as a mistake by some of the generals, who were quite vocal in their criticism of the reforms and in their condemnation of the more dovish Chief of Staff, Hilmi Özkök (Heper 2005, pp. 37–42). Yet, the option for these officers of staging a coup was closed, since public opinion at the time was pro-EU and supported the reforms (Gürsoy 2010). Indirectly, the EU-induced reforms of 1999 and 2005 contributed to the split in the military and the weakening of the armed forces, which was further accentuated with the failure of the website declaration of the General Staff in 2007.

The second event that contributed to the relative empowerment of civilians was the start of a controversial judicial investigation, known among the public as the 'Ergenekon' case. Shortly after the 2007 presidential crisis, conspiracies were uncovered revealing coups allegedly planned by civilians and military officers against the AKP government between the years 2003 and 2004. The coup plans with the code names 'Blonde Girl', 'Moonlight' and 'Phosphorescence' were first revealed with the publication of the diaries of a former navy commander in March 2007 by a weekly magazine (Nokta 2007). More plots entitled 'Action Plan to Combat Islamic Fundamentalism', 'Glove', 'Cage' and 'Sledgehammer' were also exposed between 2008 and 2010. These conspiracies allegedly planned to manipulate public opinion and the media by carrying out psychological warfare and false flag operations, such as attacking minority groups, provoking Greece into a war, organising anti-government rallies, planting bombs or assassinating political leaders and intellectuals. The aim of the plots was to provoke chaos in the country, which would create favourable conditions for the military to step in and stage a legitimate coup. Even though the connections between the conspiracies are not entirely clear, a clandestine organisation called Ergenekon is suspected of being behind some of these plots. The trials that started in October 2008 and the ongoing investigations are firsts of their kind in Turkish history, since some of the suspected plotters are retired and active-duty military officers of higher and lower ranks, including several retired commanders of the armed forces and a former deputy chief of the General Staff (Yetkin 2009).

The arrests and trials of officers are also important because, simultaneously with these developments, public debate on the role of the military in politics has increased. Some secularist groups in Turkey have raised important questions regarding the evidence that has been provided in the indictments, the manner in which this evidence has been gathered and the detention periods and conditions (Jenkins 2009, pp. 78–83; Özel 2009, p. 2). It has been suggested that there are no indisputable facts supporting the existence of an organisation called Ergenekon and that the only common denominator that brings suspected individuals together is their opposition to the AKP government (Ünver 2009, pp. 12–14; for such a view see Çağaptay 2010). There is considerable worry among some segments of the public that the aim of the investigations is to eliminate the opposition and decrease the power of the secularist military in order to establish an Islamic state (Zaman 2009, p. 2). Such views are raised by the opposition, the Republican People's Party and the National Action Party, and by columnists in newspapers that are especially keen on defending the secular principles of the Republic, such as *Cumhuriyet*, *Vatan* and *Sözcü*. Certainly, if the suspicions of these groups are true, they raise a prospect that would damage Turkish democracy in the long run. In the short run, however, the affair seems to have given an opportunity to the government to increase the democratic control of the armed forces (Cizre & Walker 2010, pp. 92–95). Some columnists in pro-government dailies and/or newspapers with Islamist leanings, such as *Star*, *Yeni Şafak* and *Zaman*, welcome the investigations, and, likewise, liberal intellectuals writing most notably in *Taraf*—the newspaper that exposed some of the alleged plots—support reducing the role of the military in Turkish politics.

Indeed, the investigations have resulted in a new drive to introduce more amendments. In the wake of the coup investigations, the government has started a second wave of reform in Turkish civil–military relations. In January 2010, the Protocol on Cooperation for Security and Public Order (EMASYA) was abolished. This protocol was signed between the military and the government in 1997 and gave the military the right to gather intelligence and, if necessary, carry out operations against internal security threats without the authorisation of the civilian administration (Bayramoğlu 2009). The shelving of EMASYA can be interpreted as an important development in civil–military relations, since the protocol had justified the involvement of the military in providing internal security.

In May 2010, parliament passed a new constitutional package, which was approved by the majority of the Turkish electorate in the September 2010 referendum. The two following amendments came into force with the package: first, it became possible to subject to judicial review the decisions of the High Military Council (HMC) on discharges from the military; second, the military courts can now try officers only on crimes committed against other officers and related to military service, while all other crimes, including those against the security of the state and the constitution, are now tried by civilian courts (Hürriyet 2010).

Another important change in Turkish civil–military relations came in August 2010, when at the meeting of the HMC the government intervened in the process of senior-level personnel promotions and appointments. In the past, the promotions of officers were decided strictly by the military, and the procedure was almost automatic in the case of the chief of staff: the HMC selected the commander of the army, who then became the chief of staff when the term of the incumbent came to an end. This procedure almost always received the rubber-stamp approval of the prime minister and the president, who officially appointed the new chief of staff. Only in one instance in the post-1980 era—in 1987—did Prime Minister Turgut Özal refuse to promote the chief of staff suggested by the officer corps, but after this incident the practice of leaving the matter in the hands of the military hierarchy continued. In what seems a radical break from the past, before the HMC meeting in August 2010 the criminal court that tried the Sledgehammer plot case ordered the arrest of around 100 officers, including several generals who were expected to be promoted. In the following HMC meeting, the government insisted on delaying the promotions of these officers and vetoed the general who was expected to become the new commander of the army. Such a showdown in the HMC, where civilians exerted influence on senior-level personnel decisions, is an important deviation from normal practices (Yetkin 2010). However, it remains to be seen whether this will be a one-off incident similar to the one in 1987, or if civilians will continue to be involved in military promotions.

Similar to changing practices in the HMC, amendments were made in the writing of the National Security Policy Document (NSPD) in October 2010. The NSPD identifies the internal and external threats facing the country and has such significance in determining policy that it is sometimes even referred to as the 'secret constitution' of the Republic (Aydıntaşbaş 2010). While in the past the NSPD was formulated by the military, in 2010 the document was rewritten by the government and accepted by the NSC. The AKP government, in fact, had played a more active role in the preparation of the previous NSPD in 2005 as well, but the final document was not significantly different from the previous ones. In particular, the 2005 document included reactionary Islam as an internal threat, indicating the continued influence of the military in the final draft (Cizre 2008, p. 139; Özcan 2006, pp. 44–45). However, the 2010 NSPD was reformulated by civilians, and as a result it includes significant changes from the previous versions of the document. Reactionary activities are not regarded as a threat any more, although organisations that take advantage of religion are still listed as a domestic danger (Radikal 2010). Such changes in the NSPD and the ascendancy of civilians in the preparation of the document are important reductions of the political autonomy of the military.

Thus, after 2007, important amendments were made in Turkish civil–military relations both in practice and also in legal texts. At the time of writing, it appears that more reforms in civil–military relations in the future will follow. For instance, the Republican People's Party leadership proposed—and the AKP government in principle agreed—to change Article 35 of the Internal Service Act of the military, which gives the armed forces the responsibility to protect the country from internal threats (HaberTürk 2010). The current climate gives reason to believe that the reform process will forge ahead, but it remains to be seen whether the new suggestions of the government and opposition will be carried out.

The Effects of the Reforms on the Political Autonomy of the Military

The reforms seem to have reduced the prerogatives of the military in Turkish politics, but the question remains: How much have they really altered the overall autonomy of the military? In order to answer this question, it is important first to identify the indicators of the military's political autonomy. Scholars of civil–military relations have established several measures to evaluate the degree of political autonomy that interventionist armed forces maintained in Latin American and South European countries after their transitions to democracy. Taking these indicators as the basic criteria, it is possible to measure how much political autonomy a military has. The indicators could be classified in two extreme variations of autonomy, such as 'high' and 'low', as Table 1 does for reasons of simplicity. However, the political autonomy of a military at a given time could be judged to be somewhere within this range, and therefore also as 'moderate' (see for instance Stepan 1988, pp. 94–97).

In Turkey, the reform process has introduced changes in the first four indicators but has not altered the remaining two prerogatives, which may still be classified as 'high'. One of the most important areas of neglect in the amendments has been the reorganisation of the defence sector. In neither of the reform waves was this reorganisation seriously suggested by the government or opposition parties. As a result, the armed forces are still responsible to the prime minister and not to the minister of defence (indicator five).

Similarly, there have been no improvements with regard to the intelligence activities of the gendarmerie (indicator six). The gendarmerie, which is controlled by the General Staff in its organisational system, promotions and training, is partly responsible for providing security in regions that do not fall under the jurisdiction of the police forces, i.e. mainly rural areas. In the past two decades, there have been accusations that the gendarmerie regularly exceeds its authority and operates in areas that are under the authority of the police. Moreover, there has been information circulating in the media which indicates the existence of an intelligence organisation in the gendarmerie called the Gendarmerie Intelligence and Counter-Terrorism Organisation (JİTEM). Since the early 1990s it has been alleged that JİTEM units have engaged in unlawful activities, including bombings, murders, extortions and abductions. It is suspected that JİTEM is especially active in the southeast and was first established to combat activities of the Kurdish terrorist organisation Partiya Karkeren Kurdistan (PKK) in the region. Military officers and civilians, including former PKK members who have confessed their association with the organisation, are thought to comprise the JİTEM units (Beşe 2006, p. 183).

Table 1 The Indicators of the Military's Political Autonomy

Selected indicators	Degree of military autonomy	
	Low	High
1. Role in internal security	The military engages in activities in order to provide internal security only in rare circumstances, with the authorisation of the executive and within limits envisioned by the legal framework.	The legal framework gives the military the duty to provide internal security and leaves it to the discretion of the military to decide when and how it will carry out its duties.
2. Role of executive, legislature and civilian courts	The executive, legislature, relevant parliamentary committees and civilian courts monitor and oversee the military budget and arms procurement.	The legislature approves the defence budget without much debate. The executive approves military's procurement requests. Civilian courts do not audit military budget and assets.
3. Role in legal system	The military has no legal jurisdiction except for cases against the discipline of the armed forces.	Military courts can try both civilians and officers. Military personnel are unlikely to be tried by civilian courts.
4. Role in senior-level personnel decisions	The military makes recommendations to the executive on promotions, retirements, appointments and purges. The executive is not constrained and can approve or disapprove the military's recommendations.	The military determines promotions, retirements, appointments and discharges on its own. The executive approves the military's decisions without changes.
5. Coordination of defence sector	The military is responsible to a defence ministry directed and controlled by civilians. Professional civil servants assist the government in designing and implementing defence and national security policies.	The military is not responsible to a civilian-controlled defence ministry. Designing and implementing defence and national security policies are directed and controlled by military officers.
6. Role in intelligence	All intelligence agencies are directed by civilians, subject to reviews of civilian-controlled boards.	Intelligence agencies are directed by military officers. The military is involved in both intelligence-gathering and carrying out operations, which are not subject to the review of civilian boards.

Source: Pion-Berlin, 1992; Stepan, 1988, pp. 94–97; Zaverucha, 1993.

A new law that went into effect in July 2005 formally established the department of intelligence controlled by the Gendarmerie General Command, and arguably this new law has brought some transparency to the intelligence activities of the gendarmerie. However, there have been no major amendments to the autonomy of the military in intelligence-gathering. Apart from the mostly civilian-controlled National Intelligence Organisation (MİT)[2] and the department of police intelligence, the General Staff also continues to have its own intelligence department, about which limited information is yet available. But it is still suspected that the gendarmerie and the military collect intelligence (including information on private lives) and also carry out operations without being subject to the review of civilian boards. Thus, with regard to the sixth indicator, there have been no changes in either period of the reform process, and military autonomy has remained high in intelligence-gathering.

The reforms enacted since 1999 have attempted to reduce the autonomy of the military, in particular by altering the first four indicators in Table 1, namely the internal security roles of the military, civilian supervision of the defence budget and arms procurement, functions of the military courts, and senior-level personnel decisions.

Until 2010, no changes had been made in the autonomy of the HMC, which decides on promotions, appointments and discharges. Thus, in the first phase of reforms, between 1999 and 2007, the military retained high levels of autonomy on this fourth indicator. However, the second phase of reforms introduced major changes, and, after the constitutional package was accepted in the September 2010 referendum, HMC decisions came under judicial oversight. If the practice of civilians being involved in decisions on military promotions continues in future HMC meetings like the one in August 2010, the military will lose an important prerogative and will have low levels of autonomy in this critical area.

The biggest achievement in Turkish civil–military relations has been experienced on indicator three, with regard to the role of the military in the legal system. In the first phase of reforms, the trial of civilians by military courts during peacetime came to an end. Although this was a major reform, armed forces personnel were still subject to the authority of military courts not only for felonies against the discipline of the armed forces, but also for general offences. This continued to give the impression that officers were exempted from civil laws (Kardaş 2009). Thus, on this indicator, the political autonomy of the military was moved from high to only relatively moderate levels until 2007. However, with the approval of the 2010 constitutional package in the referendum, armed forces personnel have come under the authority of civilian courts for crimes against the security of the state and the constitutional order. In fact, with the Ergenekon trials, this condition had been fulfilled in practice even before the referendum, since suspected officers were tried by civilian courts instead of military tribunals. The only remaining question in this area is the jurisdiction of the Military Court of Appeals and the High Military Administrative Court, which reviews disputes over administrative decisions involving military personnel even when these decisions are made by civilian institutions. However, there are proposals by the AKP government and the opposition to restrict the jurisdiction of these courts or to abolish them completely. If these proposals come to fruition, another important step will have been taken on the role of the military in the legal system.

With regard to the overview of the budget and military assets by civilians (the second indicator), the 2004 amendment to the constitution gave the Court of Auditors the authority to oversee the military budget. However, necessary amendments were not made in the Law on the Court of Auditors in the first phase of the reforms, and as a result, even though the court could 'carry out external ex-post audit of military expenditure ... based on accounting records', it could not audit some of the military assets or carry out 'on-the-spot checks' (European Commission 2009, p. 11). Moreover, one of the most important deficiencies of the first phase of reforms was that they did not cover off-budget defence expenses. For instance, neither the Court nor parliament reviewed the undersecretariat of the defence industry, which functions under the Ministry of Defence. The undersecretariat is financed by the off-budget Defence Industry Support Fund (DISF), which pays for the procurement projects of the military. The failure of the first wave of reforms to cover the DISF was detrimental to civilian oversight (Demirel 2010, p. 8; Karakaş 2009, pp. 176–177). However, the Law on the Court of Auditors, which reinforces the previous amendments, was enacted in December 2010 during the second phase of reforms. The new law enables the Court to audit military procurements, properties, assets, equipment and expenses, as well as the DISF. Yet, the overview of the Foundation of Strengthening the Armed Forces, which is responsible for the building and developing of defence industry companies, is not covered by the law and will not be subject to the Court's audit. Moreover, some of the auditing reports will not be disclosed to the public for security reasons.

The overall assessment of military autonomy on the second indicator must be considered 'moderate', additionally due to problems in implementation. Civilian oversight of the military budget is problematic partially because civilians are reluctant to exercise their legal rights. Decisions on arms procurement and production are made by the defence industry executive board, the undersecretariat of defence industry and the Ministry of Defence. Even though these institutions are controlled by civilians, 'in practice the General Staff [has been] responsible for making decisions about military needs' (Ünlü Bilgiç 2009, p. 805). Similarly, in parliament, deputies approve budgets without substantial deliberation, and the parliamentary planning and budget committee fails to review the programmes and projects of the Ministry of Defence and the military budget in a detailed manner. Deputies rarely make formal inquires about issues relating to the Turkish armed forces and national security, and the government does not provide answers to any of the few questions that are asked by deputies (Akyeşilmen 2009, pp. 13–21). These types of behaviour can be explained by the deputies' limited knowledge and their self-restraint. Since the military has enjoyed authority and high degrees of autonomy on these issues for years, politicians deliberately refrain from questioning national security matters and lack the necessary expertise on budgetary and defence matters. In fact, the attitudes of politicians are both an explanation and an expression of problematic civil–military relations in Turkey: high degrees of autonomy result in the timid behaviour of politicians, which in turn provides greater prerogative to the armed forces.

Important changes have been made in the internal security roles of the military (first indicator), but in this area as well the degree of autonomy must be classified as 'moderate'. The first phase of reforms introduced changes in the NSC and abolished the seats of the military on civilian boards. In the second phase, the EMASYA protocol was abolished and changes in Article 35 of the Internal Service Act of the military were suggested by the opposition party. However, as of December 2010, there had been no proposals to change Article 85 of the Internal Service Regulations of the military, which states that 'every soldier in the Turkish Armed Forces [has] the duty to protect the Turkish Homeland and Republic from internal and external threats, if necessary by force' (Türk Silahlı Kuvvetleri İç Hizmet Yönetmeliği 1961). In fact, the General Staff has departments, such as Internal Security Operations, Special Forces and Psychological Operations, which are geared towards providing internal security (Akay 2010, p. 14). Article 2a of the Law of the National Security Council has not been changed by the reforms either: the law still defines national security in broad terms allowing security forces, including the military, 'a wide margin of manoeuvre' (European Commission 2007, p. 9).

Besides these legal and institutional remainders of autonomy, it must be emphasised that the military's role in providing internal security is also a matter of implementation. As long as civilians use the military to fight what they believe to be internal threats and the military sees itself as having the duty to provide security at home, legal amendments may not change practices. This problem was evidenced after the first phase of reforms, as the military continued to show a willingness to treat security as its reserved domain. Some of the functions of the NSC were moved to the General Staff, and instead of the monthly meetings of the NSC the military started to conduct regular meetings with members of the media. Similarly, the HMC started to make declarations on political matters (Özcan 2006, p. 40). These practices allowed the high command to put across its views on security and political matters. The media broadcast its meetings with the General Staff to the public, as well as the various other declarations of the high command. The April 2007 website pronouncement of the General Staff is a final reminder that legal and institutional reforms do not necessarily translate into democratic practices. Even though such interventionist tendencies have decreased in the second phase of reforms, caution should still be exercised, since it remains to be seen if the attitudes of officers and the political elite towards the role of the military in providing internal security will continue to be relatively negative.

Conclusion

Table 2 summarises the amendments that have been carried out in Turkish civil–military relations in the two phases of reform and the resulting degrees of autonomy. It is clear that any changes in the future should first focus on the last two spheres of

Table 2 Summary of Reforms in Turkish Civil–Military Relations

| Selected indicators | First phase (1999–2007) | | Second phase (2007–) | |
	Amendments	Degree of autonomy	Amendments and proposed change as of December 2010	Degree of autonomy (if all the legal proposals take place and democratic practices continue)
1. Role in internal security	Changes in the NSC were introduced; the seats of the military in civilian boards were removed	Moderate	Emasya protocol was abolished; Proposal to change Article 35 of the Internal Service Act	Moderate
2. Role of executive, legislature and civilian courts	Court of Auditors was given some authority to oversee the military budget	Moderate	The Law on the Court of Auditors was enacted	Moderate
3. Role in legal system	The law was changed so that military courts cannot try civilians in peacetime; State Security Courts were abolished	Moderate	Officers cannot be tried in military courts for offences against the security of the state and the constitutional order; proposal to restrict the jurisdiction of high military courts	Low
4. Role in senior-level personnel decisions	No amendments	High	HMC decisions on purges are subject to judicial review; civilian involvement in HMC decisions regarding promotions	Low
5. Coordination of defence sector	No amendments	High	No amendments	High
6. Role in intelligence	No amendments, but some increased transparency	High	No amendments	High

TURKEY AND THE EU: ACCESSION AND REFORM

prerogatives, where no amendments have taken place and the autonomy of the military is still high. The defence sector must be reorganised by subjecting the armed forces to the authority of the Ministry of Defence and increasing the expertise of civilians working in the Ministry. In addition, attempts should be made to civilianise all internal intelligence activities and close down any organisations within the gendarmerie or other forces geared towards gathering internal intelligence.

Major changes have been carried out in the remaining spheres of autonomy, but there are still important steps that need to be taken. Civilian oversight of the military budget is still an issue that must be dealt with in practice. Similarly, the duty of the military in providing internal security must be abolished by amending and implementing the necessary laws and regulations. Moreover, and undoubtedly, important gains from the previous years, such as civilians taking part in senior-level promotions, must be protected from any future backlashes.

EU enforcement must also continue, since it was the pressure of the accession criteria that started the process of reform in the first phase. The second phase was triggered by these earlier reforms and the EU played an indirect role by empowering civilians against the generals who made the website announcement of April 2007. Such enduring support from the EU in the future may help elevate Turkish civil–military relations to the level of ideal-type democracies.

Notes

[1] For reasons of simplicity, in this article I use 'political autonomy', 'prerogatives' and 'privileges' interchangeably.
[2] MİT used to be directed by military generals, but the practice of appointing a retired or active duty officer to the position of undersecretary of MİT came to an end in 1992.

References

Akay, H. (2010) *Security Sector in Turkey: Questions, Problems, and Solutions*, TESEV, Istanbul.
Akyeşilmen, N. (2009) 'Yasama: Türkiye Büyük Millet Meclisi' [Judiciary: Turkish Grand National Assembly], in *Almanak Türkiye 2006–2008: Güvenlik Sektörü ve Demokratik Gözetim* [Almanac Turkey 2006–2008: Security Sector and Democratic Oversight], eds A. Bayramoğlu & A. İnsel, TESEV Yayınları, Istanbul, pp. 13–22.
Aydın Düzgit, S. & Çarkoğlu, A. (2009) 'Turkey: reforms for a consolidated democracy', in *International Actors, Democratization and the Rule of Law: Anchoring Democracy?* eds A. Magen & L. Morlino, Routledge, London, pp. 120–155.
Aydınlı, E. (2009) 'A paradigmatic shift for the Turkish generals and an end to the coup era in Turkey', *Middle East Journal*, vol. 63, no. 4, pp. 581–596.
Aydıntaşbaş, A. (2010) 'Kırmızı Kitap'ta köklü değişim' [Fundamental transformation in the Red Book], *Milliyet*, 28 August, available online at: http://www.milliyet.com.tr/kirmizi-kitapta-koklu-degisim/asli-aydintasbas/siyaset/yazardetay/24.05.2010/1279655/default.htm
Bayramoğlu, A. (2009) 'EMASYA: Üç Anlam, Üç İşlev' [EMASYA: three meanings, three functions], in *Almanak Türkiye 2006–2008: Güvenlik Sektörü ve Demokratik Gözetim* [Almanac Turkey

TURKEY AND THE EU: ACCESSION AND REFORM

2006–2008: Security Sector and Democratic Oversight], eds A. Bayramoğlu & A. İnsel, TESEV Yayınları, Istanbul, pp. 204–205.

Beşe, E. (2006) 'Jandarma İstihbarat (JİTEM-JİT)' [Gendarmerie Intelligence (JITEM-JIT)] in *Almanak Türkiye 2005: Güvenlik Sektörü ve Demokratik Gözetim* [Almanac Turkey 2005: Security Sector and Democratic Oversight], ed. Ü. Cizre, TESEV Yayınları, Istanbul, pp. 168–195.

Cizre, Ü. (2008) 'The Justice and Development Party and the military', in *Secular and Islamic Politics in Turkey: The Making of the Justice and Development Party*, ed. Ü. Cizre, Routledge, London, pp. 132–171.

Cizre, Ü. & Walker, J. (2010) 'Conceiving the new Turkey after Ergenekon', *International Spectator*, vol. 45, no. 1, pp. 89–98.

Cizre-Sakallıoğlu, Ü. (1997) 'The anatomy of the Turkish military's political autonomy', *Comparative Politics*, vol. 29, no. 4, pp. 151–165.

Çağaptay, S. (2010) 'What's really behind Turkey's coup arrests?', *Foreign Policy*, vol. 25, available online at: http://www.foreignpolicy.com/articles/2010/02/25/whats_really_behind_turkeys_coup_arrest

Demirel, T. (2010) *2000'li Yıllarda Asker ve Siyaset: Kontrollü Değişim ile Statüko Arasında Türk Ordusu* [Soldiers and Politics in the 2000: Turkish Military in between Controlled Change and Status Quo], Siyaset, Ekonomi ve Toplum Araştırmaları Vakfı (SETA), Ankara.

European Commission (2007) 'Turkey 2007 progress report', Brussels, available online at: http://ec.europa.eu/enlargement/pdf/key_documents/2007/nov/turkey_progress_reports_en.pdf

European Commission. (2009) 'Turkey 2009 progress report', Brussels, available online at: http://ec.europa.eu/enlargement/pdf/key_documents/2009/tr_rapport_2009_en.pdf

Gürsoy, Y. (2009) 'Civilian support and military unity in the outcome of Turkish and Greek interventions', *Journal of Political and Military Sociology*, 271, pp. 47–75.

Gürsoy, Y. (2010) 'Changing role of the military in Turkey: democratization through coup plots?', paper presented at the Annual Meeting of the American Political Science Association, Washington, 2–5 September.

Heper, M. (2005) 'The European Union, the Turkish military and democracy', *South European Society and Politics*, vol. 10, no. 1, pp. 33–44.

HaberTürk (2010) 'CHP'nin 35. Madde Teklifine AKP'den Olumlu Yanıt' [Positive response from the AKP to the CHP's proposal on Article 35], 23 July, available online at: http://www.haberturk.com/polemik/haber/535385-chpnin-35-madde-teklifine-akpden-olumlu-yanit

Hürriyet (2007) 'Gece Yarısı Uyarısı' [Midnight warning], 28 April, p. 25.

Hürriyet (2010) 'Anayasa Değişlik Paketi Kabul Edilirse Neler Olacak' [What would happen if the constitutional amendment package is accepted], 8 July, available online at: http://www.hurriyet.com.tr/gundem/15262091.asp

Jenkins, G. (2007) 'Continuity and change: prospects for civil–military relations in Turkey', *International Affairs*, vol. 83, no. 2, pp. 339–355.

Jenkins, G. (2009) 'Between fact and fantasy: Turkey's Ergenekon investigation', Central Asia-Caucasus Institute Silk Road Studies Program. Available online at: http://www.silkroadstudies.org/new/docs/silkroadpapers/0908Ergenekon.pdf

Karakaş, E. (2009) 'Askeri Harcamaların ve Askeri Malların Parlamenter ve Yargısal (Sayıştay) Denetimi' [Parliamentary and judicial (Court of Auditors) oversight of military spending and military properties], in *Almanak Türkiye 2006–2008: Güvenlik Sektörü ve Demokratik Gözetim* [Almanac Turkey 2006–2008: Security Sector and Democratic Oversight], eds A. Bayramoğlu & A. İnsel, TESEV Yayınları, Istanbul, pp. 176–177.

Kardaş, Ü. (2009) 'Askeri Yargı' [Military justice], in *Almanak Türkiye 2006–2008: Güvenlik Sektörü ve Demokratik Gözetim* [Almanac Turkey 2006–2008: Security Sector and Democratic Oversight], eds A. Bayramoğlu & A. İnsel, TESEV Yayınları, Istanbul, pp. 66–72.

Kaya, A. (2009) 'Turkey–EU relations: the impact of Islam on Europe', in *Yearbook of Muslims in Europe*, Vol. 1, eds J. S. Nielsen, S. Akgönül, A. Alibasic, B. Marechal & C. Moe, Brill, Leiden, pp. 377–402.

Michaud-Emin, L. (2007) 'The restructuring of the military high command in the seventh harmonization package and its ramifications for civil–military relations', *Turkish Studies*, vol. 8, no. 1, pp. 25–42.

Nokta (2007) '2004'te İki Darbe Atlatmışız' [We survived two plots in 2004], 29 March.

Özcan, G. (2006) 'Milli Güvenlik Kurulu' [National Security Council], in *Almanak Türkiye 2005: Güvenlik Sektörü ve Demokratik Gözetim* [Almanac Turkey 2005: Security Sector and Democratic Oversight], ed. Ü. Cizre, TESEV Yayınları, Istanbul, pp. 38–51.

Özel, S. (2009) 'The back and forth of Turkey's "Westernness"', *German Marshall Fund of the United States: Analysis*, available online at: http://www.gmfus.org/cs/publications/publication_view? publication.id=281

Pion-Berlin, D. (1992) 'Military autonomy and emerging democracies in South America', *Comparative Politics*, vol. 25, no. 1, pp. 83–102.

Radikal (2010) 'Yeni MGK'dan Yeni "Kırmızı Kitap'a" Onay' [Approval to the new "Red Book" from the new NSC], 28 October, available online at: http://www.radikal.com.tr/Radikal.aspx? aType=RadikalHaberDetayV3&Date=&ArticleID=1026024&CategoryID=98

Stepan, A. (1988) *Rethinking Military Politics: Brazil and the Southern Cone*, Princeton University Press, Princeton, NJ.

Türk Silahlı Kuvvetleri İç Hizmet Yönetmeliği [Turkish Armed Forces Internal Service Regulations]. (1961) Available online at: http://www.mevzuat.gov.tr/Metin.Aspx?MevzuatKod=7.5.5905& MevzuatIliski=0&sourceXmlSearch=t%C3%BCrk%20silahl%C4%B1

Ünlü Bilgiç, T. (2009) 'The military and the Europeanization reforms in Turkey', *Middle Eastern Studies*, vol. 45, no. 5, pp. 803–824.

Ünver, A. (2009) 'Turkey's "deep state" and the Ergenekon conundrum', *Middle East Institute*, available online at: http://mei.edu/Publications/WebPublications/PolicyBriefs/PolicyBrief Archive/tabid/539/ctl/Detail/mid/1611/xmid/597/xmfid/17/Default.aspx.

Yetkin, M. (2009) 'Ergenekon, Generaller, Suç ve Ceza' [Ergenekon, generals, crime and punishment], Radikal, 6 December, available online at: http://www.radikal.com.tr/Default.aspx?aType= RadikalYazar&ArticleID=967719&Yazar=MURAT%20YETK%DDN&Date=06.12.2009& CategoryID=98

Yetkin, M. (2010) 'Ordunun En Uzun Günü (ve Gecesi)' [The longest day (and night) of the military], *Radikal*, 5 August, available online at: http://www.radikal.com.tr/Radikal.asp? aType=RadikalHaberDetayV3&ArticleID=1011923&Date=30.03.2011&CategoryID=98

Zaman, A. (2009) 'Receding power of Turkey's military: a leap for democracy or another power struggle?', *German Marshall Fund of the United States: Analysis*, available online at: http://www. gmfus.org/cs/publications/publication_view?publication.id=370

Zaverucha, J. (1993) 'The degree of military political autonomy during the Spanish, Argentine and Brazilian transitions', *Journal of Latin American Studies*, vol. 25, no. 2, pp. 283–299.

Yaprak Gürsoy (PhD University of Virginia) is an assistant professor in the Department of International Relations at Istanbul Bilgi University. Her research interests are regime change, democratization and civil–military relations. Her work has been published in *East European Quarterly*, *Journal of Political and Military Sociology*, *Turkish Studies* and *Journal of Modern Greek Studies*.

Is Corruption a Drawback to Turkey's Accession to the European Union?

Fikret Adaman

The paper focuses on the question of whether or not the current level of corruption in Turkey constitutes a major drawback for European Union (EU) membership. After elaborating the different types of corruption in Turkey, the paper argues that a full-scale anti-corruption strategy should include not only policing-type regulations and improved institutional structures, but also systemic reforms to deal with patron–client networking, informality and tax evasion. Assuming that the EU anchor will continue to be important, the EU's impact on combating corruption in Turkey will be greater to the extent that the EU manages to better understand the full picture in Turkey with regard to corruption.

Turkey's aspirations to become a full member of the European Union (EU) span over half a century (see e.g. Grabbe 2003). Historically, matters surrounding democratisation, human rights and economic development have been instrumental in shaping how the EU–Turkey relationship has evolved. Yet this by no means implies that other issues have been only marginally important—corruption being one of them. Although fighting corruption has yet to be a point of contention in EU–Turkey negotiations, it may figure prominently in future talks with Brussels, especially when the negative consequence of corruption on democracy is considered. This raises two interrelated questions: whether or not the current level of corruption in Turkey constitutes a major drawback for EU membership; and how negotiations with the EU will affect corruption in Turkey. This paper aims to provide answers to these questions and, to this end, attempts to categorise the different types of corruption observed in the country.

Combating corruption assumed importance in EU–Turkey negotiations quite recently in fact, although this has largely been overlooked by the media, political actors and academia. After joining the European Council's Group of States against Corruption (GRECO) in January 2004, in a Council decision dated 23 January 2006,

Turkey was advised to 'fully commit at all levels to the fight against corruption, including by strengthening all institutions involved, as well as coordination between them' (European Council 2006). In line with this standpoint, the EU and the Council of Europe jointly funded a two-year project, effective from 1 December 2007, on 'Ethics for the Prevention of Corruption in Turkey', which aimed, inter alia, to support the implementation of the code of ethics across public administration and public officers, develop systems to monitor the effectiveness of prevention and other anti-corruption measures, and ensure and enhance the coordination of these measures. This project, despite its modest budget of €1.5 million, should perhaps be considered a starting point of the EU's explicit involvement in Turkey's corruption problem.[1]

Turkey's involvement in international treaties on anti-corruption is not limited to GRECO; the ratification of the UN Convention against Corruption (2006), the Criminal Law Convention on Corruption (2003), the Civil Law Convention on Corruption (2003) and the Organisation for Economic Co-operation and Development (OECD) Anti-Bribery Convention (2000) are merely a few that stand out from a rather long list. In addition to efforts conducted at the international level, a series of serious, nationwide legal initiatives were also undertaken, especially in the last decade. Lately, the government has adopted the 2010–14 strategy to develop preventive and repressive measures against corruption and enforce transparency and accountability. Prior actions included: the adoption of the Action Plan on Increasing Transparency and Enhancing Good Governance in the Public Sector (2002), which sets out disciplinary and criminal sanctions against civil servants involved in corruption; the formulation of the Emergency Action Plan (2003), which aims to strengthen specialised anti-corruption units; the establishment of the Financial Crimes Investigation Board at the Ministry of Finance (1996); and modifications made to the Criminal Code to clarify the definition of corrupt activities (2005). Efforts by civil society to oversee the implementation of national anti-corruption strategies, however limited, should also be considered in this vein: in addition to the continued work by the Turkish Economic and Social Studies Foundation (TESEV) to raise awareness on corruption and search for anti-corruption policies, a number of private anti-corruption initiatives have also been influential, including Transparency International Turkey, the Association for Combating Corruption, the Association for the Protection of Citizens' Taxes, and the Economic Policy Research Institute (TEPAV).[2]

Against the backdrop of this rather impressive palette of anti-corruption policy initiatives, the current level of corruption is strikingly alarming. The European Commission's *Progress Report on Turkey 2010* makes a rather poignant remark, claiming that 'effective implementation of the strategy is necessary to reduce corruption *which remains prevalent in many areas*' (p. 17, italics added). Corruption seems to remain a serious concern for the people of Turkey—a fact that is quite observable in public opinion surveys. For instance, according to the '2010 Corruption Perceptions Index' prepared by Transparency International (2010a), the world-acknowledged authority on this issue, Turkey ranks 56th with a score of 4.4 (an index from 0 to 10, 10 corresponding to 'no corruption at all' and 0 to 'full corruption' in the public sector)—and has oscillated around that rank in the past few years. Similarly, findings from a recent nationwide survey conducted (in 2009) exclusively on this issue (Adaman et al. 2009) revealed that most layers of both central and local governments were perceived as being seriously corrupt: traffic police, customs, deeds offices, procurement offices, municipalities and construction offices all received scores of 6 or above, on a scale of 0–10, where 0 means 'no corruption at all' and 10 'full corruption'. These findings confirm Transparency International's (2010b) '2009 Global Corruption Parameters' study, which found the perceived corruption average for political parties, parliament/legislature, public officials/civil servants and the judiciary to be around 3.5 on a scale of 1–5 (where 1 corresponds to 'not at all corrupt' and 5 to 'extremely corrupt'). Moreover, in the private sector, where the current government has been trying to create an ambitious investment climate for national and international entrepreneurs, corruption was found to severely hinder investors: 42 per cent of the companies surveyed in the *Enterprise Survey 2008* study by the World Bank and International Finance Corporation (IFC) (2008) identified corruption as a major constraint in doing business. This is reminiscent of findings from an earlier nationwide survey conducted with firms (Adaman et al. 2003), where 48 per cent stated they had been forced to pay bribes or bring gifts to public officials/civil servants in the past two years in order to 'get things done'.

Furthermore, anecdotal evidence also corroborates this rather stark picture. The daily news coverage of top-level officials (sometimes including prime ministers and ministers) facing corruption charges has became a fairly routine occurrence in the last decade. More specifically, land administration has emerged as a speculative rent-making field especially in metropolises, and is prone to corruption. Global Integrity's (2010) '2008 Report' reveals that the Istanbul Greater Metropolitan Municipality has made more than 4,000 changes to city plans since 2004—read as changes to building permits—igniting severe concern about corruptive practices. More recently, the fraud case filed in 2008 against the Deniz Feneri charity in Germany, on the grounds that some of the donated monies were (illegally) transferred to the Justice and Development Party (AKP), is worth remembering. This brought about a corruption scandal that the Doğan Media Group pounced on, leading to a public feud between its owner, media tycoon Mr Doğan, and Erdoğan (see e.g. Global Integrity 2010).[3] It should also be noted that similar cases were observed in previous coalition governments comprising different political parties.

All in all, it appears that corruption has permeated all levels of government in Turkey—this despite the fact that, recently, successive governments have ratified important international and EU conventions on anti-corruption as well as taking relevant and imperative legal and administrative measures nationally. How are we to explain this rather unintended outcome? Are we to see the announcement of such anti-corruption efforts as nothing but whitewash, viz. as non-credible commitments, by a Turkish state machinery (elected members—central and local governments alike—as well as the bureaucracy) that is not genuinely willing to enforce the legal and administrative reforms adopted so far? Or perhaps the problem is not one of unwillingness but rather one of the lack of capacity and capability of the state machinery. Could it be that, rather than engaging in comprehensive programmes, the state has been targeting only piecemeal programmes to fight corruption, and thus achieving only a little?

Motivated by these questions, this paper aims to explore the current situation described above and its implications for the two fundamental questions set out earlier. However, to arrive at an answer, it is vital to first begin by analysing and subsequently contextualising the different manifestations of corruption. Certainly, offering a police officer cash to dodge a fine when caught speeding should be categorised as bribery, regardless of cultural or political context. However, lines of definition blur: for instance, when firms, in attempts to evade taxes—say, by employing informal labour—pay the 'necessary price' to avoid auditing in an environment where this is known to be standard practice throughout the country; or when primary-school headteachers ask parents trying to enrol their children in a certain school known to be of good quality and/or in their neighbourhood to make a 'voluntary' donation, on the grounds that the school is underfunded and money needs to be collected to cover its expenses; or when people seek out friends/relatives in public institutions to ensure even the simplest task is done without getting tangled up in red tape, while simultaneously thinking this just a part of their social life. These and similar cases make it necessary to unpack the term 'corruption'.

Unpacking Corruption: A Taxonomical Approach

The standard political economy literature defines 'corruption' as the misuse of legislated power and position by public officers as well as political officials for illegitimate private gain.[4] Corruption is then seen as threatening good governance, sustainable development and the democratic process, and as promoting injustice in society and business; it is thus conceived as a type of deviant behaviour.[5]

Although upstream and downstream corruption (sharing bribes with higher- and lower-ranked officials, respectively) is widespread, making it ever more difficult to contain the extent of corruption in public institutions, the umbrella framework used to capture the economic dimension of corruption is the principal–agent theory. Since most public institutions are organised hierarchically, the relationship between superiors (principals) and subordinates (agents) may become problematic under conditions of incomplete and asymmetric information: agents, instead of working on tasks assigned by the principal, may well pursue their own interests and misuse their power or position in return for private benefits in cases where such behaviour is not easily observable.[6] For instance, suppose the Minister of the Interior is keen on reducing traffic accidents and employs tools to this end (such as punishing speeding drivers), but the traffic police see no harm in accepting bribes to overlook the transgression and not fine speeders. This is where a principal–agent problem emerges between the Ministry and its officers. If it were the government accepting kickbacks from procurements, then the problem would be between the elected government and the constituency. The literature certainly provides remedies for both kinds of cases, underlying the importance of incentive structures.[7] For the first type, introducing properly—and intelligently—designed institutions, including 'incentive-compatible' mechanisms that align agents' interests with those of the principal, increasing audits and penalties and introducing technology that will curb agents' discriminatory power may well work to halt corruption to a great extent, even if not fully. For the second type, promoting transparency and accountability and demanding commitment from political parties to combat corruption should produce similar outcomes.

Underlying this line of thinking is the fact that agents engaged in corrupt activities are indeed conscious of the deviant nature of their behaviour. The standard literature is therefore based on the assumption that agents make their own cost–benefit analyses before undertaking such activities. In the present attempt to investigate taxonomically the different manifestations of corruption, this type of corruption will certainly capture many cases and will be referred to as 'individualistic' corruption.

It is also true that in some circumstances agents may engage in corrupt activities without realising the wrongdoing dimension of their actions. Consider, for instance, public officers who extend favourable treatment to members of their network in an environment where many procedures are indeed conducted through such networks. If these officers perceive themselves, above all, as a member of their network rather than a member of society, and if such perceptions are indeed numerous in a given society, then such an action—which in fact contradicts the very basic neutrality requirement of the public sphere—will not be categorised in their mind as preferential treatment and thus illegitimate; at any rate, since money/gifts are not exchanged, it will be difficult to prove wrongdoing. Obviously, such officers are likely to be receiving similar favourable treatments from other members of their network, and their behaviour thus may reflect a kind of reciprocal relationship. However, the fact is that this reciprocity may be very indirect and realised within long-standing friendship and family/ethnic/clan/religious ties based on closeness and obligations. As largely discussed in the anthropology literature, in such environments it is conceivable that agents are not engaging in simple cost-and-benefit analysis.[8] This type of favouritism, where agents are unaware of the deviant aspect of their actions, will be labelled 'reciprocity' here. Increasing transparency and accountability at the bureaucratic level and relying more on automated procedures in the relationship between citizens/firms and public institutions would certainly curb this type of corruption, although a more decisive solution would of course be a gestalt switch, so that public officers associate themselves not with narrowly defined networks but rather with the general public.

The third category deals with situations arising from a collective-action problem that leads to the ready acceptance or internalisation of corrupt activities as legitimate, where wrongdoers lack a sense of guilt. In a country where informality is rampant due to systemic problems, evading taxes or employing labour with no social security (and bribing officers to escape auditing) could easily become the default behaviour.

The crucial point in the context of extensive informality is that, in reality, informal firms simply legitimise their actions on the grounds that 'everyone else evades taxes, or everyone else uses informal labour, so I do as well—otherwise I won't be able to compete with these firms and will eventually go bankrupt'. This third taxonomic category, labelled corruption due to 'lack of participation' here, obviously requires the existence of a large informal economy (a large part of the community not contributing to the public sphere). Literature on the informal sector refers to a set of policies to reduce informality, such as making the formal sector more beneficial, building trust and collective incentives and increasing tax compliance. Yet, especially the policy-oriented literature points out that in cases where informality is certainly not a marginal issue, then piecemeal reforms may not work effectively and an overall systemic reform initiative may be required instead.

The fourth category of corruption arises in cases where local governments or local public institutions (such as schools, hospitals, kindergartens) utilise their power to extract (additional) money from service users so as to run their activities 'properly', claiming their initial budgets are insufficient to fully cover their expenses. Although the funds raised in implicit or explicit deals are claimed to be channelled to public use, this constitutes yet another manifestation of corruption, since the funds are collected involuntarily and illicitly, most likely without reference to any principles (such as progressivity), and are not bound by the accountability rule. Here it is assumed that local institutions have an a priori definition regarding the quality/quantity of the service to be delivered (greater than what is currently available) and believe that service users can afford to pay such 'additional' taxes.[9] There is obviously a clear connection between this category, labelled 'forced donations', and the third one, in the sense that informality reduces the size of the public (central government) budget, and hence puts financial pressure on individual public institutions. Furthermore, given that tax evasion is a serious issue, these institutions may well find it legitimate to demand extra taxes from the captured service users.

Finally, the last category considers cases where the process of political clientelism, where politicians favour and look after the interests of people from their own party at the expense of violating the neutrality principle, turns politics into a bargaining process between the voting public (the clients) and the politicians who protect them (the patrons).[10] In this situation, labelled 'clientelist corruption', one would expect to see people voting for political parties or politicians they perceive as providing them special favours, and politicians granting these favours with the expectation of re-election or other political gains. State employment based on service to a party rather than public interest; distribution of public services in return for political support rather than according to need and justice; public support to certain segments of the population in return for political support, ignoring the principle of productivity—all these are clear examples of clientelism. What is observed in such cases is particularistic networks between government bodies and interest groups—hence the term 'patron–client' relationship.

These five different categories, and inevitably their combinations, should provide a suitable setting to investigate the various manifestations of corruption. A detour is required at this point to explain why this matter has been elaborated. The literature on corruption largely departs from the view that involved parties are indeed aware of the 'wrongdoing' aspect of their actions, due to the misuse of entrusted power by political leaders and/or public officials, and thus tends to analyse these actions as 'exchange' relations—some realised in a one-shot interaction, others extended to the long term; some involving nothing but cash, others coming with their own specific rituals—at the expense of public benefits. Here, however, it is explicitly acknowledged that, at the expense of social welfare, some mutually beneficial relations may possibly be perceived by their participants as being quite natural and within the spirit of societal and friendship bonds. A similar mentality of not feeling guilt is said to occur in cases where a serious informality problem exists, and evading taxes or employing informal labour, even resorting to bribery if necessary, may become the default behaviour. The taxonomic and, in my opinion, more complete categorisation of corruption provided here will help in answering the questions we put forward. Now the Turkish case will be considered on the basis of this categorisation, by employing results from field studies.

Different Manifestations of Corruption in Turkey

As framed above, 'individualistic' corruption can easily be dealt with through redesigning the institutional setting. It is a fact that some people are more opportunistic (and have lower moral values) than others, and will therefore engage in such manipulative activities if given the opportunity. Altering people's moral values towards becoming more responsible citizens should of course be the ultimate aim, yet this can only be achieved in the long run. However, changing the rules of the game— by, for instance, increasing the probability of getting caught when engaging in corrupt actions, designing incentive compatible procedures that cannot be manipulated, making it less possible for officials to make arbitrary decisions and hence curtailing their power to influence outcomes—is certainly within the reach of governments. It is telling that in a nationwide survey representative of urban Turkey conducted in late 2008, as many as 26 per cent of respondents said that if they were caught speeding (in a hypothetical setting) they would opt to bribe the officer or at least definitely consider it (Adaman et al. 2009). More interestingly, this figure has remained more or less unchanged over the last few years (it was 28 per cent in 2004; see Adaman et al. 2005). Although the share of the population ready to resort to bribery has remained almost intact, people's experiences with traffic police in real life are more telling. In both 2004 and 2008, people were asked (in the same surveys mentioned above) whether they actually made irregular payments (cash or in-kind) to various institutions in the last two years; responses revealed a very sharp decrease in payments to traffic police, from 20 per cent to 8.8 per cent. A new set of regulations (e.g. installation of automated speed cameras) has decreased the level of arbitrary action by police officers, and this decline is explicable from changes in the rules of the game. The prevalence of bribery/embezzlement in public hospitals reveals a similar picture. The 2004 survey indicated that four per cent of those who had visited public hospitals were asked to make irregular payments to be able to receive services; this figure went down to 1.7 per cent in 2008 (Adaman et al. 2005; 2009). A very likely explanation for the decrease in the hospital setting are the recent reforms in the health care system, in which many hospital procedures became automated, decreasing the leverage of health care personnel and thus opportunities for embezzlement. These two findings indicate that while the proportion of opportunistic people may not have altered much, incidences of corruption decreased between 2004 and 2008, providing clear evidence that institutional mechanisms can successfully combat the first category of corruption.

The second category, 'reciprocity', is reportedly quite prevalent in Turkey. The 2008 survey results revealed a very striking fact: when dealing with public institutions, 22.1 and 23.3 per cent of the respondents said that the best way to conduct official business would be to find a friend/relative/acquaintance in, respectively, a national or a local government office. Although there is a slight decrease in these figures compared with the 1999 data as a result of increased automation of certain official procedures (from 26 and 31 per cent, respectively), the prevailing high percentage is a clear indication of how the state–civil-society relationship is being infiltrated by 'reciprocal' networks (Adaman et al. 2001; 2009).

Evidence suggests that the third category, or corruption 'due to lack of participation', is also quite common in Turkey. The 2008 survey delivered a noteworthy finding: 45 per cent of the urban population said they agreed to make purchases without receipts, thus colluding with the shopkeeper against the value-added tax (VAT) system (Adaman et al. 2009). This should not come as a surprise, given that Zenginobuz and Tokgöz (2010) computed that in 2008 in Turkey the VAT evasion rate was 41 per cent (calculated as the difference between the potential tax people should normally pay—based on consumption figures revealed in a country-wide comprehensive household survey—and the actual amount of collected tax). Similarly, informality has reached quite high levels in Turkey: it is estimated to be around 35 per cent of gross domestic product (GDP) (Schneider 2007), and 30 per cent of the industrial labour force is known to be uninsured (Türkiye İstatistik Kurumu [TURKSTAT] 2010). Informality and the third type of corruption may very well form a self-perpetuating system, as increased informality will make more people legitimise corrupt activities in their minds, and more corruption will mean further increase in informality—and in such an environment people will have no sense of illegitimacy if it comes to be that they have to bribe state officers to avoid being caught during auditing. Unless informality is addressed as a top-priority problem, and a long-term and comprehensive reform scheme is designed, curbing this type of corruption in Turkey will remain difficult. Although Turkey has recently made an attempt to target informality (World Bank 2010), not much has been achieved so far.

The fourth category, 'forced donations', has clear links to the Turkish government's inability to collect taxes properly. As of 2008, Turkey's ratio of collected taxes to GDP was 24.5 per cent, the smallest figure among OECD countries after Mexico—the EU-15's average being 38.7 per cent (Zenginobuz et al. 2010). One likely consequence of this, as presented in the previous section, may be that local institutions feel the need to collect their own taxes to top up their budgets. There is abundant anecdotal evidence indicating that local governments request 'voluntary' donations—not cash, but in-kind donations, such as an air conditioner for the municipality building, four tyres for a road grader, an ambulance, etc.—from citizens as a requisite to conclude their requests. Although public institutions try to make it apparent that the donation will not be used for personal gains, the lack of transparency makes people feel the arbitrariness in the process.

The last category involves cases of favouritism as manifestations of 'patron–client' networks. A wide body of theoretical literature suggests, almost unanimously, that interaction between groups of people and the Turkish state is mostly being conducted through the use of patronage links.[11] Yet, unveiling these types of corrupt activities, and especially distinguishing between whether the patron–client relationship is based on explicit beneficial exchanges or long-term reciprocity with no explicit transactions, is no easy task. Again, diagnostic survey results may give some evidence. When asked, for example, about their perceived level of favouritism on a scale of 0–10 (0 = 'full favouritism' and 10 = 'no favouritism'), the respondents of the 2008 survey ranked most national and local governments' services (construction permits, inspections, auditing, tender bids, among others) around 4, suggesting the existence of patronage links. Similarly, when people were asked to reveal their perceptions of how public jobs are filled, 44 and 54 per cent of respondents indicated that clientelism played a large role in recruitment to positions in, respectively, central government and municipalities. Although reasonable improvement from the 2000 figures is apparent for both cases, these findings still indicate the perception of preferential treatment in the public sphere (Adaman et al. 2009).

Looking Forward

The discussion so far has shown that incidences of corruption in Turkey result from a variety of circumstances. These were taxonomically divided into five, and it was claimed that each category had a different set of causes. Needless to say, reality most likely involves hybrid cases. For instance, some of the money embezzled by a public office could also be used to improve the public service provided, or high school headteachers who collect 'voluntary donations' could put aside a portion of it for private usage.

What matters is that some of these types of corruption can easily be targeted with improved institutional settings, while others cannot, as there seem to be systemic problems deep rooted in the state–society relationship. Therefore, any policy suggestions to fight corruption in Turkey should take this picture as a starting point, as otherwise it may prove difficult to comprehend why the Turkish state is achieving so little despite the presence of a quite impressive legislative body. Making it possible to pay taxes online, thereby drastically reducing red tape and room for potential embezzlement (the first type of corruption) is one thing; minimising tax evasion and hence providing better public services, thus lessening the need for public institutions to raise extra funds (the third and fourth types of corruption) is quite another. It was also observed that if the state–society relationship is largely configured along clientelistic lines, these are likely to appear in decisions taken in every area of the public sector and to develop as part of the political process (the fifth type). In their relations with each other, all actors who play a role in this process are likely to act as parts of the corruption network, at different levels. Certainly, increased transparency and accountability at the state level, especially with regard to the financing of political parties and election campaigns, would help deal with patron–client networks, but presumably a more democratic environment, where civil society has a larger say in the political sphere, will be the proper cure. Finally, the question of how to achieve the gestalt switch that will make people (ordinary citizens as well as businesspeople and politicians) move away from particularistic interests, in which belonging to a network is valued highly (the third type), and begin to value the meaning of universal principles is certainly not an easy one, and requires proper enquiry into the state–society relationship, its past and its evolution.

Concerning the last dimension, it is safe to say that there exist unhealthy elements in the way the state–society relationship is construed. Let us again refer to the 2008 survey results (Adaman et al. 2009), where respondents revealed a lack of trust in public bodies/institutions in general and dissatisfaction with the services provided. This clearly indicates that corruption problems are at least partially due to misgovernance and a fracture that exists between society and the state.

To conclude, let us reiterate that, given this picture, it becomes clear that a full-scale anti-corruption strategy should include not only policing-type regulations and improved institutional structures (provided of course there is political will in that regard), but also systemic reforms to deal with patron–client networking, informality and tax evasion. Once this is acknowledged, corruption in Turkey could be seen as deeper than a mere 'technical problem', which can successfully be addressed by increasing public auditing and by designing incentive-compatible mechanisms. Since trust in public institutions is very low, it is difficult to speak of a healthy public sphere. There is a clear need, therefore, for a comprehensive reform of governance structures, in the form of increased accountability and transparency. Furthermore, when speaking of reforming the overall governance structure, there is also a question that needs to be asked regarding the political economy side of the problem: who is going to absorb the resistance from the beneficiaries of corruption, and, in the case of large-scale reforms that will also incorporate more systemic issues, who will shoulder the cost?

Last but not least, let us return to those initial questions regarding the future of the EU–Turkey relationship within the context of corruption. As mentioned at the outset, there are two (somewhat related) questions that need to be answered: first, whether the corruption issue will be a constraint for Turkey in its efforts to join the EU, and, second, how the negotiations with the EU will affect corruption in Turkey. Regarding the former, it is true that the EU is keen on fighting corruption, as Article 29 of the Treaty mentions preventing and combating corruption as one way to achieve the objective of creating and maintaining a European area of freedom, security and justice. Yet, on the question of whether the corruption level in Turkey is comparable to that in countries that have already acceded, the picture is mixed (see e.g. Michael 2004). According to Transparency International figures, although most member states have scores 7 or above on a 0–10 index and are therefore among the least corrupt countries in the world, the number of member states where corruption figures are worse than for Turkey is not negligible; for instance, Italy (an old member), Greece (a relatively newer one) and Bulgaria (a new one) all have worse scores than Turkey. Presumably, though, Turkey will be unable to ask to be considered among the 'bad examples', and the EU will likely press Turkey to combat corruption. Given the link between corruption and democracy (see e.g. Warren 2006), the EU's continued pressure on democracy and human rights in Turkey will certainly be of help in this regard, albeit mostly indirectly. Regarding the latter question, it has been already observed that the EU's engagement with corruption in Turkey seems to be focused on policing-type regulations and increasing coordination among public institutions charged with fighting corruption.

Acknowledgements

I am grateful to editors Gamze Avcı and Ali Çarkoğlu, as well as two anonymous referees, for their suggestions. I should also mention that the thoughts presented here have been largely shaped through my decade-long cooperation with Ali Çarkoğlu and Burhan Şenatalar while conducting a series of field studies on corruption. The usual disclaimer applies.

Notes

[1] The Economic Crime Division of the Council of Europe has been charged with implementing this project; see www.coe.int/t/dghl/cooperation/economiccrime/corruption/projects/TYEC/1062-TYEC-ProjectDocument-Sep07.PDF
[2] For a selection, see Adaman et al., 2001; 2003; 2005; 2009; Tarhan et al., 2005; Önder et al., 2008.
[3] In passing, let me acknowledge that cases of corruption covered in the media may be different from actual occurrences of corruption.
[4] Although corruption may well occur in the private sphere, the scope of this paper only includes those in the public sphere.
[5] For a theoretical discussion, see e.g. Rose-Ackerman, 1978; 2006; Klitgaard, 1988. For an applied research study, see e.g. Sayan, 2009. I do not question here the moral aspect per se. What if a father bribes the police not to torture his son charged with engaging in political activities in an undemocratic country?
[6] See e.g. Stiglitz, 2008.
[7] See e.g. Acemoğlu et al., 2001.
[8] See e.g. Eisenstadt & Roniger, 1984.
[9] Motivations that underlie officials actions are not pursued here.
[10] See e.g. Bhagwati, 1982; Krueger, 1994.
[11] See e.g. Heper & Keyman, 1998; Green, 2005; Keyman, 2005; Keyman & İçduygu, 2005.

References

Acemoğlu, D., Johnson, S. & Robinson, J. A. (2001) 'The colonial origins of comparative development: an empirical investigation', *American Economic Review*, vol. 91, no. 5, pp. 1369–1401.

Adaman, F., Çarkoğlu, A. & Şenatalar, B. (2001) *Hanehalkı Gözünden Türkiye'de Yolsuzluk*, [Corruption from the Turkish Household Perspective], TESEV, Istanbul.

Adaman, F., Çarkoğlu, A. & Şenatalar, B. (2003) *İşdünyası Gözünden Türkiye'de Yolsuzluk*, [Corruption from the Turkish Business Perspective], TESEV, Istanbul.

Adaman, F., Çarkoğlu, A. & Şenatalar, B. (2005) *Toplumun Kamu Yönetimine, Kamu Hizmetlerine ve Reforma Bakışı* [People's Position to Public Governance, Public Services and Public Reform], TESEV, Istanbul.

Adaman, F., Çarkoğlu, A. & Şenatalar, B. (2009) *Türkiye'de Kamu Reformu* [Public Reform in Turkey], TEPAV, Ankara.

Bhagwati, J. (1982) 'Directly unproductive profit-seeking (DUP) activities', *Journal of Political Economy*, vol. 90, no. 5, pp. 988–1002.

Eisenstadt, S. N. & Roniger, L. (1984) *Patrons, Clients and Friends: Interpersonal Relations and the Structure of Trust in Society*, Cambridge University Press, Cambridge.

European Commission (2010) *Progress Report on Turkey 2010*, Brussels.

European Council (2006) 'Council decision of 23 January 2006 on the principles, priorities and conditions contained in the Accession Partnership with Turkey', available online at: http://www.abgs.gov.tr/files/AB_Iliskileri/Tur_En_Relations/Apd/Turkey_APD_2006.pdf

Global Integrity. (2010) '2008 report', available online at: http://report.globalintegrity.org/Turkey/2008

Grabbe, H. (2003) 'Europeanisation goes east: power and uncertainty in the EU accession process', in *The Politics of Europeanisation*, eds K. Featherstone & C. M. Radelli, Oxford University Press, Oxford, pp. 303–327.

Green, P. (2005) 'Disaster by design: corruption, construction and catastrophe', *British Journal of Criminology*, vol. 45, no. 4, pp. 528–546.

Heper, M. & Keyman, E. F. (1998) 'Double-faced state: political patronage and the consolidation of democracy in Turkey', *Middle Eastern Studies*, vol. 34, no. 4, pp. 259–277.

Keyman, E. F. (2005) 'Modernity, democracy, and civil society', in *Environmentalism in Turkey*, eds F. Adaman & M. Arsel, Ashgate, Aldershot.

Keyman, E. F. & İçduygu, A. (2005) *Citizenship in a Global World: European Questions and Turkish Experiences*, Routledge, London.

Klitgaard, R. (1988) *Controlling Corruption*, University of California Press, Berkeley and Los Angeles.

Krueger, A. O. (1994) 'The political economy of the rent-seeking society', *American Economic Review*, vol. 64, no. 3, pp. 291–301.

Michael, B. (2004) 'Anti-corruption in Turkey's EU accession', *Turkish Policy Quarterly*, 34, available online at: http://papers.ssrn.com/sol3/papers.cfm?abstract_id=999350

Önder, İ., Karakaş, M. & Çak, M. (eds) (2008) *Yolsuzluk Ekonomisi ve Yolsuzlukla Mücadele* [The Economy of Corruption and the Fight against Corruption], TOBB, Ankara.

Rose-Ackerman, S. (1978) *Corruption: A Study in Political Economy*, Academic Press, New York.

Rose-Ackerman, S. (ed.) (2006) *International Handbook on the Economics of Corruption*, Edward Elgar, Cheltenham.

Sayan, S. (ed.) (2009) *Economic Performance in the Middle East and North Africa*, Routledge, London.

Schneider, F. (2007) 'Shadow economies and corruption all over the world: new estimates for 145 countries', *Economics*, available online at: http://www.google.com/search?client=safari&rls=en&q='Shadow+economies+and+corruption+all+over+the+world:+New+estimates+for+145+countries'&ie=UTF-8&oe=UTF-8

Stiglitz, J. E. (2008) 'Principal and agent', in *The New Palgrave Dictionary of Economics*, 2nd edn, eds S. N. Durlauf & L. E. Blume, Palgrave Macmillan, London.

Tarhan, R. B., Gançkaya, Ö. F., Ergül, E., Özsemerci, K. & Özbaran, H. (2005) *Bir Olgu Olarak Yolsuzluk: Nedenler, Etkiler ve Çözüm Önerileri* [Corruption as a Phenomenon: Causes, Impacts and Proposals for Solution], TEPAV, Ankara.

Transparency International (2010a) '2010 corruption perceptions index', available online at: http://www.transparency.org

Transparency International (2010b) '2009 global corruption parameters', available online at: http://www.transparency.org

TURKSTAT (2010) 'Household labor statistics', available online at: www.tuik.gov.tr

Warren, M. E. (2006) 'Democracy and deceit: regulating appearances of corruption', *American Journal of Political Science*, vol. 50, no. 1, pp. 160–174.

World Bank (2010) *Turkey: Informality; Causes, Consequences, Policies*, Ankara.

World Bank & IFC (2008) *Enterprise Survey 2008*, Washington.

Zenginobuz, Ü. & Tokgöz, E. (2010) 'Trends in tax revenues and rates in OECD countries: a comparative assessment of the Turkish tax system', mimeo, Istanbul, March.

Zenginobuz, Ü., Adaman, F., Gökşen, F., Savcı, Ç. & Tokgöz, E. (2010) *Vergi, Temsiliyet ve Demokrasi İlişkisi Üzerine Türkiye'de Vatandaşların Algıları* [Turkish Citizens' Perceptions on the Relationship between Tax, Representation and Democracy], Boğaziçi University Press, Istanbul.

Fikret Adaman (PhD Manchester University) is a professor in the Economics Department at Boğaziçi University, Istanbul. His research interests are ecological economics, political economy of Turkey and the history of economic thought. His most recent publications have been in journals such as *Ecological Economics* (2010, with D. Avcı and B. Özkaynak), *European Journal of History of Economic Thought* (2010, with Y. Madra) and *Turkish Studies* (2009). His most recent book (co-edited with B. Karapınar and G. Özertan) is *Rethinking Structural Reform in Turkish Agriculture* (Nova, New York, 2010).

Human Rights and Turkey's EU Accession Process: Internal and External Dynamics, 2005–10

William Hale

This paper attempts to assess and explain the relative strength of internal and external factors in the improvement of Turkey's human rights regime. After 1999, the European Union, which required Turkey to conform to the 'Copenhagen criteria' of civil liberties as a precondition for the start of accession negotiations, has been by far the most important element, resulting in the passage of an impressive raft of constitutional and legal reforms between 2001 and 2004. After 2005, when accession talks officially began, the pace of reform slackened markedly, as the accession process became more problematic. Nonetheless, in 2010, another package of constitutional reforms was enacted, suggesting that the cause of reform has now acquired a powerful internal dynamic.

Between 2001 and 2005, Turkey made remarkable advances in the improvement of human rights. However, over the next four years, the reform process slackened severely, causing pessimists to predict that it might evaporate altogether. A commonly given explanation for this was that, up to 2005, Turkish governments had a powerful incentive to improve Turkey's human rights regime, as demanded by the European Union (EU) as an essential condition for the start of accession negotiations. Once these negotiations had officially begun in October 2005, it was suggested, the incentive for further reform slackened significantly. This effect was compounded by the fact that some European leaders, in France and Germany in particular, now voiced open opposition to the whole principle of eventual Turkish membership, strengthening the arguments of those in Turkey who opposed further political reforms or closer alignment with the EU. Nonetheless, in 2010 the Justice and Development Party (AKP) government re-started its programme of political reform, by tabling a raft of amendments to the highly defective constitution of 1982. This package included some important improvements in human rights. In the present context, what is important about the revived effort is that it did not correspond to any distinct shift in EU policy, or Turkey's overall relations with the EU. The explanation thus has to be sought in Turkey's internal dynamics.

Against this background, this paper attempts to assess and explain the relative strength of external and internal factors in aiding or impeding the extension of civil liberties in Turkey. It starts by taking up some general questions about the relationship between democratic government and human rights, and the processes by which political liberalisation can be achieved. This is followed by a critical analysis of the historical record of Turkish–EU relations since 2001, and their effects on the drive to improve human rights.

Democracy and Human Rights: Some General Considerations

Besides their inherent importance for the future political direction of both Turkey and the EU, experiences since the official opening of accession negotiations in October 2005 have raised some crucial questions about the general relationship between democratic government and the application of human rights norms. Frequently, the assumption is made that the two will inevitably go together.[1] Unfortunately, Turkey's experiences since the 1950s undermine this bland assumption of mutual reinforcement, since the establishment of democratically elected government has not automatically led to the improvement of the human rights regime, especially where it affects the rights of minorities, whether ideologically, ethnically, or religiously defined. As in other cases, universal suffrage and free elections can lead to the tyranny of the majority, unless they are accompanied by strict limitations on the exercise of state power. Moreover, in the Turkish case, there is a tendency to promote human rights on a particularist rather than universalist basis (Plagemann 2000, pp. 440–447, 451–459). As in other spheres, human rights discourse in Turkey tends to be highly partisan, and often interpreted as 'human rights for *me*' (by implication, 'but not for those other people'). This has been reinforced by the fact that, although Turkey has been ruled by democratically elected governments for most of the period since 1950, its constitutions have been weak protectors of human rights. In particular, the constitution of 1982, most of which is still in force, re-asserted the powers of the state against democratic values and human rights. This effect has been strengthened by the highly restrictive attitudes of the high judiciary in Turkey, especially in recent years.

How can these problems be solved? Although there are some rare cases of enlightened autocracies, which extended human rights when conservative elected governments would probably have opposed them (Langlois 2003, pp. 1005–1006), in Europe and North America this process can more commonly be seen as the result of society's internal dynamics of conflict and eventual compromise between opposing social forces, something that was part of the overall process of democratisation. Following the classic proposal made by Dankwart Rustow, it is argued that this was achieved not through the prior adoption of common ideals, but through the survival tactics of previously ruling elites who saw compromise and concession as the best alternative to violent revolutionary overthrow: in the Turkish case, Rustow noted that Turkey 'received its first democratic regime as a free gift from the hands of a dictator'—referring to İsmet İnönü's decision to end the single-party regime in 1945–46—rather than through prolonged and then resolved social conflict: this, he suggested, helped to account for the subsequent weakness of Turkish democracy (Rustow 1970, p. 362).

The Turkish experience of 1945–46 also points up the importance of external influences and pressures as the third factor in political liberalisation, since it corresponded with Turkey's shift into the Western camp in the Cold War conflict, although whether this was a process of direct causation can be disputed.[2] Since 1993 the EU, in particular, has played the essential role of extending democratic government and human rights norms in Eastern Europe, by insisting on adherence to the 'Copenhagen criteria' of political as well as economic practice as a precondition for the start of accession negotiations with prospective member states. Critically, this process succeeds only if the candidate country is offered full membership, and this offer is sustained. In contrast, the Euro-Mediterranean Partnership programme launched in 1995 aimed merely at developing closer economic, political, and strategic relations between the EU and Mediterranean countries that were not candidates for full membership. Although it was supposed to support political liberalisation in the region, it has failed to achieve this, as the limited partnership it offers is too weak an incentive, given the reluctance of ruling elites in Middle Eastern and North African countries to relax their grip on power (Grigoriadis 2009, pp. 173–175).

Turkey, the EU and Human Rights: The Stumbling Journey

Between the start of the EU-inspired political reform programme in Turkey, in 2001, and the official opening of accession negotiations in 2005, the Turkish experience afforded a striking illustration of the powerful impact of an external impetus to the widening of civil liberties. This was achieved by a series of nine 'harmonisation packages' enacted by parliament between February 2002 and July 2004. Since this process has been explored elsewhere in some detail (Hale 2003, pp. 106–127; Özbudun 2007, pp. 179–96; Hale & Özbudun 2010, ch. 5) its main contents can be summarised as: the revision of the constitution so as to enhance freedoms of speech and association and the passage of a new Law of Associations; the enactment of new Criminal and Civil Codes; the complete abolition of the death penalty, and legal changes to facilitate the prosecution of public officials responsible for torture and maltreatment of prisoners; and the passage of legislation allowing broadcasting in languages other than Turkish, as a first step towards the recognition of Kurdish cultural rights.

In pushing forward with this reform programme, the government formed by the AKP after the general elections of November 2002 had two vital advantages. First, from the opposition benches, the Republican Peoples Party (CHP) generally supported the changes—an essential condition given that a number of reforms required changes to the constitution, and thus a two-thirds majority in parliament, which the AKP by itself fell just short of holding. (As an alternative, an amendment endorsed by less than two-thirds but more than three-fifths of the deputies could be enacted if then passed by a referendum, but at this stage the AKP was apparently reluctant to resort to this.) Second, although it was generally recognised that Turkey's path towards eventual EU membership would be long and at points problematic, there was committed support for the principle of Turkish accession from all the main European governments.

As time went on, however, these favourable conditions weakened. After the AKP's second election victory in 2007, the CHP was joined in parliament by the ultra-nationalist Nationalist Action Party (MHP) in opposing further constitutional changes. Meanwhile, doubts were being raised in Europe about the prospective admission of a 'non-European' country. In Germany, the Christian Democrats (CDU–CSU) proposed instead that Turkey should merely be offered an ill-defined 'privileged partnership'—in effect, a polite way of excluding Turkey from the EU. Following national elections in Germany in September 2005, the CDU–CSU became the dominant partner in a coalition with the Social Democrat Party of Germany (SPD). Officially, the new chancellor, Angela Merkel, adhered to the aim of 'privileged partnership' rather than full membership for Turkey; nevertheless, she realised she could not now reverse a process that had been endorsed by the previous German government, as well as her coalition partners. She adhered to this stance after forming her second coalition, this time with the Free Democratic Party (FDP) in October 2009 (*Today's Zaman*, 15 November 2009; NTV television, www.ntvmsnbc.com, 13 October 2009). In France, the UMP (Union pour un mouvement populaire), which was set up in 2002 to support President Jacques Chirac, also supported the idea of 'privileged partnership' for Turkey, although Chirac himself joined other European leaders in endorsing full membership as the eventual aim. However, the succession of Nicolas Sarkozy, formerly the chairman of the UMP, to the French presidency in May 2007 was a serious blow, since the new president now made 'privileged partnership' for Turkey an official part of French government policy.

Early signs of the more negative tone from Europe emerged from the wording of the 'Negotiating Framework for Turkey' that was drawn up by the European Commission in 2004 and subsequently accepted by the EU heads of state and government, meeting as the European Council, in December of that year. This stated that, although the 'shared objective of the negotiations is accession', the negotiations 'are an open-ended process, the outcome of which cannot be guaranteed beforehand', and that the process 'will take into account the absorption capacity of the Union'.[3] For the Turks, stating that the process was 'open-ended' appeared to give some sort of endorsement of 'privileged partnership' as an alternative. More ominously, no definition of the 'absorption capacity of the Union' was given—nor could it be, granted the extreme vagueness of the term. From the Turkish viewpoint, it seemed possible that the EU leaders might simply decide to break off the negotiations, citing the EU's lack of 'absorption capacity', without having to give any further explanation.

This garbled message from Brussels was compounded by specific limitations on the scope of the negotiations. After Nicolas Sarkozy's election to the Elysée Palace, the French government unilaterally blocked negotiations on five chapters of the *acquis communautaire*, which Turkey was required to accept to complete the accession process. In December 2006, negotiations on another eight chapters were blocked, thanks to Ankara's refusal to ratify an additional protocol to extend its customs union with the EU to the ten states that had joined the EU in May 2004—most notably the (Greek Cypriot) Republic of Cyprus. Moreover, it was announced that no chapters could be 'closed' (that is, the negotiations formally completed) until the additional protocol were ratified (CNNTurk, www.cnnturk.com, 15 December 2006). According to one experienced commentator, 'the very moment the Turkish political leadership lost trust in the readiness of the EU to stand by its commitments, it started to change its policy'—by for instance, failing to carry through further human rights improvements (Kramer 2009, p. 3).

This effect should not be exaggerated, since human rights reforms were not entirely abandoned by Turkey after 2005. Improvements that were effected included a new and more liberal law on foundations, passed in February 2008, which significantly improved the property rights of religious foundations established by the small non-Muslim minorities in Turkey. This had long been demanded by the EU.[4] Another issue repeatedly stressed by the Commission was the wording of Article 301 of the new Criminal Code (replacing Article 159 of its predecessor), which makes insulting the 'Turkish identity' and state institutions a punishable offence. This permits statements deemed to be 'criticism' rather than 'insult', but has allowed courts wide latitude in deciding how to interpret this. In April 2008, after repeated complaints by the European Commission, Article 301 was amended, most importantly by requiring permission from the minister of justice to launch a prosecution.[5] This resulted in a sharp reduction of the number of prosecutions—a development welcomed by the Commission—although it could be argued that it would have been better if the Article had been withdrawn altogether, and other sections of the Criminal Code restricting freedom of speech remained in force.[6]

Repeated reports and declarations by the Commission made it clear that these reforms, limited as they were, still left the government with a large unachieved agenda. Apart from the failure to further extend the cultural and other rights of the Kurdish minority, the concerns in question included continued restrictions of freedom of speech and communication, the continuation of compulsory classes in religious culture and ethics in primary and secondary schools (ignoring the interests of the Alevi minority), and restrictions on the Greek Orthodox Ecumenical Patriarchate (in particular, the closure of its seminary on the Marmara island of Heybeli). On women's rights, the Commission continued to complain that the government had failed to establish a gender equality body, and to chafe at the low level of female representation in politics as well as the serious problems of domestic violence, 'honour killings' and forced marriages. On these and other issues, the main complaint was that, although the legal framework for protecting women's rights, and gender equality generally, was in place, these reforms were not carried through in practice.[7] More surprising, perhaps, was the government's failure to amend Articles 68–69 of the constitution, or Articles 78–83 of the Law on Political Parties (Law No. 2820), under which the AKP itself had narrowly escaped closure by the Constitutional Court in 2008, on the alleged grounds that it had become a 'focus' of anti-constitutional activities aimed at ending the secular character of the state. Following pressure from its own supporters as well as well as the EU, the AKP government had promised to amend these provisions in accordance with the criteria adopted by the Venice Commission. These stipulate that the closure of political parties should only be justified 'in the case of parties which advocate the use of violence or use violence as a political means to overthrow the democratic constitutional order', adding that this provision 'should be used with utmost restraint'.[8] There were predictable complaints from the EU in November 2009, when the Constitutional Court dissolved the pro-Kurdish Democratic Society Party (DTP) on the grounds that it had become a focus for activities 'in conflict with the indivisible integrity of the state with its territory and nation' and its 'links with a terrorist organisation' (that is, the Kurdistan Workers' Party [PKK]) (*Hürriyet*, 11 December 2009).

The AKP government's failure to reform the constitutional rules could be seen as part of its apparent abandonment of a far more ambitious scheme to jettison the existing constitution and replace it with a more democratic alternative. In June 2007, Prime Minister Tayyip Erdoğan asked a group of constitutional law professors, headed by Professor Ergun Özbudun, to prepare a draft of a new constitution. Following the AKP's clear victory in the general elections of July 2007, the committee presented its proposals to the party leaders in August.[9] The original intention of the leaders of the AKP was to finalise the draft, before submitting it for public debate by a variety of social organisations, and then present it to parliament as a product of broad consensus. However, after this brave start, the project was quietly shelved. It was suggested that this was due to the government's preoccupation with the crisis over the presidential election in 2007 and the subsequent attempt by its opponents to have the AKP closed down by the Constitutional Court, but there also seems to have been serious divisions of opinion on this issue within the AKP (Hale & Özbudun 2010, p. 67).

Conditions then started to alter during the autumn of 2009. Initially, the main focus was on the Kurdish problem, rather than human rights in general, and resulted from initiatives by the United States, and domestic political considerations, rather than pressure from the EU. At this point, the Obama administration was beginning the long process of withdrawal from Iraq, and was anxious to ensure that this did not produce a dangerous collision between Turkey and the Iraqi Kurds. To achieve this, Turkey would need to reach an accommodation with the Iraqi Kurdish leadership (in which it eventually succeeded) and make effective moves to solve its own internal Kurdish problem. Domestically, the AKP government needed to overcome the alienation of much of the Kurdish population from the Turkish state, so as to reduce the risk of terrorist attacks by the PKK and strengthen its electoral position in the south-east. Hence, it launched what was referred to as the 'Kurdish initiative' (in Turkish, *açılım*, or 'opening') in September 2009. While not conceding Kurdish demands for regional autonomy within the Turkish republic, this was expected to include wider use of the Kurdish language and the winding-down of the much criticised 'village guards' system of local militias armed and paid for by the Turkish state (*Radikal*, 16 December 2009, *Today's Zaman*, 18, 24 December 2009). By exploiting its new links with the Kurdistan Regional Government in Iraq, the government also hoped to bring the PKK militants who had been based in northern Iraq since the Gulf war of 2003 'down from the mountains'. As a first step, 34 PKK members and their families presented themselves at the border crossing post of Habur on 19 October 2009; after questioning they were sent on to Diyarbakır, the biggest city in the region, where they received a rapturous welcome orchestrated by the DTP. This reaction backfired severely, since the government quickly realised that the DTP was turning the 'opening' into a propaganda victory for its own cause. On 24 October Tayyip Erdoğan announced that there would be a 'break' in the process, and the DTP subsequently declared that it no longer supported the initiative (*Hürriyet Daily News*, 25 October 2009, *Radikal*, 1 November 2009; *Today's Zaman*, 4 December 2009). With the closure of the DTP by the Constitutional Court, the 'opening' seemed to have been put in the freezer.

Rather than focus purely on the Kurdish question, the government then decided to develop its initiative as a 'democratisation package', beginning with a raft of constitutional reforms. In doing this, it decided not to resurrect the idea of a completely new constitution, as it had originally proposed, but to opt for piecemeal changes to the existing constitution. Given that the two main opposition parties in parliament—the CHP and MHP—could be expected to oppose the package, it also decided to adopt the second method of changing the constitution, by securing a three-fifths majority in parliament (that is, at least 330 votes), followed by approval in a national referendum. Given that the AKP had 336 seats in parliament—excluding the Speaker, who has no vote—it should have been able to surmount the first hurdle, assuming that virtually all its deputies toed the party line (the latter was not absolutely certain, since the constitution stipulates that amendments must be passed in a secret ballot).

The government tabled its package of amendments in parliament at the end of March 2010.[10] A large part of the package did not directly affect human rights, although these clauses were of crucial importance to the government—in particular, changes to the composition and structure of the Constitutional Court and the High Council of Judges and Prosecutors (Articles 146, 147, 149, and 159 of the constitution) and changes authorising civilian courts to try military personnel for 'crimes against the security of the State, constitutional order and its functioning', and preventing civilians from being tried in military courts except in wartime (Article 145). However, the government's package did take up several of the Özbudun committee's proposals for the improvement of individual rights, such as clauses authorising positive discrimination in favour of women, children, the elderly, and the disabled (Article 10), and those ensuring the protection of personal data (Article 20) and the protection of children (Article 41). The improvement of trade union rights included permission for workers to become members of more than one union simultaneously (Article 51), allowing unions of public servants to sign collective labour agreements, although not to declare strikes (Article 53), and removing the previous ban on 'political' and solidarity strikes (Article 54). In accordance with frequent prompting from the EU, an amendment to Article 74 paved the way for the establishment of an Ombudsman's office, while alterations to Article 148 allowed individuals to apply to the Constitutional Court 'on the grounds that one of the fundamental rights and freedoms within the scope of the European Convention of Human Rights which are guaranteed by the Constitution has been violated by public authorities'. While not perfect, this amendment, if applied effectively, should reduce the large number of applications from Turkey to the European Court of Human Rights.[11]

The Turkish parliament began its full debate on this package on 19 April 2010, completing the initial ballot on each of its individual articles ten days later, and in each case passing them by more than the minimum of 330 votes, albeit by very narrow margins in some cases.[12] This process was repeated in the second round of voting, beginning on 3 May, but with one notable casualty on 4 May, when a proposed amendment to Article 69 received only 327 votes: had it passed, this would have made the opening of a case for the closure of a political party dependent on a decision by a special commission representing all the main parties in parliament. It was reported that seven AKP deputies had failed to support the motion, suggesting that there were some serious divisions on this point within the ruling party. Nonetheless, the government pressed ahead with the rest of the package, which was finally passed as a whole by 336 votes on 7 May (*Hürriyet*, 4 May 2010; *Today's Zaman*, 8 May 2010).

Critics might complain that the reforms were insufficient, that Turkey had failed to apply the Venice criteria on the closure of political parties, and that a new constitution was still needed. Nor did the package meet all the requirements of the EU, outlined earlier. Above all, the outcome of the reform programme was still uncertain, since the CHP, supported by the tiny Democratic Left Party and a handful of independent deputies, immediately applied to the Constitutional Court for the annulment of the package. At the time of writing (June 2010), the Court still had to issue a verdict, although it had agreed to examine the petition on procedural grounds (that is, to decide whether the correct legislative procedures had been adhered to) (*Hürriyet*, 8 June 2010). After the Court ordered only minor amendments, the package was passed by the convincing majority of 58 to 42 per cent in a national referendum held on 12 September. It was clear that the 'democratic opening', for all its shortcomings, was to be an important step forward, and it had been warmly welcomed as such by the EU (*Today's Zaman*, 8 May 2010). Even though the government's critics argued that the package did not go far enough, they had to accept that half a loaf was much better than no bread.

Conclusions and Explanations

To return to the questions raised at the beginning of this paper, it is obviously impossible to make an exact assessment of the role of the EU accession process in improving

Turkey's human rights regime, since we have no way of knowing whether some reforms would not have taken place anyway, thanks to domestic political pressures or other more general effects of economic and cultural globalisation, broadly defined. On the other hand, there can be little doubt that the need to conform to the Copenhagen criteria had a powerful effect in boosting the effort for reform, especially during the first phase, up to 2004. As a contrary example, nearly all Turkey's near neighbours in the Middle East, the Caucasus, and Central Asia, which lacked the incentive offered by prospective EU membership, made virtually no effort to democratise during this period—and its other near neighbour Russia actually reversed the process. After 2004, as multiple obstacles emerged in Turkey's prospective path to EU membership, with centre-right parties in France and Germany opposing the idea in principle, the process of reform in Turkey slackened markedly. This strengthened the argument that there was a direct causal relationship between the prospects of accession and Turkish democratisation, the latter being heavily dependent on the former. Moreover, the political rhetoric of reform in Turkey rested on the EU agenda, 'harmonisation' with the Copenhagen criteria being advanced as the main reason for reforms during the first phase.

On the other hand, the resumption of reforms in 2010 weakens this assumption of a neat linkage between the Turkey–EU relationship and human rights improvements in Turkey. Admittedly, the EU continued the pressure on Ankara for progress in this direction, but it had been doing so for several years previously without much effect, and there was no noticeable change in its tone in 2009–10. In urging the adoption of the reforms, both Foreign Minister Ahmet Davutoğlu and Prime Minister Erdoğan mentioned that they would strengthen Turkey's hand in negotiations with the EU (*Today's Zaman*, 10 April 2010; *Zaman*, 24 March 2010), but this was not the main burden of the government's message. Significantly, the term 'harmonisation' was completely dropped from the official rhetoric, to be replaced by 'democratisation'—a far less specific alternative. If the external environment was referred to, it was the because of the need to keep up with a changing world—in effect, the global setting—rather than the EU. The 1982 constitution was dismissed for being outdated as well as undemocratic: in the words of Deputy Premier Cemil Çiçek, it was a 'Cold War-era relic ... focused on security, putting individuals' rights on the back burner' (*Today's Zaman*, 24 March 2010). Echoing the Kemalist attachment to political Darwinism, Tayyip Erdoğan claimed that 'we will either write history or become history' (ibid., 7 May 2010); addressing a meeting of sports officials, the former semi-professional footballer urged that 'we cannot march towards the future with our feet shackled by our recent history, with the dregs of the past'—instead, 'the time has come ... to shoot for goal' (*Radikal*, 6 June 2010). Just why the AKP had adopted the initiative was not quite clear, and would need further research, but a plausible explanation could be that it saw the need to regain democratic momentum, after its setback in the local elections of March 2009, and to breathe new life into a government that was in danger of running out of energy after nearly eight years in office. In this way, domestic political priorities took precedence over external ones. The resulting mix reflected this, by privileging some proposals that were not clearly part of the EU's agenda, while neglecting others that were, but the fact that the two streams of influence—internal and external—could be brought together was an important sign of the degree to which Turkey's politics had changed over the previous decade.

Notes

[1] See, for instance, the 'Vienna Declaration and Programme of Action', part 1, para. 8, www.unhchr.ch/huridocda/huridoca.nsf/(symbol)/a.conf, cited in Donelly 1999, p. 609.
[2] The writer has examined this in more detail in another context; see Hale 2000, pp. 110–111.
[3] Text of the Negotiating Framework from the Washington Institute for Near East Policy, Washington (www.washingtoninstitute.org/documents). In fact, 'the Union's capacity to absorb new members' was mentioned in the original Copenhagen criteria as one of the factors affecting enlargement; see European Commission, *European Council in Copenhagen 21–22 June 1993: Conclusions of the Presidency* (SN 180/1/93 REV 1), p. 13. However, this had not been referred to in any of the Commission's previous documents on Turkey. I am grateful to Joost Lagendijk for this point.
[4] *Turkey 2008 Progress Report*, Commission of the European Communities, Brussels, 5 November 2008, SEC [2008] 1334), pp. 17, 23.
[5] Ibid., p. 15.
[6] *Turkey 2009 Progress Report*, Commission of the European Communities, Brussels, 14 October 2009, SEC [2009] 1334), pp. 9, 15, 17–18.
[7] See the frequent references in ibid., pp. 6–29, *Turkey 2008 Progress Report*, pp. 6–26, and the *Progress Reports* for 2007, 2006, and 2005.
[8] Commission for Democracy through Law (Venice Commission), *Guidelines on Prohibition and Dissolution of Political Parties and Analogous Measures Adopted by the Venice Commission at Its 41st Plenary Session (Venice 10–11 December 1999)* (CDL-INF [2000] 1), Articles 3 and 5. See also Özbudun 2008.
[9] See Hale & Özbudun 2010, p. 66; Özbudun & Gençkaya 2009, p. 104. For the text of the draft, with relevant explanations by the committee, see the website of the organisation Yeni Anayasa İçin (www.yenianayasicin.org).
[10] For the English text of the amendments, as originally tabled, see Prime Ministry, Secretariat General for European Affairs, *Constitutional Amendments Proposal (5 April 2010)*, www.abgs.gov.tr/files/BasinMusavirlik/const_amendments.pdf
[11] As an alternative, the Özbudun committee had proposed that the Constitutional Court be empowered to amend a law in conflict with an international human rights treaty to which Turkey is a party. This would carry forward the amendment to Article 90, enacted in 2004, stating that in the event of a conflict between domestic law and international agreements the latter should take precedence; in practice, this amendment had had little effect. See Hale & Özbudun 2010, pp. 56, 66.
[12] For the exact voting figures, see *Radikal*, 30 April 2010.

References

Donelly, J. (1999) 'Human rights, democracy and development', *Human Rights Quarterly*, vol. 21, no. 3.
Grigoriadis, I. N. (2009) *Trials of Europeanization: Turkish Political Culture and the European Union*, Palgrave Macmillan, New York.
Hale, W. (2000) *Turkish Foreign Policy, 1774–2000*, Frank Cass, London.

Hale, W. (2003) 'Human rights, the European Union and the Turkish accession process', in *Turkey and the European Union: Domestic Politics, Economic Integration and International Dynamics*, eds A. Çarkoğlu & B. Rubin, Frank Cass, London.

Hale, W. & Özbudun, E. (2010) *Islamism, Democracy and Liberalism in Turkey: The Case of the AKP*, Routledge, London.

Kramer, H. (2009) 'Turkey's accession process to the EU: the agenda behind the agenda', Stiftung Wissenschaft und Politik, SWP Comments 25, October 2009, Berlin.

Langlois, A. J. (2003) 'Human rights without democracy? A critique of the separationist thesis', *Human Rights Quarterly*, vol. 25, no. 4.

Özbudun, E. (2007) 'Democratization reforms in Turkey, 1993–2004', *Turkish Studies*, vol. 8, no. 2.

Özbudun, E., 'European criteria for party closure', *Today's Zaman*, 4 May 2008.

Özbudun, E. & Gençkaya, Ö. F. (2009) *Democratization and the Politics of Constitution-Making in Turkey*, Central European University Press, Budapest.

Plagemann, G. (2000) 'Human rights organizations: defending the particular or the universal?', in *Civil Society in the Grip of Nationalism: Studies on Political Culture in Contemporary Turkey*, eds S. Yerasimos, G. Seufert & K. Vorhoff, Orient-Institut der Deutschen Morgenländischen Gesellschaft and Institut Français d'Études Anatoliennes, Istanbul.

Rustow, D. A. (1970) 'Transitions to democracy: toward a dynamic model', *Comparative Politics*, vol. 2, no. 2.

William Hale (PhD Australian National University) is professor emeritus in the School of Oriental and African Studies of the University of London. He is a specialist on the politics of the Middle East, especially Turkey. His publications include *The Political and Economic Development of Modern Turkey* (1981, 1984), *Turkish Politics and the Military* (1994), *Turkish Foreign Policy 1774–2000* (2000, 2002), *Turkey, the US and Iraq* (2007), and a number of papers and edited books on modern Turkish politics and history. With Ergun Özbudun, he is co-author of *Islam, Democracy and Liberalism in Turkey: The Case of the AKP* (2010).

The Kurdish Issue in Turkey: Limits of European Union Reform

Kemal Kirişci

The first half of the 2000s was characterised by unprecedented political reform in Turkey encouraged by the prospects of EU membership. These reforms helped to improve the quality of democracy as well as the cultural rights of the Kurdish minority in the country. Yet, the Kurdish problem remains far from being resolved. The paper argues that it is, at least partly, the European Union that bears responsibility for the failure of the government's Kurdish 'opening', which, when launched in the summer of 2009, had aspired to solve the Kurdish problem in Turkey.

Introduction

The first half of the 2000s was characterised by unprecedented political reform in Turkey. It has become almost established wisdom to attribute these reforms to the decision of the European Union (EU) in 1999 to engage Turkey as a candidate country for membership (Kubicek 2005; Ulusoy 2007; Keyman & Aydın-Düzgit 2007). As in the case of the EU's eastern enlargement, the principle of conditionality is invoked to explain the role of the EU in inducing candidate countries to adopt reforms and harmonise their laws and policies with those of the EU. Some of the reforms that had a bearing on the Kurdish issue in Turkey, among others, included the reduction of the influence of the military in Turkish politics and public policy, the abolishment of the death penalty and state security courts, enabling broadcasting and education in minority languages, liberalising freedom of expression and association, and the adoption of a modernised penal and civil code.

However, these reforms have fallen short of 'solving' the Kurdish question in Turkey. The violence perpetrated by the Kurdish Workers' Party (PKK) resumed in 2004 and has been continuing since. There has also been a distinct increase in both Kurdish and Turkish nationalism which at times boils over into large Kurdish protest demonstrations. Allegations of human rights abuses and torture in Kurdish-populated parts of the country accompanied by the practice of mass arrests of radical Kurds have returned. The constitutional court, in December 2009, closed down the Democratic Society Party (DTP), a pro-Kurdish political party, and two former leaders of the DTP, Ahmet Türk and Aysel Tuğluk, were expelled from parliament. Finally, the government's 'Kurdish opening' launched in July 2009 had petered out by the end of the year. The 'opening', though ill defined, had the courageous and noble intention of aspiring to solve the Kurdish question in Turkey.

Why did the impressive reforms induced by the EU fail to resolve the Kurdish question in Turkey? What is it that went wrong? What has been the role of the EU in this failure? What are the prospects for the future of the Kurdish 'opening'? This paper will attempt to answer these questions and in doing so will basically argue that the decision of the EU to grant Turkey the prospects of membership helped to empower a liberal approach on the Kurdish question. The traditional hardline approach that had long denied the existence of a Kurdish question in Turkey had been under challenge for some time and, as early as the late 1980s, there was talk in Turkey of the need to recognise the 'Kurdish reality' and reform state policy. However, it was the EU's engagement of Turkey that would finally tip the balance in favour of substantive reform. Yet, the paper will also argue that the EU, at least partly, bears responsibility for the failure of the Kurdish 'opening' and the resolution of the Kurdish problem in Turkey.

The paper is divided into three sections. The first section offers a brief assessment of the Kurdish issue in Turkey in general terms. The next section examines the role of the EU in inducing reforms in the area of cultural rights, especially after Turkey became a candidate country for membership. The final section takes a critical look at the limits of EU reform, and the challenges that stand in the way of a final resolution of the Kurdish problem in Turkey.

The Kurdish Question in Turkey

The Kurdish question in Turkey can be seen as a function of the state's failure to reconsider the definition of its national identity in a manner that allows Kurds to express and live their ethnic and cultural identity in public. Broadly speaking, two approaches to the Kurdish issue can be recognised. The dominant approach for long was what can be labelled the 'hard-line' approach. This approach, very briefly, is the one that traditionally argued that there is no Kurdish problem in Turkey, but only a problem of terror, aggravated by the economic and social problems of under-development in southeastern Turkey and the support given to the PKK by the international community. The advocates of this hardline approach insisted that once terrorism is eradicated then economic and social programmes associated with the Southeastern Anatolia Project (GAP) will resolve the problems of the region. The second, more liberal, approach to the Kurdish problem in Turkey starts with the premise that in essence the Kurdish problem is a product of increasing demands by Kurds to express their cultural and ethnic identity and the inability of Turkey to adjust to these demands. After a decades-old policy of denial, this new approach first officially surfaced in the late 1980s under Turgut Özal's presidency. It re-emerged in a much stronger shape soon after the formation of a new coalition government in 1999, when the hardline approach began to erode. At first sight this erosion was rather unlikely, since in the national elections of April 1999 the hardline approach appeared to receive public endorsement. Bülent Ecevit's Democratic Left Party (DSP), who had received the highest percentage of the votes, was followed by the right-wing Nationalist Action Party (MHP)—long a supporter of the hardline approach. However, one important factor for this erosion was Abdullah Öcalan, who was captured in Kenya and brought to Turkey to face trial in 1999. During his trial, Öcalan repented of the death and destruction caused by the PKK and promised that he would be willing to serve Turkey if his life was spared. His advocacy of greater democracy and pluralism as a panacea to the Kurdish problem coincided with the new government's aim to develop a more liberal democracy and improve Turkey's human rights record. A second factor was Ecevit, who played a critical role in this respect, and in a personal letter to the newly elected Social Democrat chancellor of Germany, Gerard Schröder, he expressed his government's determination to meet the Copenhagen criteria of the EU (*Hürriyet*, 5 June 1999). In June, the government also succeeded in removing from the state security courts the military judge who was to hear Öcalan's case. This reform had been demanded earlier by a decision of the European Court of Human Rights (ECtHR) to ensure a fair trial for Öcalan. Similarly, in December 1999 and after a long and a contentious debate, Ecevit persuaded his coalition government, including the right-wing nationalist MHP, to respect another call by the ECtHR for a stay of execution on Öcalan's death sentence. The effects of moderation became visible among the military too when the National Security Council (NSC) in December 1999 decided to gradually end emergency rule by 2002.

It is against this background that the role of the EU decision in December 1999 to declare Turkey a candidate country for membership deserves to be assessed. The direct involvement of the EU became critical in terms of Turkey's democratisation in general, as well as with respect to reform concerning the Kurdish problem, for at least three reasons. Firstly, it provided a powerful incentive based on 'conditionality' as well as a relatively clear blueprint for reform expressed in the Accession Partnership (AP) of November 2000, to be discussed below. Secondly, the promise to start accession negotiations if the Copenhagen political criteria were met provided a 'push' or 'trigger' for growing domestic demands and efforts to reform (Tocci 2005a). Thirdly, the 'trigger' role of the EU was politically very important because it tipped the balance in the country in favour of the liberal approach against a 'powerful anti-EU coalition'[1] resisting reform efforts.

Turkey's EU Transformation and the Kurdish Question

The December 1999 decision symbolised a qualitative change in the EU's engagement of Turkey's democratic transformation and handling of its Kurdish question. The 1990s had seen a growing debate on the Kurdish issue as well as a number of modest reforms such as the lifting of the ban on the day-to-day usage of Kurdish in the public. However, it was not until Turkey was declared a candidate for membership that the internal political balance in Turkey between hardliners and advocates of reform in general, and on the Kurdish question in particular, began to change conspicuously. This opened the possibility of a set of critical constitutional amendments to be adopted in 2001 that subsequently opened the way to the first package of reforms directly impacting on the Kurdish issue, which were adopted in August 2002. However, the pace of reform gathered speed when the EU was able to encourage the formation of a grand coalition between the Justice and Development Party (AKP), which came to power as a result of the November 2002 national election, and liberal circles in Turkish civil society, ranging from business associations and various pro-reform groups to academics and intellectuals (Tocci 2007b, p. 13). Furthermore, prospects of reform were also enhanced when the decision to upgrade EU relations from 'association to accession' injected a sense of security into the Turkish political system (Tocci 2007a, pp. 69–70). Reforms, with respect especially to the Kurdish issue but also, for example, to freedom of expression and association, were traditionally seen as constituting threats to Turkey's national security. The promise and prospects of EU membership helped reform-related issues to become 'de-securitised' and carried over into 'normal' politics as the influence of this syndrome upon Turkish politics receded (Polat 2009).

The EU's ability to de-securitise the Kurdish problem was a novel development. Traditionally, many EU governments, the European Commission and particularly the European Parliament had taken a very critical view of Turkey's hardline approach to the Kurdish question. The 1990s were characterised by the EU's frequent calls for a political solution to the Kurdish problem and its advocacy of 'minority rights'. This in turn played into the hands of those who argued that the EU was only interested in weakening Turkey's territorial integrity. For this very reason the first-ever report on Turkey that was prepared by the European Commission in November 1998 provoked a negative reaction. Regarding the Kurdish problem, the report noted that 'Turkey will have to find a political and non-military solution to the problem' (European Commission 1998). The references to minority rights and the need for a political solution provoked criticism and led to accusations of European aspirations to undermine Turkey's national identity and territorial integrity.

However, a drastic change occurred in the EU's position once Turkey was declared a candidate country and the AP was adopted. In a marked departure from the past, the AP document shied from using the term 'minority'. Instead, the framers of the EU document chose to use politically inoffensive and nuanced language. It called for the lifting of the restrictions that denied Turkish citizens the option to broadcast in their mother tongue. It also called for improving cultural diversity and securing cultural rights (including education in the mother tongue) of all Turkish citizens, irrespective of their origin. This helped moderates to disarm the arguments of hardliners in Turkey. The lack of references to minority rights and political solutions, especially regarding the Kurds, meant that hardliners could not argue their classic case based on threats to national security and integrity.

Slowly but surely, the engagement of the EU opened space for the advocates of reform and diminished the grip of the hardliners on national politics. This process is probably best captured by the remarks of the then Deputy Chief of General Staff, Yaşar Büyükanıt, when he unequivocally stated in 2003 that 'Turkish Armed Forces cannot be against the European Union because the European Union is the geo-political and geo-strategic ultimate condition for the realization of the target of modernization which Mustafa Kemal Atatürk chose for the Turkish nation' (quoted in Kirişci 2005). Here, the impact of the EU on Turkey's reform process might be better appreciated by considering that a year earlier the Secretary-General of the NSC, General Tuncer Kılınç, had declared, in a particularly aggressive and virulent manner, that the EU was a 'Christian Club' and that it was a 'neo-colonialist force determined to divide Turkey' (Avcı 2003, p. 164).

Getting Büyükanıt to lend his support was not an easy process. In contrast to the AP's emphasis on the removal of 'any legal provisions forbidding the use by Turkish citizens of their mother tongue in TV/radio broadcasting' and the need to ensure the 'cultural diversity and guarantee of cultural rights for all citizens irrespective of their origin' (European Commission 2000), the *National Programme for the Adoption of the Acquis* (NPAA) of 2001 was simply silent on the prospects of TV/radio broadcasting in minority languages.[2] Instead, it noted that the official language of Turkey and that of education was Turkish. Nevertheless the government was able to push through parliament a set of critical constitutional reforms in October 2001. These enabled the government to draft and get Turkey's first set of harmonisation packages adopted in an effort to meet the Copenhagen criteria in June and August 2002. The package opened the way for broadcasting and education in 'mother-tongue' languages other than Turkish as well as enabling the public use of Kurdish in publications, concerts and conferences (especially in Kurdish-populated areas). It also became possible to adopt Kurdish personal names. Ironically, these reforms went well beyond what had been envisaged in the NPAA. However, the resistance of the MHP as a member of the governing coalition to reforms, especially the one adopted in August, led this particular package to be adopted with the support of the remaining governing parties, the Motherland Party (ANAP) and the Democratic Left Party (DSP), and the main opposition party, the True Path Party (DYP). The defection of the MHP from the government coalition and the decision of the remaining parties to go ahead with the reforms led to the collapse of the government and the call for early elections in November 2002.

The AKP won the election with an overwhelming majority in November 2002. AKP's promise for greater democracy in Turkey and its commitment to EU membership played an important role in this outcome (Çarkoğlu 2002; Özel 2003). Indeed, the European Commission acknowledged the performance of the government when, in November 2004, it recommended to the European Council that accession negotiations be opened with Turkey on the grounds that Turkey had 'sufficiently' met the Copenhagen political criteria. A number of specific developments with respect to the Kurdish issue were central to this decision. Firstly, the AKP government oversaw the ending of emergency rule over the last two of the 13 Kurdish-populated provinces of Turkey. The rule had been in place for more than 15 years and was blamed for gross human rights violations against Kurds. It also was a major source of tension in Turkey's relations with the EU. Secondly, the AKP government was able to break the resistance to the implementation of the reforms adopted by the preceding government. The bureaucratic resistance to implementation was most conspicuous in the area of cultural rights.[3] Most significantly, the government was able to overcome stiff bureaucratic resistance from the state-operated Turkish Radio and Television Broadcasting Corporation (TRT) as well as the Radio and Television Supreme Council (RTUK) to the actual implementation of broadcasting in ethnic minority languages. In June 2004, both radio and TV broadcasting in a number of ethnic minority languages, including in two Kurdish dialects, Kirmanji and Zaza, finally became possible. Even if the broadcasting was limited to less than an hour a day and its content was severely restricted and controlled, it still constituted a major step in the direction of pluralism. Lastly, the government was able to implement the decision to respect a ruling of the ECtHR concerning the imprisonment of Leyla Zana and her colleagues in 1994. This led to her release, together with her colleagues, from prison.

The recommendation of the European Commission culminated in accession negotiations beginning in October 2005 with the adoption of the Negotiation Framework for Turkey. However, this led to little rejoicing in Turkey, partly because of the considerable tension and acrimonious debate that preceded the decision, and partly because of the emergence in Europe of a virulent public and governmental opposition to Turkish membership. Inevitably, this would culminate in the weakening of the grand coalition supportive of reforms, and see hardliners whip up nationalism. Very quickly, the reform process in Turkey began to slow down, and growing setbacks in the implementation of reforms began to be experienced. These developments would come to undermine the 'virtuous circle' achieved in EU–Turkish relations, reinstil mistrust between the parties and provoke the 're-securitisation' of various issues, including the Kurdish one (Narbone & Tocci 2009, pp. 23–24).

Limits of EU 'Soft Power'

The back-sliding with regard to the implementation of the reforms became quite noticeable, especially during 2006 and 2007. This period was marked with a distinct rise in Turkish nationalism and conservatism as well as a process of polarisation within society (Uslu 2008a; Verney 2009; Çarkoğlu & Kalaycıoğlu 2009). There are a number of reasons behind this backlash which can be attributed to Turkish domestic politics. Since 2005, Turkey had begun to experience a significant rise in PKK violent attacks on civilian and military targets, accompanied by emotional funerals held for the victims. The ability of the PKK to operate from northern Iraq with impunity aggravated the situation, especially after the invasion of Iraq led by the United States. This resulted in urgent and often unequivocal demands from the opposition as well as the military to mount an armed intervention into northern Iraq against PKK bases and hideouts.

The level of tension created by these calls was further aggravated by a nationalist and confrontationist discourse adopted by some Kurdish leaders in northern Iraq. The rise in PKK violence and tension with Kurds in northern Iraq also led to considerable backsliding in the Turkish military's attitude towards reforms. One conspicuous manifestation of it came from General Büyükanıt, who was promoted from his position as deputy chief to chief of general staff in 2003. He argued in April 2007 that the EU aimed to divide up Turkey by pushing for reforms that would create 'minorities' while not granting Turkey membership of the EU (*Radikal*, 13 April 2007). His remarks coincided with a period when the reform process, particularly with respect to freedom of expression, experienced important setbacks. For example, there was the opening of court cases against numerous individuals for the alleged inappropriate use of the Kurdish language and the expression of views threatening to the unity of the country.

Furthermore, the inability and unwillingness of the government, until April 2008, to adopt legislation to rescind or narrow down the content of Article 301 criminalising statements deemed offensive to 'Turkishness' was another factor contributing to a rise in nationalism. The nationalist frenzy manifested itself in an ugly and sinister manner too. During the course of 2006 and 2007 Turkey witnessed the assassination of a priest in Trabzon, two Turkish Christians and a German missionary in Malatya and a prominent Turkish-Armenian journalist, Hrant Dink. In 2005, ultra-nationalist groups created a climate that saw the indictment of Orhan Pamuk and Elif Safak for their remarks about the mass killings of Armenians and Kurds. When Pamuk won the Nobel Prize for Literature in October 2006, many were displeased and the then President of Turkey, Ahmet Sezer, refused to congratulate him.

The Prime Minister himself, too, became engulfed in this climate of nationalism and populism. During a speech in Diyarbakır in August 2005, Erdoğan had acknowledged that the Turkish state had made mistakes in the past and promised a solution to the Kurdish problem based on more democracy, more rule of law and economic prosperity (*Radikal*, 13 August 2005). Yet, just about a year later, he made a complete U-turn and barely employed the word 'Kurd' in his address to the local AKP congress in Diyarbakır. The following month in Bilecik, where a ceremony was being held to commemorate the beginning of the Ottoman Empire in the thirteenth century, he brazenly courted rising nationalist sentiments in the country. In April 2008, he publically scolded the respected head of the bar association of Diyarbakır after the latter raised the issue of education in mother-tongue languages (*Hürriyet*, 9 April 2008).

The political climate in Turkey further deteriorated when, in the spring of 2007, Turkey experienced considerable political instability and polarisation characterised by huge public demonstrations accusing the government of pursuing policies aiming to undermine secularism in Turkey. The AKP's aspiration to open greater public space for Islam in Turkey was virulently resisted. The instability turned into a state of crisis when the Turkish military in April 2007 mounted what has come to be referred to as an 'e-coup'. The 'e-coup' came on the immediate heels of the Prime Minister's announcement that Abdullah Gül, former minister of foreign affairs, would be the AKP's candidate for the upcoming presidential election. In a thinly veiled manner the military threatened to intervene if a candidate that they suspected would endanger Turkey's secular credentials were to be elected. The heightened tension and deep sense of crisis were finally diffused with the government's decision to call for an early election in July rather than in November.

This drift into nationalism and polarisation also needs to be seen in the light of the deterioration in EU–Turkish relations. There are many in Turkey as well as in Europe who argued that the slowdown in reforms and the accompanying political instability were also, even if partly, a function of the EU's weakening commitment to Turkish membership.[4] This first manifested itself during the adoption as well as problematic wording of the Negotiation Framework of October 2005. Austria and France resisted the adoption of this document. The ensuing compromise arrangements left deep doubts about the objective of the accession negotiations. The wording in the document had not been adopted either in the case of previous enlargements, or in the case of Croatia. This led many among the Turkish public as well as officials to believe that the EU held 'double standards' and was not after all committed to Turkey's eventual membership. The Turkish public had already felt there had been a double standard when Cyprus was admitted to membership in spite of the Greek-Cypriot rejection of the decision to reunify the island on the basis of the United Nations (UN) Annan Plan.

Furthermore, there was growing talk in the EU linking Turkey's accession to the EU's absorption capacity, while in some member states, such as Austria and France, accession was made conditional upon national referendums. The Turkish side increasingly began to feel that Turkish accession was indeed being treated differently and that conditions beyond Turkey's control were being introduced, seriously undermining the effectiveness of 'conditionality' (Aydın & Esen 2007, p. 133). This sense of doubt was exacerbated by the decision of the European Council in December 2006 to suspend negotiations on eight chapters on the grounds that Turkey had failed to open its harbours and airports to Cypriot shipping. In December 2007, at the end of the German presidency's term, the announcement that France would object to the eventual opening of five specific chapters, arguing that these chapters were directly linked to membership, made matters worse. Additionally, there are about half a dozen chapters whose opening was vetoed by Cyprus.

The situation has also been aggravated by the constant questioning of Turkey's membership on the grounds of identity. This has played an important role in undermining the hand of reformists in Turkey as much as it has weakened the transformation process. In particular, the discourse of Nicholas Sarkozy and his readiness to dismiss the binding nature of previous EU *acquis* on Turkey has inflicted massive damage on the EU's credibility. Furthermore, the constant rhetoric adopted by the governments of a number of member states, such as Austria, Germany, France and the Netherlands, that Turkey be given a 'privileged partnership' instead of full membership has not helped either. It has reinforced the hand of those in Turkey who have argued that the EU is after all a 'Christian Club' and that the EU has no intentions of admitting Turkey as a member. It is not surprising that, in the course of less than a few years, levels of support for membership plummeted from around 72 per cent in 2004 to well below 50 per cent in 2009, while objections to membership increased from 16 to 41 per cent during the same period (reported in *Hürriyet*, 26 May 2010).

These developments have deeply undermined the EU's 'transformative' power as well as credibility. One important consequence has been the breakdown of the coalition between the AKP and liberals as the momentum behind the government's support for reform has waned. The weakening of the EU's commitment has also revived traditional fears over Turkey's territorial unity and the intentions of Europe and the West in general. The dramatic impact of the EU's loss of 'soft power' is best captured by the remarks of retired General Edip Başer. Başer in 2004 had argued that as a former member of the Turkish military he saw EU membership as 'the ultimate guarantee of Turkish domestic and external security'. Yet, in 2008 he was noting that 'had the EU remained engaged it would be unlikely that Turkey would be experiencing the crisis and difficulties of the last two years or so'.[5]

In spite of the turmoil in the country and the difficulties in EU–Turkish relations, Turkey managed to hold peaceful national elections in July 2007, culminating in a massive victory for the governing AKP. The electorate rewarded the government primarily for its reform policies and reluctance to become drawn into the populist and nationalist politics that preceded the elections. The election was also important because for the first time since 1991 a group of Kurdish politicians representing the Democratic Society Party (DTP) were able to enter parliament as independents. Yet, instability continued well into 2008. The country went through a major crisis over the election of the new president in August 2007. The election of Abdullah Gül was virulently opposed by the opposition party, Republican People's Party (CHP), as well as the military and the hardline secularist civil society. The situation became aggravated when the government became sidetracked from its effort to launch a major effort to rewrite a new constitution and instead focused on adopting legislation to lift a ban on the wearing of headscarves (*turban*) by female students at universities. By late 2007, this had reignited concerns and fears that the government had an agenda to Islamise the country, which led to the AKP, in March 2008, being indicted on the grounds that the party was aiming to undermine secularism in Turkey. Furthermore, the rise in PKK violence continued to aggravate the tension in the country with ever rising calls in support of a military intervention in northern Iraq.

This was also a period when a large number of serving and retired officers, journalists, academics, businessmen and lawyers were indicted on the grounds of having plotted to overthrow the government. The case known as 'Ergenekon' started as a judicial process that was meant to contribute to Turkey's democratisation. However, the process provoked considerable turmoil and even led to accusations that the government was using it to suppress opposition. These accusations were fuelled by a tax-evasion case opened against one of the leading media groups in Turkey, one that often presented an editorial line critical of government policies. Many have seen this as an attempt to intimidate and silence the media, which has led to growing criticisms being levelled at the government for becoming authoritarian, nationalist and populist, while Turkish society and politics have continued to polarise between growing religious conservatism and advocates of hardcore secularism. The situation has also been aggravated by a weak opposition in parliament, led by the CHP, that has not been able to offer a vision for reform (Öniş 2009). There are even those who have compared the conflicts resulting from deep divisions within the country to a 'bloodless civil war' (Champion 2010) or a 'war at home' (Cook 2009; Turan 2008).

Nevertheless, the government, to its credit, did try to further reforms on the Kurdish question. In February 2008, it authorised the military to intervene against the PKK in northern Iraq. The striking difference in this intervention compared with the numerous preceding ones since the 1990s is that it was preceded by a long public debate in the country and also an effort to mobilise support from the international community as well as the Kurdistan Regional Government (KRG). The government not only put considerable effort into improving relations with the KRG, but also resisted nationalist calls for an intervention not just against the PKK but also the KRG to deter it from declaring an 'independent Kurdish state'.[6] Furthermore, during the actual operation, utmost care was taken to ensure that civilian Kurds would not be hurt. In a surprising manner, the intervention culminated in the emergence of an unexpected dialogue and cooperation between Turkey and the KRG. The intervention also coincided with the Prime Minister's announcement in February 2008 that the government would introduce a fully fledged TV station broadcasting in Kurdish by the end of the year.

The process of actually setting up a TV channel by the Turkish Radio and Television Corporation called TRT-Six ('Şeş' in Kurdish) took a whole year. Numerous minor reforms had to be introduced. One such reform involved the authorisation of the public use of the letters 'q', 'w' and 'x'. These letters do not exist in the Turkish alphabet and their public use was long considered a violation of a law dating back to 1928 that had Latinised the Turkish alphabet. Prosecutors regularly opened court cases against the public use of these letters even after the EU reforms. The Population Registry refused to register Kurdish names that employed these letters. Late in February 2009, another taboo was broken when the leader of the DTP, Ahmet Türk, addressed his group in Kurdish in parliament. However, the most significant and possibly exciting development came in the summer of 2009 on the heels of the AKP losing badly to the DTP in the local elections of March 2009.[7]

In July the Interior Minister, Beşir Atalay, launched the 'Kurdish opening' with the ambitious objective of 'solving' the Kurdish problem. The government had long been entertaining the idea of 'solving' the Kurdish problem. Undoubtedly, the desire to recover the Kurdish vote lost during the local elections was a critical motivation. The 'opening', which was subsequently renamed the 'democratic opening' and then the 'national unity plan', precipitated a lively and massive debate in Turkey. However, the government struggled to give the 'opening' much substance beyond promises of improved and more liberal implementation of what had already been put into place as a result of the EU reforms. The exception was a difficult effort to extend amnesty to PKK militants to encourage them to return to Turkey from northern Iraq. Late in October a small group of militants and family members did enter Turkey; however, the occasion turned into a massive display of support for Öcalan and the PKK. In turn, this provoked a nationalist backlash against the government and the process of returns was quickly discontinued. The situation went from bad to worse when massive demonstrations organised by the DTP, in coordination with the PKK, took place, and then in early December the PKK attacked a military vehicle, killing all the soldiers on board. The following week, the constitutional court finalised its decision against the DTP, pending since 2007, culminating in the closure of the party and expulsion of two of its members from parliament on the grounds of supporting and maintaining organic links with the PKK. The DTP was promptly replaced by a new Kurdish political party called the Peace and Democracy Party (BDP) led by Selahattin Demirtaş. However, for all intents and purposes, the 'Kurdish opening' had come to a dead end by the end of the year, even if the government insisted on its intention to continue with it.

The causes of why the 'Kurdish opening' ran aground are complex. Clearly, the AKP's inability or reluctance to seek consensus and mobilise broader support for it played a role. However, here the focus will primarily be on the role of the EU. There are at least three EU-related causes that can be highlighted. Firstly, and possibly most importantly, the weakening of the EU's engagement has had an adverse impact on Turkey's transformation, including on the Kurdish question, by aggravating 'Turkey's sense of uncertainty and insecurity' (Tocci 2005b, p. 26), and arming those who resist reforms with the argument that 'there would be little point in passing reforms, given that "Europe" would never accept Turkey into its club' (Tocci 2005b, p. 26). It is difficult to see how the Kurdish question could successfully be addressed without the sense of security that comes with credible prospects of EU membership. Secondly, the absence of an EU *acquis* defining minority rights going beyond cultural ones (Witte 2002) has been a mixed blessing in Turkey's case. As argued earlier in the paper, it has helped reformers in Turkey to circumvent the adverse effects of the rhetoric employed by hardliners. Yet, at the same time the absence of a blueprint has complicated the politics surrounding efforts to give the 'Kurdish opening' more robust but at the same time legitimate substance for both the 'Turkish' but also the Kurdish side. In other words, such a blueprint, accompanied with prospects of membership, would offer 'contours' of what could be expected from the 'opening', by demonstrating to hardliners on both sides that secession or even an internal territorial rearrangement could not be entertained.

Lastly, the EU was very successful in transforming and reforming Turkish politics especially on the Kurdish problem by encouraging a plurality of views to emerge. It enabled the emergence of a fledgling but growing and vocal civil society. The reform process that it triggered also helped a wide range of views on the question of how to solve the Kurdish problem in Turkey to be raised and debated. The engagement also helped a vocal civil society increasingly independent of the PKK to emerge among the Kurds too, especially during the first half of the 2000s. For example, Kurdish business interests represented by local chambers of commerce such as the Diyarbakır Chamber of Commerce (DTO) presented much more moderate views on the Kurdish problem and emphasised the importance of creating a stable environment for economic growth and employment. This led them to openly criticise the PKK and the use of violence as sources of instability that undermine economic growth.[8] Similar indications of independence from the PKK could be observed in terms of the broader civil society in the Kurdish region. A case in point is the women's rights organisation, the Women's Centre (KAMER). The leader of KAMER, a much respected Kurdish woman with a nationalist background, has distanced herself from the PKK on the grounds that it demands women's rights to be subordinated to the 'struggle for self-determination'.[9]

However, this situation has drastically changed in the last couple of years. The rise of Kurdish nationalism and the grip of the PKK over Kurdish political life have re-emerged, stifling the prospect of the development among the Kurds of a freer and more moderate as well as pragmatic debate on the substance of the solution of the Kurdish problem.[10] This became especially conspicuous after the 'Kurdish opening' was launched and the DTP was paralysed when it came to developing ideas beyond the ones 'authorised' by the PKK and Öcalan. A number of prominent liberal commentators and observers of the Kurdish scene in Turkey have criticised the totalitarian grip of the PKK over Kurdish politicians and Kurdish civil society.[11] Numerous EU member countries banned the PKK and listed it as a terrorist organisation and then mounted various EU efforts seeking DTP politicians to distance themselves from the PKK and disavow violence (Uslu 2008b). The fact that these developments have had little effect is evidence of the erosion of the EU's influence over Kurdish politics, which has clearly not helped the 'Kurdish opening' let alone the broader efforts to find a 'solution' to the Kurdish problem in Turkey.

Conclusion

Demands for reform on the Kurdish question in Turkey had begun to surface as early as the late 1980s. In the 1990s, some very modest steps were taken and the need for reform became louder. However, the advocates of reform continued to face resistance from hardliners who continued to block major reforms. The decision of the EU to declare Turkey a candidate country changed the nature of the game. It enabled the liberal approach to the Kurdish problem to acquire a growing say. The various 'harmonisation packages' adopted in an effort to meet the Copenhagen criteria opened the way for Kurds to enjoy an increasing set of cultural rights. In a country where, for a long time, talking about Kurds let alone their rights was problematic, these developments were impressive. In this sense, the EU deserves credit for having helped to create a climate that could overcome deep-seated fears and taboos. Nevertheless, this fell well short of 'solving' the Kurdish problem in Turkey. The government's 'Kurdish opening' was both courageous as well as risky. It was definitely not spurred by the accession process and was primarily a product of domestic politics. However, it came at a time when scepticism about the EU's commitment to Turkey's membership had grown, undermining the sense of security that the EU had been able to inject into otherwise jittery Turkish politics. Old fears about the country's territorial integrity and its national identity were reignited and aggravated by growing concerns about the future of secularism in Turkey.

These problems were compounded by the AKP government's failure at the kind of coalition-building they were able to achieve during their first term of office. The return of the PKK led to violence, and the way in which the PKK is stifling pluralism among Kurds has also contributed to the undermining of the 'Kurdish opening'. Furthermore, all this is occurring at a time when the country is experiencing a rise in nationalism as well as conservatism which has led to concerns about the resilience of Turkish democracy and its ability to cope with the conflicts that this polarisation is generating. Under these circumstances it is highly likely that the 'Kurdish problem' will continue to remain a major challenge for Turkey for a while to come. Meeting the challenge will greatly depend on developments within Turkey. Will Turkey be able to overcome its fears concerning secularism and national identity? How will demands for greater religious freedom be reconciled with the precepts of secular governance? How much public space can a well-entrenched unitary and homogeneous culture of national identity allow for the expression of ethnic diversity in Turkey? What form will the demands of Kurds take? Will they be content with the continuation of EU-led reforms for improved cultural rights or will more ambitious 'solutions' such as a 'territorial' solution be sought? Will the BDP, in contrast to its predecessor the DTP, be able to distance itself from the PKK and adopt more pluralist politics? These are very important but difficult questions to answer. However, it is essential to appreciate that the answers to these questions and whether Turkey is able to develop a 'solution' to its Kurdish problem will also depend on the evolution of EU–Turkish relations. The significance of this can best be appreciated with respect to the 'Kurdish opening'. However, the way in which the 'Kurdish opening' disintegrated is evidence of how, in spite of all the good intentions embedded in the Turkish Prime Minister's idea of continuing with the 'Ankara criteria' instead of the 'Copenhagen' ones, the EU's engagement remains critical.[12] Turkey needs the sense of confidence and security that comes with prospects of EU membership, not to mention actual membership. Yet, in the light of the massive financial crisis that the EU is in, it is not clear that the EU would be able to help Turkey even if it had the will to do so.

Notes

[1] This coalition composed notably of the military and security establishment was not necessarily against EU membership but was opposed to the conditions that EU demanded (Öniş 2004, p. 493). 'Europeanization' literature also points out how the engagement of the EU can impact on domestic political balances by empowering certain actors over others (see Risse et al. 2001; Börzel & Risse 2003).

[2] *Avrupa Müktesebatının Üstlenilmesine İlişkin Türkiye Ulusal Programı* (Ankara: Ankara Üniversitesi Basımevi, 2001).

[3] For example, a secret letter from the Secretary General of the NSC leaked to the press revealed that the NSC was against broadcasting in Kurdish (reported in *Milliyet*, 19 May 2003).

[4] On the link between political instability in Turkey and the weakening of the EU's engagement, see Gordon and Taşpınar (2006) as well as International Crisis Group (2007) and Narbone and Tocci (2009).

[5] The author of this article was present at a conference in Ankara in September 2004 on 'democratic governance and the military' when the General made his initial remarks. The author of this article had an opportunity to doublecheck these remarks with the General during a conference in Istanbul in June 2008 and also note his subsequent remarks on the EU.

[6] For example, during the parliamentary debate to authorise the government to mount a military intervention against the PKK, Devlet Bahçeli, the leader of the MHP, openly called for action directed against the Kurdish administration in northern Iraq, including action to prevent the emergence of an independent Kurdish state. Similar remarks were expressed by Şükrü Elekdağ, a high-ranking member of the CHP and a former permanent secretary of the Ministry of Foreign Affairs (*Radikal*, 17 October 2008, 18 October 2007).

[7] Electoral support for the AKP dropped significantly at the national level, but the loss was much more dramatic in some of the Kurdish-populated municipalities. For municipal elections results see 'Yerel Seçim 2009, *Milliyet*, 30 March 2009. See also Çarkoğlu (2009).

[8] Personal interview with the head of DTO, November 2006.

[9] Personal interview, November 2006.

[10] Personal interview with the former head of DTO as well as the former head of the Diyarbakır Bar Association, August 2009.

[11] See for example Taha Akyol's columns in *Milliyet*, 28 and 29 December 2009.

[12] The Prime Minister frequently uses the notion of 'Ankara criteria' to refer to how the reforms are done 'to fulfill the democratic dreams of our own people' independent of EU membership prospects.

References

Avcı, G. (2003) 'Turkey's slow EU candidacy: insurmountable hurdles to membership or simple Euro-skepticism?', *Turkish Studies*, vol. 4, no. 1, pp. 149–170.

Aydin, M. & Esen, T. A. (2007) 'Conditionality, impact and prejudice: a concluding view from Turkey', in *Conditionality, Impact and Prejudices in EU–Turkey Relations*, ed. N. Tocci, Istituto Affari Internazionali, Rome, pp. 129–139.

Börzel, T. A. & Risse, T. (2003) 'Conceptualizing the domestic impact of Europe' in *The Politics of Europeanization*, Oxford University Press, Oxford.

Çarkoğlu, A. (2002) 'Turkey's November 2002 elections: a new beginning', *Middle East Review of International Relations*, vol. 6, no. 4, pp. 30–41.

Çarkoğlu, A. (2009) 'The March 2009 local elections in Turkey: a signal for takers or the inevitable beginning of the end for AKP', *South European Society and Politics*, vol. 14, no. 3, pp. 295–316.

Çarkoğlu, A. & Kalaycioğlu, E. (2009) *The Rising Tide of Conservatism in Turkey*, Palgrave Macmillan, New York.

Champion, M. (2010) 'Intrigue in Turkey's bloodless civil war', *Wall Street Journal*, 4 May.

Cook, S. (2009) 'Turkey's war at home', *Survival*, vol. 51, no. 5, pp. 105–120.

European Commission (1998) Regular Report from the Commission on Progress towards Accession: Turkey, Brussels.

European Commission (2000) *Turkey: 2000 Accession Partnership*, Brussels.

Gordon, P. & Taşpinar, Ö. (2006) 'Turkey on the brink', *Washington Quarterly*, vol. 29, no. 3, pp. 57–70.

International Crisis Group (2007) 'Turkey and Europe: the way ahead', Report No. 184, Brussels, 17 August.

Keyman, F. & Aydin-Düzgit, S. (2007) 'Europeanization, democratization and human rights in Turkey', in *Turkey and the European Union: Prospects for a Difficult Encounter*, eds E. LaGro & K. Jørgensen, Palgrave Macmillan, Basingstoke, pp. 69–89.

Kirişci, K. (2005) 'Turkey and the European Union: the domestic politics of negotiating pre-accession', *Macalester International*, vol. 15, pp. 44–80.

Kubicek, P. (2005) 'The European Union and grassroots democratization in Turkey', *Turkish Studies*, vol. 6, no. 3, pp. 361–377.

Narbone, L. & Tocci, N. (2009) 'Running around in circles? The cyclical relationship between Turkey and the European Union', in *Turkey's Road to European Union Membership: National Identity and Political Change*, eds S. Verney & K. Ifantis, Routledge, London, pp. 21–34.

Öniş, Z. (2009) 'Conservative globalists versus defensive nationalists: political parties and paradoxes of Europeanisation in Turkey', in *Turkey's Road to European Union Membership: National Identity and Political Change*, eds S. Verney & K. Ifantis, Routledge, London, pp. 35–48.

Özel, S. (2003) 'After the tsunami', *Journal of Democracy*, vol. 14, no. 2, pp. 80–91.

Polat, R. K. (2009) 'The 2007 parliamentary elections in Turkey: between securitisation and desecuritisation', *Parliamentary Affairs*, vol. 62, no. 1, pp. 129–147.

Risse, T., Cowles, M. & Caporaso, J. (2001) 'Europeanization and domestic change: introduction', in *Transforming Europe*, eds M. Cowles, J. Caporaso & T. Risse, Cornell University Press, Ithaca, NY, pp. 1–20.

Tocci, N. (2007a) *The EU and conflict resolution: promoting peace in the backyard*, Routledge, London.

Tocci, N. (2007b) 'Unpacking European discourses: conditionality, impact and prejudicies in EU–Turkey relations', in *Conditionality, Impact and Prejudicies in EU–Turkey Relations*, ed. N. Tocci, Istituto Affari Internazionali, Rome, pp. 7–32.

Tocci, N. (2005a) 'Europeanization in Turkey: trigger or anchor for reform', *South European Society and Politics*, vol. 10, no. 1, pp. 72–81.

Tocci, N. (2005b) 'Conflict resolution in the neighborhood: comparing the role of the EU in the Turkish–Kurdish and Israeli–Palestinian conflicts', CEPS Working Document, No. 221.

Turan, İ. (2008) 'War at home, peace abroad!', *PrivateView*, Autumn, pp. 8–15.

Ulusoy, K. (2007) 'Turkey reform effort reconsidered, 1987–2004', EUI Working Paper RSCAS, No. 2005/28.

Uslu, E. (2008a) 'Ulusalcılık: the neo-nationalist resurgence in Turkey', *Turkish Studies*, vol. 9, no. 1, pp. 73–97.

Uslu, E. (2008b) 'The Kurdistan Workers' Party turns against the European Union', *Mediterranean Quarterly*, vol. 19, no. 2, pp. 99–121.

Verney, S. (2009) 'National identity and political change on Turkey's road to EU membership', in *Turkey's Road to European Union Membership: National Identity and Political Change*, eds S. Verney & K. Ifantis, Routledge, London, pp. 1–10.

Witte, B. de (2002) 'Politics versus law in the EU's approach to ethnic minorities', in *Europe Unbound*, ed. J. Zielonka, Routledge, London, pp. 137–160.

Kemal Kirişci (PhD City University London) is a professor at the Department of Political Science and International Relations at Boğaziçi University, Istanbul. He holds a Jean Monnet Chair in European Integration and was also the director of the Center for European Studies at the same university between 2002 and 2008. Most recently he was a fellow at the Transatlantic Academy in Washington, DC (2009–10). His research interests are European integration, asylum and immigration issues in the EU, EU–Turkish relations, Turkish foreign policy, ethnic conflicts, and refugee movements. In addition to many books, articles and reports, he recently co-edited a special issue of *New Perspectives on Turkey* (May 2009) on the transformation of Turkish foreign policy. He is also the co-author of *The Kurdish Question and Turkey: An Example of a Trans-State Ethnic Conflict* (co-authored with G. Winrow) (Frank Cass, London, 1997).

A Precarious Relationship: The Alevi Minority, the Turkish State and the EU

Ali Çarkoğlu and Nazlı Çağın Bilgili

Over the last decade, the political significance of the Alevis, the largest sectarian Muslim minority in Turkey, has notably changed. This article aims to evaluate the Alevi community's changing stance as a sectarian minority within an increasingly conservative Turkish society facing European Union (EU) membership negotiations. We first of all summarise the characteristics of the Alevi community and contextualise the changing role of the Alevi minority in Turkish politics. We focus on Alevi demands as part of the EU adjustment reforms and negotiation process, and present the official responses from the Justice and Development Party (AKP) government as well as the EU authorities.

Most depictions of the state of religious diversity in modern Turkey misleadingly simplify a deeply divided Muslim community as a homogeneous entity. Although only a tiny fraction of the country's population is non-Muslim, sizeable Muslim minorities of sectarian as well as ethnic nature continue to exist. Following the same logic, the Lausanne Treaty grants a religious definition of minorities only for non-Muslims; no such explicit recognition can be found for the sizeable Muslim ethnic groups such as the Kurds or sectarian minority groups such as the Alevis. The resistance of Kurdish ethnicity, together with elements of peripheral religious groups, posed a formidable challenge to the young Republic in its formative years. The young Republic chose to repress any ethnic or religious minority demands, and thus freeze any impending conflicts. Over the years, a domineering rhetoric developed, ignoring any recognition of minorities on any ethnic or Muslim sectarian basis.

The reluctance to recognise any Muslim minority identities and the continuation of oppressive policies towards them started to change in the aftermath of the Cold War, which marked a turning point in Turkey's domestic as well as the international political scene. A critical element in this new international environment was attributable to intensifying relations with the European Union (EU) and the start of membership negotiations in October 2005. The domineering rhetoric and the consequent public policies towards Muslim minorities in Turkey were thenceforth increasingly challenged. As a result, in the highest echelons of the Republican regime, together with the masses and important figures in Turkish civil society, there emerged an increasing recognition of Turkey's ethnic and religious diversity.

In this article, we focus only on the sectarian Alevi minority in Turkey, whose condition can best be understood with reference to the larger religious scene in the country, which is marked by two distinct cleavages. One is based on sectarian differences between the dominant Sunnis and the minority Alevis, and the other on lifestyle and cultural differences among the Sunnis.[1] The lifestyle or cultural divide is between those who adopt a lifestyle according to the tenets of an Anatolian tradition of Sunni Islam and those who take a more secular or anticlerical (*laik*) view.[2] The Alevis have historically been the minority among an overwhelming majority of Sunnis and at the same time have appeared almost uniformly to take the secularist view in terms of the cultural divide. This latter characteristic has caused Alevis to support the secularist foundations of the Republican regime, despite their historical persecution by the same regime on many different occasions.

Alevis and the EU Project

The democratisation reforms that were shaped prior to the start of the EU negotiations to meet the Copenhagen political criteria, as well as in its aftermath, have created a precarious relationship between the Alevi community and representatives of the EU and the Turkish government. The condition of the Alevi community found reflection in evaluations and consequent demands for reform from the European side.

The Alevi community pays a great deal of attention to how Alevis are defined in the EU progress reports. In the 2004 report, the group is defined as a 'non-Sunni Muslim minority' and three times in the same report it is noted that 'Alevis are still not recognised as a Muslim minority'. The use of the term 'minority' was highly significant for Alevis—especially for those who seek official minority status—as they could use the report as a reference for their demand for such official recognition. In 2005, the terminology adopted to refer to Alevis changed from 'minority' to 'community' when they were referred to as a 'non-Sunni Muslim community'. 'Large Muslim Alevi community' is the expression used in 2006, leaving out the emphasis on the Alevis being non-Sunni. As a result, over time, the EU's identification and reference to Alevis have come closer to the official definition used by the Turkish state.

Alevis do not appear to agree on what needs to be done even with respect to such definitions of fundamental factors concerning Alevi existence within Turkish society. Some Alevis are more under the influence of Eurosceptic nationalist perspectives; others believe that the EU is the only route through which they can force the Turkish state to recognise the Alevi community. In this view, an Alevi consciousness that is not alienated from its own tradition, rights and sorrows cannot reject integration with the EU. Nevertheless, even among those who take this view, reflections of the influence of

Alevi left-wing traditions can be found. According to such a left-wing interpretation, imperialists are seen as still dominant in the EU and are a cause of concern for the EU project's acceptability among the Alevi community (Aydın 2004).

The Alevi Population

The historical animosities between the Alevi and Sunni communities were kept mostly under control during the Republican era.[3] Nevertheless, over the long haul, Alevi communities have been pushed into urban settlements and have kept their sectarian identities concealed in the public realm. As a result, a solid determination of the size of their population is practically impossible (Shindeldecker 1996, p. 3).

Rough population estimates vary between 10 and 20 per cent of the population (see Çarkoğlu 2005). It appears that Alevis are on the move to urban areas, thus rendering the sectarian mix of Turkish provinces less homogenous. Such trends could potentially ease the historical tensions between the Sunnis and Alevis, who are becoming more mixed in metropolitan settings, instead of being segregated in smaller rural settlements. Yet, this could also mean the creation of new tensions when uprooted rural communities of Alevis and Sunnis start to live side by side in metropolitan settings.

There are striking contrasts of theology and religious practice between the Alevi minority and the Sunni majority. Instead of repeating the contrasts between these two Muslim communities already available in the literature, we would like briefly to contextualise the Alevi community's historical development during the modern era, and link this development to the EU membership negotiations.[4]

Alevism in Republican Turkey: A Short Historical Overview of Political Trends

With the founding of the Kemalist Republic in 1923, Alevis were relieved of considerable formal pressures. The new Republic, unlike its predecessor the Ottoman Empire, no longer had an official religion. However, the Alevis' daily problems concerning religious practice in *cem* houses, or socio-economic discrimination they may have faced within Sunni communities, were largely unresolved.[5] As part of the new Republic's secularisation policies, religious orders and their institutional backbones, the *tekkes* and *zaviyes* (dervish lodges), were closed (see Turan 1984). The Alevi community also felt the effects of these closures. While the places of worship for Sunni Muslims—the mosques—were protected as the official shrines of Muslims, Alevi *cem* houses were counted among the *tekkes* and were closed due to their 'unofficial' status. Nevertheless, the new secular Republic also provided the very basis of Alevi security. From the very beginning of the multi-party Republican regime, the Alevis' support for secularist principles and their opposition to Islamist Sunni electoral traditions have been visibly significant, since they saw a Sunni Islamist electoral tradition as the ultimate threat to Alevi survival in the country. This state of mind directed the Alevis closer to the centrist Republican centre-left political wing, over time, lost interest in the Alevi minority issue as one of its main concerns (Koçan & Öncü 2004, p. 477). Right-wing politics in

Turkey has long remained distant from Alevi communities. While the fear of losing Sunni conservative support might be one reason for the cold relations between right-wing parties and Alevis, the main reason is more likely to be an ideological incongruence arising from the progressive, egalitarian and left-wing orientation of the Alevis in the post-1960 era (Çakır 1998; Seufert 1997; Koçan & Öncü 2004; Göner 2005).

The military junta of 1980 turned the socio-political organisation of the country almost upside down through its oppression of various groups, as well as its institutional and legal reshaping of the socio-political milieu of the country. The implications of such developments for the left-wing ideological umbrella, under which the newly urbanised Alevi communities found shelter, were quite significant. Left-wing class struggle rhetoric that mobilised the Alevi communities was slowly replaced by cultural and religious argumentation focusing on the teachings and rituals of Alevi belief (see Erman & Göker 2000). This newly discovered Aleviness and glorification of Alevi identity were shaped in response to earlier left-wing ideological positions of the Alevi community and were seen as even more 'just, egalitarian and libertarian than socialism' (Poyraz 2005, p. 505).

The military takeover in 1980 put only a temporary end to the conflict between the left and the right in Turkey. To be able to control the left, which was regarded by the state establishment as the more dangerous of the two sides, the military itself used Islam and embraced a policy called 'Turkish–Islam synthesis'. Consequently, the state and its institutions allocated and promoted in the Turkish public sphere a privileged place for Islam with a clear Sunni flavour. More specifically, the explicit policy of the 1980 junta to build a mosque in all villages that did not have one effectively brought Sunni imams, earning a state salary, and the official Sunni worldview into all Alevi villages (see Zeidan 1999; Şimşek 2004, p. 128). Such a blend of factors, together with longer-term social developments in the country's conservative Islamist movement, slowly gained momentum on the Turkish political scene (Çarkoğlu & Kalaycıoğlu 2009). The attitude of the state with regard to Islam changed considerably in the 1990s. The state elite were eventually alerted to what they perceived to be an uncontrollable rise in fundamentalist Islam and have since taken defensive measures against this rising influence of Islamic conservatism.

As threat perceptions changed, the elusive secularist state elite aimed to render the Alevi community an integral part of a safety policy against Islamic fundamentalism. The Alevi community was considered suitable for such a role because they were well known for lending 'support to democratic and tolerant ideals, while shying away from some of the more fundamentalist practices found in the Sunni religion' (Poyraz 2005, p.506). The Alevi stance towards democracy and secularism was congruent with the defensive standpoint of the Turkish state and its elite against the rise of political Islam. This fact fostered proximity between the state elite and the Alevis, and prevented the complete marginalisation of the Alevi community.

Given the theological contrasts and historical hostility between the Alevi and Sunni populations, it should come as no surprise that the relationship between the Justice and Development Party (Adalet ve Kalkınma Partisi, AKP) and the Alevis has been strained from the very beginning. The AKP follows the conservative Islamist tradition of the National Outlook (Milli Görüş) Movement. Despite its close ties to the elite cadres of this movement, the AKP elites are of a younger generation with distinctly more liberal stances on critical issues such as EU membership and the reforms needed to achieve this end (Hale & Özbudun 2010; Yavuz 2009b; Turunç 2007). The decisive approach of the AKP government towards a resolution of differences between the Alevis and the Turkish state and its Sunni stance can be heard at the highest levels. Prime Minister R. Tayyip Erdoğan, for instance, asserts,

> We do not discriminate between our citizens on the basis of their ethnic origin, their being ... Alevi or Sunni ... We know that the rights of all are sacred. We respect the rights of all our people to live their own values and to express themselves as they wish ... For long years, our Alevi citizens could not find a collocutor to explain their conditions and needs. We now listen to them. (Cumhuriyet 2009)

The Alevi community has always remained sceptical of this liberal and tolerant self-presentation of the AKP, despite a number of political overtures by the AKP administration aiming to appeal to their demands.[6] The political scene in Turkey is currently shaped by a new divide around the democratisation reforms for EU membership. While the AKP claims these reforms to be necessary for a well-functioning democracy in the country, the opposition views the same reform attempts as first steps on the way to an Islamist takeover of the secularist Republican regime. The Alevis appear indecisive upon the appropriate stance to take in this debate, despite their widespread conviction that the state establishment has long ignored the Alevis' identity and demands. Below, we follow the state of Alevi complaints during the EU membership negotiations, together with EU perspectives regarding these complaints and responses voiced by the AKP administration.

Progress or Stagnation: Alevi Complaints and Demands

At the core of Alevi complaints lies the claim that they are not recognised by the Turkish state. The state institutions, they believe, impose Sunni Islam on their community even though the Turkish Republic is officially proclaimed to be a secular state. The Directorate of Religious Affairs (DRA), which is accused of favouring Sunni Islam at the expense of the Alevis, is the main target of Alevi criticisms (see Ayata 1996; Keyman 2007). The DRA claims to be above sectarian divides and that it embraces Islam as a whole. Yet, Alevis complain about obligatory religion classes at primary and secondary education levels which, by and large, ignore the Alevi belief system, imposing an exclusively Sunni interpretation of Islam upon students. The EU regards these practices by the Turkish state as violations of human rights and has called for reform in this area (see European Commission 2005).

Various policy options for dealing with inequalities created by the DRA appear to deeply divide the Alevi community. While some seek legal recognition of their belief system through the provision of official cadres within the DRA for Alevi religious authorities and ask for financial support for the *cem* houses, others are harshly critical of such a stance and blame members of this first group for being adulators of the state. The group that favours government financial aid to *cem* houses argues that the government should provide electricity and water to *cem* houses as it does for mosques, churches and synagogues. The more cooperative former group argues for the integration of Alevis into the DRA whereas the latter supports abolishment of the DRA, as they believe that this institution creates a formal bias towards Sunni Islam in Turkey (Dressler 2008, pp. 289–290). This latter view asserts that in a secular state religious affairs should be run by civil society at the grassroots level. Indeed, what makes this group nervous with respect to Alevis' relationship with the DRA is a fear that they will lose their independence from the state once they are integrated into the strictly bureaucratic DRA.

The official view of these demands is far from sympathetic. The DRA's perspective is that Alevism is just a mystical interpretation of Islam. The DRA defines itself as independent of Muslim groups and sects, and claims that its voice is the voice of Islam as a whole. The DRA also warns that these discussions are not only about the organisation and the structure of the DRA, but are also directly related to the definition and implementation of secularism in Turkey, which is constitutionally protected. Pulling the debate to an undisputed area in Turkey, the DRA aims to stop the discussions revolving around the nature, composition and functioning of the institution.

The Cem Foundation, acting in the name of the Alevi community, filed a lawsuit against the Prime Ministry in order to force a change in this DRA policy that provides no recognition of Alevi identity. The Sixth Administrative Court in Ankara decided that no cadres and no portion of the budget can be earmarked for Alevis, accepting the argument of the Prime Ministry that all sects and groups within Islam are embraced in Turkey under the single label of Islam. Accordingly, the DRA represents all Muslims and the mosque is the only common place for their worship (*Hürriyet*, 2007).

The official status of *cem* houses is another major concern for Alevis. Representatives of Alevi organisations maintain that they often face obstacles when attempting to build new *cem* houses. Approximately 100 cem houses exist in the country; a number that Alevis claim is insufficient to meet their needs (United States [US] Department of State 2008). In addition, while the places of worship of the Lausanne minorities are legally recognised and the state covers utility costs of all officially recognised shrines in Turkey, the same is not provided for the Alevis. Such an official recognition is expected to render the granting of construction permits for *cem* houses much easier, and exemption from the costs of utilities, such as water and electricity, will facilitate the establishment of new *cem* houses for the Alevis to satisfy their communal needs.

Important developments concerning the official recognition of *cem* houses as places of worship have taken place in the last few years. In 2006, Taşdelen municipality of Istanbul allocated land for the construction of a new *cem* house. The first *cem* house with official recognition—in the form of an open declaration of its status as a *cem* house in the building registration—was opened in July 2007. In 2008, three municipal councils—two districts of the Aydın province (Kuşadası and Didim) and the city municipal council of Tunceli (a province in eastern Anatolia with a predominantly

Alevi population)—agreed to officially recognise *cem* houses as sites of worship. These municipalities decided that the *cem* houses would be exempt from utility costs. The same decision was taken in the Mediterranean coastal province of Antalya in 2009. However, such a policy is not being implemented nationwide, as Parliament has not ratified such a decision yet. The opposition policy circles of influence have also been at work around this issue of official recognition of the Alevi identity; in 2008, the Sixth Administrative Court in Ankara refused the demands of Cem Vakfı, including the recognition of *cem* houses as places of worship (*Hürriyet*, 2007).

It is hard to interpret these isolated incidents of recognition of *cem* houses as representing a changing political stance from any party or ideology in Turkey. When the composition of the municipal councils that decided in favour of Alevis is taken into account, quite diverse political affiliations are observed. For example, the Kuşadası municipal council had five members from the AKP, six independents (two of whom were elected from the AKP and four from the DYP (the True Path Party-Doğru Yol Partisi) but all of whom later resigned from their parties) and four from the CHP (The Republican People's Party-Cumhuriyet Halk Partisi). The mayor was from the ruling AKP. The mayor of the second municipality, Didim, was from the CHP, yet, the members of the municipality council again had a varied political affiliation, as they were from the ANAP (The Motherland Party-Anavatan Partisi), AKP and CHP. The mayor of Tunceli was elected as an independent candidate. The members of the council were mostly from the left-wing SHP (The Social Democratic Populist Party-Sosyal Demokrat Halkçi Parti), DSP (The Democratic Left Party-Demokratik Sol Parti) and CHP, as well as the AKP. The mayor of Antalya, on the other hand, is from the CHP, and the members of the council are from the CHP, AKP and MHP (The Nationalist Action Party-Milliyetçi Hareket Partisi). Putting all this information together, it is not easy to claim that these individual attempts to officially recognise the cem houses as places of worship represent the strategy of a single political party that aims to satisfy Alevi demands. All these councils have members from the AKP as well as from various other parties. However, there is still a lack of information about which members of the council voted for or against these proposals for the recognition of *cem* houses as places of worship. Only the report on Taşdelen's decision gives this detail and makes clear that the four members of the council who voted against the decision were all from the AKP.[7]

The DRA's answer to Alevi demands regarding the official recognition of *cem* houses as places of worship emphasises that the concept of the *cem* house is a relatively new phenomenon that has arisen as a result of extensive urbanisation. Alevi worship activities were previously carried out in *tekkes* or even in private Alevi houses. References to unknown scientific works defining *cem* houses as places of 'rule of conduct' and 'spiritual courtesy', rather than as shrines like mosques, churches or synagogues, are used to strengthen the stance of the DRA. Focusing on the need to distinguish the shrine of a religion from places where mystic, scientific or cultural activities related to that religion are conducted, the DRA mentions that *cem* houses have never been considered an alternative to mosques during the 14-century-long Islamic tradition. In this explanation, the mosque is accepted as the place of worship and *cem* houses are regarded as places of customary mystic and spiritual significance, and as not having a theologically legitimate status. However, this argument is always followed by a statement of the need to protect these places as evidence of the cultural plurality and wealth of Islam and Anatolian Turkish culture. The DRA ends its explanation by claiming that it has already declared, many times, that these places need to be supported socially, economically and culturally. However, such support remains unofficial, as it does not recognise *cem* houses as shrines equivalent in status to mosques, synagogues or churches.

The EU progress reports also mention difficulties experienced by Alevis in establishing *cem* houses. The problem of *cem* houses not having official recognition as places of worship has been mentioned in progress reports every year, and details of policy changes concerning this issue are closely monitored. In the 2008 report, a municipality's decision to recognise a *cem* house as a place of worship and to apply mosque tariffs to its water charges is also mentioned (European Commission 2008). The expectation of the EU with respect to this particular issue is that the decision should not be taken in an isolated manner by municipalities, and that the legal framework as a whole should be brought in line with the European Court of Human Rights (ECHR) decisions, so that Alevis throughout Turkey can perform their religious practices without limitations. The 2009 report announces the increase, from one to three, in the number of municipalities recognising *cem* houses as places of worship; however, Turkey is still being criticised for not turning these decisions into a national policy (European Commission 2009).

Besides the status of the *cem* houses, the compulsory religious education courses throughout secondary education in Turkey that were introduced by the 1980 military coup are a vital point of Alevi criticism of the established system; the Alevis consider these courses to be part of an assimilation policy (Stewart 2007, p. 55). They believe that the state is forcing Alevi students to learn the Sunni interpretation of Islam and to ignore Alevi identity totally while claiming to be talking about Islam as a whole; on the other hand, students belonging to the Lausanne minorities are exempt from this requirement. For nearly three decades, no mention of Alevism was to be found in textbooks, even when different interpretations of Islam were being discussed. The Alevi proposed that the content of these courses should maintain the same distance from all different religious beliefs and hence be informative about all of them, or, alternatively, that these courses should at least be turned into elective courses so that only students who would like to learn about the Sunni interpretation of Islam would select them. Although little progress has been made on turning these courses into electives, the decision to include sections about Alevism within compulsory religion coursebooks was taken partly as a result of pressure from the EU.

The 2005 progress report prepared by the European Commission mentions a case pending before the ECHR, in which an Alevi family from Turkey argued that their child should not be forced to receive Sunni religious education in school (European Commission 2005). As mentioned in the 2007 report, in October of that year, the ECHR decided that 'there had been a violation of Article 2 of Protocol No.1 (right to education) to the ECHR'. The ECHR also mentioned that 'the religious instruction syllabus in Turkey' does not 'meet the criteria of objectivity and pluralism necessary in a democratic society'; its suggestion was that 'Turkey should bring its educational system and domestic legislation into conformity with the ECHR' (European Commission 2009). This ECHR decision was reported as not yet implemented in its 2008 report even though some information on Alevi beliefs and practices was added to the curriculum in the final year of religious instruction at secondary school level in January 2008 (US Department of State 2008).

Alevis additionally complain that the new textbooks include not only superficial but also misleading information on their community heritage, beliefs and practices. For instance, the sixth-grade textbook coverage of Haci Bektas Veli—influential in spreading Islam among the Turks—is found unsatisfactory. Without much emphasis of his significance in Alevi tradition, his teachings on tolerance and mystical (*tasavvufi*) thinking are highlighted, and it is underlined that he went to Mecca on pilgrimage before arriving in Anatolia. Alevis question the historical accuracy of this information and do not believe in pilgrimage as an obligation. Another incident of biased coverage of theological differences can be found in the eighth-grade textbook, where the discussion of Alevism takes place in Chapter 3 on mystical interpretations in Islam. Before covering the mystical interpretations, different interpretations of Islamic jurisprudence are given and, in this part, Sunni and Shia Islam and schools of law within these branches (i.e. Hanafi, Caferi and Shafi'i) are mentioned, but not Alevism. The placing of Alevism among other mystical interpretations reveals that it is not recognised as a sect or a different branch of jurisprudence within Islam, but just as a different 'mystical mindset' of the religion. These mystical interpretations are mentioned as phenomena that pioneered the spread of a culture of tolerance in Anatolia. So, rather than dealing with more practical issues such as performing different worship practices or defining different interpretations of obligations within Islam, the Alevi belief system is given the inferior status of a spiritual approach rather than a sect or branch of Islamic jurisprudence. The above-stated examples from various areas indicate that the official perspective is dismissive towards Alevi expectations of recognition, both in practical and theological matters, comparable to other branches of jurisprudence within Islam. The Alevi tradition is never condemned, but its acceptance is only as a sign of the cultural wealth of the Anatolian interpretation of Islam.

The 2008 International Religious Freedom Report prepared by the US Department of State reports more than 4,000 court cases against the Ministry of Education regarding discrimination in compulsory religious education (US Department of State 2008). The Council of State (CoS), the high court for administrative justice decided in two different cases in 2008 that children of Alevi families were entitled to exemption from these religious education classes. 'Administrative courts in Antalya, Ankara and Istanbul also ruled that Alevi students should be exempt from attending the mandatory religion and ethics course' (European Commission 2009). Alevis claim that the decisions of the courts are binding and hence the government should act to put these decisions into effect. They use the example of the practice in Germany and argue that Alevis might even be permitted to have their own religious courses, as is the case in four different German provinces (*Milliyet*, 2008). Such achievements in various countries of Europe have fostered Alevi support for Turkey's EU membership, as they believe that similar recognition of their status will be achieved if Turkey becomes an EU member state.

Alevis also complain about difficulties they face in the Turkish public sector. With each and every election, most of the officeholders in the public sector change, as each ruling party prefers to selectively appoint their own supporters to various influential positions. Alevis believe that they do not receive such preferential appointments in any significant way under any government's tenure.

> The complaint of the Alevis regarding political representation is about holding public office. The Alevi claim is that there are no Alevi governors among the 81 provinces in Turkey, and none of the 400 general managers in the public sector organisations are Alevis. (Özalay 2006, p. 18)

Besides all these issues, the sections of the Turkish ID cards noting one's religion have also been considered a problem. Such explicit revelation of religious identity is claimed to cause trouble in social life. In April 2006, the obligation of completing these parts of the ID cards was removed in answer to EU demands on the issue. The ID cards still have the same format, yet an individual is free to fill in that section or to keep it empty. The Alevis, however, do not interpret this as a real solution; people who leave this part blank will face problems, as it will be clear that they do not accept being defined as a Muslim of Sunni orientation. Hence, many Alevis will not dare to leave the space blank. While some Alevis seek official freedom to remove the religious section in their IDs completely, others argue that they are Muslims and see no problem in keeping that part of the ID card filled in as 'Muslim'. The former view is shared by some secular Sunnis as well, who claim that a secular state should not deal with its citizens' religious orientation (Minority Rights Group International 2007).

Conclusions

Alevis have generally played a major supportive role in the development of Turkish secularism and its relation to religious groups. During the EU negotiations they have undertaken a particularly important role of setting the stage for evaluations of the state of religious freedoms in the country.

Over the years, the perceived threat of the Sunni Islamist electoral tradition has directed Alevis towards the secular Republican wing. The reactions of many Alevi groups continue to be shaped along these familiar lines despite many well-publicised overtures by the AKP government. Although the AKP tries hard to distance itself from earlier Islamist parties, many Alevi groups continue to be sceptical of the party, owing to the earlier record of its members as well as the ambiguous positions of the present leadership. Steps taken by the AKP towards fulfilling certain demands by the Alevi community have not been uniformly favoured by Alevi groups. The multiplicity of voices on both sides has made it harder for the AKP to try to fulfil the Alevi demands.

Although the Alevi community agrees on the main problems, there seems little agreement among them as to the possible solutions. There also appears little agreement among the largely Sunni-controlled state apparatus as to a diagnosis of the Alevi community's problems, despite the fact that the EU progress reports already provide a comprehensive framework on this issue.

A major problem in this respect seems to be that, within the Sunni establishment, there is an almost total theological disagreement that the Alevi identity is a legitimate reality to be reckoned with. As long as this theological disagreement remains unresolved, there seems to be little hope of bridging the gaps between the Alevis and the ruling AKP government or, for that matter, with any potential competing party for executive office.

Despite concerted efforts by the AKP government since their coming to power in 2002, the Alevi demands remain largely unresolved. The European Parliament

> emphasises freedom of religion as a universal fundamental value and calls on Turkey to safeguard it for all; welcomes the dialogue entered into by the Turkish Government with representatives of religious communities, including the Alevis, and encourages the authorities to intensify the inter-religious dialogue

while it also

> regrets that uncertainty persists concerning the recognition of *cem* houses as Alevi places of worship and concerning compulsory religious education in schools; calls on the Turkish Government systematically to remedy this situation. (European Parliament 2010)

As such, the expectations of Alevi communities are largely unfulfilled, and this leaves them in search of a new representative in the political arena, since their traditional preference in the party system, the CHP, also seems to have largely abandoned their cause. The immediate future for the Alevi community is thus likely to reflect an assertive demand for recognition of their distinct sectarian identity and a search for a new representative in the political arena to defend their social and political rights and further enlarge their limited power in Turkish society. The EU once appeared to be a source of help to advance the Alevi community's conditions. However, the developments outlined above appear to have left the fate of the community in the hands of domestic power circles.

Notes

[1] For a comprehensive overview of Alevi issues and Alevi involvement in Turkish politics, see White and Jongerden (2003) and Shankland (2007).

[2] For comprehensive reviews of the large and growing literature on this divide between the secularists and Islamists, see Kuru (2009) and Yavuz (2009a).

[3] Notable exceptions to this peaceful coexistence of the Alevi and Sunni communities can be seen in bloody clashes between the two communities in the late 1970s in Çorum and Kahramanmaraş. In early July 1993, an Alevi group called the Pir Sultan Abdal Association sponsored a conference in Sivas which was confronted by Sunni reactionists who set fire to the

TURKEY AND THE EU: ACCESSION AND REFORM

hotel where the conference was being held. As a consequence, 37 participants died in the flames and smoke (see Doğan 2007; Sökefeld 2008; White & Jongerden 2003).

[4] For accessible accounts of the religious characteristics of Alevism, see Zeidan (1999), Shindeldecker (1996) and Shankland (2007).

[5] See Toprak and colleagues (2009) for an authoritative depiction of the state of the Alevi community in diverse Anatolian towns.

[6] For reasons for this failure on the part of the AKP initiatives to appeal to the Alevi community, see Çarkoğlu and Bilgili (forthcoming).

[7] See *Radikal* (2006). However, as Çarkoğlu (2005) notes, despite the commonly held view that Alevis support the CHP, they appear in significant numbers in other major party constituencies as well. Thus, such a partisan variation in decisions to recognise *cem* houses as places of worship is not surprising.

References

Ayata, S. (1996) 'Patronage, party and state—the politicization of Islam in Turkey', *Middle East Journal*, vol. 50, no. 1, pp. 40–56.

Aydın, E. (2004) 'Aleviler ve Avrupa Birliği', [Alevis and the European Union], *Pir Sultan Abdal*, no. 57, available online at: www.psakd.org/yazarlar/avrupa_birliği_aleviler.html

Cumhuriyet. (2009) 'Erdoğan Ulusa Seslendi', [Erdoğan spoke to the nation], 26 November, available online at: http://www.cumhuriyet.com.tr/?im=yhs&hn=96914

Çakır, R. (1998) 'Political Alevism versus political Sunnism: convergences and divergences', in *Alevi Identity: Cultural, Religious and Social Perspectives*, eds T. Olsson, E. Özdalga & C. Raudvere, Swedish Research Institute, Istanbul, pp. 63–98.

Çarkoğlu, A. (2005) 'Political preferences of the Turkish electorate: reflections of an Alevi-Sunni cleavage', *Turkish Studies on Religion and Politics in Turkey*, vol. 6, no. 2, pp. 273–292.

Çarkoğlu, A. & Bilgili, N. Ç. (forthcoming) 'Alevis in Turkish politics', in *Power and Powerlessness: Religious Minorities in the Middle East*, eds A. N. Longva & A. S. Roald, Brill, Leiden.

Çarkoğlu, A. & Kalaycıoğlu, E. (2009) *The Rising Tide of Conservatism in Turkey*, Palgrave, New York.

Doğan, S. (2007) *Sivas: 2 Temmuz 1993*, [Sivas: July 2, 1993] Ekim Yayınları, Istanbul.

Dressler, M. (2008) 'Religio-secular metamorphoses: the remaking of Turkish Alevism', *Journal of the American Academy of Religion*, vol. 76, no. 2, pp. 280–311.

Erman, T. & Göker, E. (2000) 'Alevi politics in contemporary Turkey', *Middle Eastern Studies*, vol. 36, no. 4, pp. 99–118.

European Commission. (2005) 'Turkey, 2005 progress report', available online at: http://ec.europa.eu/enlargement/archives/pdf/key_documents/2005/package/sec_1426_final_progress_report_tr_en.pdf

European Commission. (2007) 'Turkey, 2007 progress report', available online at: http://ec.europa.eu/enlargement/pdf/key_documents/2007/nov/turkey_progress_reports_en.pdf

European Commission. (2008) 'Turkey, 2008 progress report', available online at: http://ec.europa.eu/enlargement/pdf/press_corner/keydocuments/reports_nov_2008/turkey_progress_report_en.pdf

European Commission. (2009) 'Turkey, 2009 progress report', available online at: http://ec.europa.eu/enlargement/pdf/key_documents/2009/tr_rapport_2009_en.pdf

European Parliament. (2010) 'European Parliament resolution of 10 February 2010 on Turkey's progress report 2009', available online at: http://www.mfa.gov.cy/mfa/mfa2006.nsf/All/1E690E46004D36D6C22576C70042B105/$file/2009%20progress%20report%20on%20Turkey%20en%20_2_.pdf

Göner, Ö. (2005) 'Transformation of the Alevi collective identity', *Cultural Dynamics*, vol. 17, no. 2, pp. 107–134.

Hale, W. & Özbudun, E. (2010) *Islamism, Democracy and Liberalism and in Turkey: The Case of the AKP*, Routledge, New York.

Hürriyet. (2007) 'Cem Vakfı Davası Duruşması Yapıldı', [The trail of the Cem Foundation Case was held], 20 June, available online at: http://www.hurriyet.com.tr/gundem/6744929.asp

Keyman, F. (2007) 'Modernity, secularism and Islam, the case of Turkey', *Theory Culture and Society*, vol. 24, no. 2, pp. 215–234.

Koçan, G. & Öncü, A. (2004) 'Citizen Alevi in Turkey: beyond confirmation and denial', *Journal of Historical Sociology*, vol. 17, no. 4, pp. 464–489.

Kuru, A. (2009) *Secularism and State Policies toward Religion, The United States, France and Turkey*, Cambridge University Press, New York.

Milliyet. (2008) 'Almanya'da Alevilik Din Dersleri Yayılıyor', [The religious courses on Alevism are spreading in Germany], 11 October, available online at: http://www.milliyet.com.tr/almanya-da-alevilik-dindersleriyayiliyor/guncel/haberdetayarsiv/22.10.2010/1001779/default.htm

Minority Rights Group International. (2007) 'Bir Eşitlik Arayışı: Türkiye'de Azınlıklar', [A search for equality: minorities in Turkey], available online at: www.minorityrights.org/download.php?id=433

Özalay, E. (2006) 'Cultural minorities in Turkey: the identity of the Alevis in accordance with the EU legislation', IP Student Papers, San Sebastian

Poyraz, B. (2005) 'The Turkish state and Alevis: changing parameters of an uneasy relationship', *Middle Eastern Studies*, vol. 41, no. 4, pp. 503–516.

Radikal. (2006) 'Türkiye'de Bir İlk: Cemevi arsasına törenle tapu verildi', [For the first time in Turkey: an official register has been given to the land of the *cemevi*], 9 July, available online at: http://www.radikal.com.tr/Radikal.aspx?aType=RadikalHaberDetay&ArticleID = 785497&Date = 13.01.2010&CategoryID = 97

Seufert, G. (1997) 'Between religion and ethnicity: a Kurdish-Alevi tribe in globalizing Istanbul', in *Space, Culture and Power: New Identities in Globalizing Cities*, eds A. Öncü & P. Weyland, Zed Books, London, pp. 157–176.

Shankland, D. (2007) *The Alevis in Turkey: The Emergence of a Secular Islamic Tradition*, Routledge, London.

Shindeldecker, J. (1996) 'Turkish Alevis today', available online at: http://www.alevibektasi.org/xalevis1.htm

Sökefeld, M. (2008) *Struggling for Recognition: The Alevi Movement in Germany and Transnational Space*, Berghahn Books, New York.

Stewart, M. (2007) 'Modernity and the Alevis of Turkey: identity, challenges and change', *Journal of International Relations*, vol. 9, no. 1, Spring, pp. 50–60.

Şimşek, S. (2004) 'New social movements in Turkey since 1980', *Turkish Studies*, vol. 5, no. 2, pp. 111–139.

Toprak, B., Şener, N., Bozan, I., & Morgül, T. (2009) *Türkiye'de Farklı Olmak: Din ve Muhafazakârlık Ekseninde Ötekileştirilenler Mahalle Baskısı Araştırma Raporu*, [Being Different in Turkey: The Ones Othered on the Axis of Religion and Conservatism. The Report on Neighbourhood Pressure] Metis Yayınları, Istanbul.

Turan, İ. (1984) 'Continuity and change in Turkish bureaucracy: the Kemalist period and after', in *Atatürk and the Modernization of Turkey*, ed. J. Landau, Westview Press, Boulder, CO, pp. 99–124.

Turunç, H. (2007) 'Islamicist or democratic? The AKP's search for identity in Turkish politics', *Journal of Contemporary European Studies*, vol. 15, no. 1, pp. 79–91.

US Department of State. (2008) 'International religious freedom report 2008 Turkey', available online at: http://2001-2009.state.gov/g/drl/rls/irf/2008/108476.htm

White, P. J. & Jongerden, J. (eds) (2003) *Turkey's Alevi Enigma: A Comprehensive Overview*, Brill, Leiden.

Yavuz, H. M. (2009a) *Secularism and Muslim Democracy in Turkey*, Cambridge University Press, New York.

Yavuz, H. (2009b) 'Adalet ve Kalkinma Partisi (AKP)', in *The Oxford Encyclopedia of the Islamic World*, available online at: http://www.oxfordislamicstudies.com/article/opr/t236/e0924

Zeidan, D. (1999) 'The Alevi of Anatolia', *Middle East Review of International Affairs*, vol. 3, no. 4, pp. 74–89, available online at: http://meria.idc.ac.il/journal/1999/issue4/zeidan.pdf

Ali Çarkoğlu (PhD State University of New York—Binghamton) is a professor of political science in the Department of International Relations at Koç University, Istanbul. His research interests are in comparative politics, voting behaviour, public opinion and party politics in Turkey. His publications have appeared in the *European Journal of Political Research, Electoral Studies, Turkish Studies, New Perspectives on Turkey, South European Society and Politics, Middle Eastern Studies, Political Studies* and in many edited volumes. His most recent book is *The Rising Tide of Conservatism in Turkey* (Palgrave-Macmillan 2009, co-authored with E. Kalaycıoğlu).

Nazlı Çağın Bilgili (PhD Sabancı University) teaches at Istanbul Kültür University. Her research was on the relationship between religiosity and democratic attitudes with a special focus on the empirical analysis of tolerance in Turkey. She has participated in several studies on the role of institutional and social Islam in Turkey. Her research interests include political sociology, political culture, Islam in social and political life and democratization in the Middle East.

Diagnosing Trends and Determinants in Public Support for Turkey's EU Membership

Ali Çarkoğlu and Çiğdem Kentmen

Despite scholarly interest in the process of Turkey's candidacy for European Union (EU) membership, what is missing in the literature is a detailed examination of Turkish public opinion on the issue. Using Turkish Election Surveys, Eurobarometer surveys and International Social Survey Programme data, we test whether economic considerations, support for democracy, attachment to national identity and religiosity affect Turkish individuals' attitudes towards Turkey's EU membership. Perceived national economic conditions and national identity have a negative impact while satisfaction with democracy is positively linked to support for EU membership. Contrary to expectations, religion exerts no significant influence over membership preferences.

Although Turkey has a long and troubled relationship with the European Union (EU), there are only a few empirically informed studies analysing the determinants of Turkish public support for membership of the EU (Çarkoğlu 2003; 2004; Kentmen 2008; Şenyuva 2006; 2009). This is in contrast to the fact that there is a rich literature on EU–Turkey relations, emphasising the rationale of EU and Turkish decision-makers, and the underlying socio-economic and cultural challenges these relations entail.[1] The EU's decision to grant Turkey candidate status in 1999 following a reform process in Turkey to meet the Copenhagen political criteria, and the beginning of accession negotiations in 2005 have attracted vibrant interest among scholars seeking to explain the EU's decisions relating to Turkey. However, time and time again, the EU enlargement process has been blockaded by resistance of mass public opinion as exemplified in the Norwegian, Dutch and French referendums of the past decades. These historical turning points have clearly shown the fragility of enlargement when faced with resistant public opinion in member countries as well as in applicants. The ensuing analyses are primarily based on the historical development of popular support for EU membership in Turkey over the last decade. This showed, once again, that popular backing for EU membership may, depending on the circumstances prevailing, act as a hindrance as well as a solid basis of support for the EU membership project.

We base our analysis first on the historical development of Turkish mass public support for EU membership. Diagnosing an unmistakable decline in support for EU membership, we explore what factors account for variation in the attitude of Turkish citizens, using cross-temporal and cross-sectional data analysis. We examine the validity of three models—the winners and losers in economic circumstances model, the winners and losers in democratic transitions model, and identity-based models within the context of Turkey. Previous studies addressing similar models have produced contradictory findings, mostly because they each relied on different sample survey data in their empirical analyses and used different measures of variables. This paper aims to clarify the determinants of support for EU membership in Turkey by comparing results from four different fieldwork exercises: the 2002 Turkish Election Survey (TES), the 2002–03 Eurobarometer (EB) pooled surveys, the 2007 TES and the 2009 International Social Survey Programme (ISSP) survey. The Eurobarometer and ISSP surveys adopt a conceptual framework that is more comparable across nations passing through the same membership negotiations, whereas the TES survey, which was initiated by Turkish experts, was keener to grasp country-specific phenomena A major problem with previous studies was that there were differences in the way they measured their dependent variable—support for Turkey's EU membership—since the related survey questions were worded differently across different surveys. Such differences raise doubts about the degree to which we can generalise from the existing analyses. We thus used a hypothetical referendum question to measure our dependent variable to compare results from EB, TES and ISSP in this study.

Historical Developments

A descriptive account of public support for EU membership can be obtained on the basis of two different series of questions. The one obtained from Eurobarometer studies asks, 'Generally speaking, do you think that our country's membership of the European Union is a good thing? A bad thing? Or neither a good nor a bad thing?' As such, it reminds respondents that there might be a downside to EU membership as well as good aspects. It also avoids asking a final assessment about individuals' support for membership as a function of net benefits. Accordingly, this wording typically diagnoses a lower level of positive evaluations of membership compared with questions asking respondents how they would vote in a hypothetical referendum on EU membership such as 'If there were to be a referendum tomorrow on the question of your country's membership in the European Union, would you personally vote for or against membership?'

Another series of observations can be obtained from various ad hoc surveys usually designed to grasp measurements concerning phenomena other than EU membership and related issues. Çarkoğlu (2003; 2004) has assembled a collection of such data since 1996. Çarkoğlu and Kalaycıoğlu (2009, p. 122) report an updated version of this collection, which is brought further up to date below, to cover a total of 14 different surveys over the 1996–2009 period.

Figure 1 summarises the Eurobarometer data from 2004 to 2009. We clearly observe here that the Turkish public increasingly regards membership in the EU as not necessarily a good thing. In the second half of 2007, 49 per cent of the public found membership a good thing and at the end of 2009 this group was about 45 per cent. In the meantime, those who consider membership a bad thing slowly rose to and settled at around 25 per cent. Five years earlier, in 2004, this group was nine per cent while at the same time those who considered membership a good thing was about 70 per cent.

A similar picture of developments in public opinion is observed using the referendum evaluation question. Figure 2 shows the dynamics of Turkish public opinion providing a longer time trace than Figure 1. Obtained from various national surveys, these data indicate an oscillating pattern since the mid 1990s. In 1995, at the time of the signing and ratification of the Customs Union Agreement, only a little over 50 per cent of the Turkish adult population seemed supportive of EU membership.[2] Following the Customs Union Agreement and its implementation from 1 January 1996, the public mood quickly turned positive. However, primarily due to the rising anti-EU campaign from nationalist circles and diplomatic bottlenecks in EU–Turkey relations, significant setbacks may be observed.[3] With the recognition of the Turkish

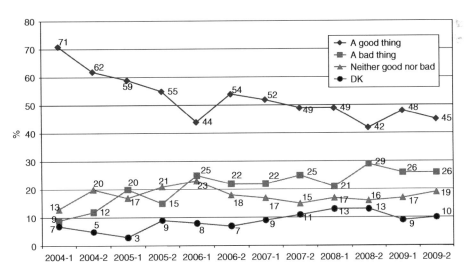

Figure 1 'Generally speaking, do you think that [our country]'s membership of the European Union is … ?'
Source: Eurobarometer surveys 2004–09.

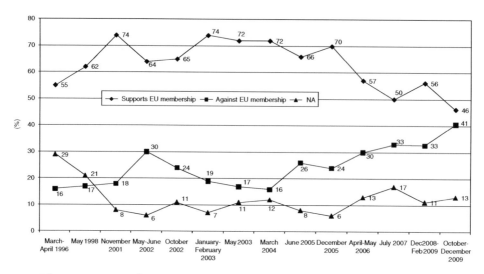

Figure 2 Support for EU Membership in a Referendum Setting, 1996–2010.

candidacy in 1999 and then the coming to power of the Justice and Development Party (AKP) at the end of 2002, we observe a three-year-long high level of public support for membership in the country. However, from spring 2006 public support faltered and went down to the level of support at the end of 1996.[4] What is notable in these figures is that by the end of 2009 support for EU membership in a possible referendum had also dropped below 50 per cent for the first time since the start of our data collection in the first half of 1996.

These two series of observations indicate similar trends for the time period between 2004 and 2009. Spring 2006 appears to be the turning point in both series. This is when anti-EU circles appear to have become violently rejuvenated in some smaller Anatolian provinces, where lynching attempts occurred when left-wing and Kurdish activists attempted to spread their propaganda. Although these events were not directly linked to EU policies and the EU reforms undertaken by the government, since then the public mood has produced a backlash of mistrust towards the EU.

From a comparative perspective, such a drop in public opinion support for membership in the EU perfectly parallels findings from similar candidate countries. What is typical in a candidate country is that such support for membership normally appears to be high before the start of accession negotiations. However, these high levels of support normally evaporate during the negotiation process. The candidate country public typically becomes disenchanted with the EU membership project upon the realisation that there will be an inevitable loss of sovereignty, and that the European bureaucracy will be structurally weak in handling country-specific sensibilities. What is atypical in the Turkish case is that such a drop appeared so early in the negotiation phase.

What Do We Know About the Determinants of Mass Preferences for EU Membership?

Hypotheses that are used to account for a changing likelihood of support for EU membership can be grouped under three main headings. First is the utilitarian expectations hypothesis, which claims that individuals who believe that EU membership will positively affect national and their personal economic circumstances will be more likely to support membership (Ehin 2001; Gabel & Whitten 1997). Human capital arguments expect occupational status and educational attainment of individuals to explain variation in levels of likelihood of support for EU membership. Those with higher human capital who are more likely to benefit from free movement within a larger European market are more likely to support European integration than others (Gabel 1998). However, we claim that the expectations of labour in Turkey will be different from those in the EU. This is because Turkey is a low-skilled country compared with the Western European member states' average, and the unification of Turkey with the EU will be a unification of a skill-scarce country with a skill-abundant group of states. Unskilled labour might move from Turkey to the rest of the EU member states to find better jobs, or European firms might move their business to Turkey to benefit from low-cost unskilled labour. In line with human capital arguments, we claim that EU membership would bring positive personal repercussions to unskilled labour in Turkey, and thus unskilled labour would support integration with the EU.

Similarly, perceptions of a country's economic conditions are linked to support for membership. Such sociotropic models claim that if national economic spaces, structures and regulations have been modified to comply with EU rules and if national economic conditions sour, citizens will blame the EU (Hooghe & Marks 2004; 2005). However, it is questionable whether Turkish individuals would base their evaluations of national economic conditions on the impact of the EU on Turkish economy. The Customs Union between Turkey and the EU, and the loans received from the EU since the signing of the Association Agreement in 1963 have not made as significant an impact on macroeconomic indicators as in the Central and Eastern European Countries (CEECs) (Ataç & Grünewald 2008). Therefore, expectations regarding subjective evaluations of the EU's economic benefits for the national economy might be different in Turkey from in other candidate countries.

A second set of hypotheses that accounts for a changing likelihood of support for EU membership claims that the EU's impact on a candidate country's democracy is linked to support for membership. The EU has been one of the most effective international promoters of democracy, since the benefits of accession and the costs of being left out of the EU are so high that candidate country elites are naturally inclined to agree to meet the democratic criteria for EU membership. Scholars have suggested that if citizens are satisfied with how democracy is working in their country they will be supportive of EU membership because of the EU's significant impact on democratisation (Cichowski 2000).

Many studies document the fact that the EU has accelerated the democratisation process in Turkey as it has done in former candidate countries (Güney & Karatekelioğlu 2005; Öniş 2003). However, three military interventions have suspended Turkey's competitive party system since 1950. The authoritarian heritage of the very last military regime of 1980–83 has shaped the dynamics of EU–Turkey relations since 1999, when Turkey became an official candidate for membership. Turkey needed to make substantial progress in its efforts to promote rights and freedoms and to consolidate its democracy to fulfill the EU membership criteria. However, democratisation reforms potentially pose challenges to the analysis of public support for EU membership. One of these reforms concerns the role of the military and another the expansion of minority rights. As Turkish public opinion is highly supportive of the role of Turkish armed forces in the political structure (Sarıgil 2009) and the majority are concerned about broadening the rights of minorities (Güneş-Ayata 2003), there is a high possibility that many citizens might be uncomfortable with democratisation and liberalisation reforms associated with EU membership. One vital question here is whether Turkish citizens who are opposed to the efforts of democratisation are also against Turkey's EU membership. There is a possibility that there may be individuals who value the economic benefits of accession over the costs of democratisation and thus may still want EU accession even if they are not happy with the democratisation reforms.

A third set of hypotheses concerns national and ethnic identities and religiosity. The stronger an individual's national identity, the less likely they are to be supportive of EU membership. National identity, like any other social identity, will provide individuals with feelings of belonging, distinctiveness and increased self-esteem, which can result in inter-group discrimination. Of course, it is possible that one may have a national and a European identity simultaneously (Risse 2001); however, scholars claim that national identities are 'more deeply rooted in respondents' minds' than a distant and newly emerged European integration (Hooghe & Marks 2005, p. 433). Another reason why the EU (out-group) might be seen as a threat to national identity is that the EU may appear to some individuals to be a discrete supranational entity that weakens the sovereignty and traditional roles of the nation-state (in-group) (Murphy 1999). For example, the use of qualified majority voting in the Council of Ministers and the increased legislative powers of the European Parliament have limited the decision-making powers of member states regarding economic and monetary issues and have decreased nation states' capability to represent and mediate domestic interests (Marks, Hooghe & Blank 1996). Also, the EU has minimised member states' distinctiveness by eroding physical boundaries and creating common symbols such as a common currency, an EU flag and an anthem (Carey 2002). Thus, as individuals might worry that European integration undermines national authority and identity, they may try to maintain the integrity of the national group to protect the national identity and, to this end, may oppose European integration (Castiglione 2009).

The central questions remain: How different is Turkish national identity from European identity and how does this difference affect Turkish citizens' attitudes towards the EU? A review of the historical roots of Turkish nationalist ideology and its modern reflections in electoral politics is beyond the scope of this article.[5] However, studies clearly reveal a vibrant multi-dimensional nationalist movement that is closely tied to developments in Turkey's relations with the EU.[6] This movement typically perceives democratisation reforms as a threat to national unity, and the whole EU project as a campaign to undermine the Turkish national identity. Given that Kemalist policies sought to base the identity of the new republic on the Turkish nation while assimilating minorities, one might also question how minority ethnic and sectarian groups view Turkey's integration with the West. As EU membership has a protective stance regarding ethnic and sectarian minority rights and freedoms, it is plausible to argue that Kurdish and Alevi groups would support Turkey's EU membership.

Religious identity also provides a source for Euroscepticism. Moral codes associated with religious identities will signify to individuals that 'a particular mode of conduct or that a particular end-state of existence is personally and socially preferable to alternative modes of conduct or end-states of existence' (Rokeach 1968, p. 550). Religion also provides individuals with feelings of predictability in a rapidly changing world, since religions are based to a large extent on concrete doctrines, traditions and role expectations. The EU has obviously brought major economic, political and social changes such as the euro, the European Central Bank and cooperation in foreign and security affairs to the everyday lives of citizens, and when evaluating these changes individuals may rely on more familiar and stable religious values, so Turkish individuals who are strongly attached to their Muslim identity might view the EU as a Christian club. If that be the case, the stronger the religiosity of an individual, the less likely they will be to support membership in the EU.[7]

In addition, although in the current Turkish political scene some Islamist groups appear worried that the West has introduced Muslims to non-moral values, others have been supportive of Westernisation in the hope that it will guarantee rights and freedoms in highly secular Turkey.[8] Thus, given such different stances by Islamist groups, there is no clear directional hypothesis for the effect of religiosity on EU attitudes.

Evaluations of these three main sources of expectations rely on a large set of socio-economic, political and demographic factors. Obviously, one's political ideology and party preferences are expected to play a mediating role in shaping one's support for EU membership. Similarly, individuals' income level and age, as well as differences of perceptions and evaluations between men and women, are expected to exert some influence upon one's likelihood of support for EU membership.

There is a burgeoning empirical literature that relies on survey data to identify the impact of utilitarian expectations, national identity and religiosity on support for EU membership. However, these studies mostly report contradictory evidence. For example, Çarkoğlu (2003), Kentmen (2008) and Elgün and Tillman (2007) offer little evidence that human capital affects Euro-attitudes. All three studies provide evidence that occupation does not exert a statistically significant effect on public support in Turkey. Similarly, Çarkoğlu (2003) and Elgün and Tillman (2007) report no significant influence from the level of education of respondents while Kentmen (2008) finds only that respondents of low education level are more likely to be supportive of EU membership. However, while Çarkoğlu's (2003) analysis reveals that individuals' self-evaluation of how EU membership would change their personal life affects their Euro-attitudes, Kentmen's (2008) findings show instead that perceptions of national economic circumstances shape support for EU membership. Elgün and Tillman (2007) test neither of these arguments. Moreover, while Çarkoğlu claims that religiosity is significantly and negatively linked to EU support, Kentmen finds no significant influence of religiosity.

A possible explanation of why these findings are contradictory is that different studies use different survey data and test diverse sets of control variables. Çarkoğlu (2003) uses a 2002 nationwide survey and operationalises religiosity by creating an index of respondents' attitudes concerning religious issues, including the ban on Islamic headscarves and the freedom of religious conscience. His indicator chiefly measures Islam's influence over individuals' political positions. Kentmen relies on 2001, 2003 and 2003 pooled Eurobarometer data and creates a religiosity measure by forming interactions between a respondent's religion and the number of times they attend religious services other than weddings and funerals. Thus, these two authors test the impact of different aspects of attachment to Islam on Euro-attitudes and reach different conclusions.

Empirical Results

Given this background, we now embark upon a temporal comparison of different cross-sectional samples of data available to us on support for EU membership in Turkey. For this purpose we use the EB Series 2002.2 (European Commission 2002) and 2003.2 (European Commission 2003), the two pre-election surveys from TES 2002 and 2007 and the ISSP Religion III survey. Our dependent variable is measured using the question asking, 'If there were to be a referendum tomorrow on the question of Turkey's membership of the European Union, would you personally vote for or against it?' Answers to this question are coded 1 for 'for' and 0 for 'against'. 'Don't know' answers are coded as missing. Since this variable is dichotomous, we use logistic regression to estimate our models.

With regard to the independent variables, we unfortunately do not have the same set of questions across these five surveys and whatever is available is not necessarily worded exactly the same way. However, we made use of all available data in as suitably comparable a way as possible. For this purpose, whenever possible, we adopted the same variable definitions and transformations.[9] We present the results of our models of support for EU membership in Table 1.[10] The chi-squared statistics for all our models allow us to reject the null hypotheses that our independent variables have no influence over Turkish citizens' attitudes towards integration with the EU. What then are the emerging patterns from these five surveys over the seven-year span between 2002 and 2009?

Education appears statistically significant only for the EB 2002–03 data. In all others, when control variables are included, it drops out of significance. This finding

Table 1 Logit Results for Support for EU Membership in Turkey, 2001–09

		EB 2001–02	TES 2002	TES 2007	ISSP-2009
Intercept		−4.73***	0.19	−2.33	−0.45
National, ethnic and religious identity	Attachment to Turkish identity	−0.28*** (0.76)	−0.11 (0.9)	—	—
	Attachment to Islam	−0.02 (1.02)	−0.04 (0.96)	0.03 (1.03)	0.02 (1.02)
	Self-evaluated religiosity	—	0.05 (1.05)	0.06 (1.06)	—
	Religious belief	—	0.001 (1.00)	—	—
	Support for Shari'a-based regime	—	—	−0.51*** (0.6)	—
	Kurdish identity	—	0.39 (1.47)	−0.06 (0.94)	−0.39 (0.68)
	Alevi identity	—	—	−0.2 (0.82)	—
Utilitarian calculations	Sociotropic calculations (STC)	2.04*** (7.69)	—	0.45*** (1.57)	0.7*** (2.01)
	Perceived personal benefit (PPB)	1.23*** (3.42)	—	—	—
	Professionals	−1.98 (0.14)	−0.45*** (0.64)	—	−1.17 (0.31)
	Professionals* STC	—	—	—	0.3 (1.35)
	Professional* PPB	0.59 (1.81)	—	—	—
	Manual workers	1.13 (3.08)	—	—	−0.09 (0.91)
	Manual workers* STC	—	—	—	−0.02 (0.98)
	Manual workers* PPB	−0.23 (0.79)	—	—	—
	Whitecollar workers	—	−0.48 (0.62)	—	—
	Bluecollar workers	—	−0.21 (0.81)	—	—
	Unemployed	—	−0.53** (0.59)	−0.21 (0.81)	—
	Education	−0.27** (0.77)	0.02 (1.02)	−0.09 (0.91)	−0.06 (0.94)
	Index of perceived economic benefits	0.43*** (1.54)	—	0.001 (1.001)	−0.10** (0.9)
	Sum of bad economic evaluations	—	−0.04 (0.96)	—	—
Satisfaction with democracy		—	—	0.07** (1.07)	—
	N	1322	1435	1194	1082
	Cox and Snell R^2	0.395	0.086	0.397	0.499
	Log likelihood	−353.541	1566.276	1566.276	684.579

* Significant at 0.05 level; ** significant at −0.01 level; *** significant at 0.001 level in two-tailed test of significance.

implies that education does not affect how individuals view the EU in Turkey; those who have higher education do not necessarily think that they would benefit more from European integration and they do not have more favourable attitudes towards the EU. Moreover, occupational groups do not have any impact on Euro-attitudes. Only the 2002 TES survey results reveal that professionals are less likely to support EU membership as expected by the utilitarian calculations literature. Skilled labour in skill-scarce Turkey may be concerned that Western professionals will come to Turkey and effectively steal their jobs; thus, their opposition to Turkey's integration with the EU is not surprising.

Evaluations of a family's economic condition, from a retrospective or prospective perspective, have a statistically significant impact on Euro-attitudes. As the positive evaluations of the national economy rise, the likelihood of support for EU membership rises significantly. In contrast, for 2009, as individuals become more optimistic in their economic evaluations, they appear to be less likely to support EU membership.

Political utilitarian calculations are also influential in individuals' attitudes towards the EU. Similar to Cichowski's (2000) findings, those who are satisfied with the way democracy works in Turkey are more likely to support Turkey's EU membership.

Eurobarometer data reveal that national identity has a significant negative impact on attitudes, as expected. However, the rest of the analysis shows that ethnic Kurdish and Alevi backgrounds, religious practice and self-evaluated religiosity do not exert statistically significant influence over attitudes towards EU membership. This finding is interesting because earlier studies found that devout Catholics are more likely to support European integration when controlled for political engagement, partisanship and socio-demographic factors (Hagevi 2002; Nelsen & Guth 2003; Vollaard 2006). Yet, in the case of Turkey, only the analysis of the 2007 TES data reveals that those who would like a Shari'a-based regime in Turkey are less likely to support EU membership.

Our results show that significant differences between men and women respondents appear for the TES 2002 survey. Men, rather than women, appear more likely to be supportive of EU membership, after controlling for other influences. Age appears significant only in the sample for EB 2002–03 pooled data. Partisan differences exert a significant influence in the 2002 pre-election study and in the 2009 ISSP study. As expected, Nationalist Action Party (MHP) voters are consistently less likely to be supportive of EU membership. While supporting a Kurdish party appears to have a significant effect on support for EU membership, the survey results show that Republican People's Party (CHP) voters were more likely and AKP voters less likely to be supportive of EU membership in 2002. The CHP and AKP voters are not significantly different from others on attitudes towards the EU in all other years.

Conclusion

In this paper, we have examined factors that are critical in explaining public attitudes towards Turkey's EU membership. Relying on four different sources of data collected over the 2001–09 period, we have provided a full picture of the dynamics and nature of Turkish public opinion. Our findings support the utilitarian expectations that individuals who perceive that the EU would positively affect their personal or Turkey's national economic circumstances tend to support membership. In contrast, human capital has little to no impact on Euro-attitudes. National identity is negatively and satisfaction with democracy positively linked to Turkish public opinion on the EU.

Our analyses show that religion is insignificant in determining support for EU membership. This finding needs further corroboration with a multi-dimensional representation of religiosity, taking into account separately belief, practice, self-evaluation and political attitudes shaped by religiosity.

When we move beyond the simple religious practice question into religiously significant social attitudes reflective of a more comprehensive conservative ideological worldview, the latter appear significant in the shaping of preferences concerning EU membership. However, such attitudinal measures are clearly related to political predispositions of individuals as well. This may be suggestive of a more complex set of relationships between variables that shape EU preferences and thus may be indicative of a need for a system of equations modelling.

Our analysis also suggests that government performance and partisan preferences are also influential in shaping attitudes concerning EU membership. This clearly has implications for the way EU adjustment reforms are shaped in Turkey. Given an overall successful government in policy areas only indirectly related to the EU process, reforms and the successful continuation of negotiations may be difficult to obtain. In contrast, a stable and domestically confident and successful government may find it easier to mobilise the masses in favour of EU membership. Further analyses are needed to uncover the intricacies of such complex interactions that shape preferences concerning EU membership in Turkey.

Our analyses also clearly document that, despite expectations to the contrary, we find no evidence that Kurdish ethnicity or Alevi sectarian orientation exert any significant influence upon support for EU membership. Although this may be partially attributable to our operationalisation of the Kurdish and Alevi variables, we nevertheless have to underline a more general observation concerning the nature of the influences diagnosed for the national, religious and sectarian identity variables as a whole. As a group, these variables show no significant influence unless a clear political intervening variable evaluation such as support for a Shari'a regime in the country is reflected in their operationalisation. As a result, utilitarian economic benefit calculations and partisan evaluations appear to be the dominant factors shaping support for EU membership.

The question that remains concerns the clear fall in support for EU membership over the period in question. While at the end of 2001 the support level exceeded 70 per cent, by 2009 it had declined to just below 50 per cent. Our results above provide a framework within which this phenomenon can at least partially be explained. The economic crisis of 2001 soured the public mood at the beginning of 2002 and hence judgements as to how EU membership would affect the country as well as personal economic circumstances were predominantly positive, pushing support levels upwards. As our analyses above indicate, partisan influences were yet to become potent in shaping preferences concerning EU membership at the end of 2001. However, in contrast, by 2009 not only had the partisan nationalist influences become apparent in the shaping of EU preferences, but the economic evaluations had also changed in character. Compared with the 2001–02 results, our 2009 results show that the sign of perceived economic benefits had switched from a significant positive to a significant negative. In other words, those perceiving positive economic benefits were more likely to be supportive of membership in 2001–02 whereas in 2009 there was less likelihood of support for EU membership from these individuals.

Equally noticeable is the rising partisan rejection of the EU project by the increasingly nationalistic rhetoric in the few years preceding 2009. Identification of the EU with intensely debated democratisation efforts targeting improvements in minority rights appear to be the underlying reason for the rising partisan cleavage around EU issues, and declining support for membership. Although we have no variables representing nationalist sentiment among the voting age population, there is reason to believe that, on the basis of historical observations of developments in Turkish politics, behind this rising partisan divide lie nationalist rhetoric and sentiment fuelled by democratisation reforms and Kurdish minority issues. As a result, the popular backing for the EU project appears weaker only a few years after the start of negotiations. Our data cannot grasp the influence of negative approaches of European leadership cadres towards Turkish membership of the EU as they are perceived by the Turkish masses. However, these developments that effectively block the negotiations and create a negative public image of the EU in Turkey are also expected to have played a key role in the drop in Turkish public support for membership in the EU. Analyses of the relationship between these developments and public opinion in Turkey have yet to be carried out by researchers in this area.

Notes

[1] See Müftüler-Baç (2008a) on a foreign policy perspective, Müftüler-Baç (2008b) on the interplay of utility-based and identity-based factors and the EU's internal dynamics, Nugent (2007) on the explanatory role of the rationalist approach plus political pressures and rhetorical commitments, Font (2006) on interest-based calculations, polity norms and institutional arrangements, Müftüler-Baç and McLaren (2003) on the interplay of constructivism, historic institutionalism and EU members' preferences and Oğuzlu (2002) on identity and culture from a security perspective.

[2] For details of the question wording and sources for the data presented in Figure 2, see Çarkoğlu and Kalaycıoğlu (2009, pp. 122–130, p. 165 n. 3). The last two observations for December 2008 to February 2009 and October–December 2009 were obtained from ISSP's Religion III and Social Inequality surveys carried out by Ali Çarkoğlu and Ersin Kalaycıoğlu with the financial support of the Scientific and Technological Research Council of Turkey (TÜBİTAK).

[3] Considering the drop in public support for EU membership, one has to take into account the negative developments on the European side of the relationship. One major issue in these developments was the bottlenecks the Turkish side encountered on the Cyprus issue, especially in the aftermath of the Annan Plan referendum in April 2004. Despite expectations and promises of normalisation if not a complete resolution of the long-standing conflict, the

Turkish side was not able to achieve any significant progress that could benefit the lives of the Turkish Cypriots on the island. To what extent such a development is linked to public opinion's negative image of the EU and the membership project is not clear from empirical data. However, taking this together with the lukewarm, if not completely negative stances of the German and French authorities towards Turkey's membership, it appears that the Turkish public at large has persistently received an unwelcoming signal from the European side. Such a signal is thus typically linked in daily political conversations to declining public support for membership. However, there is yet no empirical evidence as to whether the public is attentive to the mutual policies of Turkey and European States, nor do we know whether such developments in international politics have an influence on evaluations of EU membership at comparable magnitudes to other factors to be underlined below.

[4] See Çarkoğlu (2004) and Çarkoğlu and Kalaycıoğlu (2009) for a long-term historical evaluation of these trends in public support for EU membership.

[5] See Canefe and Bora (2003) for a review of this literature.

[6] See Avcı (2011) in this volume.

[7] Some scholars argue that the compatibility of Turkey's predominant Muslim population with the predominantly Christian EU might be another factor that would affect how Turkish citizens view accession to the EU. See Müftüler Baç (2000). For a detailed discussion of the relationship between religion and Turkey–EU relations see Jung and Raudvere (2008).

[8] See Atacan (2006), Çarkoğlu and Toprak (2006), Dağı (2004), Kuru (2005), Toprak (2006), Yavuz (1997) and Yılmaz (2005) on the divisions within the Islamist movement towards Europe, democratisation and value differences within Turkish society.

[9] Details of variable transformations and coding are available from the authors upon request.

[10] Coefficients for control variables are not reported in Table 1 in order to facilitate the interpretation of the table. However, they are available on request from the authors.

References

Atacan, F. (2006) 'Explaining religious politics at the crossroad: AKP–SP', in *Religion and Politics in Turkey*, eds A. Çarkoğlu & B. Rubin, Taylor & Francis, London, pp. 45–58.

Ataç, I. & Grünewald, A. (2008) 'Stabilisation through Europeanisation? Discussing the transformation dynamics in Turkey', *Debatte*, vol. 16, no. 1, pp. 31–54.

Carey, S. (2002) 'Undivided loyalties: is national identity an obstacle to European integration?', *European Union Politics*, vol. 3, no. 4, pp. 387–413.

Canefe, N. & Bora, T. (2003) 'The intellectual roots of anti-European sentiments in Turkish politics: the case of radical Turkish nationalism', in *Turkey and the European Union, Domestic Politics, Economic Integration and International Dynamics*, eds A. Çarkoğlu & B. Rubin, Frank Cass, London, pp. 127–148.

Çarkoğlu, A. (2003) 'Who wants full membership? Characteristics of Turkish public support for EU membership', *Turkish Studies*, vol. 4, no. 1, pp. 171–194.

Çarkoğlu, A. (2004) 'Societal perceptions of Turkey's EU membership: causes and consequences of support for EU membership?', in *Turkey and European Integration, Accession Prospects and Issues*, eds N. Canefe & M. Uğur, Routledge, New York, pp. 19–45.

Çarkoğlu, A. & Kalaycıoğlu, E. (2009) *The Rising Tide of Conservatism in Turkey*, Palgrave-Macmillan, New York.

Çarkoğlu, A. & Toprak, B. (2006) *Değişen Türkiye'de Din, Toplum ve Siyaset* [Religion, Society and Politics in Changing Turkey], TESEV, Istanbul.

Castiglione, D. (2009) 'Political identity in a community of strangers', in *European Identity*, eds J. T. Checkel & P. J. Katzenstein, Cambridge University Press, Cambridge, pp. 29–51.

TURKEY AND THE EU: ACCESSION AND REFORM

Cichowski, R. A. (2000) 'Western dreams, Eastern realities: support for the European Union in Central and Eastern Europe', *Comparative Political Studies*, vol. 33, no. 10, pp. 1243–1278.

Dağı, I. (2004) 'Rethinking human rights, democracy, and the West: post-Islamist intellectuals in Turkey', *Middle East Critique*, vol. 13, no. 2, pp. 135–151.

Ehin, P. (2001) 'Determinants of public support for EU membership: data from the Baltic countries', *European Journal of Political Research*, vol. 40, no. 1, pp. 31–56.

Elgün, Ö. & Tillman, E. R. (2007) 'Exposure to European Union policies and support for membership in the candidate countries', *Political Research Quarterly*, vol. 60, no. 3, pp. 391–400.

European Commission, Directorate-General Press and Communication, Public Opinion Analysis Sector. (2002) 'Candidate countries Eurobarometer 2002.2', *Inter-university Consortium for Political and Social Research*, Ann Arbor.

European Commission, Directorate-General Press and Communication, Public Opinion Analysis Sector. (2003) 'Candidate countries Eurobarometer 2003.2', *Inter-university Consortium for Political and Social Research*, Ann Arbor.

Font, N. (2006) 'Why the European Union gave Turkey the green light', *Journal of Contemporary European Studies*, vol. 14, no. 2, pp. 197–212.

Gabel, M. & Whitten, G. (1997) 'Economic conditions, economic perceptions, and public support for European integration', *Political Behavior*, vol. 19, no. 1, pp. 81–96.

Gabel, M. (1998) 'Public support for European integration: an empirical test of five theories', *Journal of Politics*, vol. 60, no. 2, pp. 333–354.

Güneş-Ayata, A. (2003) 'From Euro-scepticism to Turkey-scepticism: changing political attitudes on the European Union in Turkey', *Journal of Southern Europe and the Balkans*, vol. 5, no. 2, pp. 205–223.

Güney, A. & Karatekelioğlu, P. (2005) 'Turkey's EU candidacy and civil–military relations: challenges and prospects', *Armed Forces and Society*, vol. 31, no. 3, pp. 439–462.

Hagevi, M. (2002) 'Religiosity and Swedish Public Opinion on the European Union', *Journal for the Scientific Study of Religion*, vol. 41, no. 4, pp. 759–769.

Hooghe, L. & Marks, G. (2004) 'Does identity or economic rationality drive public opinion on European integration?', *PS: Political Science and Politics*, vol. 37, no. 3, pp. 415–420.

Hooghe, L. & Marks, G. (2005) 'Calculation, community and cues: public opinion on European integration', *European Union Politics*, vol. 6, no. 4, pp. 419–443.

Jung, D. & Raudvere, C. (eds) (2008) *Religion, Politics, and Turkey's EU Accession*, Palgrave Macmillan, London.

Kentmen, Ç. (2008) 'Determinants of support for EU membership in Turkey: Islamic attachments, utilitarian considerations and national identity', *European Union Politics*, vol. 9, no. 4, pp. 487–510.

Kuru, A. T. (2005) 'Globalisation and diversification of Islamic movements: three Turkish cases', *Political Science Quarterly*, vol. 120, no. 2, pp. 253–274.

Marks, G., Hooghe, L. & Blank, K. (1996) 'European integration from the 1980s: state-centric v. multi-level governance', *Journal of Common Market Studies*, vol. 34, no. 3, pp. 341–378.

Müftüler-Baç, M. (2000) 'Through the Looking-glass: Turkey in Europe', *Turkish Studies*, vol. 1, no. 1, pp. 21–35.

Müftüler-Baç, M. & McLaren, L. M. (2003) 'Enlargement preferences and policy-making in the European Union: impacts on Turkey', *Journal of European Integration*, vol. 25, no. 1, pp. 17–30.

Müftüler-Baç, M. (2008a) 'The European Union's accession negotiations with Turkey from a foreign policy perspective', *Journal of European Integration*, vol. 30, no. 1, pp. 63–78.

Müftüler-Baç, M. (2008b) 'Turkey's accession to the European Union: the impact of the EU's internal dynamics', *International Studies Perspectives*, vol. 9, no. 2, pp. 201–219.

Murphy, A. (1999) 'Rethinking the concept of European identity', in *Nested Identities*, eds G. H. Herb & D. H. Kaplan, Rowman & Littlefield, Lanham, MD, pp. 53–74.

Nelsen, B. F. & Guth, J. L. (2003) 'Religion and Youth Support for the European Union', *Journal of Common Market Studies*, vol. 41, no. 1, pp. 89–112.

Nugent, N. (2007) 'The EU's response to Turkey's membership application: not just a weighing of costs and benefits', *Journal of European Integration*, vol. 29, no. 4, pp. 481–502.

Oğuzlu, T. H. (2002) 'The clash of security identities: the question of Turkey's membership in the European Union', *International Journal*, vol. 54, no. 3, pp. 579–603.

Öniş, Z. (2003) 'Domestic politics, international norms and challenges to the state: Turkey–EU relations in the post-Helsinki era', *Turkish Studies*, vol. 4, no. 1, pp. 9–34.

Rokeach, M. (1968) 'The role of values in public opinion research', *Public Opinion Quarterly*, vol. 32, no. 4, pp. 547–559.

Sarıgil, Z. (2009) 'Deconstructing the Turkish military's popularity', *Armed Forces and Society*, vol. 35, no. 4, pp. 709–727.

Risse, T. (2001) 'A European identity? Europeanisation and the evolution of nation-state identities', in *Transforming Europe: Europeanisation and Domestic Change*, eds M. G. Cowles, J. A. Caporaso & T. Risse, Cornell University Press, Ithaca, NY, pp. 198–216.

Şenyuva, Ö. (2006) 'Turkish public opinion and European Union membership: the state of the art in public opinion studies in Turkey', *Perceptions*, vol. 11, pp. 19–32.

Şenyuva, Ö. (2009) 'Türkiye kamuoyu ve Avrupa Birliği 2001–2008: beklentiler, istekler ve korkular [Turkish public opinion and the European Union 2001–2008: expectations, wishes and fears]', *Uluslararası İlişkiler*, vol. 6, no. 22, pp. 97–124.

Toprak, B. (2006) 'Islam and democracy in Turkey', in *Religion and Politics in Turkey*, eds A. Çarkoğlu & B. Rubin, Taylor & Francis, London, pp. 25–44.

Vollaard, H. (2006) 'Protestantism and Euro-Skepticism in the Netherlands', *Perspectives on European Politics and Society*, vol. 7, no. 3, pp. 276–297.

Yavuz, H. (1997) 'Political Islam and the Welfare Party in Turkey', *Comparative Politics*, vol. 30, no. 1, pp. 63–82.

Yılmaz, I. (2005) 'State, law, civil society and Islam in contemporary Turkey', *Muslim World*, vol. 95, no. 3, pp. 385–411.

Ali Çarkoğlu (PhD State University of New York–Binghamton) is a professor of political science in the Department of International Relations at Koç University, Istanbul. His research interests are in comparative politics, voting behaviour, public opinion and party politics in Turkey. His publications have appeared in the *European Journal of Political Research, Electoral Studies, Turkish Studies, New Perspectives on Turkey, South European Society and Politics, Middle Eastern Studies, Political Studies* and many edited volumes. His most recent book is *The Rising Tide Conservatism in Turkey* (Palgrave-Macmillan, New York, 2009, co-authored with E. Kalaycıoğlu).

Çiğdem Kentmen (PhD University of Missouri, Columbia) is an assistant professor in the Department of International Relations and the EU, at Izmir University of Economics, Turkey. Her research interests are public opinion in the EU as well public opinion in Turkey regarding Turkey's prospective membership of the EU. Her work has been published in journals such as *European Union Politics, International Political Science Review* and *Turkish Studies*. She has also published a book entitled *Why Do People Abstain from the European Parliament Elections? An Empirical Test of Second Order Theory 1979–1999* (VDM, Berlin, 2008).

Interacting Actors: The EU and Civil Society in Turkey

Ahmet İçduygu

Civil society organisations in Turkey have remained highly visible in the country's relations with the European Union (EU). Given the particular incentives that the EU offered for the empowerment of civil society actors during the pre-accession process, it has often been assumed that the EU context played an important role in this vibrant situation. However, this article argues that the EU's impact was highly ambivalent, and the contribution of civil society organisations to the EU membership process was frequently indecisive. It concludes that this ambivalent climate is mostly due to various aspects of the ill-functioning mechanisms of the EU's enlargement regime, on one hand, and particular problems inherited from the state–society relations and socio-political culture in Turkey that are associated with the civil society arena in the country.

Civil Society has become a paradigmatic concept in the European integration process. When the European Union (EU) developed a strategy to draw the countries of Eastern Europe closer to the prospect of European integration, the issue of civil society development was a significant element of the demanding criteria of Europeanisation as set by the Copenhagen criteria, which required aspirant states to have stable institutions guaranteeing democracy, the rule of law, human rights and respect for minorities, a functioning market economy and the ability to take on the obligations of EU law. In this context, the conditionality mechanism associated with a well-functioning civil society seems to have proven to be effective in the case of the countries of the so-called fifth enlargement (Knezović 2009; Schimmelfennig 2007; Grugel 1999).

Likewise, a key feature of the ongoing debates on Turkey's potential membership is the attention paid to the issue of civil society, to what extent it exists, what form it takes, and its role in the integration process. This interest in civil society has emerged within two academic discourses: the progress of civil society within EU candidate countries, and the impact of civil society organisations (CSOs) on Turkey's Europeanisation process and prospects of EU membership (Alemdar 2008; İçduygu 2008; Göksel & Güneş 2005; Boztekin 2004; Diez et al. 2005). The changing nature of the civil society discourse points to an increasing awareness in Turkey of the need for a more democratic and liberal state–society relationship than a conventional modernity project based on a strong-state tradition and an organic vision of society. At issue is the extent to which the country's nascent civil society can be considered vibrant enough for a full democratisation of state–society relations. This is also an issue of the contribution of civil society to the country's Europeanisation process. It is possible to argue that, as far as Europeanisation is concerned, the emerging agenda on civil society points to the need to more fully understand the dynamics of the issue as they relate to the state, the market and the family.

The main aim of this article is three-fold. First, it evaluates the linkage between Turkey's EU affairs and civil society, focusing on how these two forces influence each other. Second, it examines the civil-society–democratisation nexus, emphasising how Europeanisation has produced new discourses and practices. Third, the article critically analyses the current nature and status of civil society in Turkey and the future prospects offered by the EU accession process. Most of the arguments in this article are predominantly based on the data gathered from the two CIVICUS-STEP projects conducted in 2006 and 2009 by the Third Sector Foundation of Turkey (TÜSEV) on the status of civil society in Turkey.[1]

Civil Society in Turkey: An Overview

Even though the Westernisation-based modernity project was able to bring its own notion of associational life into the late Ottoman Empire in the nineteenth century, the development of civil society in Turkey was very slow, even after the establishment of the modern Turkish Republic. In fact, neither Turkish society, which was primarily agrarian, nor Turkish politics, which constantly reflected the nature of a strong-state tradition, provided the country with a fertile ground for the advancement of civil society (Yerasimos 2000). If civil society is defined only as 'an associational life outside of the state', one can possibly argue that civil society has a long history in Turkey: for example, foundations emerged in the Ottoman Empire as 'philanthropic institutions', which created social solidarity outside political and economic spheres through charitable activities (TÜSEV 2006). Similarly, following the declaration of the Turkish Republic as a modern nation-state, the associational sphere emerged as an integral component of modernisation and of social and political life, though it was often closely controlled by the state. However, if we view civil society as something more than an associational life outside of the state and instead as a sphere that contributes to public participation and democratisation on a voluntary basis, then the history of civil society in Turkey will be rather short, since such a civil society only gained importance partly after the 1960s and partly after the 1980s. Hence, it is widely argued that there is a paradox involving the simultaneous existence of a long history of civil society as associational life and a new history of a civil society contributing to democratisation in Turkey (TÜSEV 2006; Yerasimos 2000).

As the modern nation-state project was conceived on the principle of a nation existing for the state, in the early republican period (1923–45), it is assumed that associations of citizens existed on the basis of serving the state and state interest, not on the basis of social relations derived from individual interest or economic class (Pope 1997). Consequently, the sociological grounding of associations of citizens was viewed through an organic vision of society that defines society not with reference to such categories as class or individual, but in terms of duty to the state. Civil society organisations experienced a steady growth after the transition to democracy in 1946 and had a particularly strong boost with the adoption of the (liberal) 1961 constitution (Özbudun 2000, p. 5). The increasing importance of civil society development in the 1960s and 1970s was notable, as civil society gradually incorporated business chambers, unions and township associations. However, it is wrong to take an optimistic viewpoint that state control over civil society disappeared. In fact, the three military interventions (1960, 1971 and 1980) occurred during harsh periods when the state took severe repressive measures to control and even to prohibit the activities of civil society.

As far as the discourses and practices of civil society are concerned, the post-1980 period opened up a new era in modern Turkey's social and political spheres. Of course, what happened in the country's pre-1980s modernisation also had implications for the wider social change and democratisation process, but any discussion of that period is beyond the scope of this article. As discussed elsewhere (Keyman & İçduygu 2003), several internal and external factors were influential in prompting these openings, and, by linking the internal with the external, globalisation has been furthering this change even more. *Internal* developments such as the restoration of democracy after the 1980 military intervention, the making of the 1982 constitution and the economic liberalisation of the 1980s and 1990s, and *external* developments such as the end of the Cold War, the emergence of the 'New World Order', the rise of European integration and finally the start of Turkey's EU accession negotiations, have all paved the way for the beginning of a new era in Turkey. Perhaps one of the most essential causes behind the linkages of these internal and external factors is the process of globalisation, which often implies the widening, the deepening and the speeding up of the interconnectedness of the related actors and processes. Consequently, not only the ongoing interplay of domestic and international factors, but it is also the interaction of the past (tradition) and the present (modern/post-modern) that have operated together to shape the current status of civil society in Turkey in general, and the characteristics of the CSOs in particular (İçduygu 2008).

Probably one of the simplest indicators of the quality of civil society formation in a country is the nature of its main constituent elements, namely CSOs. In Turkey, there are *four* basic types of CSOs, based on their differing legal status: (a) associations, (b) foundations, (c) public professional organisations and (d) cooperatives. While an *association* is a 'participatory'- or 'community'-based organisation that requires a system of membership, a *foundation* is usually established through an initial endowment. In addition, a *cooperative* comprises a commercial entity owned by its members, with no passive shareholders, while *public professional organisations* involve establishments primarily engaged in promoting the professional interests of their members and the profession as a whole. Available data on the number and types of CSOs in Turkey are not very reliable; however, it is estimated that in the latter part of the 2000–10 decade, the total number of CSOs was nearly 200,000, only less than half of which are currently active.[2] With nearly 80,000 associations, 60,000 cooperatives, 45,000 foundations (over 40,000 were established in the Ottoman period, and 5,000 were established in the republican era) and 3,000 professional organisations, Turkey's civil society picture is very complex. Despite their deficiencies, which are deeply rooted in their ongoing weak status in the country's social and political spheres, CSOs have begun to gain importance in Turkey's societal and political affairs. This is partly due to the predictions of political modernisation that are inherited from the Western political ideologies, and partly due to the critical conclusions of post-modern and post-national developments, such as the process of EU integration. For the former, as modernisation theory predicts, an emerging middle class demands civil society; for the latter, processes such as globalisation first lead to social transformation, which in turn results in new forms of political activity, such as identity claims that translate into civil demands.

Turkey's EU Affairs and Civil Society: A Cause-and-Effect Relationship

The relationship between civil society and democratic consolidation is not a new phenomenon, nor an issue peculiar to Turkey's accession to the EU. Not surprisingly, Turkey's involvement in European integration concerns civil society in two related ways: as an object of structural change and as a participant in European integration. In the case of the former, the civil society arena is characterised by growing numbers of CSOs and by their activities and discourses. As agents of change, CSOs participate in the process of European integration not only by supporting or opposing the EU, but also by promoting the idea of civil initiation. These activities, and the conditions surrounding them, imply a change in domestic affairs, in state–society relations and in the social, political and economic context of the Turkey–EU relationship (İçduygu 2008; Öniş 2003; Diez et al. 2005).

While Turkey was dealing with the re-installation of democracy in the 1980s, the consolidation of democracy in the 1990s and accession to the EU in the 2000s, civil society actors not only struggled for their own existence and development, but also in some cases simultaneously attempted to contribute directly or indirectly to the process of democratisation, and consequently to the country's intention to be integrated into Europe as a full member of the EU (Kubicek 2005; Uğur & Canefe 2004; Keyman & İçduygu 2003; Rumford 2003). It is possible to argue that, while not a causal determinant of successful democratic consolidation in Turkey, the promise of EU membership helped Turkey's democratisation and consolidation process, partially by overcoming its notorious deficiency in voluntary associations. In addition, the EU also exerted significant influence on prominent segments of civil society, most notably influential associations and foundations as well as professional organisations, which helped shape the context for state–society relations. This essay draws attention to two facets of civil society: 'as an object of structural changes' and 'as a participant in European integration'. My discussion and analysis is chiefly guided by the question: How does civil society in Turkey work with respect to EU–Turkey relations or to areas relevant to EU integration? It is not my intention to give a full historical account of this contribution or to provide a comprehensive overview of the literature; rather, I provide an overview of civil society involvement in the country's EU affairs.

Civil society is central not only to the EU's conceptual approach to promoting and consolidating democracy in a candidate country like Turkey, but also to its overall integration process (Uğur & Canefe 2004; Keyman & İçduygu 2003; Rumford 2003). Hence, the EU supports the civil society dimension of the whole European integration project very enthusiastically. As the development of civil society in all areas is seen as indispensable for the consolidation of democracy, the EU has overwhelmingly emphasised its wish to support that process, particularly by developing direct exchange between civil society actors in Turkey and the EU's institutions and processes. It is assumed that CSOs make a vital contribution to strengthening civil society and promoting the development of democracy. The EU often stresses the importance of this contribution. Within this context, this paper considers what role civil society plays in accompanying these two crucial processes, namely democratisation and European integration.

When the Helsinki Summit in 1999, which recognised the candidacy status of Turkey, and later the Presidency Conclusions in 2004, which confirmed the start of accession negotiations initially generated an optimistic prospect of EU membership, the role of civil society in the entire process became very clear: the EU clearly and repeatedly underscored the importance of civil society for full membership. On the other hand, having secured the support of the EU, a vast majority of the well-known CSOs, which are mainly located in big urban centers, became important actors retaining a pro-EU perspective, albeit for a short period of time. During this period, various prominent, Istanbul-based CSOs, such as the Turkish Industrialists' and Businessmen's Association (TUSİAD), Economic Development Foundation (IKV), Helsinki Citizens' Assembly, Association for Supporting and Training Women Candidates (KADER), Women Entrepreneurs Association (KAGİDER), History Foundation and ARI Movement lobbied for Turkey's EU membership in Brussels as well as at a national level. For instance, the Movement for Europe, a civic platform founded by 175 CSOs in 2002, pressured the government towards alignment with the EU and contributed to a rapid adoption of EU alignment packages in parliament. In 2004, the same platform with more participants under the leadership of IKV intensely and successfully lobbied for the EU to open membership negotiations with Turkey.[3]

Established in 1965, the IKV aims to inform the Turkish public and business community about developments in EU–Turkey relations. Today, besides providing an updated online resource for recent developments in Turkey's EU negotiation process, IKV has been running a number of projects mainly focused on raising awareness about the EU and on targeting different subgroups within the wider public. For example, in this context a pilot project was run in 2008 to raise awareness about the EU at the grassroots level. The project entailed the preparation and dissemination of course materials covering the basics of the EU, as well as training seminars for primary school teachers designed to help them transfer a basic knowledge of the EU to their pupils. Among many other initiatives, one project of the IKV targeted members of the chambers of trade in the Bandırma region and aimed to prepare them for changes that the gradual implementation of the EU *acquis communautaire* would bring for their business activities. In this project, particular attention was paid to technical fields such as environment and food security, as the regulations in such fields have a direct impact on most of the small businesses in the region.

In the last decade, IKV also organised, participated in and hosted seminars at national and international levels in an effort to gather together different actors involved in Turkey's EU negotiation process. The main goal of these activities was to initiate communication networks in which professionals outside Turkey would get acquainted with Turkey, and the Turkish public with the EU. One of these seminar series, for instance, brought together journalists in Brussels writing on Turkey with their counterparts in Turkey working on Turkey–EU relations. Another seminar series on the EU was initiated in 2005 with the aim of reaching CSOs, universities, local governments and professionals' and business organisations in 27 city centres in Turkey. Conferences on Turkey's EU accession were organised in various European capitals by the IKV and included the participation of high officials of the EU.

Another CSO that played a notable role in Turkey–EU relations was the ARI Movement, an organisation that promotes participatory democracy in Turkey (Göksel & Güneş 2005, p. 59). By giving updates on statements and directives from the EU, the ARI Movement was quite active in pushing forward its EU-related reform agenda. For instance, nearly two-fifths of the press bulletins of the Movement in 2004 related to EU affairs, discussing a variety of issues ranging from the number of women parliamentarians in Turkey compared with EU standards, to the educational system in comparison with those of EU member states, to the level of human development in comparison with the EU average, and so on. The ARI Movement has also been very active in advocacy work to communicate the EU-related views of Turkish civil society to officials and public in both Turkey and Europe.

Various CSOs in Turkey, like the IKV and the ARI Movement, have been very energetic not only in promoting the general idea of EU integration, but also in formulating certain concrete EU-related reforms. In this context, a leading example of civil society contributing to policy using the EU as both motivation and framework is the active lobbying by the women's movement in Turkey for amendments to the Criminal and Civil Codes. The women's movement, which had been active in Turkey since the 1980s, benefited from the EU negotiation process and successfully eliminated or changed the content of articles with discriminatory clauses against women.

Through their efforts, necessary amendments were made to the Civil Code in 2001 and to the Criminal Code in 2004 (Göksel & Güneş 2005, p. 68). In particular, the women's movement worked hard against the government's proposal for the codification of adultery as a crime, and strived to keep the issue high on the agenda. Their campaign against the proposal gained intense support from the EU. It is also thought-provoking that success stories generated by the women's movement were the first examples of the successful impact-making campaigns in the field, as repeatedly cited on various occasions since 2001 in the context of the EU and civil society.

In particular, two of the women's associations, KADER and KAGİDER, have played active roles in Turkish–EU relations by introducing a gender-sensitive approach to the pre-accession process (Bayraktar 2009). These two associations have expanded their objectives to target a wider scope of gender policies. By doing so, they act as political entrepreneurs for the pre-accession process in Turkey. While KADER launches advocacy campaigns for good representation of women in parliament, mainly targeting public opinion and political candidates, KAGIDER advocates on the issue of entrepreneurship. Moreover, both associations aim to increase sensitisation to gender through publications, projects, conferences and educational activities. These activities lead to a transfer of European models to non-statist actors.

Consequently, change has been observed in advocacy activities following the integration of a frame of reference on Europeanisation. There has been a shift of action towards lobbying, a shift of discourse to a more Europeanised one, and increased inter-association relations in order to form coalitions in Turkey that will influence a greater number of people. The lobbying activities are neither restricted to a unilateral relationship of the organisations with public action, nor organised only within domestic coalitions; for instance, the women's organisations tend to coordinate their actions at multiple levels. The participation of the women's movement in the European Women's Lobby through a national coordination built by KADER is an illustration of such networks. However, since Turkey is a non-EU member country, this non-membership status limits their effort to be involved in European women's networks or to access European institutions. Hence, here one may use the concept of 'velvet triangles' that refer to the networks between three types of agents that may enhance gender policy at international as well as domestic levels: femocrats and feminist politicians, expert academicians and women's movement or nongovernmental organisations (NGOs) (Bayraktar 2009). In this regard, both KADER and KAGIDER were successful in managing the formation of velvet triangles. For example, the opening day of the Brussels Bureau can be analysed as a demonstration of KAGIDER's wish to create a velvet triangle by bringing together the State Minister responsible for Women and the Family, Nimet Çubukcu, academician Ayşe Soysal, writer Elif Şafak and the European Parliament (EP) Turkey Rapporteur, Ria Oomen-Rujiten.

In terms of exerting influence over the Europeanisation process, most strikingly, KAGIDER and KADER appended the EU institutions in the boomerang pattern, which involves risks in their campaigns to international networks, because the governments which should be the primary guarantors of rights often become the primary violators. Participation in the EP Women's Report writing process has been a major step in the construction of the boomerang pattern for the Turkish women's movement. It all started in 2006 when the EP decided to draw up a report for the case of women in Turkey, to be appended to its regular country reports on Turkey. Participation in the EP Women's Report was organised by KADER through assembling actors from the women's movement. The EP acted as the mediator between the EU and the Turkish state and urged the state to adjust the areas of misfit on gender policies. As the policy objectives of the associations return to the Turkish state through EP reports, this process has blocked the state's dialogue with NGOs. As expected, the state authorities in Turkey have been sceptical of the collaboration of the EP with its own national NGOs to put pressure on them.

Turkey's long-established will towards EU membership served as a framework for older demands for the deepening of democracy in Turkey. Although Turkey–EU relations are occasionally prone to tensions and ruptures, and although the Turkish government has become less interested in EU-related reform since 2007, it can fairly be argued that civil society in Turkey retains its EU perspective to a large extent. However, unlike in earlier times, use of the EU as a tool or a framework for every occasion is no longer highly preferred by CSOs in Turkey.

It is obvious that there have also been diverse competing views of civil society actors on EU affairs; in particular, some strict, ideology-based CSOs, which originated from the extreme edges of the left–right spectrum, have been highly critical of the country's EU membership process. In order to better understand these anti-EU positions together with their pro-EU counterparts, one must refer to a typology of the CSOs in Turkey. Regardless of their legal status, *four* main distinctive types of CSOs in Turkey are observed in terms of ideological positions or normative aspects of civil society: (a) 'conventional/apolitical', (b) 'Western-oriented/modern', (c) 'primordial' and (d) 'religion based'. In addition to these four, there are also hybrid types that mix characteristics from the aforementioned groups. Of course, this unsophisticated typology is neither fully comprehensive nor totally mutually exclusive, but it is exploratory. This typology of five seems to be an outcome of the recent process in which not only the local and global but also the traditional and modern have influenced how these organisations operate within the parameters of democratisation and Europeanisation. These organisations are differentiated as follows. *Conventional* organisations are politically state-centric, organisationally old-fashioned and norma-tively issue-specific. *Western-type* organisations are independent of and prepared to oppose the state. *Primordial* organisations include traditional networks of solidarity based on primordial communities of kinship and patronage. *Religion-based* organisa-tions are those in which a community of believers operates according to the values and ethics of their faith (Islam). Although these conventional, primordial, and religious elements are ubiquitously found within CSOs in Turkey, *all* types of CSOs tend to engage in EU-based activities and discourses – even if they are ideologically opposed to the idea of European integration.

It is also necessary to identify the 'demand' and 'supply' factors that affect the nature of civil society involvement in EU affairs (Mazey & Richardson 2006; Mahoney 2004). After recognising the inherent opportunities at the intersection of the activities of civil society and the practice of European integration, it is possible to argue that, from the side of the EU, strengthening and consolidating civil society remains fundamental to the ultimate goal of sustainable integration in Europe. As for CSOs, they have vigorously tried to lobby the EU institutions to gain the necessary support for their activities. Within this mutually complementary context, reflecting an image of Western-type CSOs that are independent of and strong enough to oppose the state, those CSOs in Turkey that are highly politicised or critical of the state were able to receive an overwhelming share of EU assistance. This support has often been mistakenly conceived as a means of strengthening civil society capacity, whereas in practice many of these organisations are either based on primordial ties (for instance, some of those with pro-Kurdish or liberal-Islamist tones) or are issue-based small foundation-type organisations (such as human rights or women organisations). Thus, the partnership between CSOs in Turkey and the EU institutions has sometimes been established without broad-based involvement of civil society at large. This uneven relationship, combined with the ineffective organisational structure of the CSOs, has often been affected by some important socio-political issues of the country, such as the identity claims of Islamists and Kurds, among others. There is no doubt that EU-originated support for these types of CSOs has a profound impact on the overall democratisation process in Turkey, particularly regarding identity-based social and political claims. In other words, even if a direct contribution to the strengthening of civil society and the reinforcing of democratisation in this context is questionable, an overall input into both arenas has gradually become more salient.

The EU's engagement with CSOs in Turkey with politically toned religious or ethnic-based, nationalist (Kurdish) agendas has to be questioned in a context that requires a much more structured process with a clearer agenda. Such a questioning should certainly take the chief characteristics of a mature civil society into consideration, such as participation in the political and social development of the country, tolerance and rejection of violence, democratic governance, and independence from the state, private business and primordial structure (Heinrich 2007). In addition, the EU has often failed to recognise the weaknesses of the conventional types of civil society and professional organisations in Turkey, where such organisations are usually tied to the state through patronage networks. Indeed, among other things, clientelism is one negative legacy of the past which renders the development of well-functioning civic activities in the country more difficult. On the other hand, while foundation-type organisations, which are exclusive in terms of membership, representation and participation, are able to receive EU assistance, some large-sized membership organisations cannot get support from the EU, mostly because of their lack of capacity to establish a partnership with EU-based institutions. The competence of some Western-type, modern foundations justifies a role in addressing democratisation issues that often emerges as an issue of conditionality in the European integration settings. Some even make vital contributions to Turkey's steps toward European integration.

The uneven structures and activities of CSOs, combined with ineffective communication between these organisations and the EU institutions, has led to a process that is disrupted by various levels of uncertainties. For instance, organisations in civil society with the most to contribute in terms of their wide range of membership and grassroots character are typically marginalised because of their weak infrastructure and resources. The EU side has been hesitant about developing close relationships with certain CSOs, thereby opening itself up to accusations of bias. However, as noted earlier, one should not underestimate the EU's impact at different stages of the overall democratisation process in Turkey, nor should one underestimate its impact on CSOs. Despite its general success, such as in helping to secure a more rapid and transparent transition, problems of resource(s), strategy and coordination have persisted. Of course, other limiting factors have emerged, many related to the characteristics of CSOs, such as their administrative frameworks and their too limited or over-ambitious agendas. The involvement of civil society in European integration has also been hampered by legal problems that are a direct reflection of the uneasy state–civil-society relationship in the country, although in this area improvements have recently been made. These changes on the legal side demonstrate both the potential for transformation and the difficulty of reconciling different perspectives to provide a coherent focus on democratic consolidation and European integration.

What is often seen as a striking feature of the differing types of CSOs in Turkey is their membership profile: the more conventional, primordial or religious an organisation is, the larger its membership, and the higher its rates of participation are. Indeed, and probably more in the case of Western-type organisations and less in that of other groups, there is a small cadre of organisational activists who tend to emerge as civil society elites and whose enthusiasm for democracy may be a signal to the rest of the society. As participation is often viewed as the foundation of democratic settings, some likely reasons behind the relatively slow development of the qualities of civil society in Turkey should be carefully analysed, particularly given the rapid growth in numbers of CSOs. In the last decade, for instance, the number of associations registered in Turkey increased from around 61,000 in 2000 to nearly 71,000 in 2005, and to over 85,000 in 2010.[4] An understanding of the gap between resisting weak qualities and increasing quantities can be partly achieved by analysing the resources CSOs possess and the constraints they face, and partly by examining citizens' willingness or unwillingness to become active citizens and active civil society members. Beyond the participation problem that plagues Turkish civil society, the internal organisational problems of the country's CSOs are also significant, as they too lead to inefficiency. Together, inefficiency and the participation problem profoundly influence civil society's involvement in the processes of democratic consolidation and European integration. In order to provide a comprehensive picture of the role played by CSOs in the processes of democratisation and European integration, it is imperative to refer to the example of the Civil Society Development Programme (CSDP), which has been implemented by the EU in all candidate countries, including Turkey. In general this programme aims at making civil society more active and allowing CSOs to play a more effective role in the process of democratisation by enhancing their capacities.[5] As noted by a civil society member in Turkey, what is fairly clear from the case of CSDP is that the organisations of civil society in the country seem to be responsive enough to adopt the principles and approaches of the EU-originated civil society concept on a rhetorical level, but despite their use of fancy words pertaining to a Western-type of civil society, they often fail to implement such approaches in practice (Genel 2002, p. 305).

It is often seen that the concepts related to the enhancement of civil society in Turkey have been imported and are symbolically there, but in practice are not usually applied at the organisational level. For instance, these organisations are not very successful at achieving certain goals such as clearly advancing their own institutional changes, constantly promoting the idea of democracy and civil participation and consequently building up their civil discourses and activities for the development of a civil society movement in the country. It is rather in more practical areas that the interrelationship between the EU settings and the CSOs demonstrates some success. For example, limited success has been achieved in refining organisational structures and procedures, improving fundraising methods and strengthening the advocacy role.

In the process of European integration, it seems that two main lines of development cross each other: while some minor civil society groups in Turkey are becoming more particularistic and orthodox as they increasingly enjoy the relative freedom of the civil society arena, most of the other such groups are transforming from organisations based on traditional commitments, religious ties and other primordial forms of relations, into organisations based on universal values, which are shaped mainly by the claims of global civil society. These universal values are closely connected to changes taking place at the local level, exerting an influence on particularistic values. This results in flows of interaction between global civil society and grassroots initiatives. In this sense, CSOs at the national level play a crucial role in forming the link between the global and the local within a given nation-state. However, values promoted at the national level, shaped mainly by nation-state politics, can sharply contrast with those of a universalist and equally particularistic character. In fact, what happens in Turkey in this field is a clear reflection of the interplay between these universalist and particularistic views, as the articulation of CSOs occurs in the processes of democratic consolidation and European integration. This situation currently prevails in Turkey with respect to the discussion of the issues of democratic consolidation and European integration. Civil society organisations, represented mainly by associations and foundations as NGOs, are trying to bring closer together the national discourses and practices of democracy and the changes in the notion of democracy at the global level, with reference to European integration. It is the role of national CSOs in Turkey, then, to ease the tension with respect to the clash of values between universalist and particularistic levels as shaped by the institutions and processes of European integration. On a global scale, CSOs have started filling the gap between the top-down policies of the EU settings and the bottom-up demands of local grassroots activity. The three-tier relationship between the EU, civil society and the state is becoming increasingly complex due to the internal as well as external forces at play.

Concluding Remarks

Certainly, the relationship between the EU and Turkish civil society should be examined within a historical context highlighting the ongoing diffusion of Western democratic values and practices into the country since the late Ottoman and early republican eras. There is no doubt that Turkey's EU pre-accession process has brought a new tenor to the discourses and practices of the civil society arena in the country. Now, in the early twenty-first century, Turkey finds itself at a critical juncture in its democratic evolution. This turning point has been precipitated by Turkey's desire to enter the EU and the recent governing crisis that Turkey has faced, both of which have fuelled the need for the creation of a strong and democratic Turkey. Within this process, civil society in Turkey has been subject to radical changes as it has moved into a Europeanisation process. These changes reflect a growing interest in limiting state power, promoting an active citizenry and lobbying for European integration. It seems that, built upon different conditions and a different infrastructure, and developed through different political socialisation processes, various civil society actors are taking varying positions on the role of the state in state–society relations, hence on the nature of democratic state–society affairs and consequently on the idea of Europeanisation and on EU affairs. Overall, however, it is difficult to deny the efforts and work of civil society actors towards Turkey's integration into the EU settings. The consequences of these efforts and work, however, are open to debate in terms of their success and failures.

The discussion in this article has signalled the range of critical issues which need to be addressed in relation to the theoretical and practical issues of civil society in Turkey. As far as recent developments are concerned, very few seem unconvinced that civil society in Turkey plays a significant role in the country's democratic consolidation process as well as its steps towards integration into Europe. However, the involvement of CSOs in EU integration has been very much preoccupied with interest-based, pragmatic approaches, such as involvement through capacity-building, fund-demanding or -providing, or pro-EU campaigning. There is no doubt that this involvement should go beyond the questions of organisational strengthening or EU promoting. This involvement should transform the efforts of strengthening CSOs into contributing to the normative aspects of civil society in state–society relations in both Turkey and Europe. Along these lines, *firstly*, it appears that the agenda of strengthening a civil society would be most effectively executed by drawing on the idea of normatively developing civil society in Turkey, which requires a higher profile, more efficient operations and the coordinated skills and resources of a range of organisations both locally and abroad. *Secondly*, a project of this nature will provide the perfect opportunity for ordinary citizens and organisations of civil society to involve themselves in the work of institutions of European integration. Thus, it seems that the involvement of CSOs in the EU settings is crucial and symbiotic, where both stand to gain from collaborating on issues of European integration. In this context, a failure to fully empower civil society in Turkey as a key role-player should become a concern for the future. This concern should bolster the argument that democracy consolidation and European integration both presuppose the existence of a variety of elements that define the very quality of a country's system of governance. Obviously, one of these necessary elements is a well-functioning, high-quality civil society.

Notes

[1] For the detailed elaboration of the two CIVICUS-STEP projects conducted in 2006 and 2009 by TÜSEV, see http://www.step.org.tr.

[2] Figures presented here were compiled by the author through the examination of various documents and consultation with the officials of the Department of Associations of the Ministry of the Interior and the General Directorate of Foundations of the Prime Ministry.

[3] Information gained from Zeynep Özler of the IKV.

[4] These figures were compiled by the author from the Department of Associations of the Ministry of the Interior.

[5] This capacity-enhancing includes: (1) providing training for the managers of the CSOs to improve their abilities, (2) facilitating the CSOs' diversification of their funding base by providing training in fundraising and public relations, and (3) supporting them for (a) leadership development, (b) policy research and advocacy, (c) information access, use and dissemination, (d) building alliances, coalitions, networks, North–South partnership, and inter-sectoral partnership, and (e) financial sustainability.

References

Alemdar, Z. (2008) *Turkish Civil Society and the European Union: Domestic Politics through International Organisations*, Springer-Verlag, Berlin.

Bayraktar, D. (2009) *Crossing the Bridges: The Europeanisation of Women's NGOs in Turkey*, Institut D'Etudes Politiques de Paris, Paris.

Boztekin, N. (2004) *AB Uyum Süreci ve STK'lar* [EU Harmonisation Process and NGOs], Tarih Vakfı Yurt Yayınları, Istanbul.

Diez, T., Agnantopoulos, A. & Kaliber, A. (2005) 'File: Turkey, Europeanisation and civil society introduction', *South European Society and Politics*, vol. 10, no. 1, pp. 1–15.

Genel, S. (2002) 'NGOs as the link between state and society: women's community centers in southeast Turkey', PhD dissertation, Bilkent University, Ankara

Göksel, D. N. & Güneş, R. B. (2005) 'The role of CSOs in the European integration process: the Turkish experience', *South European Society and Politics*, vol. 10, no. 1, pp. 52–72.

Grugel, J. (1999) *Democracy without Borders*, Routledge, New York.

Heinrich, V. F. (2007) *CIVICUS, Global Survey of Civil Society, Vol. 1: Country Profiles*, Kumarian, Bloomfield.

İçduygu, A. (2008) 'The anatomy of civil society in Turkey: toward a transformation', in *Remaking Turkey*, ed. F. Keyman, Lexington, Lanham, MD, pp. 179–197.

Keyman, F. & İçduygu, A. (2003) 'Globalisation, civil society and citizenship in Turkey: actors, boundaries and discourses', *Citizenship Studies*, vol. 7, no. 2, pp. 219–234.

Knezović, S. (2009) 'EU's conditionality mechanism in South East Europe – lessons learned and challenges for the future, european perspectives', *Journal on European Perspectives of the Western Balkans*, vol. 1, no. 1, pp. 93–113.

Kubicek, P. (2005) 'The European Union and crossroads: democratisation in Turkey', *Turkish Studies*, vol. 6, no. 3, pp. 361–377.

Mahoney, C. (2004) 'The power of institutions: state and interest group activity in the European Union', *European Union Politics*, vol. 5, no. 4, pp. 441–461.

Mazey, S. & Richardson, J. J. (2006) 'Interest groups and EU policy making', in *European Power and Policy Making*, ed. J. J. Richardson, Routledge, Abingdon, pp. 248–268.

Öniş, Z. (2003) 'Domestic politics, international norms and challenges to the state: Turkey–EU relations in the post-Helsinki era', *Turkish Studies*, vol. 4, no. 1, pp. 9–34.

Özbudun, E. (2000) *Contemporary Turkish Politics*, Lynne Reinner, Boulder, CO.

Pope, P. (1997) *Turkey Unveiled*, John Murray, London.

Rumford, C. (2003) 'European civil society or transnational space? Conceptions of society in discourses of EU citizenship, governance and the democratic deficit: an emerging agenda', *European Journal of Social Theory*, vol. 6, no. 1, pp. 25–43.

Schimmelfenning, F. (2007) 'European regional organisation, political conditionality and democratic transformation in Eastern Europe', *East European Politics &Societies*, vol. 21, no. 1, pp. 126–141.

TÜSEV (2006) *Civil Society in Turkey: An Era of Transition. Index Country Report for Turkey*, Istanbul.

Uğur, M. & Canefe, N. (2004) *Turkey and European Integration*, Routledge, Abingdon.

Yerasimos, S. (2000) 'Civil society, Europe and Turkey', in *Civil Society in the Grip of Nationalism*, eds S. Yaresimos, G. Seufert & K. Vorhoff, Orient-Institut, Istanbul, pp. 11–24.

Ahmet İçduygu (PhD Australian National University) is a professor in the Department of International Relations of Koç University, Istanbul, where he also directs the Migration Research Program (MiReKoc). His research and teaching interests include policies and practices of international migration, citizenship, civil society and international organizations, and research methods in social sciences. Along with numerous articles and book chapters on these topics, he has two co-edited books: *Citizenship in a Global World: European Questions and Turkish Experiences* (Routledge, London, 2005, with E. F. Keyman) and *Land of Diverse Migrations: Challenges of Emigration and Immigration in Turkey* (Bilgi University Press, Istanbul, 2009, with K. Kirişçi).

The Turkish Parliamentary Elite and the EU: Mapping Attitudes towards the European Union

Sait Akşit, Özgehan Şenyuva and Işık Gürleyen

This study aims to map out the opinions and attitudes of the Turkish parliamentary elite regarding Turkey's membership of the European Union in general and the future of Europe in particular. The parliamentary elite group consists of political party representatives present in the current Turkish Grand National Assembly. The study uses the findings of the Turkish Elite Survey 2009 conducted by the Center for European Studies, Middle East Technical University. The article argues that while Turkish parliamentarians support Turkey's entry into the EU, particularly on security grounds, there are significant signs of lack of trust in EU institutions.

Turkey's longstanding relationship with the EU gained momentum following the December 1999 European Union (EU) Helsinki Summit decision to grant Turkey the status of a candidate state. In the aftermath of this summit, the political reforms required to meet the membership conditions of the EU topped the agenda of Turkish politics. Turkey initiated a series of constitutional and legal amendments with the aim of fulfilling the requirements of membership. The political reform process took on a new phase with the start of the negotiations on 3 October 2005 and is still continuing even though its pace has slowed down. This foreign policy priority of Turkey, first and foremost, involves the parliamentary elite—the members of the Turkish Grand National Assembly (Türkiye Büyük Millet Meclisi—TBMM)—who play a significant role as the legislative power in the EU-related reform process.

In spite of the fact that European integration is often described as an elite-driven process, the elite dimension is strikingly under-researched; in particular, there is a lack of systematic data on parliamentary elites. The few political elite studies on

Turkey–EU relations have mostly been based on individual open-ended interviews, or have primarily concentrated on party positions towards the EU with an inherent assumption that Turkish members of parliament (MPs) in actual fact assume positions identical to their parties (see, for instance, Avcı 2006; Gürleyen 2008; Öniş 2009). There is a shortage of studies that take the individual MPs as the main unit of analysis. An important exception that provides an overview with replicable and structured data is the pioneering study by McLaren and Müftüler-Baç (2003) which analysed the perceptions on EU membership of Turkish MPs in 2002. With the 2002 elections, a new parliamentary elite has emerged (Sayarı & Hasanov 2008), but a systematic study on the perceptions of this new elite has not been carried out. Hence, this study aims to fill the gap in the Turkey–EU literature on the approaches of the parliamentary elite towards the EU.

This article provides a systematic descriptive analysis of the results of the *Turkish Elite Survey 2009*[1] by focusing on the attitudes of the Turkish parliamentary elites regarding Turkey's membership of the European Union in general and the future of Europe in particular. Since the data are retrieved from one wave of interviews, this study will remain mainly an exploration rather than a far-reaching analysis. The parliamentary elite were interviewed in order to address the following questions: What are the main characteristics of the attitudes of the Turkish political elite towards the issue of EU membership? How do the Turkish political elite perceive the future of Europe (mainly in terms of further integration and EU competences on key issues)?

The article starts with a brief theoretical background, examining the discussion of the role of elites in the foreign policy formation process in general. This section in particular addresses the political elite as a major driving force for European integration and stresses the role of the political elite in Turkey's ongoing negotiations for EU membership. The literature review is followed by a description of the survey sample and methodology. The following two sections of the article provide the data analysis: the first part focuses on the general attitudes of MPs towards the EU and Turkey's membership, while the second focuses on their views on the future of the EU.

The Political Elite and Turkey's EU membership

The role of elites in the foreign-policy-making process has long been debated in international relations (IR) literature. On the one hand, traditional IR scholars question the consideration of elites as a unit of analysis, except for the state elite; others, following the liberal approach, focus more on elite attitudes. The motivations of elites have been explored by putting forward either utilitarian concerns, which signify cost–benefit calculations of material interests such as economic and security interests, or ideational sources such as identity, universal norms and values (Holsti 2004; Goldstein & Keohane 1999).

European integration literature focuses essentially on elites, particularly on political elites, and this focus stems from the fact that the process has been driven by European elites, be they political, bureaucratic or societal (Haller 2008, p. 3; Bellamy & Warleigh

2001, p. 9). In this context, scholars have analysed the motivations, discourses and stances of elites in member states and/or candidate countries.

The attitudes of Turkish MPs towards Turkish membership of the EU are quite significant, particularly in the pre-accession phase. As a negotiating country, Turkey is obliged to undertake a large set of legal, technical and administrative changes. Despite the large scale of reforms already undertaken, the government needs to initiate another battery of legislative changes and obtain the approval of the TBMM to open further chapters or provisionally close the ongoing ones. The need for further reforms and legislative changes makes the Turkish parliament one of the most important actors in the membership process.

The importance of the elite as a major actor in Turkey–EU relations is firmly recognised in the literature. The reason for such a focus may be the fact that, since its inception in 1959, Turkey's membership process on both the EU and Turkish sides has been solely led by the political elite in a manner very detached from other segments of society. Nonetheless, the Turkey–EU literature is strikingly different from other case studies of European integration in terms of the lack of empirical-analytical analyses. While political elites are widely studied empirically in the broader European integration literature, it is a rather new tendency to analyse empirically the motivations/positions of Turkish elites in initiating the process. Since the 1990s, empirical analysis of the attitudes of elites in Turkey has been gradually growing.

The research on the Turkish elite shares similarities with the broader literature regarding the lack of attention paid to certain groups; for instance, the economic elite is a powerful but frequently neglected elite group in the European integration literature and also in the analyses of Turkey–EU relations.[2] In general, the support of economic elites is taken for granted because the EU provides ample opportunities for the business sector. While the cultural elite are rather neglected in the broader context, with the exception of the media elite, they are is particularly overlooked in the literature on Turkey.[3] Methodologically, it is a major weakness that a comparative perspective—comparing elites in different countries—is rarely employed in the analyses.[4] Furthermore, the relationships between different elite groups, on the one hand, and between elites and non-elites, on the other, have not received sufficient attention from scholars.[5] Above all, the fact that there are very few empirical analyses on the Turkish political elite is a remarkable weakness of the literature. As mentioned above, the study by McLaren and Müftüler-Baç (2003) is an exception in this regard. Since the latter, the only example until the present is the survey of the opposition Republican People's Party (Cumhuriyet Halk Partisi—CHP) deputies in 2005 (Gülmez 2008).

This study aims to contribute to the empirical work on the Turkish political elite with data obtained from interviews. Utilitarian and ideational sources of Turkish elite perceptions on Turkey–EU relations and the EU are identified using a structured questionnaire. It is hoped that outcomes of this study will also facilitate comparisons with the results of other surveys on the positions and attitudes of the parliamentary elite in Turkey and other European states.

Sample and Methodology

The findings of this study are based on the Turkish Elite Survey 2009[6] conducted in cooperation with the IntUne project[7] in order to create systematic and comparative data. The respondents consisted of political party representatives present in the current TBMM (formed after the 2007 elections). As part of the survey, 62 MPs—out of a total of 550 MPs in the TBMM—were interviewed in the period of June–December 2009. The interviews were conducted face to face, with a structured questionnaire based on close-ended questions. Each interview took on average 40 minutes. All analyses included in this article are given in valid percentages, calculated as a proportion of total valid answers, excluding 'Don't know' and 'Refusal'.

The sample of the 62 interviewed Turkish MPs was selected through quota sampling according to the methodology set by the IntUne project. The number of MPs from different parties reflected the distribution of seats among the parties in the assembly: 39 of our respondents were Justice and Development Party (Adalet ve Kalkınma Partisi—AKP) representatives, ten CHP, eight National Action Party (Milliyetçi Hareket Partisi—MHP), four Democratic Left Party (Demokratik Sol Parti—DSP) and one Democratic Society Party (Demoktratik Toplum Partisi—DTP). In the sample, the DSP was over-represented, as it had only eight seats in the TBMM at the time our survey was conducted. On the other hand, the DTP was under-represented, as its representation in the assembly amounted to 20 seats. We were able to interview only one DTP representative, due mainly to inability to contact members of that party, their refusal to be interviewed, or the judicial process that the party was going through: the DTP, which represents Kurdish voters, was banned by the Constitutional Court on 11 December 2009 and two of its MPs were expelled from parliament, subsequent to which the remaining party members established the Peace and Democracy Party (Barış ve Demokrasi Partisi—BDP).

Our sample took into account the gender balance in parliament (12.9 per cent of our respondents were female while the female representation in parliament was 8.85 per cent) and was representative in terms of age (the average age of the MPs in the TBMM was 54.3 and in our sample 53.2). The discussion below refers to the political elite in general, as the parliamentarians interviewed include 16 former ministers, former or present standing committee chairs/deputy chairs or chairs of international parliamentary groups. Twelve of this group of frontbenchers were AKP members, two MHP, one CHP and one DSP. Their average age was 56.75. In addition, 18 of the MPs we interviewed were deputy chairs or parliamentary assembly members. Thirteen of these MPs were AKP members, three CHP and two MHP. The average age of these respondents was 50.11. Given the small size of the sample, the deviations do not present problems with regard to representation. Thus, we did not weight the results.

Having the frontbencher MPs included in our sample resulted in a particular picture in terms of the basic characteristics of the respondents, particularly with regard to their level of education. Of the MPs in the TBMM 94.5 per cent held a university degree (Sayarı & Hasanov 2008, p. 354), yet the level of education of the MPs in our sample was higher than the average: 37 per cent of the respondents had a PhD degree, and 32 per cent had a master's degree. These figures indicate that the frontbench MPs are selected from among the better educated, who tend to be specialised and more experienced compared with other MPs.

General Attitudes and Ideas About the EU and Turkey's Membership

A major portion of the Turkish Elite Survey 2009 focused on opinions on the EU and Turkey's membership. The respondents were asked a large set of questions regarding the EU, its institutions, Turkish membership and policy-making. The results presented in this article focus on the three dimensions of Europeanness: the *emotive dimension*, level of attachment to country and Europe; the *cognitive-evaluative dimension*, the EU's structure and functioning and the progress and nature of Turkey's negotiations; and the *projective dimension*, the future of the EU and the role of Turkey in the future.[8] The main aim of this set of questions was to gain insights on the thoughts and motivations of the individuals responsible for making necessary legislative reforms and changes during accession negotiation as well as communicating these to the general public.

One of the important findings of the survey was the unified support for Turkey's membership of the EU among the MPs. When asked if Turkey's membership in the EU would be 'a good thing' or a 'bad thing', an overwhelming majority of the MPs (98.4 per cent) stated that it would be a 'good thing' while only one respondent believed it would be 'neither a good nor a bad thing'. When asked to evaluate if 'Turkey would benefit from membership', again a similar majority (96.8 per cent) indicated that Turkey would benefit from eventual membership, while only 3.2 per cent believed Turkey would not benefit. These two indicators show us that among the MPs there is a high level of support on the issue of Turkey's membership of the EU, regardless of individual differences. This also points to a broad consensus among the MPs from the governing and the opposition parties.

When asked how they perceived the EU, a large majority of MPs responded that they have a 'positive' image of the EU: 9.8 per cent have a 'strongly positive' image and 68.9 per cent have a 'somewhat positive' image. Only 11.5 per cent of the MPs interviewed have a 'somewhat negative' image of the EU and 9.8 per cent have neither a positive nor a negative image.

Despite the clear support for Turkey's membership of the EU and the rather positive image of the EU, our survey revealed certain problematic issues among the attitudes of the MPs. One of the important dimensions is the issue of trust/distrust in EU institutions, which signifies both utilitarian and ideational sources of elite attitudes. The positive approach of Turkish MPs does not translate into a feeling of trust in European institutions (Table 1). This attitude towards European institutions is somewhat negative when compared with EU member states considered by the IntUne project. On a 0–10 scale, 10 being the highest level of trust, the trust in the European Commission of the Turkish MPs interviewed is 5.04 against an average of 5.90 in South European member states (SEU4) (Italy: 5.5; Portugal: 5.9; Greece: 6.0; Spain: 6.2) and

TURKEY AND THE EU: ACCESSION AND REFORM

Table 1 Level of Trust in EU Institutions (0–10 scale)

	N	Mean	Standard deviation
The European Commission	62	5.04	1.86
The European Parliament	62	4.33	1.71
The European Union Council	62	4.82	1.54

Source: Turkish Elite Survey 2009.

5.6 for the EU17[9]; with regard to trust in the European Parliament (EP) it is 4.33 points compared with 6.4 in the SEU4 and 6.1 in the EU17; and as far as trust in the European Union Council is concerned it is 4.82 points against 6.0 in the SEU4 and 5.8 in the EU17 (See Conti, Cotta & de Almeida 2010, p. 128).

Previous studies argue that it is plausible that institutions, their functioning and individuals' evaluation of their performance shape the development of identifications and level of support (Brewer, Hermann & Risse 2004). The negative attitude of our respondents towards the EP was not surprising given the critical approach of the EP towards Turkey. Various EP reports have widely criticised Turkey on the issues of democracy and human rights; what is more, some of the issues brought forward by the EP are perceived in Turkey as attempts to create new conditions on the route to membership, leading to widespread suspicion of EU institutions among Turkish parliamentarians.

This low level of trust in EU institutions has potential importance in our analysis, for the pace and success of the ongoing negotiations. If the parliamentary elite harbour certain question marks about the nature of EU institutions' decisions, it may prove highly problematic for the European Commission to make reform demands in the accession process. This low level of trust may also stem from the constant mixed signals from the EU regarding Turkey's membership, and from the increasing debate on 'privileged partnership'.

The other issue that appeared along with the low level of trust was the widespread belief that Turkey's interests are not being taken into account by the decision-makers within the EU. The majority of Turkish parliamentarians (strongly agree: 22.6 per cent; agree somewhat: 62.9) felt that those who make decisions at the EU level did not take Turkey's interests into account. Only 14.5 per cent of the respondents disagreed with such a statement. This is contradictory to the overall supportive stance of elites towards Turkey's EU membership.

Our survey also revealed that among the MPs there is a strong feeling of 'being ignored' in their relations with decision-makers within the EU. When presented with the statement, 'Decision makers in the EU do not take into account what people like me think,' 70 per cent of the respondents agreed (strongly agree + agree somewhat). While this perceived feeling of exclusion seems to be a cross-party issue, it appears to be stronger among the MPs from the opposition parties. Ninety per cent of the MPs interviewed from the main opposition party, CHP, agreed with the statement, while the agreement rate fell to 56 per cent among the MPs from the governing party.

In addition to the questions on the EU and its institutions, we also included a battery of questions on the issues of identity and belonging. A longstanding assumption in the research on European support accepts that elites tend to be more European than the masses (Hooghe 2003). When asked how they would define themselves primarily, Turkish MPs overwhelmingly identified themselves with nationality (Figure 1). While 35.5 per cent identified themselves as Turkish only, 55 per cent of the respondents indicated that they see themselves primarily as Turkish and then as European. While only 6.5 per cent of the interviewed MPs identified themselves primarily as European and later Turkish, none of the respondents declared 'European only' as their main personal identification.

The self-definition of the respondents was also confirmed by their degree of identification with Turkey as well as the EU. The respondents predominantly identified themselves with nationality, and the low level of attachment to the EU became more apparent with the answers to these questions. Of the Turkish parliamentarians 98.4 per cent stated that they feel attached to Turkey, in comparison with 57.6 per cent who feel attached to the EU. While there is only one MP who feels 'not very attached' to Turkey, almost 40 per cent of the respondents do not feel attached to the EU. Five per cent of the participating MPs refused to answer a question on attachment to the EU.

As our analysis reveals, Turkish MPs have a low level of attachment to the EU, corresponding to a low level of trust in EU institutions. This result is consistent with Roux and Verzichelli's assumption that 'a very high degree of identification with the

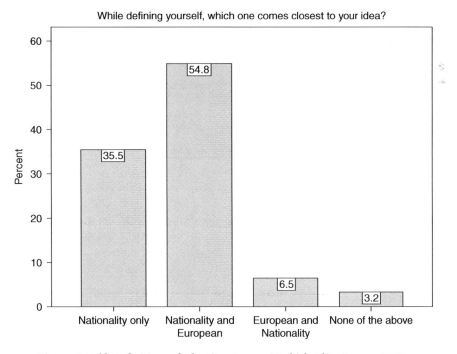

Figure 1 Self-Definition of Identity. *Source:* Turkish Elite Survey 2009.

supranational polity should correspond to a high degree of trust in EU institutions' (Roux & Verzichelli 2010, p. 14).

A striking outcome of our analysis was the threat perception among Turkish parliamentarians. A general assumption is that threat is a relevant factor for collective identity building, and Lauren McLaren (2006) argues that a perceived cultural threat results in decrease in support for further European integration. Other studies (Carey 2002) have shown that this is particularly true for public opinion. Our respondents do not perceive the EU as a danger to the cultural integrity of Turkey: 97 per cent disagree (disagree somewhat + strongly disagree) with the idea that the EU poses a threat, whereas only three per cent agree somewhat. This outcome indicates that the reasons for the low level of trust in the EU institutions and low level of attachment to the EU should be sought elsewhere than in a perceived threat to cultural integrity.

All the general perceptions regarding the institutions and policies of the EU are intimately linked with the level of knowledge of the respondents. The survey also included a self-assessment question on one's level of knowledge of the EU, its institutions and its policies. On a 0–10 scale, with 10 representing the highest level of knowledge, the mean score of the MPs' responses was rather high: 6.9, with a standard deviation of 1.67.

Turkish Parliamentarians and the Future of EU–Turkey Relations

Each enlargement round of the EU has brought about changes within the EU in terms of redefining political dynamics, institutional structure and policy priorities. Considering the size and potential weight of Turkey, its own characteristics and priorities will be of utmost importance for the EU in the event of membership, especially given the provisions of the Lisbon Treaty.[10] According to article 2 of the Lisbon Treaty, the standard system of voting in the Council of Ministers will be 'Qualified majority voting' (QMV), based on the principle of double majority. This indicates that any decision will need the support of 55 per cent of the member states (currently 15 out of 27 EU countries), representing a minimum of 65 per cent of the EU's population. This point is important given the population of Turkey, which is more than 70 million as of 2011. The same article in Lisbon Treaty also increased the number of policy areas where co-decision procedure will be applied, increasing the weight of the EP, where Turkey will also have a sizeable number of members owing to its population. However, while there is a multiplicity of surveys dealing with this question at the public level, the perceptions of the elite on the future of the EU are often neglected. We believe that the policy priorities of Turkey's leading elite, as well as their opinions on the structure, policies and characteristics of the EU, deserve special attention for the future dynamics of the EU. As such, Turkey's eventual membership in relation to the future of the EU was an important part of our survey, within which a detailed series of questions aimed to elicit the preferences and policy choices of Turkish parliamentarians.

One of the important findings of the survey concerned the Turkish parliamentarians' strong support for further European unification. When asked if the level of integration has gone too far or should be further strengthened, on a 0–10 scale with 0 representing

'Unification has gone too far' and 10 representing 'Unification should be strengthened', the mean score of the responses came out as 7.05 with a standard deviation of 2.5. This support for further unification was also reflected in opinions on the institutions and policies of the EU: 93.4 per cent of the MPs agreed that the EU needs a common constitution and 77 per cent of them were in favour of having a president of the EU. Turkish parliamentarians also tended to support the European Commission becoming the true government of the EU: 64.5 per cent of the MPs agreed (strongly agree + agree somewhat) with the statement on the European Commission, while 30 per cent of the respondents disagreed (disagree strongly + disagree somewhat).

In line with utilitarian perspectives of integration, we asked questions relating to the perceived material benefits of membership. The 'main purpose of the EU' emerged as a polarising issue among the Turkish MPs. When they were asked whether the main purpose of the EU should be to make the European economy *more competitive* or to provide better *social security* for citizens, their responses were evenly distributed. The percentage of the MPs arguing for a more competitive EU (42.9 per cent) was slightly higher than the percentage of the MPs supporting the idea of a social Europe (35.7 per cent). Although it was not spelled out as an option, 21.4 per cent of the respondents chose both.

Turkish MPs were generally more enthusiastic about the notion of security— compared with other dimensions of integration—as a defining feature of the European integration process. On the question of a European army, they were supportive: 75.8 per cent of the MPs expressed that they would like to see both a national and a European army, while 16.1 per cent stated that they supported the existence of a national army only. Those who said that there should only be a European army and no national armies were only 6.5 per cent of the respondents. The notion of European integration also received support on the issue of European security. When asked which authority should be responsible for providing European security, 51.6 per cent named the EU, compared with 22.6 per cent who named the North Atlantic Treaty Organisation (NATO).

However, Turkish parliamentarians tended to be less enthusiastic about the delegation of authority when it comes to security policy. Only 27.4 per cent of the MPs stated that decisions regarding security policy should be taken at the EU level when Turkey becomes a member. On the other hand, almost half of the respondents (48.5 per cent) stated a preference for keeping security-policy-making at the national level. The ratio of MPs who think that there should be close cooperation, and that security policy should be made at both national and EU levels, was only 21 per cent. This indicates that, despite strongly supporting a European security policy and favouring the establishment of a European army that would coexist with the national army, Turkish parliamentarians are very reluctant to delegate policy-making on security issues. These results are also supported by Turkish resistance to the establishment of a full-fledged relationship between the EU and NATO. Turkey's elite would like to see more joint initiatives, but is not willing to support any integration process that would exclude Turkey from decision-making.[11]

The parliamentary elites were more likely to delegate authority on issues they consider 'soft', such as environment and energy policies. While 42 per cent of the respondents thought that energy policy should be handled at the EU level when Turkey becomes a member, 16.1 per cent believed energy policy should be dealt with at both the national and the EU levels. The preference for EU policy-making was even clearer on environmental policy: 60 per cent of the MPs believed the EU should be in charge, and 11.3 per cent argued that authority should be assigned to both national and EU levels.

Where Do We Go from Here?

The descriptive analyses presented above point to certain conclusions and potential hypotheses for future research. To begin with, the support for the EU among Turkish parliamentarians from both the government and the opposition is strong. Similarly, the EU has a rather positive image in the eyes of the MPs, and they believe that Turkey would benefit from being an EU member.

In contrast to the strong support for membership, the MPs appear to have a low level of trust in the EU and its institutions. The European Commission enjoys the highest level of trust, whereas the EP is the least-trusted institution. The low level of trust may prove to have serious repercussions in the formulation of necessary legislation during the accession negotiations; without the necessary credibility, the EU institutions are very likely to face serious opposition on certain issues. One potential explanation for the low level of trust was reflected in the widespread agreement among the MPs that Turkey's interests were being ignored by European decision-makers. This belief suggests that in their dealings with the EU Turkish parliamentarians have a mindset of a win–lose situation. Such a widespread low level of trust among the political elite is an important issue that deserves further investigation and analysis.

Our survey, moreover, demonstrated that among Turkish parliamentarians national identity and attachment to nationality are very strong and European identity and European attachment are much weaker. This may prove to be an important factor in further analysis of motivations and determinants of policy actions in the course of Turkey–EU relations. In spite of the strong national identity and attachment, members of the Turkish parliament do not perceive the EU and Turkey's membership as a potential threat to Turkish cultural integrity.

Security matters appeared to be a policy area on which it may prove easier for the Turkish and European sides to cooperate. Taking into consideration the enthusiasm of Turkish parliamentarians for further European unification, and especially the formation of a European security structure as well as a European army, one may argue that successful security cooperation may have a spillover effect on other dimensions of Turkey–EU relations.

When considered with reference to the three dimensions of Europeanness, it seems that, while on the *projective dimension* there is strong enthusiasm for future integration, there are variations in the *emotive dimension*, with low levels of attachment to Europe, and a low level of identification and low scores on the *cognitive-evaluative dimension*, particularly on the issue of trust.

Finally, five issues stand out as areas that may deserve further research and analysis. The first possible research area is the changes over time in the opinions and attitudes of Turkish parliamentarians on the European issues, and how they have been affected by different actors and dynamics involved in the accession process. A second area is the relationship between individual MPs and party structure/-hierarchy. By outlining the interaction between the party leadership and individual MPs, and focusing on the inner party mechanisms, one could find out how many of the individual MPs' attitudes are reflected in their actions. Another area of investigation is the convergence and divergence between elite and public opinion. A fourth area is the detailed analysis of the attitudes towards EU issues of various Turkish elites—political, economic and social. Important issues, such as whether there is consensus or divergence among different elites, and the causes of and motivations for any divergence should be analysed. A final potential research area is applying the theoretical dimension of elite opinions and attitudes to elite research in Turkey.

Turkish parliamentarians certainly take into account cost–benefit considerations besides evaluating Turkey's accession process as one that strengthens democratic norms and values as well as freedoms and liberties in Turkey. This duality deserves further attention and may also be approached with an analysis of diffuse versus specific support.[12]

Notes

[1] The research was funded by a grant from the project on Strengthening and Integrating Academic Networks (SInAN) financed by the Central Finance and Contracts Unit of the Republic of Turkey under the 'Promotion of Civil Society Dialogue between the EU and Turkey: Universities Grant Scheme' (TR0604.01-03/092).

[2] Two early examples of empirical analyses regarding economic elites are Keyman (2001) and Öniş and Türem (2001).

[3] An important exception is the article by Mclaren (2000).

[4] Among the few exceptions are Öniş (2004), Lundgren (2006), Verney (2007) and Gürleyen and Tamvaki (2008).

[5] See Gürleyen's (2008) comparison of 12 Turkish actors with respect to their attitudes towards European integration and EU's political conditionality.

[6] The survey was constructed to cover different elite groups. For more information on the Turkish Elite Survey see Akşit, Şenyuva and Üstün (2009).

[7] The IntUne project (Integrated and United? A Quest for Citizenship in an Ever Closer Europe) financed by the Sixth Framework Programme of the EU, Priority 7, Citizens and Governance in a Knowledge Based Society (CIT3-CT-2005-513421) was conducted in 19 countries including Turkey. For some of the first results of the IntUne project see the special issue of *South European Society and Politics* on 'European Citizenship in the Eyes of National Elites: A South European View', vol. 15, no. 1, 2010.

[8] The three dimensions of Europeanness are taken from IntUne.

[9] EU17 refers to EU member states where the IntUne survey was conducted, namely, Austria, Belgium, Czech Republic, Denmark, Estonia, France, Germany, Greece, Hungary, Italy, Lithuania, Poland, Portugal, Slovakia, Spain, United Kingdom, and Bulgaria.

TURKEY AND THE EU: ACCESSION AND REFORM

[10] See the Treaty of Lisbon amending the Treaty on European Union and the Treaty establishing the European Community, 2007/C 306/01. Official Journal of the European Union, C 306, v 50, 17 December 2007.

[11] For a detailed analysis of Turkish security culture and Turkey–EU relations on security matters from a historical perspective, see Üstün (2010).

[12] For a detailed analysis of diffuse versus specific support, see Şenyuva (2008).

References

Akşit, S., Şenyuva, Ö. & Üstün, Ç. (2009) *MYTHS AND ELITES, Turkish Elite Survey 2009: Initial Findings*, Centre for European Studies, Middle East Technical University, Ankara.

Avcı, G. (2006) 'Turkey's EU politics: consolidating democracy through enlargement', in *Questioning EU Enlargement: Europe in Search of Identity*, ed. H. Sjursen, Routledge, Abingdon and New York, pp. 62–77.

Bellamy, R. & Warleigh, A. (2001) *Citizenship and Governance in the European Union*, Continuum International, London.

Brewer, M., Hermann, R. & Risse, T. (eds) (2004) *Identities in Europe and the Institutions of the European Union*, Rowman & Littlefield, Lanham, MD.

Carey, S. (2002) 'Undivided loyalties. Is national identity an obstacle to European integration?', *European Union Politics*, vol. 3, no. 4, pp. 387–413.

Conti, N., Cottta, M. & de Almeida, P. T. (2010) 'Southern Europe: a distinctive and more pro-European region in the EU?', *South European Society and Politics*, vol. 15, no. 1, pp. 121–142.

Goldstein, J. & Keohane, R. (1999) 'Ideas and foreign policy', in *International Relations Theory*, eds P. R. Viotti & M. V. Kauppi, Allyn & Bacon, London, pp. 297–306.

Gülmez, S. B. (2008) 'The EU policy of the Republican People's Party: an inquiry on the opposition party and Euro-skepticism in Turkey', *Turkish Studies*, vol. 9, no. 3, pp. 423–436.

Gürleyen, I. (2008) *Impact of the European Union on Turkey's Democracy: Turkish Elite Attitudes towards the EU and Democratization*, VDM, Berlin.

Gürleyen, I. & Tamvaki, D. (2008) 'A promising comparison: Greek and Turkish elite attitudes to European integration', in *Turkey–European Union Relations: Dilemmas, Opportunities, and Constraints*, eds M. Müftüler-Baç & Y. A. Stivachtis, Rowman & Littlefield, Lexington Books, Lanham, MD, pp. 257–278.

Haller, M. (2008) *European Integration as an Elite Process: The Failure of a Dream?* Routledge, Abingdon and New York.

Hooghe, L. (2003) 'Europe divided? Elites vs. public opinion on European integration', *European Union Politics*, vol. 4, no. 3, pp. 281–304.

Holsti, O. (2004) *Public Opinion and American Foreign Policy*, University of Michigan Press, Ann Arbor.

Keyman, F. (2001) 'Cultural globalization and Turkey: actors, discourses, strategies', EUI Working Papers, Robert Schuman Center, no: 38, EUI, Florence.

Lundgren, A. (2006) 'The case of Turkey: are some candidates more European than others?', in *Questioning EU Enlargement: Europe in Search of Identity*, ed. H. Sjursen, Routledge, Abingdon and New York, pp. 121–141.

Mclaren, L. (2000) 'Turkey's eventual membership in the EU: Turkish elite perspectives on the issue', *Journal of Common Market Studies*, vol. 38, no. 1, pp. 117–129.

McLaren, L. (2006) *Identity, Interests and Attitudes to European Integration*, Palgrave Macmillan, Basingstoke.

McLaren, L. M. & Müftüler-Baç, M. (2003) 'Turkish parliamentarians' perspectives on Turkey's relations with the European Union', *Turkish Studies*, vol. 4, no. 1, pp. 195–218.

Öniş, Z. (2004) 'Diverse but converging paths to EU membership: Poland and Turkey in comparative perspective', *East European Politics & Societies*, vol. 18, no. 3, pp. 481–512.

TURKEY AND THE EU: ACCESSION AND REFORM

Öniş, Z. (2009) 'Contesting for the "center": domestic politics, identity conflicts and the controversy over EU membership in Turkey', Bilgi University European Institute Working Paper No. 2 EU/2/2010, Istanbul, available online at: http://eu.bilgi.edu.tr/docs/working%20paper2_101209.pdf

Öniş, Z. & Türem, U. (2001) 'Business, globalization and democracy: a comparative analysis of Turkish business associations', *Turkish Studies*, vol. 2, no. 2, pp. 94–120.

Roux, C. & Verzichelli, L. (2010) 'Italy: still a pro-European, but not a fully Europeanised elite?', *South European Society and Politics*, vol. 15, no. 1, pp. 11–33.

Sayarı, S. & Hasanov, A. (2008) 'The 2007 elections and parliamentary elites in Turkey: the emergence of a new political class?', *Turkish Studies*, vol. 9, no. 2, pp. 345–361.

Şenyuva, Ö. (2008) *Public Support for European Integration and Public Support for Turkish Membership*, Ankara University Press, Ankara.

Üstün, Ç. (2010) *Turkey and European Security Defence Policy: Compatibility and Security Cultures in a Globalised World*, I.B. Tauris, London.

Verney, S. (2007) 'The dynamics of EU accession: Turkish travails in comparative perspective', *Journal of Southern Europe and the Balkans*, vol. 9, no. 3, pp. 307–322.

Sait Akşit (PhD Middle East Technical University) is an assistant professor at the Department of International Relations at Gediz University, İzmir, Turkey. His main research interests are economic and political transformations in Eastern Europe and the Balkans, Turkish foreign policy, EU enlargement and Cyprus. He was one of the coordinators of the Turkish Elite Survey 2009. His most recent publications include an edited book, *Turkey Watch: EU Member States' Perceptions on Turkey's Accession to the EU* (Zeplin İletişim, Ankara, 2009, coedited with Ö. Şenyuva and Ç. Üstün).

Işık Gürleyen (PhD University of Siena) is an assistant professor at the Department of International Relations and the EU at Izmir University of Economics, Turkey. Her research interests include European integration, Turkey–EU relations, democratisation and dynamics of regime change. Her latest publications include an edited book entitled *International Relations: Textbook for High Schools* (MEB, Ankara, forthcoming in 2011). She has written a book on the *Impact of EU on Turkey's Democracy: Elite Attitudes towards the EU and Democratization* (VDM, Berlin, 2008).

Özgehan Şenyuva (PhD University of Siena) is an assistant professor in the Department of International Relations and researcher in the Center for European Studies at the Middle East Technical University, Ankara, Turkey. He mainly works on public and elite opinion and the EU. He was one of the coordinators of the Turkish Elite Survey 2009. His most recent works include 'Nationalism, Europeanization and football: Turkish fandom transformed?', in *Football, Europe et regulations* (co-authored with T. Bora, edited by G. Robin, Presses Universitaires du Septentrion, Paris, 2011, pp. 35–52) and *Turkey Watch: EU Member States' Perceptions on Turkey's Accession to the EU* (Zeplin, Ankara, 2009, coedited with S. Akşit and Ç. Üstün).

The Justice and Development Party and the EU: Political Pragmatism in a Changing Environment

Gamze Avcı

The article focuses on the Justice and Development Party (Adalet ve Kalkınma Partisi, AKP) and assesses whether the AKP has given up on Turkey's European Union (EU) membership goal since the beginning of negotiations in 2005. The article first reviews the AKP's EU policy, and then analyses shifts in the domestic and institutional contexts of cooperation and their effects on the AKP's EU policy preferences and policy action in the form of reforms. The article concludes with the observation that the AKP has reverted to a 'passive activism' in its approach to the EU due to the high cost of passing high-stake reforms.

Since 1999, and particularly since the election of Recep Tayyip Erdoğan's Justice and Development Party (AKP, Adalet ve Kalkınma Partisi), a centre-right Islamist party, in November 2002, there have been far-reaching political reforms in Turkey. The European Union (EU) goal has been very important in sustaining these reforms and uniting different groups around reform, yet since 2005 the reforms have slowed down and, increasingly, there seem to be problems and obstacles along the way. At this point, reforms are not complete and it appears that there are persistent bottlenecks in the EU integration process. The general feeling is that the AKP is exhibiting less of a commitment to Europeanisation and has shifted to a so-called soft Euro-Asianism (Öniş & Yılmaz 2009). This essay will focus on the AKP and evaluate the claim that the party halted or reversed its EU course with the beginning of negotiations in 2005. The paper will first briefly review the literature on the AKP's EU policy and discuss relevant aspects of scholarly works on EU enlargement. It will then employ an institutional analysis and focus on shifts in the domestic and institutional contexts of cooperation and their effects on the AKP's EU policy preferences and policy action in the form of reforms.

The AKP and the EU

Scholars frequently label the AKP party or the AKP leadership as pragmatic (Çavdar 2006; Doğan 2005; Dağı 2008; Öniş & Keyman 2003; Göl 2009), and this trait also defines the AKP's attitude towards the EU. For the AKP leadership, the pursuit of EU membership is a useful way of staying away from conflict, staying in power and carrying out their declared political programme (Doğan 2005, p. 430). Accordingly, the party pursues a 'democratisation via Europeanisation' strategy that de-emphasises ideology and focuses on Turkey's project as one that is 'above politics' (Çınar 2006, p. 471). More specifically, it has been argued that the AKP is engaged in some sort of two-level game: it uses and strives for accomplishments at the EU level to secure its position domestically. The AKP draws on the EU to 'domesticate and force not only the state but also the anti-systemic actors to change their perceptions and strategies and to take on EU norms as the point of reference to create a new social contract in Turkey' (Yavuz 2006, p. 3). This is considered a significant break with the past of pro-Islamic movements. The 'rethinking' process of the AKP is tied to the logic that the party aims 'to cooperate with global forces to break the resistance of the bureaucratic and ideological centres' (Dağı 2006, pp. 92–94). However, since 2005, the EU has increasingly ceased to function as an empowering tool and no longer provides an 'opportunity space" for the AKP (Duran 2007, pp. 81–89). Evaluating the shift in 2005, some have even argued that the AKP actually did not really ever use the EU for tactical purposes and that it lacks a practical democratisation agenda independent of EU membership requirements (Çınar 2007).

The argument that the AKP is using the EU for domestic gains matches Europeanisation studies that concentrate on EU conditionality. The latter is extensively discussed in the context of the EU accession processes in Central and Eastern Europe (Dimitrova 2005; Grabbe 2006; Hughes, Sasse & Gordon 2004; Pridham 2005; Schimmelfennig & Sedelmeier 2005; Vachudova 2005). These studies argue that EU conditionality has spread because it opens windows of opportunity for policy reform for domestic actors by decreasing the political costs of controversial reforms. The rationalist institutionalist branch of the literature, in particular, suggests that candidate country governments adopt EU rules if the benefits of the EU rewards exceed the domestic adoption costs. The EU's 'conditionality' mechanism offers rational incentives for domestic actors to undertake reforms in expectation of the credible perspective of EU membership (Schimmelfennig & Sedelmeier 2005; Vachudova 2005). The studies point out that the effectiveness of EU conditionality differs across countries and issues, but that there are certain factors that are crucial for the success of conditionality. Most notably, two factors are singled out: a credible membership perspective offered as the key reward by the EU, and domestic adjustment costs that are not excessively high for governments and do not endanger their power base (Schimmelfennig & Sedelmeier 2005).

The credibility issue is a longstanding factor in Turkish–EU relations. Mehmet Uğur (1999), in his pioneering work, claims that Turkey's European focus is based on a non-credible commitment and that the EU has failed to become a real anchor for Turkey's policy reform. Although Uğur's argument explains a large part of Turkish–EU relations, it does not account for the progress during Turkey's EU candidacy period. Endogenous factors in Turkish–EU relations have been discussed as 'facilitators' during the candidacy process (Tocci 2005) but so far not much has been written about the role of shifts in institutions or domestic costs of reform that can empower or constrain political actors involved in EU reform in Turkey.

The Challenge of 'Negotiating'

Turkey has been a candidate for EU membership since 1999 and has been negotiating with the EU since 2005. The former period represents a high-incentive and -credibility stage, whereas the latter has been more of a low-incentive and -credibility period. This can be attributed to the specific technical characteristics of the two periods, the flow of negotiations, but also Turkey-related politics in the EU and, in particular, in some member states. A particularly harmful development has been that during the negotiations period a weakness in EU commitment (which relates to the lingering fundamental question of whether Turkey could ever actually become a member of the EU) has become a major issue again. Specifically, the discussions about offering Turkey a privileged partnership rather than full membership have diminished the credibility of EU membership. This is rather different from the Central and East European (CEE) enlargement experience, where the credibility of the threat of exclusion from membership *decreased* during negotiations (Dimitrova 2005, emphasis added).

From an institutional perspective, the candidacy as well as the negotiations periods have been marked by conditionality: the candidate does its homework and in return, ideally, moves on to the next stage. In both there is a clear asymmetry of power between the applicants and the EU, which gives the EU coercive routes of influence in the applicants' domestic policy-making processes. At the heart of the candidacy are the 'Copenhagen criteria' – especially the political ones – and if these political criteria are fulfilled the EU will consider beginning negotiations with the candidate. These political criteria were decided in Copenhagen in 1993, and they state that membership requires that a candidate country has achieved stability of institutions guaranteeing democracy, the rule of law, human rights and respect for and protection of minorities.[1] They are requirements that also apply to the Turkish case. Turkey's candidacy began in 1999 with the Helsinki Summit and 'ended' in 2004 when negotiations began. During this candidacy, the prospect of opening negotiations (with an unambiguous membership perspective) with the EU was an important incentive for the AKP to accomplish the necessary reforms. This prospect was helped by a number of factors. After Helsinki, consensus in Turkey on joining the EU was broad and the project enjoyed great popularity among all social groups, so the government was able to push through massive reforms. The decision to open negotiations was based on the decision of the European Council which would act upon the basis. The role of the Commission was not questioned by either side and the reports were judged to be fair and precise. The unprecedented amount of reforms in Turkey and the Commission's report and recommendation made it difficult for the European Council to claim that the requirements had not been fulfilled and to withhold negotiations. Ultimately, in December 2004, the European Council decided to open accession negotiations with Turkey, without delay.

However, on 3 October 2005, the EU Council in its 'Negotiating Framework' gave the first sign of 'weak commitment' through its decision to include an understanding that the upcoming negotiations would be open-ended, meaning eventual full membership could not be guaranteed. This complicated the already difficult nature of negotiations. Negotiations are more strenuous because, unlike the candidacy period, there is no possibility for package deals to be struck at intergovernmental conferences where sceptics can be won over. Furthermore, unanimity prevails at all levels with regard to whether and, if so, when enlargement negotiations are opened or closed on individual chapters. All member states have veto powers and there is no room for deliberation because the *acquis communautaire* is indivisible, which consequently gives opponents of enlargement in general or of the accession of a particular state the excuse to hold up the negotiations.

A particular hurdle during Turkey's negotiations has been the frustration with the suspension and vetoing of various chapters. Only 14 out of the 35 chapters have been opened since the beginning of negotiations. The EU has frozen eight chapters due to Ankara's refusal to open its ports and airports to Greek vessels and aircraft. Countries such as France, Germany, Greece and Greek Cyprus have blocked numerous other chapters. As a result, the negotiation process, which is generally concerned with screening the candidate country's legislation, preparing budgets and establishing timetables, has not crystallised, chiefly because EU member states have blocked the process at low political costs and weakened the merit-based character of accession (see Vachudova [2005] for a discussion on the meritocratic nature of accession). This has also precluded a snowballing effect of negotiating with the EU, reduced EU incentives for further reform and stretched the overall negotiations period. In the past, the pace of each negotiation depended on the degree of preparation by each applicant country and the complexity of the issues to be resolved. For this reason, it is not possible to estimate the likely length of each negotiation in advance. However, if we look at the recent past, we can recognise a pattern ranging from three to five years among the CEEC accession countries, Malta and Cyprus. In the case of Croatia, EU negotiations started at the same time as Turkey and Croatia is expected to close all 35 chapters by the end of 2011. In the Turkish case, only one chapter has been concluded in five years.

Shifts in Domestic and European Politics

Developments such as the Cyprus issue since 2004, increasing political violence and polarisation in Turkey and declining political and public support in the EU and Turkey have been particularly critical in undermining cooperation on EU reform and making the costs of political reform very high for the AKP. Cyprus, in particular, has been a thorny issue for the AKP given Turkish public opinion, which is very defensive and increasingly more nationalist. Concerning the 2004 referendum to approve the Annan Plan, the AKP played a critical role in pushing for a settlement despite massive opposition at home. For the first time in the recent era, a Turkish government was willing to consider an internationally acceptable solution to the Cyprus dispute along the lines of the proposed United Nations (UN) plan. The result was that the Turkish Cypriots, who had rigidly resisted unification for 30 years, overwhelmingly endorsed the proposal; yet, the referendum was rejected by an overwhelming majority on the Greek Cypriot side in April 2004. A short time later, in May 2004, Cyprus became an EU member. The AKP was disappointed with the EU because it did not come through with either pressure on Greek Cyprus or economic aid for the Turkish Cypriot side; instead, the EU facilitated the role of Cyprus as a veto player within the EU.

The disagreements around Cyprus have ultimately sabotaged the flow of the negotiation process. On 30 July 2005, Turkey signed the Protocol regarding the adoption of the Ankara Agreement (Customs Union), taking into account the accession of ten new member states (including Cyprus) before the actual start of accession negotiations, but simultaneously issued a unilateral declaration noting that its signature did not amount to the recognition of the Republic of Cyprus and did not prejudice Turkey's rights and obligations emanating from the treaties of 1960. On 21 September, the EU declared that Turkey's unilateral declaration had no legal effect on its obligations under the Protocol: in other words, Turkey had to open its ports and airports to Greek Cypriot ships and planes. On 29 November, after the evaluation of the Implementation of the Ankara Protocol in the Progress Report on Turkey, the Commission recommended partial suspension of accession talks. The EU foreign ministers followed the recommendation of the Commission and on 11 December suspended talks on eight of the 35 negotiation chapters. The dilemma for the AKP concerns making a decision on whether to open Turkey's ports to Greek Cypriot shipping without assurances on ending Turkish Cyprus's isolation. This has high political costs, given the more nationalist mood in the country and, at the same time, risks establishing the Cyprus issue as a permanent one and collateral in Turkish–EU membership negotiations.

After 2005, political violence and polarisation escalated in Turkey to the extent that it took the domestic political agenda hostage and undermined the AKP's ability to spearhead political reform. The Kurdistan Workers' Party (PKK) had suspended violence after the capture of Öcalan in 1999 and during the 1999–2004 unilateral ceasefire there was little violence in south-eastern Turkey. But in 2005 the PKK re-embarked on its violent campaign. Besides the challenge of dealing with increased political violence in the country, the AKP has also faced major political clashes with key players within Turkish society. In particular, the second part of the AKP reign (beginning 2007) was marked by struggles between the government and the secular Turkish state establishment, including the armed forces, the judiciary and the bureaucracy. The first major political crisis emerged in spring 2007, when the AKP sought to elect the then Foreign Minister, Abdullah Gül, as president. The crisis was temporarily resolved via early national elections on 22 July 2007, when the party was re-elected with 47 per cent of the vote and its strength was reinforced. Eventually, on 28 August 2007, Gül was elected president of Turkey in the third round of voting in the Turkish assembly. During this period and after the first round of balloting, a communiqué appeared on the Turkish General Staff website supporting the secular constitution of the republic – referred to widely as an 'e-ultimatum' – which raised the question of the military's continued influence on politics. Around the same time, hugely popular rallies organised by civic groups in support of the secular constitution, but also critical of military interference, took place in various cities in Turkey. But the AKP also faced other crucial domestic battles. In March 2008, the Turkish Constitutional Court narrowly rejected allegations that the AKP 'had become the centre for activities against secularism'. The case was launched on the basis that the AKP was engaged in unconstitutional anti-secular activities, citing statements by the AKP leadership and the government's attempt by parliamentary vote in February 2007 to lift the constitutional ban on wearing the headscarf on university campuses. If accepted, the allegations would have led to the banning of the party. The Court issued a serious warning, but refrained from banning the governing party, which had received 47 per cent of the popular vote. The headscarf ban on university campuses was re-imposed.

The AKP's more persistent attitude towards the headscarf shortly after the 2007 elections, which escalated into a political showdown eventually leading to the above-mentioned court case, further widened the divide between secularists and Islamists. It also may have been critical for the AKP because, in the past, many argued that the AKP would use Europe's liberal attitude to push through more liberalisation on the headscarf front. However, in 2005, when the European Court of Human Rights (ECHR) approved the ban on wearing the headscarf on university premises, the AKP was disappointed and even became alienated from its European Union membership target. The decision and the silence of the Commission's Progress Reports about the rights and liberties of Islamic identity undermined the AKP's attempts to redefine secularism as a matter of democracy and pluralism. Although the ECHR is not organically related to the EU, for many AKP supporters this came to mean that there was no room for the representation of Islamic identity in Europe (Çınar 2006, p. 482; Çavdar 2006, p. 489). The AKP's move to lift the headscarf ban was not only in defiance of the ECHR decision, but also suggested that the party had chosen to revert to a selective approach with reforms.

The AKP's struggle involved not only the secularists but also different branches of government and the media. October 2008 saw the beginning of the still-ongoing Ergenekon trial, in which many members of the military and security establishment were accused of initiating unrest. The opposition Republican People's Party (CHP) has claimed that Ergenekon was created by the AKP for the purposes of revenge and intimidation. In this context, the nationalist opposition has became more influential in weakening Turkey's bid to join the EU as the Kemalist elite has increasingly become anti-Europe. A crucial development that has increased nationalism has been a resurgence in violence by the PKK since 2005. The main opposition party, the CHP, has established itself as an important component of the nationalist bloc and has tried to capitalise on rising nationalism (see Celep in this volume). The AKP's political rivals have portrayed the party as too soft on threats to Turkish national interests and, in particular, PKK terrorism. This has frequently put the AKP on the defensive. The AKP also has an ongoing dispute with the Doğan Media Group, which owns more than half of the country's newspapers, magazines and TV channels, and claims that the media group is running a hostile campaign against it using alleged corruption stories. A tax fine of US$2.5 billion imposed on the Doğan group has been seen as a way of exerting pressure on the free media and has been condemned by the European Commission.

A broad political consensus on political reform has been further hampered by the decline in public support for the EU. Opposition to Turkey's EU membership by politicians such as German Chancellor Angela Merkel and French President Nicolas Sarkozy, and the EU Council's suspension of chapters of the accession negotiations in December 2006 have had a crucial impact on Turkish public opinion and Turkish elites. Ultimately, polls show that public support for EU membership has slipped dramatically in Turkey in recent years (see Çarkoğlu and Kentmen in this volume).

AKP's EU Commitment: Continuity and Change

Due to its pro-Islamist heritage, the AKP's EU commitment has been questioned since the party's rise to power. In the past, Islamist discourse in Turkey often concentrated on being anti-Western and anti-European (Duran 2004; Dağı 2001), yet immediately after its election to office the AKP announced that the EU would be prioritised in foreign policy and that their government would be committed to EU-related reforms. Furthermore, it stressed that the reforms would be carried out for the sake of Turkey rather than that of the EU. The AKP's election manifestos demonstrated its commitment to the EU: in its 2002 election manifesto, the party emphasised that it deemed EU membership an inevitable consequence of Turkey's modernisation process and that, regardless of EU membership, it was inevitable that the EU political and economic criteria would be implemented. However, it pointed out that the fulfilment of the Copenhagen criteria had been delayed due to circles that opposed the EU on the basis of ideological approaches linked to issues such as national sovereignty, national security, national interest and local culture. The AKP preferred to re-evaluate these terms – which they considered to be a continuation of the bureaucratic statist regime understanding – from a democratic, civil and pluralist perspective that safeguarded the rights of the individual and was based on popular participation (AKP 2002, p. 8). The AKP repeated twice in the 2002 election manifesto that the EU membership criteria pertaining to economic and democratic standards were essential, regardless of membership. The manifesto underlined that the party would fulfil the requirements for EU membership as soon as possible, and would try to prevent 'artificial' problems from filling the agenda (AKP 2002, p. 82). In its subsequent election manifesto of 2007, the AKP repeated that the EU remained an integration project as well as a modernisation initiative that would raise political, economic, social and legal standards in Turkey (AKP 2007, p. 224). The manifesto stated that even if negotiation chapters were not opened, the necessary reforms would be undertaken (AKP 2007, p. 226). The AKP's commitment was also evident in the 58th through 60th government programmes and official statements from Erdoğan himself and other senior AKP party officials.

Publically, Prime Minister Erdoğan has continuously asserted Turkey's commitment to the EU, yet a defensive tone has been noticeable since the beginning of negotiations. In 2005, Erdoğan noted that 'There is no "slowing down" in the EU process. The process continues as usual. We cannot slow down because we need it' (TGRT Haber TV, 10 March 2005). A year later, in 2006, Erdoğan drew attention to the nature of the process and claimed that 'the beginning of actual negotiations will speed up [our] reform efforts' (ABHaber, 20 January 2006). However, and increasingly over time, Erdoğan has brought attention to the unfairness and obstacles in the negotiation process. He has expressed concern about new rules being made up as the 'game' goes along, but despite this he has emphasised that, as a government, the AKP is determined that Turkey should join the EU (AB Vizyon, 16 September 2008). In 2009, Erdoğan repeated that the EU was one of their government's most important goals and that they were continuing, with determination, the negotiations that began in 2005. But by now the Prime Minister was referring to problems along the way: 'Even if there are or they [the EU] put obstacles in our path, we do our homework. One by one, we put in place the reforms that our people and country need' (*Radikal*, 4 May 2009). Erdoğan also responded to accusations that the AKP's focus was shifting somewhere else by stating that

> there can be no talk of a gliding axis. It is clearly a normalisation process. Turkey continues on its path within the normalisation process. If there is an axis shift, then this is within the EU. This should be analysed immediately and seriously. (*Zaman*, 8 December 2009)

Erdoğan also referred to opposition in Europe. He argued that

> among leaders in Europe there are those who have prejudices against Turkey, like France and Germany. Previously under Mr. Chirac, we had excellent relations [with France] and he was very positive towards Turkey. But during the time of Mr. Sarkozy, this is not the case. It is an unfair attitude. The EU is violating its own rules.[2]

But despite the criticisms he and his party received Erdoğan was keen on reiterating that 'the EU accession process is the very first item on the AKP's agenda'.[3] He assured the public that Turkey's EU vocation was not sliding, but noted that Turkey's enthusiasm for the EU is often hampered by the EU's attitudes rather than a decline in Turkey's commitment (*Zaman*, 12 August 2010).

EU-Related Reforms and Initiatives under the AKP

Although there has been doubt concerning the credibility of the AKP's EU commitment, in the end what matters is policy action. The period between 2002 and

2004 was clearly a time when the AKP accomplished much in terms of EU-related reforms, in particular by means of the harmonisation packages. The reforms were momentous and included the abolishment of the death penalty, the extension of minority rights to the Kurds, and broader definitions of freedom of association and expression. In 2004, in addition to the harmonisation packages, Erdoğan's government pushed through far-reaching changes to Turkey's 78-year-old Penal Code to bring it in line with European norms (Avcı 2004).

After 2005, and compared with the first AKP government, the record of EU reforms is scanty and no longer substantial. Some of the reforms faced the resistance of the judiciary. For instance in 2006, Turkey adopted a law for the establishment of an ombudsman that the EU believed would help fight corruption, increase transparency and allow better control of military spending. In 2006, former president Ahmet Necdet Sezer vetoed the bill and contested its legality before the Constitutional Court. In December 2008, as a major setback to the government's EU-related reform efforts, the Constitutional Court annulled the law concerning the ombudsman's office. Overall, the European Commission considered the reforms in 2007 insufficient and stated that 'Turkey now needs to renew the momentum of political reforms. Significant further efforts are needed in particular on freedom of expression, on civilian control of the military, and on the rights of non-Muslim communities' (EU Commission 2007). The Law on Foundations was adopted in February 2008. In addition, and after more than four years of delay, the AKP government finally enacted the new National Programme for the Adoption of the Acquis (NPAA) on 31 December 2008.

A number of institutional changes were enacted around the Secretariat General for EU Affairs (EUSG) – Turkey's main coordination body for EU affairs – with the idea of empowering the EU reform process. In 2007, the EUSG, had been placed under the Ministry of Foreign Affairs, but in 2009 it was moved to the Prime Ministry. At the same time, and for the first time since the beginning of accession negotiations, the government appointed a full-time EU negotiatior, Egemen Bağış (taking over the portfolio from the foreign minister), with the status of state minister to take charge of the EUSG.

Although there was some movement in EU-related reforms in 2009, it remained limited. In June 2009, Parliament passed a law that gives civil courts the power to try military personnel for crimes threatening national security or linked to organised crime. Furthermore, the new legislation lifted the remaining powers of military courts to try civilians in peacetime, thus aligning Turkey with EU practices. The government approved the judicial reform strategy in August 2009. Furthermore, Parliament ratified the UN Convention on the Rights of Persons with Disabilities, which entered into force on 18 December 2008. Overall, however, little progress was reported on effective implementation of political and constitutional reforms.

After 2009, there were a number of initiatives where the AKP sought to tackle diversity issues in Turkey. The Kurdish initiative was launched with a view to extending cultural and linguistic rights to the Kurdish minority, whose condition was seen as a major problem in EU accession talks. A full-time, state-run Kurdish-language television channel began broadcasting. In 2009, the AKP initiated serious discussions to address the concerns of the Alevi minority (see Carkoğlu and Bilgili in this volume). The government also took some steps towards normalising relations with Armenia. Two sticky, yet key, issues on the EU reform agenda remained Article 301 and a new civilian constitution. The AKP has been hesitant to scrap Article 301 of the Turkish Penal Code.[4] This article has been used in the past as a mechanism for restricting free speech on the grounds of insulting Turkishness, the Turkish state and the Turkish nation. Well-known writers such as Nobel laureate Orhan Pamuk and journalists like Hrant Dink have been charged and tried under this article.[5] Dink was murdered on 19 January 2007, and many have argued that his prosecution and conviction under Article 301 made him a target for ultranationalists. The most vocal opposition to the proposed abolition of Article 301 of the Penal Code has come from the CHP, which has also played the nationalist card on this issue. The article was eventually amended on 30 April 2008 by the AKP. With the amendment, it is a crime to insult the Turkish nation, rather than Turkishness, and the justice minister's permission will be required to open a case under Article 301. Nonetheless the European Parliament still believes that the amendment to Article 301 of the Penal Code adopted in April 2008 does not go far enough.[6]

The lack of progress on a new civilian constitution has been criticised by international non-governmental organisations (e.g. see International Crisis Group [ICG] 2008) but the allocation of seats in the Turkish Parliament based on the general elections of 2007 has made it difficult for the government to push ahead with a new constitution. The AKP formed an independent commission in 2007 to prepare a draft of a new civilian constitution but shelved it later when fighting the closure case against the party. In May 2010, the AKP secured parliamentary approval for a 26-article package of constitutional amendments, but since the reforms failed to secure the support of a large enough majority in Parliament to be enacted automatically they were put to a referendum on 12 September 2010. The package included items such as removing obstacles to positive gender discrimination; granting civil servants union rights and allowing them to engage in collective bargaining; introducing the right of appeal against summary dismissal from the military; preventing civilians from being tried in military courts except in times of war; making military personnel liable to trial in civilian courts; allowing those responsible for the 1980 military coup to be taken to court; and creating the office of ombudsman. However, there were also controversial items that pertain to the appointments to the Supreme Board of Prosecutors and Judges (HSYK, Hakimler ve Savcılar Yüksek Kurulu) and the Constitutional Court. Critics argued that with these changes the AKP would seize control over the judiciary. The referendum was endorsed by 58 per cent of the voters (with a turnout of 77 per cent). This was a boost for the AKP and a preview for the AKP's strong performance in the 12 June 2011 elections, where the AKP won a third term with 49.9 per cent. Yet, at the same time, the 42 per cent 'no' vote – with an especially strong showing in the secular Aegean and Mediterranean provinces – signals that politics in Turkey remains deeply polarised.

Conclusion

The AKP's basic long-term EU commitment has not changed fundamentally, but it has been affected and constrained by the dynamics and nature of negotiations with the EU, and changes in domestic and European politics. Typically, the EU exerts active leverage through its conditionality mechanism by establishing rewards and opportunities at the EU level that help overcome domestic challenges. In the Turkish case, the EU's active leverage has significantly decreased during the negotiations period. Negotiations have stalled and become rather irrelevant. The EU has also lost its empowering appeal. At the same time, domestic costs of undertaking reforms have risen (further) in Turkey, and they have limited not only the AKP's motivation but also its capacity and resources to push through ambitious EU reforms. With increased nationalism and hardening Euroscepticism among the main opposition parties (Nationalist Movement Party [MHP] and CHP), as well as within different branches of government, for the AKP the EU accession process no longer serves as the basis for compromise with the secular establishment and an effective tool in avoiding conflict between key actors in the country. The AKP has realised that passing high-stake reforms in an environment like this could be a threat to its own existence and domestic sources of political power. The developments around Cyprus have also limited the party's room for manoeuvre. Negative public opinion in Turkey and Europe together with mixed political messages from political leaders in Europe have added to reform costs.

The result is that the AKP has reverted to a 'passive activism' in its approach to the EU – it delivers the minimum to stay in the game. It does not openly revert from the EU goal – instead, it continues to pay lip service to the goal, but EU enthusiasm and reforms remain limited. In other words, the AKP has verbally remained committed to the goal of EU membership but the motivation and incentive to reform have been hampered. It is not an option to drop the EU quest, as this would be too damaging for the AKP's credibility and would be perceived as a sign of inconsistency (and confirm for many the 'hidden' agenda of the AKP). But, given that the payoff from pursuing the EU goal is minimal, the AKP has kept EU reforms on the backburner. In the long run, this attitude may endanger the EU project, with reforms being treated à la carte rather than as a set menu that would transform Turkey radically.

Notes

[1] EU Presidency Conclusions, Copenhagen European Council, 12 and 13 December 2002, paragraph 18.

[2] Interview with Robert Tait in *The Guardian*, 6 October 2009.

[3] Prime Minister Erdoğan's speech to his Political Group, 3 March, 2010, available online at: http://www.akparti.org.tr/tbmm/grupkon.asp.

[4] This article was adopted in June 2005 but there were other similar versions of it in the past, such as Article 159 and Article 312.

[5] Resolution by the European Parliament Foreign Affairs Committee, 10 February 2009.

References

AKP (2002) *AK Parti Seçim Beyannamesi*, [AKP Election Manifesto], Ankara.

AKP (2007) *AK Parti Seçim Beyannamesi*, [AKP Election Manifesto], Ankara.

Avcı, G. (2004) 'Turkish political parties and the EU discourse in the post-Helsinki period: a case of Europeanisation', in *Turkey and European Integration. Accession Prospects and Issues*, eds M. Uğur & N. Canefe, Routledge, New York, pp. 194–214.

Cizre, Ü. (2007) *Secular and Islamic Politics in Turkey: The Making of the Justice and Development Party*, Routledge, New York.

Çavdar, G. (2006) 'Islamist new thinking in Turkey: a model for political learning?', *Political Science Quarterly*, vol. 121, no. 3, pp. 477–497.

Çınar, M. (2006) 'Turkey's transformation under the AKP rule', *Muslim World*, vol. 96, no. 3, pp. 469–486.

Çınar, M. (2007) 'The Justice and Development Party and the Kemalist establishment', in *Secular and Islamic Politics in Turkey: The Making of the Justice and Development Party*, ed. Ü. Cizre, Routledge, New York, pp. 109–131.

Dağı, I. (2001) 'Islamic political identity in Turkey: rethinking the West and Westernisation', CPS Report, International Policy Fellowship Program, available online at: http://pdc.ceu.hu/archive/00001804/01/Dagi.pdf

Dağı, I. (2006) 'The Justice and Development Party: identity, politics and human rights discourse in the search for security and legitimacy', in *The Emergence of a New Turkey: Islam, Democracy and the AK Parti*, ed. H. Yavuz, University of Utah Press, Salt Lake City, pp. 88–106.

Dağı, I. (2008) 'Turkey's AKP in power', *Journal of Democracy*, vol. 19, no. 3, pp. 25–30.

Dimitrova, A. L. (2005) 'Europeanisation and civil service reform in Central and Eastern Europe', in *The Europeanisation of Central and Eastern Europe*, eds F. Schimmelfennig & U. Sedelmeier, Cornell University Press, Ithaca, NY, pp. 71–91.

Doğan, E. (2005) 'The historical and discoursive roots of the Justice and Development Party's EU stance', *Turkish Studies*, vol. 6, no. 3, pp. 421–437.

Duran, B. (2004) 'Islamist redefinition(s) of European and Islamic identities in Turkey', in *Turkey and European Integration: Accession Prospects and Issues*, eds M. Uğur & N. Canefe, Routledge, New York, pp. 125–146.

Duran, B. (2007) 'The Justice and Development Party's "new politics": steering towards conservative democracy, a revived Islamic agenda or management of new crises', in *Secular and Islamic Politics in Turkey: The Making of the Justice and Development Party*, ed. Ü. Cizre, Routledge, New York, pp. 80–106.

EU Commission (2007) *Progress Report Turkey*, Brussels.

Göl, A. (2009) 'The identity of Turkey: Muslim and secular', *Third World Quarterly*, vol. 30, no. 4, pp. 795–811.

Grabbe, H. (2006) *The EU's Transformative Power: Europeanisation through Conditionality in Central and Eastern Europe*, Palgrave MacMillan, Basingstoke.

Hughes, J., Sasse, G. & Gordon, C. (2004) *Europeanisation and Regionalisation in the EU's Enlargement to Central and Eastern Europe: The Myth of Conditionality.* Palgrave MacMillan, Basingstoke.

ICG. (2008) *Turkey and Europe: The Decisive Year Ahead – Europe Report Nº197*, Istanbul/Brussels.

Öniş, Z. & Keyman, E. F. (2003) 'Turkey at the polls: a new path emerges', *Journal of Democracy*, vol. 14, no. 2, pp. 95–107.

Öniş, Z. & Yılmaz, S. (2009) 'Between Europeanisation and Euro-Asianism: Foreign policy activism in Turkey during the AKP era', *Turkish Studies*, vol. 10, no. 1, pp. 7–24.

Pridham, G. (2005) *Designing Democracy: EU Enlargement and Regime Change in Post-Communist Europe*, Palgrave MacMillan, Basingstoke.

Schimmelfennig, F. & Sedelmeier, U. (2005) 'Conceptualising the Europeanisation of Central and Eastern Europe', in *The Europeanisation of Central and Eastern Europe*, eds F. Schimmelfennig & U. Sedelmeier, Cornell University Press, Ithaca, NY, pp. 1–29.

Tocci, N. (2005) 'Europeanisation in Turkey: trigger or anchor for reform', *South European Society and Politics*, vol. 10, no. 1, pp. 73–83.

Uğur, M. (1999) *The European Union and Turkey: An Anchor/Credibility Dilemma*, Ashgate, Aldershot.

Vachudova, M. (2005) *Europe Undivided: Democracy, Leverage, and Integration After Communism*, Oxford University Press, Oxford.

Yavuz, H. (2006) 'The role of the new bourgeoisie in the transformation of the Turkish Islamic movement', in *The Emergence of a New Turkey: Islam, Democracy and the AK Parti*, ed. H. Yavuz, University of Utah Press, Salt Lake City, pp. 1–22.

Gamze Avcı (PhD University of Georgia) is currently a lecturer at University College Utrecht at Utrecht University. She previously worked as assistant professor in the Department of Political Science and International Relations at Boğaziçi University, Istanbul (1997–2002). Her research is primarily on Turkey's relationship with the EU and Turkish migration into Western Europe. Her work has appeared in journals including *European Foreign Affairs Review, European Journal of Political Research, European Journal of Migration and Law* and *International Migration*.

The Republican People's Party and Turkey's EU Membership

Ödül Celep

As the founder of the Turkish secular state, the Republican People's Party (CHP) has defended the Westernisation of Turkish society, supported Turkey's acceptance to the EU as a full member, and played crucial roles in Turkey–EU relations. Nevertheless, the CHP's language towards the EU started to sound critical during the 2000s. This study argues that the CHP's seeming scepticism towards the EU is not an ideological U-turn, but a conditional situation. The CHP's Euroscepticism is an outcome of its distrust of the Justice and Development Party government's honesty and ability in implementing the required reforms for Turkey's EU membership.

Turkey's relations with the European Union (EU) have been an important issue of political debate in Turkish politics, reflecting the extent of Turkey's willingness to become a part of the 'West'. In this debate, the founding party of the Turkish state, the Republican People's Party (Cumhuriyet Halk Partisi, CHP) has historically represented the pro-Western side in favour of both the EU process itself and of Turkey becoming a part of it. In the past decade, however, the CHP's language towards the EU and Turkey's never-ending EU accession process seems to have been more sceptical than before. This recent scepticism was unexpected from the party, given its long history of engagement in and contribution to the development of Turkey–EU relations.

As a result of its commitment to the founder of the modern Turkish state, Mustafa Kemal Atatürk, the CHP has defended Atatürk's founding principles, which collectively comprise its ideology, Kemalism. Even though the CHP and Kemalists were inspired by Western civilisation, their perception of the West was paradoxical. On the one hand, they advocated Turkey's complete adaptation to the values and institutions of the West, but, on the other, they supported Turkey's economic and political independence from the West (Ayata & Ayata 2007, p. 214). In other words, Kemalists have been both pro-Western and anti-imperialist. Their anti-imperialism can be interpreted as a reaction to the Western powers that Turkey had to fight during the Turkish War of Independence as well as the struggles against foreign impositions after the post-World-War-I defeat of the Ottomans. Kemalists feared the West's potential challenges to Turkey's integrity, independence, and national sovereignty, a fear arising mainly from the 'Sèvres complex' of Kemalist nationalists (Uslu 2008).[1]

The CHP's paradoxical perception of the West and the EU can be largely explained by the unique history of modern Turkey and the unique role the CHP played in the emergence of modern Turkey from the ashes of the Ottoman Empire. Turkey's geographical location is at the crossroads of a variety of different cultures, which makes it difficult to compare the country to either East and West Europe or the Middle East. After the Republic of Turkey was proclaimed, the early Republican elite undertook a series of reforms in order to 'catch up' with the West. They contended that the major reason behind the fall of the Ottoman state was its 'backwardness' – its falling behind the civilised West – and in order to make up for so many centuries of lost time in such a short period the early Republican elite perceived 'Westernisation' as the only cure. This perception thus relied on a Eurocentric model of modernisation and development.[2]

The CHP has played critical roles in the key events throughout the history of Turkey–EU relations. The Ankara Agreement was signed when İsmet İnönü's CHP government was in office in 1963, the purpose of this agreement being Turkey's accession to the Customs Union and the European Economic Communty (EEC) as a full member. Further developments took place during the later periods of right-wing or military interim governments.[3] During the two-party coalition between the centre-right True Path Party (Doğru Yol Partisi, DYP) and the CHP, Turkey took one major step to full integration as the Customs Union between Turkey and the EU came into effect in December 1995.[4] Deniz Baykal, the then CHP leader and the minister of foreign affairs, played a major role in the signing of the Customs Union by the European Parliament (Doğan 2005; Kaleağası 2008).

Despite its pro-Western identity and attempts to develop Turkey–EU relations, during the AKP government period the CHP has sounded relatively more sceptical towards the EU than ever before. Some have interpreted this as a radical U-turn in the CHP's EU position, as if it has become an anti-EU party altogether.[5] This study argues that the CHP's reaction towards Turkey's EU membership process in the past decade has been a product of being in opposition in parliament, and therefore fighting electorally and politically with the ruling Justice and Development Party (Adalet ve Kalkınma Partisi, AKP). The year 2002 was a critical year, as the AKP won a landslide election and the European Commission presented a report that listed particular reforms to be accomplished before Turkey could satisfy the requirements of EU membership. After winning the elections, the AKP government passed a series of legal and institutional reforms in accordance with the EU harmonisation package. The CHP reacted not to the idea of Turkey joining the EU in principle, but to the way in which the AKP government interpreted and implemented the reforms: in other words, the construction of the CHP discourse on Turkey's EU membership process during the 2000s was juxtaposed with its opposition to, and competition with, the AKP government.

In essence, the CHP has criticised the AKP government's implementation of the EU reforms on two major counts. First, it claimed that the AKP government was using the EU membership process as an instrument to further its socially conservative agenda. Second, it accused the AKP of failing to defend Turkey's national interests during the EU membership process (Gülmez 2008, pp. 425–427). It is then fair to argue that the CHP's scepticism towards Turkey's EU membership in recent years is a conditional situation, and an outcome of its distrust of the AKP government's honesty and ability in implementing the required reforms. The next section in this study examines a brief history of the secular–religious cleavage in Turkish politics, which has proved to be highly influential in the positions taken by the political parties vis-à-vis Turkey's EU membership. The study then reviews the explanations of the recent factors that conditioned the CHP's reactive stance on the EU and Turkey's membership process during the 2000s. These two steps help us to understand the diverse effects of long- and short-term factors on the CHP's stance and language on the EU in general, and on Turkey joining the EU in particular. Its sociological origins make the CHP a pro-EU party, while recent developments in Turkey's accession have led to a growing level of resentment in the party towards both the EU and the AKP government.

It is, however, important to clarify at this point that 'Euroscepticism' is neither a novel concept nor a concept that applies only to the CHP. Even though this term began to be voiced during the 1980s, its history goes back to earlier decades in Britain (Spiering 2005, p. 131). From the mid-1980s to the mid-1990s, the EU experienced rapid economic development as an integrated economy (Pollack 2000), and later developments such as the Single European Act (1986) and the Maastricht Treaty (1993) laid the foundations for an economic and monetary union within a supranational policy that undermined the sovereignty of member states. Consequently, European integration became an increasingly salient issue for European national political parties and their mass publics (Marks, Wilson & Ray 2002, p. 586).

Taggart defines Euroscepticism as 'the idea of contingent or qualified opposition, as well as incorporating outright and unqualified opposition to the process of European integration' (Taggart 1998, p. 366). Taggart and Szczerbiak (2008) further define two types of Euroscepticism. 'Hard Euroscepticism' includes a fundamental opposition to the EU as an institution and European integration as a process; hard Eurosceptic parties therefore generally advocate that their countries stay away from the EU or withdraw from the EU altogether. 'Soft Eurosceptics' do not oppose the idea of European integration in principle. Their scepticism comes from policy disagreements with the EU or where they see an incompatibility between the EU rules and their countries' national interests (Taggart & Szczerbiak 2004, p. 4). Hard Eurosceptics are generally single-issue parties with an anti-EU agenda only, or parties that are highly ideology-driven such as communists and conservatives (Taggart & Szczerbiak 2008, pp. 7–8).

The existing studies on Euroscepticism of political parties generally focus on cases from European democracies and the EU member countries. The number of studies on the Euroscepticism of Turkish parties in general and the CHP in particular is limited. In principle, the CHP should not be expected to take a hard Eurosceptic approach to

Turkey's membership process because 'Europeanisation' is a component of its political cause and history. Taking a hard Eurosceptic approach would also mean that the CHP did not want to see Turkey as a part of Europe, something that contradicts its very ideology. It is more likely that the CHP is taking a soft Eurosceptic approach. It has, in fact, criticised the way the AKP government has been handling the membership process rather than the idea of membership itself. CHP's criticism has come mostly out of policy disagreements and lack of trust in the EU, which have fostered its concerns about protecting Turkey's national interests during the membership process. Nevertheless, a comprehensive argument about CHP's Euroscepticism first requires a sociological overview of the party and its historical origins.

The Cleavage in EU Politics in Turkey

The opinions of political parties on different issues can be determined by short-term factors as well as long-standing historical and sociological factors. From a sociological perspective, parties are regarded as institutions that represent particular sides of social divisions or 'cleavages' in society. The cornerstone of the sociological analysis of political parties is Lipset and Rokkan's (1967) study on the historical formation of political parties in Europe. In their study, they mention particular social cleavages that shaped European political parties in their history such as the 'centre–periphery,' 'secular–religious' and 'bourgeois–proletariat' cleavages (see also Zuckerman 1982; Ware 1996).

These cleavages have played major roles in determining European parties' stances on the EU integration process. For instance, both social democrats and conservatives face a dilemma because the EU integration process brings about mixed outcomes for both. On the one hand, right-wingers like the integration because it intensifies international economic competition and undermines Keynesian solutions to this intensifying competition at the global level. On the other hand, the process creates a supranational government for the EU as a whole to regulate markets when necessary, which appeals to left-wingers. Similarly, the religious cleavage drives Catholic parties of Europe towards a pro-EU position due to their long-standing anti-national biases and supranational aspirations (Marks & Wilson 2000, pp. 437–438). Green parties are moderately and the extreme right-wing parties strongly opposed to integration, for their own ideological reasons (Marks, Wilson & Ray 2002, p. 587).

In his classic study, Şerif Mardin (1973) applies the cleavage-based perspective to the political parties of Turkey. He argues that the CHP has represented the interests of the 'centre' while its adversaries[6] have represented the 'periphery.' In this argument, the 'centre' refers to urban, relatively wealthy, and well-educated people who have secular, modern, and Western lifestyles, including an elite group of military and civilian bureaucrats who have had control over the state apparatus. On the other hand, the 'periphery' pertains to a combination of more rural, traditional, religious, and socially conservative groups. The difference in value systems between the two sides is mostly attributable to the concept of religiosity (Kalaycıoğlu 1994; Çarkoğlu 2007). In other words, the centre–periphery cleavage can be reduced to the existing secular–religious divide in Turkey (see Çarkoğlu & Toprak 2000), which can be understood via a careful analysis of secularism and religiosity in Turkish society.[7]

In this regard, Turkey's EU membership has been contextualised in the framework of Turkey's Europeanisation and the extent to which legal, political, and social institutions in Turkey should resemble their European counterparts. The differences of opinion mostly depend on the answers to these two questions: Should Turkey Westernise? To what extent should Turkey Westernise? The two sides of the secular–religious cleavage have provided two opposing answers to these questions. Those on the secular side have argued that Turkey's Westernisation requires the society's total adaptation to a European type of life; Europeanisation should be embraced in terms of not only the West's material culture, but also its social and political culture. The opposite side in this debate is the group of pro-Islamists. This party tradition adopted an ideology named the 'National View' (*Milli Görüş*), and has relied on a number of principles, including traditional morality, family values, establishing closer ties with Muslim countries, heavy industrialisation, and religious education (Alkan 1984; Atacan 2005).

The pro-Islamist ideology strongly opposed the idea of Turkey's Westernisation as it perceived this idea as 'Christianisation' of Turkish society. It generally distinguished the 'material' and 'moral' culture of the West. In this context, 'material culture' pertains to Europe's science, technology, and economic development while 'moral culture' means European societies' values, beliefs, and lifestyles. The idea was that Christian culture was developed in terms of science, technology, and economics, but 'morally corrupt' or simply 'immoral' and could not serve as an example to Turkish society. This reactive idea was justified on the grounds of Islamic values and social conservatism. Pro-Islamists argued that the EU would never accept Turkey as a member due to cultural differences between the West and Turkey. For instance, the pro-Islamist Welfare Party strongly denounced Turkey's EU membership on the grounds that 'Turkey would be a province of Israel' if it joined the EU (Atacan 2005, p. 188).

What distorted the traditional sides of this cleavage were the consequent closures of pro-Islamist parties in recent years. After the closure of the Welfare Party and the Virtue Party in 1998 and 2001, respectively, two successor parties were founded: the Felicity Party (Saadet Partisi, SP), representing the traditionalist pro-Islamists, and the AKP, representing the revisionists. During the AKP's early years, Tayyip Erdoğan, the party chair, defined the party as a 'conservative democratic' movement and broke ties with the National View past. He argued that the AKP was not a party on a religious axis. The AKP endorsed the idea of Turkey joining the EU, which was contrary to almost all former pro-Islamist views.

With the pro-EU AKP forming the government since 2002, the nature and context of the debate on Turkey–EU relations changed. The AKP's new conservatives sounded like the champions of Turkey's EU membership, while the CHP's seculars sounded more Eurosceptical than ever. In reality, however, the CHP's attitude was the outcome of a combination of several conditional factors. Its leader Deniz Baykal pursued a reactive attitude to most of the AKP government's policy agenda and brought serious accusations against it, such as that it undermined secularism and endangered Turkey's national unity. This reactive attitude naturally shaped the CHP's discourse on AKP–EU relations as well. Eventually, the CHP gave the distinct impression of being a Eurosceptic party, as it showed almost no enthusiasm for most of the AKP government's proposed democratisation reforms.

The AKP's EU Agenda and the CHP's Response

With respect to its sociological origins, the CHP represents the pro-EU, secular side. However, a combination of conditional factors has reshaped the CHP's discourse on Turkey–EU relations recently. The CHP's successive electoral failures together with the AKP's uninterrupted single-party government since 2002 are the major conditions that have affected the former's EU discourse. It was the AKP that shaped the agenda of Turkey's EU membership process, and the CHP's discourse was constructed as a response to the AKP's agenda. The CHP's cynical attitude towards the EU (independent of its reaction to the AKP government) was another major factor that shaped its EU discourse during the 2000s. Some CHP officials expressed concerns that the EU's purpose could be to maintain Turkey's candidate status for ever or to treat Turkey as a second-class partner, because both scenarios served the EU's interests better (Gülmez 2006, p. 9).

After the official recognition of Turkey as an EU candidate in December 1999, the AKP undertook a series of legal and political reforms in accordance with the European Commission's list. These reforms included the abolishment of the death penalty and the State Security Courts (Özbudun 2007, p. 186), and the CHP supported both reforms. The EU had raised concerns about the heavy involvement of the military bureaucracy in Turkish civilian politics, in reply to which the AKP government passed a reform package that changed the political role of the military by limiting the executive powers and areas of responsibility of the National Security Council (Milli Güvenlik Kurulu, MGK) and increasing the civilian presence on the Council (Çağaptay 2003). CHP deputies voted in favour of such changes at the national legislature, even though they expressed their concerns about the changes in the legislation on the MGK.[8]

One of the controversial issues was the AKP government's efforts to ban adultery, which had been decriminalised in Turkey since 1996. The AKP's justification for the adultery ban was the public support behind it, particularly from housewife women living in rural parts of Anatolia (Korkmaz 2004). The CHP referred to the AKP's insistence on this issue as an 'reactionary attempt'[9] and said it would not challenge it, provided that men faced the same penalties as women for adultery.[10] The CHP's initial decision not to obstruct the AKP's efforts to impose the ban was interpreted as a reserved one. Nevertheless, the CHP's language changed radically after its women representatives and other women's groups reacted to the AKP's adultery agenda (İlkkaracan 2008, p. 271). The adultery ban was eventually withdrawn from the political agenda as a result of expressions of disappointment from the EU.

Another major issue was the long-standing debate between Turkey and Greece over Cyprus. Since the Turkish military intervention on the island in 1974, Cyprus has been divided into two separate ethnic and territorial communities, the (Greek) Republic of Cyprus and the Turkish Republic of Northern Cyprus (TRNC). The international community recognises the Greek Cypriot state, while the TRNC is recognised by Turkey only. The Cyprus question has turned into a major challenge for Turkey's EU membership since the accession of the Republic of Cyprus to the EU in May 2004, as subsequently the Republic of Cyprus has shown signs of willingness to block Turkey's EU membership. There have also been Turkish concerns about the possibility of the international community considering that Turkey was occupying territories of the EU after the entry of the Republic of Cyprus into the EU (Dodd 2002, p. 54). Therefore, the Cyprus question has been intimately connected to EU–Turkey relations.

In April 2004, the two communities of Cyprus were asked to choose between ratifying and rejecting the fifth revision of a UN proposal to settle the Cyprus dispute, known as the Annan Plan. Most Turkish Cypriots supported it with the hope that the Annan Plan would bring connection to the outside world and ease EU accession. A majority of Greek Cypriots objected to the Annan Plan on the account that it was extremely unbalanced and pro-Turkish (Palley 2005, p. 224).

The CHP reacted strongly to all these developments and the AKP's compliance with the EU's demands on the Cyprus question, justifying its reaction on three major counts. First, the CHP was against connecting Turkey's EU membership to the Cyprus question, as Deniz Baykal argued that this connection would require Turkey's recognition of the (Greek) Republic of Cyprus as a precondition to becoming an EU member. Second, Baykal criticised the content of the Annan Plan on the grounds that it brought disadvantageous outcomes for both Turkey and the TRNC, and challenged the status quo of bi-zonality at the expense of the Turkish Cypriot community. Third, the CHP accused the AKP government of being overly submissive to the EU on the Cyprus question and radically changing the long-standing foreign policy principles of Turkey (Gülmez 2006, pp. 38–39; 2007, p. 127).

Another significant issue concerning Turkey–EU relations is the need for a major constitutional reform in Turkey. After the 1980 coup, the interim military government (1980–83) initiated a new constitution which was ratified by a popular referendum in 1982. The Constitution of 1982 was written under military rule, with an authoritarian instead of a liberal, democratic mentality. It has been criticised for restricting rights and freedoms, and protecting the state against the citizen instead of the other way round, and it has been modified several times by the national legislature (Turkish Grand National Assembly) in order to extend individual and collective rights and liberties. The EU has encouraged Turkey to adopt a new constitution for several years, and the AKP government has initiated a series of constitutional amendments in a reform package recently.

The AKP's reform package was approved in a public referendum in September 2010. The EU supported the AKP government's constitutional amendments, despite concerns that the proposals were not as comprehensive or liberal as Europe would have really liked.[11] The reforms package pertains to a variety of domains such as labour and collective bargaining rights, closure of political parties, the domains of authority of military courts, as well as changes in the institutional structures of the high courts. The package aims to limit the power of top judicial bodies, change the make-up of a key body that deals with the appointment of judges and prosecutors, and make it more difficult to ban political parties (*Hürriyet Daily News* 2010).

The CHP's initial reaction to the package was mixed, as it supported some but objected to other aspects of the proposed reforms. Baykal, the CHP's former leader, proposed to separate the reforms regarding the Constitutional Court, the Supreme Council of Judges and Public Prosecutors (Hakimler ve Savcılar Yüksek Kurulu, HSYK), and the new arrangements for party closures from the rest of the items. The AKP ignored Baykal's proposal, and the latter later announced that the CHP would not support the government's constitutional reforms. He argued that the proposed reforms were to serve the AKP's ambitions with regard to the legal system and political interests. One of Baykal's major concerns was that the package would increase the AKP's leverage on the existing judicial system and the high courts' judges.

Considering the whole picture of the CHP discourse on Turkey–EU relations during the AKP government period gives the impression of a soft Eurosceptic party rather than a hard one. Hard Euroscepticism, in principle, goes totally against the historical cause of the CHP party tradition. The CHP did not question the principle of Westernisation or the idea of joining the EU; it is even possible that the CHP would have pursued some of those reforms if it had been the governing party. CHP politicians were mainly concerned with the way the AKP government handled the membership process. In accordance with Taggart and Szczerbiak's (2008) definition of soft Euroscepticism, the CHP showed resentment towards the EU and AKP due to policy differences and the issue of national interest.

Conclusion

The CHP's historical origins go back to the foundation of the modern, secular Turkish state. A major component of its historical cause is secularism and Turkey becoming a part of the West. It has played a significant role in the major developments between Turkey and the EEC and the EU. In recent years, the CHP discourse towards Turkey's EU membership process has sounded more resentful than ever before. This was interpreted by some scholars and columnists as a turn towards Euroscepticism. This study has put forward the argument that the CHP's seemingly negative attitude to this process was the outcome of particular contextual factors.

The AKP government undertook a series of legislative reforms in accordance with the EU's expectations of Turkey during the early 2000s, and the CHP's reaction was predominantly negative and reactive. At first, the CHP supported some initial reforms such as the abolition of the death penalty and the State Security Courts. Later, however, a series of developments in the course of the government's reforms led to controversy and opposition between the two parties. The CHP developed a resentful response to both the AKP government and the EU. It accused the government of using the membership process as grounds for broadening its conservative agenda as well as undermining secularism. The CHP also accused the government of being overly acquiescent to the EU and failing to protect Turkey's national interests. In addition, there were signs of cynicism towards the EU as well, mostly expressed as accusations of hypocrisy. Several CHP members put forward their belief that the EU has been purposefully prolonging Turkey's membership process because they either did not want Turkey as a full member or preferred to treat Turkey as a second-class partner.

After Baykal's departure, a new and popular figure, Kemal Kılıçdaroğlu, was elected as the new party leader. Kılıçdaroğlu's language reveals signs of a more optimistic approach to Turkey's EU membership. In a recent interview, he makes a distinction between Turkey's EU membership in general and the AKP's way of dealing with this process in particular. Even though he criticises the AKP for being dishonest in its willingness to make Turkey a member, he refers to the EU as a 'project of civilisation' (Zaman 2010).

One of the current EU-related issues is changing the Turkish law that says that the chief of the General Staff is accountable to the prime minister. This constitutes a significant obstacle to Turkey–EU negotiations for membership. The EU demands that the Turkish chief of the General Staff work under the minister of defence, as in Western democracies (Sarıibrahimoğlu 2006, p. 56). In contrast to Baykal's conservative approach on the military structure, Kılıçdaroğlu supports this change (Zaman 2010). It is too early yet to know whether Kılıçdaroğlu's CHP will be able to accomplish real changes in the party or will simply maintain the status quo and Baykal's legacy. However, developing a more constructive and intellectually profound discourse and strategy on Turkey's EU membership is critical for convincing the public that the CHP is indeed changing.

Notes

[1] The Treaty of Sèvres (1920) was a peace treaty signed between the defeated Ottoman state and the Allied powers at the end of World War I. It imposed several restrictions on Turkey, including the foundation of Greek and Armenian states within the current territory of Turkey. It was invalidated by the Treaty of Lausanne after the War of Independence in 1923, which led to the recognition of the new Republic of Turkey as the successor of the dead Ottoman state. Nevertheless, its legacy remained as a paranoia among Kemalists about a possibility that foreign powers such as Armenia might still claim territorial rights.

[2] What Turkey officially regards as the 'Turkish Revolution' refers to a unique set of direct adaptations of European codes to the Turkish legal system. For instance, the civil code was directly adopted from the Swiss civil code of the time. Similarly, the Italian penal code was taken directly and adopted as the Turkish penal code. The administrative code was adopted from France. In addition, the European calendar and metric system were also adopted, and the alphabet was changed from old Ottoman to Latin. Women were given the right to vote and be elected as representatives. This type of rapid and radical adaptation to European legal and cultural systems in a Muslim society does not fit the European theories of modernisation. On Turkish modernisation, see: Çınar 2005; Berkes 1998; Zürcher 2004.

[3] These developments include the signing of the First Enlargement Agreement (Complementary Protocol) in June 1973, the suspension of EU–Turkey relations after the 1980 military coup, and the normalisation of relations in 1986.

TURKEY AND THE EU: ACCESSION AND REFORM

[4] The Customs Union between Turkey and the EU entailed free movement of goods between the two entities with no customs restrictions except in some areas, such as agriculture.

[5] For instance, in an interview with the daily conservative *Yeni Şafak* in 2009, Joost Lagendijk, the then joint chairman of the Turkey–EU Parliamentarians delegation, expressed the following: 'The Europeans were expecting the demands for change from the left, the CHP. However, the change and democracy came from the AKP ... The AKP is now the address for change and reforms. This is a surprising atittude from the European perspective' (*Yeni Şafak*, 20 April 2009). Members of the European Parliament compose delegations to several parliaments of countries outside of the EU, including the candidate countries such as Turkey. The purpose of such delegations is to promote cooperation between the legislative assemblies of different countries.

[6] These adversaries include major right-wing parties in Turkish political history, such as the Democrat Party during the 1950s, Justice Party during the 1960s and 1970s, Motherland Party during the 1980s and 1990s, and AKP since 2002.

[7] The history of the religious–secular cleavage goes back to pre-Republican, late Ottoman years, as late Ottoman intellectuals also debated Westernisation in their time (see Lewis 2002, pp. 210–293). The 'secular–religious' division is most of what constituted the 'centre–periphery' cleavage. The major issue of controversy between the centre and the periphery was their perception of 'secularism' and 'religiosity', which constituted the two sides of the same coin. The people of the centre have been committed to the early Republican principles of the Turkish Revolution, particularly secularism. They have stood strongly against the use of Sunni religious symbols in public space or for political purposes. The periphery has been more sensitive on religious issues and religious freedoms. For more information on the issues that divide the secular and religious people, see Çarkoğlu and Toprak (2000).

[8] *Radikal*, 30 July 2003.

[9] *Radikal*, 1 September 2004.

[10] BBC News, 2 September 2004.

[11] European Enlargement Commissioner Stefan Füle referred to the proposed constitutional reforms as the 'broadest possible consultation' needed to improve democratic standards, human rights, the rule of law, and improvement of the daily lives of Turkish citizens (see *Sofia Echo*, 31 March 2010). 'The 27-nation bloc fully supports the reform package,' Spain's Foreign Minister Miguel Angel Moratinos said at a news conference in Brussels in May 2010 (see *Today's Zaman*, 12 May 2010). Also see Katcher (2010).

References

Alkan, T. (1984) 'The National Salvation Party in Turkey', in *Islam and Politics in the Modern Middle East*, eds M. Heper & R. Israeli, Croom Helm, London, pp. 79–102.

Atacan, F. (2005) 'Explaining religious politics at the crossroad: AKP–SP', *Turkish Studies*, vol. 6, no. 2, pp. 187–199.

Ayata, S. & Ayata, A. G. (2007) 'The center-left parties in Turkey', *Turkish Studies*, vol. 8, no. 2, pp. 211–232.

Berkes, N. (1998) *The Development of Secularism in Turkey*, Routledge, New York.

Çağaptay, S. (2003) 'European Union reforms diminish the role of the Turkish military: Ankara knocking on Brussels' door', *Turkish Yearbook*, vol. 34, pp. 213–217.

Çarkoğlu, A. (2007) 'The nature of left–right ideological self-placement in the Turkish context', *Turkish Studies*, vol. 8, no. 2, pp. 253–271.

Çarkoğlu, A. & Toprak, B. (2000) *Türkiye'de Din, Toplum ve Siyaset* [Religion, Society and Politics in Turkey], TESEV, Istanbul.

Çınar, A. (2005) *Modernity, Islam, and Secularism in Turkey: Bodies, Places, and Time*, University of Minnesota Press, Minneapolis.

Dodd, C. H. (2002) *Storm Clouds over Cyprus: A Briefing*, Eothen Press, Huntingdon.

Doğan, Y. (2005) 'Gümrük Birliği Fatihi, Hoşgeldin', [Welcome, the Customs Union conqueror], *Hürriyet*, 14 October, available online at: http://hurarsiv.hurriyet.com.tr/goster/haber.aspx?id=3380768&p=2

Gülmez, S. B. (2006) 'The Republican People's Party (CHP) and Turkish foreign policy, 2003–2005', MA thesis, Middle East Technical University, Ankara.

Gülmez, S. B. (2007) 'The Cyprus policy of the CHP: change or continuation?', *Insight Turkey*, vol. 9, no. 1, pp. 127–138.

Gülmez, S. B. (2008) 'The EU policy of the Republican People's Party: an inquiry on the opposition party and Euro-skepticism in Turkey', *Turkish Studies*, vol. 9, no. 3, pp. 423–436.

Hürriyet. (2004) 'İşte AKP'nin Zina Gerekçesi', [Here is the AKP's justification for adultery], 28 August, available online at: http://www.hurriyetdailynews.com/n.php?n=akp-to-tour-opposition-for-package-2010-03-21

Hürriyet Daily News (2010) 'AKP to tour opposition for constitutional reform package', 21 March.

İlkkaracan, P. (2008) 'How adultery almost derailed Turkey's aspirations to join the European Union', in *Deconstructing Sexuality in the Middle East: Challenges and Discourses*, ed. P. İlkkaracan, Ashgate, Burlington, VT, pp. 41–64.

Kalaycıoğlu, E. (1994) 'Elections and party preferences in Turkey: changes and continuities in the 1990s', *Comparative Political Studies*, vol. 27, no. 4, pp. 402–425.

Kaleağası, B. (2008) 'CHP AB'ye giriyor', [CHP is entering the EU], *Star*, 26 May, available online at: http://www.stargazete.com/acikgorus/chp-ab-ye-giriyor-haber-104217.htm

Katcher, B. (2010) 'Europe will back Turkey's constitutional reform', *Washington Note*, 10 May, available online at: http://www.thewashingtonnote.com/archives/2010/05/searching_for_e/

Korkmaz, S. (2004) 'Anatolian Women Wants Adultery to be Punished' [Zinaya Ceza Verilmesini Anadolu Kadını İstiyor], Hürriyet, 28 August. Available online at: http://hurarsiv.hurriyet.com.tr/goster/haber.aspx?id=253079&p=2

Lewis, B. (2002) *The Emergence of Modern Turkey*, Oxford University Press, New York.

Lipset, S. M. & Rokkan, S. (1967) *Party Systems and Voter Alignments: Cross-National Perspectives*, Free Press, New York.

Mardin, Ş. (1973) 'Center periphery relations: a key to Turkish politics?', *Daedalus*, vol. 102, no. 1, pp. 169–190.

Marks, G. & Wilson, C. J. (2000) 'The past in the present: a cleavage theory of party response to European integration', *British Journal of Political Science*, vol. 30, no. 3, pp. 433–459.

Marks, G., Wilson, C. J. & Ray, L. (2002) 'National political parties and European integration', *American Journal of Political Science*, vol. 46, no. 3, pp. 585–594.

Özbudun, E. (2007) 'Democratisation reforms in Turkey, 1993–2004', *Turkish Studies*, vol. 8, no. 2, pp. 179–196.

Palley, C. (2005) *An International Relations Debacle: The UN Secretary-General's Mission of Good Offices in Cyprus 1999–2004*, Hart, Portland.

Pollack, M. A. (2000) 'The end of creeping competence? EU policy-making since Maastricht', *Journal of Common Market Studies*, vol. 38, no. 3, pp. 519–538.

Sarıibrahimoğlu, L. (2006) 'The Turkish armed forces', in *Almanac Turkey 2005: Security Sector and Democratic Oversight*, ed. Ü. Cizre, TESEV, Istanbul, pp. 56–85.

Spiering, M. (2005) 'British Euroscepticism', in *Euroscepticism: Party Politics, National Identity and European Integration*, eds R. Hamsen & M. Spiering, Rodopi, Amsterdam, pp. 127–150.

Taggart, P. (1998) 'A touchstone of dissent: Euroscepticism in contemporary Western European party systems', *European Journal of Political Research*, vol. 33, no. 3, pp. 363–388.

Taggart, P. & Szczerbiak, A. (2004) 'Contemporary Euroscepticism in the party systems of the European Union candidate states of Central and Eastern Europe', *European Journal of Political Research*, vol. 43, no. 1, pp. 1–27.

Taggart, P. & Szczerbiak, A. (2008) 'Introduction: opposing Europe? The policy of Euroscepticism', in *Opposing Europe? The Comparative Party Politics of Euroscepticism Volume 1. Case Studies and Country Surveys*, eds A. Szczerbiak & P. Taggart, Oxford University Press, Oxford, pp. 1–15.

Uslu, E. (2008) 'Ulusalcılık: the neo-nationalist resurgence in Turkey', *Turkish Studies*, vol. 9, no. 1, pp. 73–97.

Ware, A. (1996) *Political Parties and Party Systems*, Oxford University Press, Oxford.

Zaman, A. (2010) 'Hayır, AKP ile Koalisyon Kurmayız', [No! We shall not have a coalition with the AKP], *HaberTürk*, 11 June, available online at: http://www.haberturk.com/yazarlar/522707-hayir-akp-ile-koalisyon-kurmayiz

Zuckerman, A. S. (1982) 'New approaches to political cleavage: a theoretical introduction', *Comparative Political Studies*, vol. 15, no. 2, pp. 131–144.

Zürcher, E. J. (2004) *Turkey: A Modern History*, I. B. Tauris, New York.

Ödül Celep (PhD State University of New York – Binghamton) is an assistant professor of political science at the International Relations Department of Işık University, Istanbul. His research interests are political parties and voting behavior in Turkey and Western Europe. His dissertation *The Extreme Right and Democracy* (2006) was recently published in 2009, in both Turkish (Istanbul, Turkey) and in English (Saarbrücken, Germany).

The Nationalist Movement Party's Euroscepticism: Party Ideology Meets Strategy

Gamze Avcı

This article explores what conditions or what specific issues lead to shifts in the positioning of the Nationalist Movement Party (Milliyetçi Hareket Partisi, MHP) towards Turkey's European Union (EU) membership goal. The article first examines the MHP's background and characteristics and compares it with similar parties in Western Europe. Subsequently, the MHP's EU stance during 1999–2002 and in the post-2002 period is discussed. The article concludes that ideology matters for the MHP but that shifts in degrees of Euroscepticisim during particular periods can be explained by strategic considerations of the MHP, which respond to the party's electoral gains or losses, its position in the party political spectrum and whether it is in government, in opposition or outside parliament.

This paper focuses on the Nationalist Movement Party (Milliyetçi Hareket Partisi, MHP) in Turkey and how the MHP positioned itself on the issue of the European Union (EU) during the period of 1999–2010. The aim of the paper is to seek and offer explanations for changes in the MHP's attitude towards Turkey's potential membership in the EU during the last decade. Does the MHP consistently reject membership in the EU for Turkey? If not, what conditions or what specific issues lead to shifts in the MHP's positioning towards membership? To understand the changes in MHP's responses to the EU, the paper will refer to factors identified in the established literature on political parties and European integration which have been used to explain how the European issue is politicised by political parties. Therefore, the paper will first review the existing literature on political parties and European integration. After a cursory assessment of the MHP's background and the characteristics that make it comparable to extreme-right parties in Europe, the paper will identify and discuss the MHP's experience as a coalition partner during 1999–2002 and how the MHP has changed its views on the EU in the post-2002 period. The paper will conclude with a discussion on the relevance of the existing literature on political parties and European integration for the case of the MHP in Turkey.

Political Parties and the EU

Research on political parties and European integration concentrates on how political parties have positioned themselves towards the EU and whether and how party opinions on Europe can be explained. Three different streams can be identified. The first group focuses on Euroscepticism, which in general analyses the range of negative attitudes towards the EU (Szczerbiak & Taggart 2000; Taggart 1998). In this literature, it has been argued that the political mainstream produces more moderate views on European integration, whereas Euroscepticism has been employed by political parties on the fringes of the party system: the extreme right or extreme left. Within Euroscepticism, two types are differentiated: economic and cultural opposition to integration. Parties oppose European integration in order to defend national sovereignty and national community and/or reject the European project on the basis of its neoliberal character, which undermines the national welfare state (Hooghe, Marks & Wilson 2002; Marks & Wilson 2000). The main hypothesis is that extremist parties on the right draw on feelings of cultural insecurity to reject further integration and to shield national sovereignty from EU intervention or domination (de Vries & Edwards 2009). Scholars in this field distinguish between 'hard' and 'soft' forms of Euroscepticism (Szczerbiak & Taggart 2000; Taggart 1998). Hard Euroscepticism is the 'outright rejection of the entire European project and EU membership'. Soft Euroscepticism is 'qualified and contingent opposition, which does not imply the rejection of membership itself'.

A second group of scholars maintains that views on European integration are based on cleavages (originally Lipset and Rokkan [1967]) or rooted in ideology – left/right or 'new politics' (Hooghe, Marks & Wilson 2002; Kopecky & Mudde 2002; Marks & Wilson 2000; Marks, Wilson & Ray 2002). It is generally agreed that the EU does not produce a new cleavage but that European integration is incorporated into already existing ideologies of party leaders, activists and constituencies.

Finally, a third group argues that, as the EU issue becomes politicised, parties act 'opportunistically', by adopting a pro- or anti- EU position in order to gain new votes (Iversen 1994; Ladrech 2002). More specifically, the claim is that ideology and interest affect a party's position on European integration in the long term but political parties may change tactics and electoral strategies in order to make the most of the 'EU issue' in the short term (Sitter 2002). Shifts in strategy are based on assumptions about voters' issue positions or public opinion, and are related to efforts to participate in government or tactics that require the display of critical opposition.

The MHP's Past and Trajectory up until 1999

In many ways, the MHP is similar to the radical right in Europe.[1] The MHP uses themes that are comparable to the ones used by the radical right in Europe. The traditional platforms of nationalism, ethnocentrism, the protection of territory and a focus on the struggle between nations can easily be detected within the MHP. The MHP promotes Turkishness and has a romantic and racist notion of Turkish history and culture with the broader understanding that all Turks share a common ancestry. The MHP's core ideology has its roots in its long-time leader Alparslan Türkeş's much cited pamphlet titled *The Nine Lights and Turkey*, which, among other things, advocates anti-Marxism and anti-communism but also underlines the MHP's belief in a parliamentary multi-party democracy (see also Landau 1982).[2] Hence Landau, in the 1980s, described the MHP as a 'typical best for everyone ideology with obvious emphasis on nationalism, idealism and morals in a popular vein' (Landau 1982, p. 602). During the last decade, the MHP has increasingly claimed that it has its own brand of conservatism and cultural nationalism which brings it close to the Christian Democrats in Western Europe (Öniş 2003).

The 'other' is an important issue for the extreme right, and it also plays a crucial role in the articulation of the MHP's identity (Yavuz 2002). However, some scholars suggest that the MHP's definition of the 'other' has changed over time: in the 1970s it was communism, in the 1980s it was the Kurdistan Worker's Party (Partiya Karkeran Kurdistan, PKK), in the 1990s it became political Islam and nowadays it is the EU (Arıkan 1998, p. 37). Yet, it should be noted that, unlike the MHP's other enemies, the PKK has remained more of a constant thread due to, and especially during periods of, terrorist insurgency. By and large, the MHP has portrayed the other as enemies of the state and the Turkish nation.

Compared with some of the European radical-right parties, the MHP is a rather recent phenomenon. The roots of the MHP go back to the establishment of the conservative rural Republican Farmers Nation Party (Cumhuriyetçi Köylü Millet Partisi, CKMP) in 1948 (Arıkan 1998, p. 131). In 1965, Alparslan Türkeş, a colonel in the coup of 1960 and a former member of the ruling junta, gained control of the CKMP and during the 1969 Party Congress he changed the party's name to the Nationalist Movement Party. During the 1970s, the party, especially its youth wing the Grey Wolves, was considered a protagonist of the violent left–right struggle in Turkey. When the Turkish army seized power on 12 September 1980, the MHP was banned together with all other active political parties at the time, and many of its leading members were imprisoned. The party was re-founded in 1983 as the Conservative Party (Muhafazakar Parti, MP), then changed its name to the Nationalist Task Party (Milliyetçi Çalışma Partisi, MÇP) and then back to its former name in 1992. In 1993, Muhsin Yazıcıoğlu and other five deputies left the MHP and founded the Great Union Party (Büyük Birlik Partisi, BBP), an ultranationalist and Islamist splinter party. The MHP was led by its ultranationalist leader Alparslan Türkeş from 1965 until his death in 1997. In 1997, Devlet Bahçeli took over and was highly successful in creating a new image for the MHP. He focused on creating a centrist image and downplayed ultranationalist and extremist views. Another significant change has been that, particularly under Bahçeli, the party has distanced itself from the use of violence.[3] This shift represented a clear demarcation from the pre-1980 MHP, which had a legacy of extensive violent acts (for more on the nationalist rhetoric, see Bora 2003).

Similar to its European counterparts, the MHP rejects any loss of sovereignty to a centralised European bureaucracy. However, what obviously does not appear in the MHP's rhetoric is discussion of the idea of a 'nation of Europe' (which, for the far right in Europe, generally, excludes the Turks) which coexists with the focus on traditional nationalism. Another difference is that the MHP does not typically possess deploy anti-immigration rhetoric, at least not any that is comparable to its European counterparts'. In a similar vein, it cannot be seen as a single-issue party that is openly racist and xenophobic (see also Öniş 2003, p. 39). Nonetheless, it is a party that prefers hierarchical arrangements, a limitation of diversity and individual autonomy. It is also, at this point, no longer opposed to free market economics,[4] which explains its permissive attitude towards the EU's economic criteria (see also Öniş 2003).

The MHP's nationalist outlook has always considered the party and the nationalist movement at large as aligned with and attached to the state, and this tradition has fortified a political stance whose goal has been to strengthen the state. However, this natural alliance was harmed in the aftermath of the 12 September 1980 military coup by the aggressive stance of the state against the MHP and its traditions. After the coup, the leadership of the MHP was arrested and prohibited from active politics, which eventually led to a rethinking within the MHP in terms of its attitude towards the state. In the context of its relations or attitude towards the state, another significant issue for the MHP has been the role of the state with regard to religion. While the MHP has high respect for the state and key institutions such as the military, since the post it has taken a clear position against restrictions placed on religious freedoms such as wearing a headscarf in public places. In general, the MHP's understanding of nationalism does not exclude a role for religion. As a matter of fact, the MHP has fused ethnic Turkish nationalism with Islam, although the former has always dominated the latter component to varying degrees. These features combined with the rise of the pro-Islamic vote pool explain, to a certain extent, the MHP's recent success in attracting some Islamist votes.[5]

An important issue when discussing political parties is their relative position in the political party system. Although the MHP has remained on the fringes of Turkish electoral space, it could be argued – despite dips and upheavals – that its significance has increased relatively over time. In the 1960s, the MHP's electoral vote rose gradually from 2.2 per cent in 1965 to 6.4 per cent in 1977, as it became part of the governing coalition in 1975–77 and then again briefly in 1977.[6] In 1981, the MHP was closed down by the military regime and returned to electoral politics under Türkeş in 1987. The 1987 election had dismal results for the MHP, which received only 2.9 per cent of the vote. In 1991, it participated in the general election as a coalition with the pro-Islamist Welfare Party (Refah Partisi, RP), receiving a total of about 17 per cent of electoral support. The MHP participated in the 1995 elections alone and remained below the 10 per cent threshold (which was established in the 1980 Constitution), and thus received no seats in parliament. The breakthrough for the MHP came with the 1999 election, making it evident that the ethnic nationalism of the MHP rose to a dominant role in Turkish electoral politics of the late 1990s (Çarkoğlu & Hinich 2006, p. 12).

A further critical issue is the MHP's potential as a governing partner in coalitions. The European continental party systems have bred far-right – and far-left – parties that feature a harder form of Euroscepticism. Generally, extreme-right parties in Western Europe tend to evince centrifugal electoral competition, and therefore do not have much incentive to moderate their Eurosceptic attitudes. However, the few that have had the chance of participating in government have modified their stances. For instance, the Norwegian and Danish Progress Parties and the Italian National Alliance party have all discarded some of their more extreme elements in high-profile splits over the last few years. This is in line with the argument that Eurosceptic parties are expected to modify or avoid Euroscepticism to the extent that they aspire to or actually participate in governing coalitions. Between 1999 and 2002, we observe a similar trend with the MHP while in government together with the Motherland Party (Anavatan Partisi, ANAP) and the Democratic Left Party (Demokratik Sol Parti, DSP). As the literature suggests, being in a governing coalition during this period mitigated and provided countervailing forces to MHP's traditional stances (see Avcı 2004).

Finally, EU support is not typical of the MHP's constituency, since the MHP voter is considered to be rather Eurosceptic (Çarkoğlu & Kalaycıoğlu 2007, pp. 197–200). Traditionally, the core of MHP support is found in the central and west Anatolian provinces of Turkey. It is weakest in the southeast because MHP's nationalist line does not appeal to the ethnic Kurdish vote. In the 1990s and in the most recent election of 2007, the party made strong gains along the Mediterranean coast and moderate gains in the Aegean region. The party has also become, relatively speaking, stronger in the larger cities of the northwest region, such as Istanbul, Ankara and Izmir.

1999–2002: The MHP in Coalition Government

From 1999 to November 2002, the MHP's role became more noticeable as a coalition partner and a key actor in passing (or blocking) reforms required under the Copenhagen criteria. The MHP was in the coalition government led by Ecevit, together with the ANAP. Ecevit's DSP received 22.3 per cent of the votes in 1999, and his coalition partners the MHP and ANAP received 18.1 per cent and 13.3 per cent, respectively. On 18 March 2000, the new government announced that the three coalition partners had finally reached a compromise on the commitments Turkey would make in the context of the EU accession process. The National Programme for Adoption of the *Acquis* (NPAA) listed the short- and medium-term reforms, which required 89 new laws, amendments to 94 existing laws and a significant overhaul of Turkish politics. This occurred only after long deliberations and much struggle in parliament. The NPAA appeared to be a joint declaration by the three coalition partners but also, in a way, was a symbol of all the difficulties the coalition partners had faced when trying to agree on sensitive issues. Many of the reforms required by the EU's Accession Partnership were either watered down or dealt with in a vague manner. Despite the commitment made in the NPAA, progress was inconsistent, particularly in some of the substantial areas such as minority rights, freedom of speech and the abolition of the death penalty. Most of the delay was due to protracted discussions concerning 'national interest'. Although nationalist tendencies existed in all three coalition parties, they tended to be more pronounced in the MHP. Consequently, the MHP acquired a critical role in the coalition when it came to EU reforms. Parties either responded to the MHP's objections or compromised despite some degree of internal protest. Frequently, the MHP's attitude led to deadlocks within the frail coalition.

The MHP did not reject EU membership totally: for instance, Bahçeli stated that 'we want to take part in this Union', yet in the same breath he also stated that 'this participation should be in compliance with the magnitude, history and potential of our country'. Moreover, he added that 'it is hard to claim that the EU administration is quite aware of Turkey's efforts and contributions to the Union so far' (Anadolu Agency, 18 June 2002).

A key issue for the MHP was Cyprus's bid to join the EU. The bid itself and its implications were considered problematic. Bahçeli believed that the EU would create a fait accompli in Cyprus because of the EU's support for the Greek and Greek Cypriot positions (Avcı 2004). Yet another important issue of contention for the MHP was the abolition of the death penalty, as this had direct implications for the Öcalan case. Abdullah Öcalan, the former leader of the PKK, was found responsible for the death of an estimated 35,000 people in the guerrilla war between 1984 and 1999. He was sentenced to death for high treason by an Ankara State Security Court after his capture in 1999, even though Turkey had maintained a moratorium on executions since 1984. The MHP and other nationalists within the Ecevit government coalition wished to retain the right to order the execution of Öcalan. In October 2001, an amendment to the Constitution abolished capital punishment except in time of war, under the imminent threat of war and for terrorist crimes. Bahçeli's view was that Turkey wanted to unite with Europe in an honourable, fair and full membership, and that in order for it to do that there should be 'no bargaining concerning Öcalan' (Türkiye, 1 December 1999).

MHP leaders were worried that if they accepted the lifting of the death penalty while in government as a coalition partner, it would be very harmful for the party; indeed, one of the MHP's election pledges in 1999 was that if it came to power it would ensure the execution of Öcalan (Sabah, 6 December 1999). This pledge explains why the MHP changed its position during the course of the discussion despite the fact that it had initially suggested that it would not oppose the abolition of the death penalty if the DSP and ANAP legislated the measure through parliament with the support of the opposition (Turkish Daily News, 24 May 2002).

The use of Kurdish in education and on television constituted another issue for the MHP. The problem with extending rights to the Kurdish minority had much to do with the violent struggle between the PKK and the Turkish army. Quite often, the enlarged package of 'cultural rights' is seen as rewarding terrorism or approving violence, and in that context Bahçeli called the EU's attitude concerning terrorism 'double-faced and not serious'. He argued that 'most European countries continue to embrace terrorists who are the enemies of Turkey' and that this demonstrates that Turkey is justified in its concerns (*Cumhuriyet*, 21 November 2001). Finally, the MHP opposed the proposed amendment of article 312 of the Turkish Penal Code, which bans the incitement of hatred on religious or ethnic grounds. Similarly, the European Security and Defence Identity (ESDI) became an intractable problem. The final issue dividing the coalition parties in the EU debate was early elections (at some point in conjunction with the EU reform package): Bahçeli wanted to call for early elections to end the political uncertainty that had grown in recent months as Ecevit's illness kept him from work while coalition members clashed over EU reforms. The debate on early elections overlapped with a final attempt to pass a number of necessary EU reforms. Parliament finally approved elections to be held on 3 November 2002, and also approved on 3 August 2002 a package (the third package) of human rights reforms that it hoped would clear the way for EU membership. This package was adopted after a marathon overnight session. It included the abolition of the death penalty in peacetime, to be replaced with life imprisonment with no possibility of parole. It also legalised broadcasting and education in languages other than Turkish, notably Kurdish. Furthermore, the package did away with penalties for criticising state institutions, including the military, eased restrictions on demonstrations and associations and allowed non-Muslim religious foundations to buy and sell real estate. The package was presented by Yılmaz's ANAP and was passed with the support of the DSP, ANAP and opposition parties, despite the opposition of the MHP. The MHP voted 'no' en bloc. The other parties – despite their various prior statements – supported the package. There were defections from all parties (government and opposition) but there was no consistent resistance to the package as a party line. In remarks made on 4 August 2002, Bahçeli stated that the MHP would appeal to the Constitutional Court in a bid to force parliament to reverse its decision regarding the death penalty and minority rights: the reason behind this was that the MHP wanted to retain the right to execute Öcalan. Furthermore, the MHP also believed that cultural and ethnic rights would lead to ethnic clashes and separatism (*Turkey Update*, 14 November 2000). The Constitutional Court eventually rejected this petition in December 2002.

The 2002 election proved to be disastrous for the MHP. The party received 8.34 per cent of the vote and remained, therefore, without parliamentary representation according to Turkish election laws, which specify a ten per cent nationwide threshold for entry into the Turkish Grand National Assembly (TGNA). This was a major loss compared with the 1999 election, when the MHP received the second-highest vote with 17.98 per cent of the national vote and was apportioned 129 representatives in the

TGNA. This meant that from 2002 (up until the next election) the MHP was no longer either in government or in parliament.

MHP in Opposition after 2002

The years 2002 and 2003 were a turning point for the MHP. The 2002 election manifesto of the MHP clearly underlined its overall commitment to the EU: 'The MHP supports Turkey's EU membership which is one of Turkey's basic political targets' (p. 91). The same manifesto explained the moderation that the MHP exhibited during the 57th government (1999–2002) as a dual strategy. It proudly pointed out accomplishments concerning the EU such as the signing of the EU Accession Partnership document. The MHP was described as making important contributions to the EU path while looking out for the national interest when accepting the National Program and passing related legal and institutional adjustments (pp. 9–10). EU membership was presented as being beyond ordinary political discussion, but an issue that required a realistic and national perspective (p. 11). At the same time, the MHP explained that due to their 'national responsibilities' they had put up a red flag when it came to topics such as the death penalty and education/publication in Kurdish. These national responsibilities, or, in other words, sensitivities, were identified in almost all of Bahçeli's speeches touching on the EU: the Cyprus issue, Greek–Turkish relations, PKK-related terrorism, issues concerning minorities in Turkey (such as the reopening of the Greek Orthodox Halki seminary, which has been closed since 1971), and Armenian genocide claims. These are generally issues that are perceived as a threat to national unity or identity and also continue to recur as themes in the MHP's later research and development documents (titled Araştırma Geliştirme [ARGE] documents) (MHP ARGE 2004; 2005a, b and c; 2006; 2009). In a similar vein, the MHP stated that it would like to reform the domestic legal system and adopt EU and international legal norms but without hurting national unity and harmony (MHP 2002, p. 74).

Nevertheless, once in opposition in 2003, Bahçeli hardened his rhetoric and began to harshly attack the Adalet ve Kalkınma Partisi (Justice and Development Party, AKP) which was now in charge of Turkish government policy towards the EU. The MHP's attacks targeted the EU and AKP simultaneously. Bahçeli viewed the AKP's behaviour towards the EU as 'submissive'. Based on a Turkish idiom, he describes the AKP's attitude as 'I'll close my eyes and get my duty done,' hinting at quiet and passive obedience.[7] The AKP was the EU's political subcontractor and ignored the threats and dangers aimed at Turkey; in particular, the AKP was insensitive towards Cyprus and ignored threats aimed at the Lausanne Treaty.[8] By keeping the EU project alive, the AKP sought to secure legitimacy for itself and a political future.[9] The EU's reform packages were renamed and mocked as 'demolition packages'.[10] When evaluating the AKP's attainment of a negotiation date with the EU, Bahçeli claimed that 3 October 2005 was like an empty shell. It was a date that led nowhere and had been obtained by sacrificing Cyprus.[11] He said that ultimately there was no final date and clear timeline for Turkey's membership of the EU. The EU process was symbolic and only for purposes of display.[12]

Another defining moment for the MHP came at the end of 2006, with the discussions concerning the recognition of Cyprus. It reacted strongly to the EU summit and stated that 'the EU train has derailed at the Cyprus intersection'.[13] The AKP was blamed for this and Bahçeli argued that the 'AKP government is a serious security risk for Turkey's national interests'.[14] The emphasis was on Cyprus being sacrificed and Turkey being at a turning point.[15] From 2006, the MHP began to describe the EU process as thwarted, relations were likened to a sickness (gangrene) and the prediction was that the inevitable breaking point was now visible on the horizon.[16] Consequently, from 2007, Bahçeli ended his tradition of evaluating EU Progress Reports or EU summits that relate to Turkey.

This further hardening is reflected in the MHP's 2007 election manifesto, which described Turkey's recent past with the EU as 'a story of disappointment filled with blackmail, ultimatums, preconditions, unfair demands and pressure'. According to the MHP, Turkey was being treated as if it were handicapped and it was clear that the EU did not want Turkey as a member with equal rights. The impaired relationship no longer worked and a period of strategic thinking was required (MHP 2007, p. 119). As it happened, the 2007 election was a success for the MHP, which doubled its votes compared with 2002 to 14.3 per cent and obtained 71 seats in parliament, making it the third-largest party.

The MHP also benefited from a nationalist political environment at large in Turkish politics. There were a number of developments that fuelled nationalism in Turkey, most crucial of which were particular developments surrounding the PKK, Cyprus, the attitudes of some EU politicians towards Turkey, and US foreign policy in the Middle East. In 2004, the PKK abandoned its ceasefire of six years and PKK-related violence has escalated since, prompting anti-terrorism protests, often strongly nationalist in character. Open hostility towards Turkey's EU membership among the leadership of EU countries such as France and Germany, a general anti-Western attitude as a reaction to US foreign policy, and the perceived hypocrisy of the EU's decision to admit Cyprus after Turkey had backed the 2004 Annan Plan added to the more nationalist atmosphere (see also Öniş 2007). The rising tide of nationalism in Turkey was and is well embraced by the MHP.

Increasingly, the MHP also acted opportunistically and used a dual strategy. It has argued that Turkey is not obliged, sentenced to and/or in need of EU membership, which may come at a very high price (MHP ARGE 2009, p. 9). Most recently, the MHP's programme published after its Ninth Ordinary General Congress on 8 November 2009 gave a glimpse of the party's current view regarding foreign policy. The new program asserted that

> The characteristics, grounds and framework of relations between Turkey and the EU should be redefined. Turkey's relations with the Union should neither been seen as 'fate' nor 'a problem of identity.' No matter what the result is, we are not obliged to be swept around the EU's orbit.

At the same time, the MHP also stated explicitly that it will continue to 'support the EU–Turkey negotiations [but] only as long as the EU shall not harm the national unity and union, terror and separatism and does not harm Turkish interests in issues such as Cyprus, Greece and Armenia' (MHP 2009). Furthermore, the MHP maintained it would not accept any option other than full membership (MHP 2009). Alternatives to the EU were not explicitly mentioned but the MHP has suggested a diversification of Turkish foreign policy by focussing more on the Turkic world, Russia and the Middle East.

Conclusion

The MHP has traditionally been critical towards European integration due to its extreme-right political position. In the party leadership's own words, until the early 1990s it exhibited a more 'distanced' attitude towards the EU. During the run-up to the 1999 elections, Bahçeli focused on the move towards the political centre, which was well received by parts of the electorate and secured the success of the MHP in the elections. Once in government, the MHP argued that, since EU membership had evolved into a 'state policy', and symbolised for Turkey 'much more than a simple cost–benefit analysis', it needed to eventually consider a 'multidimensional and cool-headed approach' towards the EU issue.[17] As a coalition partner in government between 1999 and 2002, the MHP faced many critical hurdles related to the passage of EU reforms. The MHP's own key message was that joining the EU was in the national interest although some of the required political reforms were not, but despite these difficult issues, and while still in government in 2002, the MHP stated that it wholeheartedly supported Turkey's EU membership. In its 2002 election manifesto, it even boldly stated that the progress on the EU front accomplished until 2002 primarily owed to the MHP's commitment (p. 144), whereas in reality the measures involved were passed despite the MHP. To its credit, however, the MHP did not desert the coalition over the rather extensive EU reform packages. With the massive electoral loss in 2002, the MHP shifted to an openly more hostile EU stance, now calling the relationship 'unhealthy' and granting it only 'conditional support'. This coincided with declining public support for the EU, rising nationalism and a general disappointment surrounding the developments around the Cyprus issue.

Between 2002 and 2010, the MHP's EU criticism increased in dosage, scope and intensity although it still does not qualify as hard Euroscepticism, an outright rejection of European integration. In its discussions and criticisms of the EU, the MHP has primarily relied on 'sovereignty-based Euroscepticism' but it has never rejected the European project fully. Two different time periods can be distinguished: the period between 1999 and 2002 and the period after the electoral loss in 2002 until 2010. Between 1999 and 2002, the MHP sought to present the image of being a more open and cooperative party. But the 'mainstreaming' effect' of being in government, ultimately, did not benefit the party. In 2002, after its coalition experience, the MHP was perceived as too nationalistic by its recently acquired more mainstream voters, and as not delivering enough by its core ultranationalist constituencies. Therefore, the MHP quickly drew its own lessons and reverted to its ultranationalist roots, and eventually, by 2007, it was back as an opposition party in parliament. Since then, the MHP has exhibited harsh opposition to the AKP pro-EU government. It is also taking advantage of rising nationalism in the country.

The MHP clearly is a Eurosceptic party whose critical attitude is primarily defined by its ultranationalist character. The MHP's concern about so-called 'national sensitivities', and the way these issues are evaluated, is a reflection of its ideological concerns; however, this has not meant that these stances are not negotiable. In particular, the periods when the MHP shifted back and forth between a softer Euroscepticism and something closer to hard Euroscepticism can be explained by strategic considerations. These strategic considerations have responded to the MHP's electoral gains or losses, its position in the party-political spectrum and whether it is in government, in opposition or without seats in parliament The MHP is currently the third-largest party in parliament, and should it gain further ground in future elections the party will face the dilemma of whether to play down its 'conditional' opposition stance to the EU in pursuit of more votes and office, and thereby risk the alienation of its core voters, yet again.

Notes

[1] There is a large literature on the radical right in Europe; for an overview, see Kitschelt and McGann (1995).

[2] The full list is nationalism, idealism, moralism, societalism, scientism, independentism, ruralism, progressivism and populism, and industrialism and technologism.

[3] For a more recent statement, see Bahçeli (2006).

[4] This latter comparison is to a large extent based on, and in line with, Kitschelt and McGann's (1995) description of new radical-right parties in Europe.

[5] For an in-depth discussion on the MHP's appeal to the religious vote, see Çarkoğlu (2000) and Çarkoğlu and Toprak (2000).

[6] 1965: 2.2 per cent (11 seats); 1969: 3.0 per cent (one seat only, Türkeş himself); 1973: 3.4 per cent (3 seats) and 1977: 6.4 per cent (16 seats).

[7] Bahçeli on the EU Reform Package, 22 March 2003, available online at: http://www.mhp.org.tr

[8] Bahçeli's evaluation of the Sixth Reform Package, 19 June 2003, available online at: http://www.mhp.org.tr

[9] Bahçeli's press conference on the EU's Turkey Report, 7 October 2004, available online at: http://www.mhp.org.tr

[10] Bahçeli on the Sixth EU Reform Package, 19 June 2003, available online at: http://www.mhp.org.tr

[11] Bahçeli on the Brussels Summit, 21 December 2004, available online at: http://www.mhp.org.tr

[12] Bahçeli's press conference on the EU's Turkey Report, 7 October 2004, available online at: http://www.mhp.org.tr

[13] Bahçeli on the EU and Turkey's bargaining process on Cyprus, 8 December 2006, available online at: http://www.mhp.org.tr

[14] Bahçeli on the EU and Turkey's bargaining process on Cyprus, 8 December 2006, available online at: http://www.mhp.org.tr

TURKEY AND THE EU: ACCESSION AND REFORM

[15] Bahçeli on the Decisions of the Brussels Summit, 15 December 2006, available online at: http://www.mhp.org.tr
[16] Bahçeli on the EU Progress Report, 9 November 2006, available online at: http://www.mhp.org.tr
[17] Bahçeli's opening speech at the Sixth Ordinary General Congress, 5 October 2000, available online at: http://www.mhp.org.tr

References

Arıkan, B. E. (1998) 'The programme of the Nationalist Action Party: an iron hand in a velvet glove?', *Middle Eastern Studies*, vol. 34, no. 4, pp. 120–134.

Avcı, G. (2004) 'Turkish political parties and the EU discourse in the post-Helsinki period: A Case of Europeanization', in *Turkey and European Integration. Accession Prospects and Issues*, eds M. Ugur & N. Canefe, Routledge, Abingdon, UK, pp. 194–214.

Bahçeli, D. (2006) 'Ülkücü kardeşlerim hain tahrikler karşısında sokağa çıkmayacak' [Despite callous provocations, my nationalist brothers will not go onto the streets], *Milliyet*, 19 September.

Bora, T. (2003) 'Nationalist discourses in Turkey', *South Atlantic Quarterly*, vol. 102, nos 2–3, pp. 433–451.

Çarkoğlu, A. (2000) 'Geography of April 1999 Turkish elections', *Turkish Studies*, vol. 1, no. 1, pp. 149–171.

Çarkoğlu, A. (2003) 'Who wants full membership? Characteristics of Turkish public support for EU membership', *Turkish Studies*, vol. 4, no. 1, pp. 171–194.

Çarkoğlu, A. & Hinich, M. J. (2006) 'A spatial analysis of Turkish party preferences', *Electoral Studies*, vol. 25, no. 2, pp. 369–392.

Çarkoğlu, A. & Kalaycıoğlu, E. (2007) *Turkish Democracy Today: Elections, Protest and Stability in an Islamic Society*, I. B. Tauris, London.

Çarkoğlu, A. & Toprak, B. (2000) *Türkiye'de Din, Toplum ve Siyaset* [Religion, Society and Politics in Turkey], TESEV, Istanbul.

De Vries, C. & Edwards, E. (2009) 'Taking Europe to its extremes: extremist parties and Public Euroscepticism', *Party Politics*, vol. 15, no. 1, pp. 5–28.

Hooghe, L., Marks, G. & Wilson, C. J. (2002) 'Does left/right structure party positions on European integration', *Comparative Political Studies*, vol. 35, no. 8, pp. 965–989.

Iversen, T. (1994) 'The logic of electoral politics: spatial, directional, and mobilisational effects', *Comparative Political Studies*, vol. 27, no. 2, pp. 155–189.

Kitschelt, H. P. & McGann, A. (1995) *The Radical Right in Western Europe: A Comparative Analysis*, University of Michigan Press, Ann Arbor.

Kopecky, P. & Mudde, C. (2002) 'The two sides of Euroscepticism: party positions on European integration in East Central Europe', *European Union Politics*, vol. 3, no. 3, pp. 297–326.

Landau, J. M. (1982) 'The Nationalist Action Party in Turkey', *Journal of Contemporary History*, vol. 17, no. 4, pp. 587–606.

Ladrech, R. (2002) 'Europeanisation and political parties', *Party Politics*, vol. 8, no. 4, pp. 389–403.

Lipset, S. M. & Rokkan, S. (eds) (1967) *Party Systems and Voter Alignments*, Free Press, New York.

Marks, G. & Wilson, C. J. (2000) 'The past and the present: a cleavage theory of party response to European integration', *British Journal of Political Science*, vol. 30, no. 3, pp. 433–459.

Marks, G., Wilson, C. J. & Ray, L. (2002) 'National political parties and European integration', *American Journal of Political Science*, vol. 46, no. 3, pp. 585–594.

MHP (1999) 'MHP Seçim Beyannamesi' [MHP party programme], 18 April.

MHP (2002) 'MHP Seçim Beyannamesi' [MHP party programme], 3 October.

MHP (2007) 'MHP Seçim Beyannamesi' [MHP party programme], 22 July.

MHP (2009) 'Ninth Ordinary General Congress on November 8', available online at: http://www.mhp.org.tr

MHP ARGE (2004) 'Avrupa Komisyonu'nun 2004 Yılı İlerleme Raporu-Etki Raporu ve Tavsiyeleri' [EU progress report 2004 impact assessment and recommendations], October, available online at: http://www.mhp.org.tr

MHP ARGE (2005a) *Çıkmaz Sokak AKP'nin Avrupa Birliği Yol haritası*, [At a Dead End: The EU Road Map of the AKP], MHP, Ankara.

MHP ARGE (2005b) '2005 Yılı İlerleme Raporu ve Katılım Ortaklığı Belgeleri' [Progress report 2005 and accession partnership documents], October, available online at: http://www.mhp.org.tr

MHP ARGE (2005c) 'AKP'nin Avrupa Birliği Yol Haritası' [The AKP's EU road map], available online at: http://www.mhp.org.tr

MHP ARGE (2006) '2006 Yılı AB İlerleme Raporu ve Strateji Belgesi' [EU progress report and strategy document 2006], October, available online at: http://www.mhp.org.tr

MHP ARGE (2009) 'Avrupa Birliği' [European Union], available online at: http://www.mhp.org.tr

Öniş, Z. (2003) 'Globalisation, democratisation and the far right: Turkey's Nationalist Action Party in critical perspective', *Democratisation*, vol. 10, no. 1, pp. 27–52.

Ray, L. (2007) 'Mainstream Euroscepticism: trend or oxymoron?', *Acta Politica*, vol. 42, nos 2–3, pp. 153–172.

Sitter, N. (2002) 'Opposing Europe: Euroscepticism, opposition and party competition', Opposing Europe Research Network, Working Paper No. 9.

Szczerbiak, A. & Taggart, P. (2000) 'Opposing Europe: Party Systems and Opposition to the Union, the Euro and Europeanisation', Opposing Europe Working Paper No. 1, Sussex European Institute, available online at: http://www.sussex.ac.uk/Units/SEI/pdfs/wp36.pdf

Taggart, P. (1998) 'A touchstone of dissent: Euroscepticism in contemporary Western European party systems', *European Journal of Political Research*, vol. 33, pp. 363–388.

Türkeş, A. (1965) *Dokuz Işık ve Türkiye* [The Nine Lights and Turkey], Ankara.

Yavuz, H. (2002) 'The politics of fear: the rise of the Nationalist Action Party (MHP) in Turkey', *Middle East Journal*, vol. 56, no. 2, pp. 200–221.

Gamze Avcı (PhD University of Georgia) is currently a lecturer at University College of Utrecht University. Between 1997 and 2002, she worked as an assistant professor in the Department of Political Science and International Relations at Boğaziçi University, Istanbul. Her research is primarily on Turkey's relationship with the EU and Turkish migration to Western Europe. Her work has appeared in journals such as *Turkish Studies, European Foreign Affairs Review, European Journal of Political Research, European Journal of Migration and Law* and *International Migration*.

Between Reason and Emotion: Popular Discourses on Turkey's Membership of the EU

Bernard Steunenberg, Simay Petek and Christiane Rüth

In this article we research the main discourses in Germany and Turkey on Turkish accession to the European Union. As we argue, these discourses may easily affect the current accession negotiations, through statements made by national political leaders. We identify three distinct discourses in Germany (multiculturalism, European consolidation and cultural incompatibility) and three in Turkey (Euro-optimism, pacta sunt servanda and Turkish pride and independence). Most of the discourses we found, in both Germany and Turkey, are incompatible with Turkish accession and will make Turkish accession a tough call. Even if further enlargement has significant economic benefits, emotional arguments appear to play an important role in setting the pace of European integration.

Despite its long-lasting relationship with the European Union (EU), Turkey's membership bid has become more and more controversial in several EU member states. Faced with changing moods within their electorate, possibly reinforced by the current economic recession, national political leaders have become more careful in expressing their support for Turkey's membership or are even rejecting this possibility. Among the opponents has been French President Sarkozy, who declared, 'I do not believe that Turkey belongs in Europe, and for a simple reason: because it is Asia Minor. What I wish to offer Turkey is a true partnership with Europe, but not integration into Europe' (MG & Sedat Laçiner 2008). Also, German Chancellor Merkel is hesitant about full Turkish membership, suggesting that Germany may also prefer a 'privileged partnership'. After the recent elections, and forming a new coalition with the Liberals, Merkel's position has changed somewhat towards a more positive outlook on Turkish membership.

The statements of Sarkozy and Merkel reflect the mood of the public in several European states that no longer unconditionally support enlargement: the last round of enlargement, including the accession of Romania and Bulgaria, has led to an 'enlargement fatigue'. Furthermore, the popular rejections of the European Constitution in France and the Netherlands, together with the bothersome passage of the Lisbon Treaty, have made political elites more aware that the times of 'permissive consensus' on European integration are over. European political leaders need to be more sensitive to the preferences of their domestic electorates, which can express their dissent through popular elections or referendums.

In this article, we will analyse the existing domestic discourses on the relationship between Turkey and the EU. We focus on discourses because they provide normatively broader perspectives on issues by providing the reasons why people have certain opinions. A discourse is defined as 'a shared set of capabilities which enable the assemblage of words, phrases, and sentences into meaningful "texts" intelligible to readers or listeners' (Dryzek 1988, p. 710). It is a shared conceptual framework that allows us to understand and interpret topics and their discussion. Discourses also structure our ideas and provide an internal logic to our thoughts. By analysing discourses we deviate from public opinion studies (see, for instance, McLaren 2007; Kentmen 2008), which do not investigate these underlying, more stable normative frameworks.

We link domestic discourses with the accession process through the statements of political leaders. If a discourse is opposed to, or even incompatible with Turkish accession to the EU, political leaders – whether in the EU or in Turkey – may have to address these concerns in order to maintain their popular support. These statements affect the accession negotiations, in which credibility plays an important role. Even if politically unfavourable statements are only made rhetorically (Schimmelfennig 2009) they may erode the credibility of the negotiating parties, leading to the postponement of accession (Steunenberg 2002; Dimitrova 2005). Based on this link between national discourses and the accession process, our main expectation is that the more the main national discourses oppose or are even incompatible with Turkish EU membership, the more the current negotiations will be slowed down, postponing accession.

To identify the main discourses we use Q methodology (Brown 1993; McKeown & Thomas 1988). An important advantage of this methodology is that it is reflexive. By using authentic statements from the concourse[1] on Turkey and the EU and allowing a number of participants in this concourse to score these statements, Q methodology produces results that are not defined by preconceived notions of the researcher. As a qualitative methodology, it differs from the more interpretive work, including a frame-based content analysis (Koenig et al. 2006) using newspaper commentaries and articles (Schäfer & Zschache 2008; Wimmel 2009).

For the empirical analysis we focus on two national concourses, namely those in Turkey and Germany. The role of Turkey is of course obvious, since the Turkish population needs to accept the reforms imposed by the EU. If EU membership becomes too costly and is therefore no longer preferred, enlargement is not an option. The choice for Germany is based on two considerations. First, in comparison with other EU countries, the German population seems to take a more negative position towards Turkish accession, with about three-quarters of the population against accession (Schoen 2008). Like France, the current German government prefers a partnership with Turkey, not membership. It is therefore representative of the more 'reluctant' camp within the EU opposing Turkey's full membership. Second, Germany, as a large member state, has always been involved in the making of crucial decisions of the EU (Moravcsik 1991).

The article is organised as follows. In the next section, we first discuss the various views on Turkey and the EU, before we present our methodology to identify discourses in Germany and Turkey. In the following section, we present our findings for each country and make an inter-discourse comparison. We conclude the article by discussing our findings within the context of the current negotiations and the literature on EU enlargement.

Turkey and the EU

The problems related to Turkey's possible membership of the EU are much debated and cover a wide range of issues. Recent research has suggested a number of findings relevant to this article. Using newspaper articles, Koenig and colleagues (2006, pp. 158–165) indicate that the German media use three kinds of interpretative frames: an ethno-nationalist version of a clash of civilisations indicating how culturally or historically different Turkey is from other European states; an economic perspective emphasising the financial burden of Turkish accession; and liberal multiculturalism expressing that cultural differences should be tolerated. Using public opinion data, Schoen (2008) also finds that the German debate concentrates on the first two perspectives, which concern Europe's natural borders and the political and economic consequences of accession for the EU.

For Turkey, Koenig and colleagues (2006) find strong nationalism opposing EU accession next to liberal multiculturalism emphasising that Turkey has responded favourably to conditions set by the EU related to minority rights. A third discussion concentrates on the economic gains of EU membership. Remarkably, the meaning of these similarly labelled frames differs per country, which underscores the diversity in national concourses.

Somewhat different findings are reported by Schäfer and Zschache (2008), Walter and Albert (2009) and Wimmel (2009), who qualitatively analysed national newspaper articles and commentaries. Schäfer and Zschade (2008) and Wimmel (2009) show that conservative and liberal newspapers define Europe differently. Conservative newspapers like the *Frankfurter Allgemeine Zeitung* conceive Europe to be a 'cultural' or 'geographical union', while Turkey is defined as 'culturally different' so that its accession would destroy the political union. On the other hand, liberal newspapers like the *Süddeutsche Zeitung* refer to Europe as a 'security-political actor' or 'economic entity' (Schäfer & Zschache 2008, p. 12). Finally, Walter and Albert (2009, p. 236) point out that the conservative political-cultural and liberal geostrategic discourses in Germany seem to be based on an underlying conception of 'Turkish otherness' in which Turkey is not only described as a backward-oriented nation-state, but also the great mass of 'Turks' are seen as poor, blindly obeying authority, religious and uncultured. In the British media, on the other hand, Turkey's European identity is not contested (Walter & Albert 2009, p. 238).

These findings suggest that Turkey's accession is mainly discussed nationally and is not part of a broader 'European public sphere' (Koenig et al. 2006, p. 158). Additionally, the domestic discourses on Turkey's accession differ in terms of their content and support. These differences on what 'Europe' or 'Turkey' is shape the receptiveness to Turkish accession.

Method and Data Set

The Search for and Selection of Statements

Our identification of the main discourses is based on Q methodology, which seeks clusters of categories and concepts. These clusters indicate, in a consistent manner, what people think about Turkish membership in the EU.

In our analysis, we have drawn on statements from various media on Turkey and the EU, including newspapers, radio, political speeches and statements as well as web discussions. We aimed to find statements from a wide range of different sources from every kind of medium. In the case of newspapers, for example, we searched for statements from different national newspapers, including the yellow press. In the case of internet sources like discussion boards, we used more than one platform, trying to capture as diverse a range of statements as possible.[2] The statements were collected in the period from October to December 2009, although the sources from which we took our initial set of statements cover a much broader time frame.

Based on this search, we collected 150 statements in total from the German media and 130 statements from the Turkish media on the concourse about Turkey and the EU. It is important for our method that these statements be as authentic as possible, so they were not edited and were presented as we found them in their original language – German or Turkish; only obvious spelling mistakes were corrected. For the presentation in this article, we have translated the statements into English.

From the initial set of statements, we selected 64 statements for further analysis. To have as much variation as possible, we used a method proposed by Dryzek and Berejikian (1993). They suggest first sorting all statements according to two dimensions that characterise political discourses: the elements or aspects of a discourse, and the kind of claims made in a discourse. With regard to the elements of a discourse, and following Dryzek (1988, p. 711), we distinguished between ontology (which entities are distinguished), agency (the degree of agency assigned to these entities), motivations (what motivates agency) and natural relationships (what links are made between entities). Concerning the kind of claims made in a discourse, we used the classification developed by Toulmin and used by Dryzek and Berejikian (1993, p. 51) in their study of discourses on democracy. We distinguished between definitive (establishing meaning), designative (pointing to a 'fact'), evaluative (making a judgment) and advocative (pointing to a preferred situation or outcome) claims.

Combining these two dimensions, each with four categories, we have a four-by-four matrix with 16 cells in total. We selected four statements for each combination of both dimensions. In this process we tried as much as possible to avoid selecting 'similar' statements, so that our sample would be as diverse as possible. If one of the cells had less than four statements, which was rarely the case, we added a statement from one of the 'neighbouring' combinations to our sample. With four statements per cell and a total of 16 cells, we therefore had a total number of 64 statements in our sample (of statements).

The P-Set and the Sorting of Statements

For the Q-sort – the scoring of the various statements – we selected persons (the so-called P-set) ensuring a variety of general characteristics such as age and gender, since these often seem to affect opinions. In the German context, we considered whether the respondents were from West or East Germany (old or new Bundesländer). Based on findings by Schoen (2008, p. 78), respondents in West Germany attach great value to a historical and geographical demarcation between Europe and Turkey, while for respondents in East Germany cultural differences play a much greater role. In addition, West Germans fear an increasing immigration of Turkish citizens to Germany, which reinforces resistance to Turkish accession (McLaren 2007, p. 270), while this factor is irrelevant to East Germans (Schoen 2008, p. 84). In the case of Turkey, the perception of one's economic situation is seen as an important element determining views on EU membership.[3]

Potential participants were individually approached, and 40 persons in Germany and 30 in Turkey completed an online questionnaire based on FlashQ freeware.[4] The German participants were from East and West Germany, both men and women from different age groups and with varying years of education; the Turkish participants were relatively younger with a higher education, while the perceived, personal economic situation varied. In the Q-sort, the respondents had to score all 64 statements we selected in our research. The scores that could be attached to statements varied between -5 (strongly disagree) to $+5$ (strongly agree). The available scores follow a normal distribution so that the number of extreme values is the lowest, increases as one moves closer to the mode of the distribution, and is highest for a score of 0 (indifferent).

The resulting data were analysed using a dimension reduction technique in order to uncover underlying similarities in the way in which respondents scored their statements. In the analysis, the statements were the unit of analysis, so the number of cases was 64. We used centroid analysis as suggested by Brown (1993), since our aim was to explore existing discourses on EU–Turkey relationships.[5] Moreover, we used varimax rotation to increase the contrast between subjects being associated with possible factors. Using the eigenvalues, the extent to which these factors can be associated with particular subjects, and whether these factors can be interpreted based on distinguishing and characterising statements, we identified three different main discourses in Germany and Turkey.[6]

Main National Discourses

Germany: Between Multiculturalism and Cultural Incompatibility

In Germany, the discussions on EU–Turkey relationships can be traced back to three different main discourses. In presenting these discourses we use the distinguishing and characterising statements presented in Table 1 (see the note under the table for our definition of these terms). The table also presents the idealised Q-sort, which is the score a subject would give to this statement if his or her beliefs fully fitted with this discourse.

The first discourse we found in Germany can be labelled *multiculturalism*, since its participants favour Turkey's accession and believe that this will bridge different cultures. It consists of various statements with a Z-score in bold. The most prominent are statements 45 and 59. The second discourse can be labelled *European consolidation*, in which the participants stress the need for further development of the EU without Turkey (see statements 39, 23, 49, 64, 12, 42, 48 and 41). The last discourse we found expresses a *cultural incompatibility* between Turkey and the EU, and specifically Germany, which is illustrated by the assertion that 'Islam and democracy are incompatible' (statement 18; other statements are 3, 35, 38, 12, 2, 24, 52, 19 and 55).

Turkey: Between Pride and Optimism

Discussions in Turkey on EU–Turkey relationships appear to cluster around at least three different main discourses. Table 2 presents the scores of the various statements.

The first discourse can be labelled *Turkish Euro-optimism*, expressing that Turkey and the EU can mutually benefit from Turkish membership (see statements 12, 23, 32, 46 and 48). The second discourse is labelled *pacta sunt servanda* (commitments have to be honoured), in which Europe should keep its promise and only full membership should be offered to Turkey (see statements 55, 37, 36, 49, 31, 53, 61 and 51). The last discourse can be labelled *Turkish pride and independence*, suggesting that Turkey should not aim for EU membership (see statements 60, 64, 3, 27, 49, 29 and 2).

Discourses Compared

The main discourses in both Germany and Turkey evaluate Turkey's EU membership differently, which has implications for the accession process. Only the multiculturalism discourse in Germany and the Euro-optimism discourse in Turkey fully support Turkish membership in the EU. The *pacta sunt servanda* discourse in Turkey supports EU membership, but it also finds that the EU is obliged to grant full

TURKEY AND THE EU: ACCESSION AND REFORM

Table 1 Discourses in Germany: Z-scores and Idealized Q-scores of Statements for Different Factors*

	Factor 1		Factor 2		Factor 3	
	Z-score	Idealized Q-score	Z-score	Idealized Q-score	Z-score	Idealized Q-score
1. Not all Muslims are terrorists, but all terrorists are Muslims	−1.96	−5	−2.31	−5	−0.65	−1
2. Turkey was never as open, as wealthy and as democratic as today	0.40	0	−0.57	−1	−*1.21*	−*3*
3. Turkey is a Muslim country: it lacks the traditions of Christianity and Enlightenment that are necessary for a liberal-democratic order and economic success	−*1.09*	−*2*	−0.16	0	*1.43*	*3*
4. Turkey's development is only of Turkey's concern	−0.53	−1	−*1.13*	−*3*	−0.14	0
5. He who wants to enter the EU must accept our Christian idea of man	−0.15	−1	0.20	0	0.94	2
6. A referendum about Turkish EU membership is necessary in Germany	−0.91	−2	0.35	1	0.03	1
7. He who looks at the 67 million Turks only as a mass of immigrants, and not as a promising market, will regret this one-dimensional view in 10 to 15 years	0.60	1	0.20	1	−0.25	−1
8. Who can guarantee that Turkey will remain secular? Islamic fundamentalist tendencies cannot be overlooked	−0.43	−1	0.34	1	0.75	2
9. The Europeans want to see the actions of Turkey, not just nice words	0.37	0	0.86	2	1.22	2
10. The Europeans want Turkey first of all to establish democracy and the rule of law	1.30	3	1.55	4	1.94	5
11. The accession of Turkey is to be opposed because the EU already has too many members	−*1.58*	−*4*	−0.21	0	−0.71	−2
12. The accession of Turkey is to be supported because Turkey geographically is part of Europe	−0.04	0	−*1.97*	−*5*	−*1.02*	−*3*
13. A privileged partnership is more adequate than full membership	−0.25	−1	1.19	3	1.59	4
14. Geo-strategically, it must be in the interest of the EU, to have a dependable partner in the turbulent area of the Near and Middle East	1.42	4	0.04	0	1.08	2

(*continued*)

TURKEY AND THE EU: ACCESSION AND REFORM

Table 1 – *Continued*

	Factor 1		Factor 2		Factor 3	
	Z-score	Idealized Q-score	Z-score	Idealized Q-score	Z-score	Idealized Q-score
15. Turkey is important for Europe as a turnstile for energy streams	0.55	1	− 0.48	− 1	− 0.24	0
16. Not because it is an Islamic country, but because it is part of Europe, Turkey should become an EU member	0.37	0	− 1.16	− 3	− 0.85	− 2
17. Domestic violence, honour killings and early forced marriages are still serious problems in Turkey	1.11	3	1.65	4	1.77	5
18. Islam and democracy are incompatible	*− 1.96*	*− 4*	− 0.96	− 2	*1.59*	*4*
19. Turkey is too poor to join the EU	− 0.79	− 2	− 0.06	0	*− 1.53*	*− 4*
20. Turkey is too big: it would sooner or later be the biggest EU member, and for this reason also have the most votes	− 0.65	− 1	0.85	2	0.41	1
21. Turkey applies to the EU to be a member, not as an ambassador of the Islamic world	*1.03*	*3*	0.35	1	0.03	1
22. As long as the military perform political functions, which it has done since Kemal Atatürk, Turkey is no Western democracy	0.56	1	0.71	2	1.27	3
23. The EU can't handle Turkey	− 1.24	− 3	*1.40*	*3*	− 1.03	− 3
24. Even in the case of extremely explosive religious questions, a traditional Christian country and a traditional Muslim country, which often have contradictory positions, can take the same political path	*1.30*	*4*	0.04	0	*− 1.15*	*− 3*
25. Turkey wants to use the gas crisis between Russia and Ukraine to push its accession to the EU forward	− 0.49	− 1	0.16	0	− 0.19	0
26. The accession of Turkey is to be opposed because many immigrants will come to other EU countries	− 1.33	− 3	− 0.61	− 2	− 0.85	− 2
27. The accession of Turkey is to be opposed because, due to the low production costs, many companies will move to Turkey	− 1.17	− 2	− 0.40	− 1	− 0.62	− 1
28. The accession of Turkey is to be supported because Turkey has already made great efforts in the process of modernisation to enter the EU	0.54	1	− 1.11	− 3	− 0.95	− 2

29. Turkey does not look to the West, but seeks a close connection to the Islamic world	− 1.17	− 3	0.26	1	− 0.12	0
30. A partnership with Turkey is important to secure Europe's energy security	0.24	0	− 0.01	0	− 0.08	0
31. If the EU won't let Turkey enter, Turkey will orient itself towards the Islamic countries	0.03	0	− 0.38	− 1	0.41	1
32. The accession of Turkey would bring many unsolved conflicts into the EU's field of responsibilities. The conflicts in Turkey's neighbour states, which are little influenced by the EU so far, could play a greater role in EU policy-making	0.77	1	0.95	2	1.09	2
33. Europe has to understand that Turkey is no burden, but a benefit for the EU	0.90	2	− 1.41	− 4	− 0.66	− 1
34. The violations of the freedom of speech in Turkey are incompatible with a European perspective	1.39	4	1.70	5	1.76	4
35. After four years of assumed Western integration, Turkey presents itself as more Eastern than ever before	− 0.70	− 1	− 0.06	0	*1.28*	*3*
36. Never and nowhere has a political union that crossed cultural borders endured	− 0.83	− 2	− 0.86	− 2	− 0.27	− 1
37. No matter how Turkey changes, the Christian club will never let Turkey enter	− 1.39	− 3	− 0.80	− 2	− 0.93	− 2
38. Probably the most unpopular vision of the European future one could imagine is the full membership of poor, non-European countries full of dark-skinned people of Muslim belief	*− 1.15*	*− 2*	− 0.48	− 1	*1.01*	*2*
39. The consolidation of the European institutions must have priority before further accessions, to keep the EU capable of acting	0.00	0	*1.70*	*4*	0.34	1
40. An accession of Turkey, against the will of the majority of the EU's citizens, could increase the dissatisfaction with the EU	0.91	2	2.01	5	1.46	3
41. The Turks are right when they are angry regarding the everlasting debate about their accession to the EU	0.02	0	*− 1.32*	*− 3*	− 0.37	− 1

(continued)

TURKEY AND THE EU: ACCESSION AND REFORM

Table 1 – *Continued*

	Factor 1		Factor 2		Factor 3	
	Z-score	Idealized Q-score	Z-score	Idealized Q-score	Z-score	Idealized Q-score
42. Setting aside condescension and moralisation, one will realise that Europe needs Turkey more than is often assumed	0.94	2	−*1.17*	−*3*	−0.34	−1
43. If the EU wants to strengthen the reforms in Turkey, it must be clearer than thus far in committing to the goal of Turkey's accession to the EU	*1.18*	*3*	−0.93	−2	−0.01	0
44. The fact that Turkey did not sign the UN declaration against the persecution of homosexuals must be addressed in the accession negotiations	0.85	2	1.35	3	0.23	1
45. Turkey's accession to the EU could build a bridge between Europe and the Islamic world, increase mutual understanding and make a contribution to the peaceful coexistence of different cultures	*1.86*	*5*	−0.43	−1	−0.02	0
46. Since the eastern expansion, the EU has too often given a discount on its accession criteria, and accepted candidates that were not ready to enter the EU	0.01	0	0.93	2	−0.75	−2
47. With Turkey as a member, the EU could expand its role as a world power	0.88	2	−1.10	−2	−1.84	−5
48. Turkey deserves a chance, and Europe can only profit from that	0.48	1	−*1.79*	−*4*	−0.31	−1
49. Turkey mustn't become an EU member	−*2.08*	−*5*	*1.47*	*3*	0.29	1
50. The accession of Turkey would destroy the prospect of a politically united Europe, and the consensus in Europe that has grown over five decades	−*1.46*	−*4*	−0.17	0	−0.33	−1
51. The EU members should be honest in denying the accession of Turkey, declare themselves a Christian club, abandon the accession negotiations and build new walls in Europe	−1.30	−3	−1.02	−2	−1.23	−3
52. An EU including Turkey would be a positive thing for the rest of Europe, as it would reflect today's manifold beliefs in the EU	*1.03*	*3*	−0.36	−1	−*1.57*	−*4*

53. Turkey is asking the EU for something, so it should convince its critics	0.97	2	0.77	2	1.53	3
54. Accession to the EU would also make the integration of the Turks living here easier	*1.01*	*2*	− 1.38	− 4	− 1.43	− 4
55. EU accession would present Islam as a peaceful religion, help to show the positive sides of Islamic culture and marginalise extremist, anti-democratic movements	0.42	1	− 0.32	− 1	*− 2.21*	*− 5*
56. We cannot estimate what effect Turkey's accession would have on the EU's energy policy	− 0.13	− 1	0.30	1	0.76	2
57. The EU has to stop the accession negotiations if it does not want to lose its credibility	− 0.98	− 2	− 0.25	− 1	− 0.18	0
58. The EU would overburden itself economically and financially by letting Turkey and other states enter	− 0.50	− 1	0.71	2	− 0.24	0
59. With Turkey's accession, the EU would send an important signal against the often evoked 'clash of civilisations'	*1.44*	*5*	− 0.75	− 2	− 0.05	0
60. EU membership would mean less military autonomy for Turkey. With an army depending on the EU, it would become impossible for Turkey to react to regional developments and contingently to decide for military action, or against it	0.83	1	0.56	1	− 0.96	− 2
61. The leaders in Ankara should not forget that not geo-, but domestic politics will decide on its accession	0.07	0	0.53	1	0.86	2
62. Opening the border to Armenia would be a great plus for Turkey towards the EU	0.47	1	0.51	1	− 0.78	− 2
63. If Ankara were a member of the EU, Europe's borders would touch the central conflict areas of the world	0.96	2	1.10	2	0.59	1
64. As a member of the EU, Turkey would change the EU's culture in a way that would cause massive resistance	− 0.95	− 2	*1.38*	*3*	0.40	1

* In bold are *distinguishing* (that is, significantly different at $p < 0.01$) and *characterizing* (that is, Z-score larger than 1 or smaller than − 1) statements.

TURKEY AND THE EU: ACCESSION AND REFORM

Table 2 Discourses in Turkey: Z-scores and Idealized Q-scores of Statements for Different factors*

	Factor 1		Factor 2		Factor 3	
	Z-score	Ideal Q-score	Z-score	Ideal Q-score	Z-score	Ideal Q-score
1. Turkey is richness, not a burden for the EU	0.40	1	− 0.36	− 1	0.39	1
2. We have a mentality that performs in accordance with the will of the EU rather than with our own benefit	− 0.31	− 1	− 0.02	0	*− 1.16*	*− 3*
3. Our accession to the EU is a top priority for Turkey	− 0.62	− 2	− 0.61	− 2	*− 2.20*	*− 5*
4. Turkey is a success story for the EU	0.01	0	− 0.44	− 1	− 0.21	0
5. Turkey is an independent country. It does not need the EU	− 1.43	− 3	− 1.26	− 3	− 0.36	− 1
6. It is the EU that is slowing down the process	− 0.23	− 1	0.00	0	− 0.69	− 2
7. We don't ask for privileges. What we ask for is equal and fair treatment	1.19	3	1.63	4	0.80	2
8. Grant us the same rights that you gave to those who came before us. That is all we ask from the EU	0.57	1	1.09	3	0.97	3
9. Turkish society believes that it deserves EU membership	− 0.18	0	− 0.05	0	− 0.23	0
10. We will not accept anything less than full membership: full membership or nothing	− 0.06	0	0.55	1	− 0.88	− 2
11. Whatever democratic rights EU countries are offering their own citizens, we want the same for our country's people	1.15	3	1.27	3	0.39	1
12. We do not want to be in a Christian union. We want to belong to an identity such as Europeanness	*1.15*	*3*	0.05	0	− 0.69	− 2
13. Problems that the EU confronts today cannot be solved without Turkey's membership	0.00	0	− 0.68	− 2	− 0.45	− 1
14. We hope that the issue of Cyprus will be eliminated from being an obstacle in Turkey's EU process	− 0.11	0	0.19	1	*1.08*	*3*
15. There is no consensus in Turkey on joining the EU	− 0.27	− 1	0.12	0	0.67	1
16. The only concern the EU has is not to take Turkey, a Muslim country, in the EU. The EU is a Christian club	− 1.06	− 3	− 0.73	− 2	− 1.15	− 3
17. It is anticipated that the negotiation talks between Turkey and the EU will continue to be open-ended	0.13	0	− 0.26	− 1	− 0.69	− 2
18. Turkey is a rich cultural but also political and especially economic resource for Europe	1.72	5	0.19	1	1.10	3

19. The decisions taken by the EU to start negotiations with Turkey were not sincere. The heads of states took a decision that did not reflect their intentions	−0.81	−2	0.37	1	0.15	0
20. Turkey's accession to the EU will prove that the EU is not a Christian club	−0.40	−1	0.91	2	0.77	1
21. Many Turks are making plans to reject the EU before it rejects Turkey	−0.36	−1	−0.19	−1	−0.50	−1
22. There is prejudice against us in Europe and it is impossible to break this	−1.26	−3	−1.03	−2	−0.18	0
23. Turkey can play an effective role in many of the problems that the EU is facing and in fact can be a source of inspiration for other Muslim countries	*1.65*	*4*	−0.07	0	0.06	0
24. Turkey is not an ordinary candidate for the EU	1.69	4	1.03	2	0.48	1
25. Turkey's membership of the EU is a solution that will bring gains to both sides	0.76	2	0.44	1	1.11	3
26. We are coming as a country that contributes to peace and stability	0.56	1	−0.27	−1	0.03	0
27. We need membership of the EU for Turkish modernisation	−0.49	−2	−0.14	−1	*−1.90*	*−4*
28. Since we will not get into the EU in the end, we can talk about neither its benefits nor its costs	−2.01	−5	−0.79	−2	−1.55	−4
29. They are afraid of us and they are holding us back. Because of the very nature of Turkey, they are right; we are talking about a country with 70 million people	0.98	2	0.19	0	*−1.42*	*−3*
30. If the EU wants to become a strategic power, it cannot do so without Turkey	1.11	2	−0.14	0	1.52	4
31. Although we missed the train during Ozal's time, Turk–Arab and Turk-Turkic relations make more sense than being a small fish in the big sea	−0.79	−2	*−1.98*	*−5*	0.16	0
32. Once Turkey becomes a member of the EU, our economy is going to get stronger and per capita income will increase	*1.15*	*3*	0.38	1	−0.29	−1
33. The negotiation process, although slow, is still proceeding and we are happy with that	−1.01	−2	−1.42	−3	−0.54	−2
34. Above all, we would perceive Turkey's joining the EU as an ethical problem	−0.95	−2	−1.08	−2	−0.92	−2
35. Turkey is joining not to become a burden but to bear one	0.96	2	−0.55	−2	0.15	0

(continued)

TURKEY AND THE EU: ACCESSION AND REFORM

Table 2 – *Continued*

	Factor 1		Factor 2		Factor 3	
	Z-score	Ideal Q-score	Z-score	Ideal Q-score	Z-score	Ideal Q-score
36. It is not logical for a country that joined the Customs Union to insist on a full membership. Without becoming a full member, fulfilling the option of 'privileged partnership', we can both protect our sovereignty and reach an agreement we like with the EU	−0.23	−1	*−1.62*	*−3*	−0.40	−1
37. Focusing on 'privileged partnership' for Turkey instead of a full membership is an indignity	−0.63	−2	*1.51*	*4*	0.60	1
38. No other candidate nation has been subjected to this kind of treatment	−0.06	0	0.98	2	0.68	1
39. There is no interest for us in babysitting the clumsy and old population of Europe	−1.75	−4	−1.80	−4	−1.43	−3
40. Turkey could not draw her road map for the EU very well	0.70	2	1.05	2	0.61	1
41. Turkey's young population will play a key role in carrying on EU's economic dynamism	1.43	3	0.83	2	1.57	4
42. We do not need the EU. It will disappear ten years later anyway. The future is in Asia. We had better leave the EU option behind and return to where we came from	−1.75	−4	−1.78	−4	−0.46	−1
43. The potential contribution in energy security, labour force, decreasing the geopolitical risks, preparation for dialogue between civilisations as an alternative to clash of civilizations, bringing stability and peace in the Middle East region makes Turkey an actor that is very hard for the EU to discard	1.77	5	0.19	0	1.48	4
44. It is very difficult; the religious aspect is not mentioned but the Europeans are more prejudiced than us on this point	−0.42	−1	−0.22	−1	0.83	2
45. If we enter the EU, the European Parliament will turn into a Turkish parliament. And this is not desirable to any power	−1.76	−4	−1.39	−3	−1.00	−2
46. It is Turkey who is the giving party. It is not important to be a member by giving everything	*−1.51*	*−3*	−0.44	−1	−0.48	−1
47. It is too easy to simply claim that we can continue in our path without the EU	0.19	1	0.87	2	0.80	2

48. Europe keeps us waiting; they will benefit from us and then will not accept us	− *2.13*	− *5*	− 0.21	− 1	− *1.09*	− *3*
49. For us there should be no alternative to becoming a member	− 0.41	− 1	*1.27*	*3*	− *1.55*	− *4*
50. Turkey's full membership of the EU is important and necessary for speeding up the development of democracy	1.63	4	1.19	3	0.80	2
51. Turkey's accession to the EU will not last for 20–30 years. Nobody should have any doubt on that	0.24	1	− *1.49*	− *3*	− 0.05	0
52. EU member states should not make Ankara's accession to the EU a domestic issue	0.19	0	0.71	1	− 0.02	0
53. Instead of raising the requirements constantly, the EU should decide on a date for Turkey's full membership	− 0.15	0	*1.29*	*3*	− 0.30	− 1
54. Turkey should not become a member of the EU. Right now it should not spend energy on that	− 1.47	− 3	− 1.87	− 4	− 0.54	− 1
55. Europe should keep its promise to Turkey	0.49	1	*1.67*	*5*	0.95	2
56. One should also question whether the EU is ready for Turkey	0.55	1	0.41	1	0.81	2
57. Full membership is not a must. Turkey should also consider that	− 0.44	− 1	− 2.08	− 5	− 2.45	− 5
58. Turkey should speed up both the political and economic reform process for harmonisation with the EU	0.99	2	0.97	2	0.91	2
59. The important point should not be the issue of having a blue emblem on the number plates of cars; it should be the issue of how many people can afford to buy a car in our country	0.72	2	0.31	1	0.89	2
60. Everyone must be aware of Turkey's importance. Without the contribution of Turkey, the problems in the Middle East and the Caucasus cannot be solved	1.06	2	− 0.73	− 2	*1.90*	*5*
61. We should admit that in today's relations between Turkey and the EU there is an anxiety over trust, which is gradually deepening	0.26	1	*1.31*	*4*	0.59	1
62. The same criteria that were put forward for all the member countries should be applied to Turkey	0.22	1	1.65	5	1.90	5
63. The EU should be more encouraging, so that we can convince the Turkish public to adopt changes	0.06	0	0.91	2	− 0.63	− 2
64. We shall join the EU but not give up our customs and traditions. They should admit us only if they accept us the way we are	− 0.62	− 2	0.19	0	*1.26*	*3*

⋆ See the explanation for Table 1.

TURKEY AND THE EU: ACCESSION AND REFORM

Table 3 Discourses in Germany and Turkey and the Likelihood of Enlargement

Germany: Turkey:	Multiculturalism	European consolidation	Cultural incompatibility
Euro-optimism	+	–	–
Pacta sunt servanda	±	–	–
Turkish pride and independence	–	–	–

Note: ' + ' = positive and '–' = negative likelihood.

membership within a reasonable time frame. This idea of obligation runs against the conditionality the EU applies to induce Turkey to adapt to the pre-accession *acquis* and the *acquis communautaire*. This makes the *pacta sunt servanda* discourse less useful as a discourse supporting the Turkish accession process. Moreover, the participants doubt whether the EU will, in the end, grant Turkey membership.

The other discourses do not support Turkish accession. The German participants in the European consolidation and the cultural incompatibility discourses reject the idea that Turkey could join the EU. In the first discourse, the EU is not yet ready for Turkey and should focus on its current challenges after the last enlargement. The second discourse perceives the cultural and religious differences between the current member states (including Germany) and Turkey as the main obstacle to further cooperation. The Turkish pride and independence discourse indicates that Turkey should not aim for EU membership and should refocus itself on the Arabic world. Furthermore, these participants also seem to be unwilling to give up Turkish sovereignty in return for closer European cooperation.

In both countries, some groups do not aim for closer ties between the EU and Turkey and do not prefer enlargement. These opinions, rooted in the main discourses opposing Turkish EU membership, could easily motivate national political leaders to make statements for domestic use that are not supportive of the accession negotiations. The discourses we identified in this article are the main discourses in Germany and Turkey.

In Table 3, we summarise the extent to which the discourses we found fit in terms of the possible accession of Turkey to the EU. Only if national political leaders limit their statements to the multiculturalism and Euro-optimism discourses, respectively, will the accession process not be burdened by a possible erosion of credibility.

Conclusions

In this article, we have researched the main discourses in Germany and Turkey on Turkish accession to the EU. In both countries we have identified a number of distinct discourses. In Germany, we found a multiculturalism discourse supporting Turkish membership and two discourses rejecting it. The latter two are the European consolidation discourse focusing on strengthening the current EU, and the cultural incompatibility discourse that straightforwardly claims that Turkey is not part of 'Europe'. These distinct and parallel discourses relate to some of the earlier findings on discussions in Germany. The multiculturalism discourse relates to a similar frame noted by Koenig and colleagues (2006, p. 162) and the liberal view found in some German newspapers by Schäfer and Zschache (2008), while the European consolidation discourse fits a more conservative perspective. Schoen (2008) and Stelzenmueller (2007) emphasise some of the elements of these three discourses, such as what 'Europe' should be, and the economic and political consequences of Turkish membership (see also Koenig at al. 2006, p. 164). Finally, the cultural incompatibility discourse related to the ethno-nationalist frame is also reported by Koenig and colleagues (2006, p. 159). The important benefit of the current analysis is that these single elements are placed within a more comprehensive perspective of three coherent discourses.

In Turkey we have identified the Euro-optimism discourse supporting EU membership. This discourse seems to be related to the economic consequences frame as mentioned by Koenig and colleagues (2006, p. 164). A second one is the *pacta sunt servanda* discourse, which points to Europe's obligation to admit Turkey into the EU. This discourse is less supportive of the current accession process, since its participants just want Turkey to be accepted as a member without much more trouble. A third discourse is Turkish pride and independence, which indicates that Turkey should not aim for EU membership and should instead refocus on the Arabic world. This discourse relates to the nationalist frame reported by Koenig and colleagues (2006, p. 163). These three discourses provide a nuanced impression about current views and debates in Turkey.

Other studies sometimes tend to suggest a major cleavage between secular and more religious groups in Turkey (Bouwman 2009, p. 155). While secular Turks feel that Turkey is part of Europe, the more religious part of the population perceives Europe more as a 'Christian club', which may not accept them as members. Interestingly we do not find strong, religiously motivated statements in our discourses. This finding is in line with results reported earlier by Kentmen (2008), who claims that religion does not explain support for the EU (in contrast to Carkoglu [2003]).

Q methodology used in this article also has some important advantages compared with earlier qualitative work. It allows us to distinguish between different existing discourses, whereas this is less clear in the studies of Schäfer and Zschache (2008), Wimmel (2009) and Walter and Albert (2009). Their analyses tend to push for more unifying conclusions in which sometimes arbitrary anchor points are used. Compared with analyses based on survey data (see, for instance, Schoen 2008; Carkoglu & Kentmen 2011), discourse analysis is less affected by short-term, intertemporal changes in opinion. The reason for this is that it focuses on the underlying reasons why people support or oppose certain measures.

The consequences of the discourses identified in this article are that Turkish accession might be a tough call. Most of the discourses we found in both Germany and Turkey are incompatible with Turkish accession. Only the combination of the German multiculturalism and the Turkish Euro-optimism discourses may lead to a route of enlargement, depending on the efforts made by the negotiators. The other discourses suggest a political course in which the EU and Turkey go their own ways for various reasons. Whether there are important economic benefits or not, emotional arguments play an important role in setting the pace of European integration.

Acknowledgements

The research for this article was conducted in the framework of an MSc capstone project led by Bernard Steunenberg. We thank Antoaneta Dimitrova, Dimiter Toshkov and the referees of this journal for helpful comments.

Notes

[1] A 'concourse' is defined as the set of all statements in society related to some topic or issue.
[2] Our research in Germany used newspaper articles, searched via the database Factiva. To avoid a one-sided perspective, both liberal and conservative newspapers were selected: on the one hand *taz, Frankfurter Rundschau* and *Süddeutsche Zeitung* as liberal newspapers, and on the other hand *Frankfurter Allgemeine Zeitung* and *Die Welt* as conservative newspapers. Finally, we used *Bild* and *Hamburger Morgenpost* as newspapers from the yellow press. Furthermore, comments were taken from political statements, radio shows, and reports of different thinktanks and civic associations. For Turkey, we used the following sources: AB Haber, which is an online platform that collects, in particular, all relevant news about Turkish–EU relations; similarly Haberturk as another news channel; some famous daily newspapers like *Milliyet* and *Hurriyet*; and releases from thinktanks like USAK, the International Strategic Research Organization in Turkey. Moreover, different kinds of newspaper articles were obtained via the database TumGazeteler.com, which embraces multiple perspectives on news in Turkey.
[3] See Carkoglu and Kentmen's paper in this issue.
[4] See www.hackert.biz/flashq (last consulted 1 February 2010).
[5] We used the PQMethod statistical programme (http://www.lrz-muenchen.de/~ schmolck/qmethod/downpqx.htm; last consulted 23 April 2010). Replicating the analysis with central component analysis, as implemented in SPSS, leads to rather similar results.
[6] For the association of subjects to factors ('flagging'), we used a factor loading of 0.4 or higher as significant (which is based on a significance level of about 0.1 per cent or higher based on the fact that we used 64 statements in both analyses). In the process of flagging these subjects, we did not mark a subject if they had a value of 0.4 or higher or more than one factor.

References

Bouwman, B. (2009) *Tussen God en Atatürk: Turkije achter de schermen* [Between God and Atatürk: Turkey Behind the Scenes], Prometheus/NRC Handelsblad, Amsterdam.
Brown, S. R. (1993) 'A primer on Q methodology', *Operant Subjectivity*, vol. 16, pp. 91–138, available online at: http://facstaff.uww.edu/cottlec/QArchive/Primer1.html.
Carkoglu, A. (2003) 'Who wants full membership? Characteristics of Turkish public support for EU membership', *Turkish Studies*, vol. 4, pp. 171–194.
Carkoglu, A. & Kentmen, Ç. (2011) 'Diagnosing trends and determinants for public support for Turkey's EU membership', *South European Society and Politics*, vol. 16, no. 3, pp. 365–379.

TURKEY AND THE EU: ACCESSION AND REFORM

Dimitrova, A. L. (2005) 'Europeanisation and civil service reform in Central and Eastern Europe', in *The Europeanisation of Central and Eastern Europe*, eds F. Schimmelfennig & U. Sedelmeier, Cornell University Press, Ithaca, NY, pp. 71–91.

Dryzek, J. S. (1988) 'The mismeasure of political man', *Journal of Politics*, vol. 50, pp. 705–725.

Dryzek, J. S. & Berejikian, J. (1993) 'Reconstructive democratic theory', *American Political Science Review*, vol. 87, pp. 48–60.

Kentmen, C. (2008) 'Determinants of support for EU membership in Turkey', *European Union Politics*, vol. 9, pp. 487–510.

Koenig, T., Mihelj, S., Downey, J. & Gencel-Bek, M. (2006) 'Media framings of the issue of Turkish accession to the EU: a European or national process?', *Innovation*, vol. 19, pp. 149–169.

McKeown, B. & Thomas, D. (1988) *Q Methodology*, Sage, Newbury Park, CA.

McLaren, L. M. (2007) 'Explaining opposition to Turkish membership of the EU', *European Union Politics*, vol. 8, pp. 251–278.

MG & Sedat Laçiner. (2008) 'Sarkozy: la France et l'Asie mineure' [Sarkozy: France and Asia Minor], 16 January, available online at: http://turquieeuropeenne.eu/article2371.html.

Moravcsik, A. (1991) 'Negotiating the Single European Act: national interests and conventional statecraft in the European Community', *International Organisation*, vol. 45, pp. 651–688.

Schäfer, M. S. & Zschache, U. (2008) *Vorstellungen über die EU in der öffentlichen Debatte: Eine Analyse deutscher Pressekommentare* [Ideas about the EU in the public debate: an analysis of German press comments], Freie Universität Berlin, Institut für Soziologie, Berlin.

Schimmelfennig, F. (2009) 'Entrapped again: the way to EU membership negotiations with Turkey', *International Politics*, vol. 46, pp. 413–431.

Schoen, H. (2008) 'Die Deutschen und die Türkeifrage: eine Analyse der Einstellungen zum Antrag der Türkei auf Mitgliedschaft in der Europäischen Union', [The Germans and the issue of Turkey: an analysis of attitudes to Turkey's application for membership in the European Union] *Politische Vierteljahresschrift*, vol. 49, pp. 68–91.

Stelzenmueller, C. (2007) 'Turkey's EU bid: a view from Germany', in *Conditionality, Impact and Prejudice in EU–Turkey Relations*, ed. N. Tocci, Quaderni IAI/Instituto Affari Internazionali, Rome, pp. 105–118, available online at: www.iai.it/pdf/Quaderni/Quaderni_E_09.pdf; last consulted 02/06/2010.

Steunenberg, B. (2002) 'Enlargement and reform in the European Union', in *Widening the European Union: The Politics of Institutional Change and Reform*, ed. B. Steunenberg, Routledge, London, pp. 3–20.

Walter, J. & Albert, M. (2009) 'Turkey on the European doorstep: British and German debates about Turkey in the European Communities', *Journal of International Relations and Development*, vol. 12, pp. 223–250.

Wimmel, A. (2009) 'Beyond the Bosphorus? Comparing public discourses on Turkey's EU application in the German, French and British quality press', *Journal of Language and Politics*, vol. 8, pp. 223–243.

Bernard Steunenberg (PhD University of Twente) is Jean Monnet Ad Personam Chair in European Politics and Professor in Public Administration at Leiden University, the Netherlands. His main research interest is the analysis of European politics and policymaking, including the relationship between the EU and its member states on the transposition and implementation of European policy. His work has appeared in journals such as *Journal of European Public Policy, European Union Politics, West*

European Politics, British Journal of Political Science and Journal of Theoretical Politics.

Christiane Rüth studied European studies at the University of Bremen, Germany and Public Administration at the University of Leiden, the Netherlands. Currently she is a student assistant for the Konrad-Adenauer-Stiftung e.V. in Berlin.

Simay Petek (MSc Leiden University) is currently a project assistant and researcher at Code-X International in the Netherlands, working with EVS (European Voluntary Service) projects and youth exchange programmes.

Turkish Accession and Defining the Boundaries of Nationalism and Supranationalism: Discourses in the European Commission

Senem Aydın Düzgit and Semin Suvarierol

The European Union in general and the European Commission in particular are characterised by supranational governance. The enlargement policy gives the Commission the opportunity to export and promote supranational norms and define the boundaries of Europe as a supranational polity through the conditionality of membership and intensive contact with the candidate countries. This article analyses the discourses of the Commission on Turkey and gives us insights into how well Turkey fits the supranational model in the eyes of Commission officials. It demonstrates how the boundaries of supranationalism are set and even challenged by the prospects of Turkey's accession.

The European Union (EU) is characterised by its supranational mode of governance according to which member-states pool sovereignty. As such, the EU diverges from the neo-realist conceptions of international relations with their visions of the world as consisting of antagonistic nation-states. Whereas this view of inter-state relations rests on the tenets of nationalism wherein 'the 'other' was almost always something to fear, to attack, to colonise, to dominate and to keep at bay' (Urry 2000, p. 1), the EU's supranationalism rests on a Kantian conception according to which states peacefully work *with* each other instead of against each other (Aydın Düzgit 2006). This Kantian worldview is translated in practice into the supranational governance of the EU. Supranationalism is most pronounced in the European Commission, whose task is to represent the common interests of the whole EU. This role endows the Commission not only with the duty to represent European interests, but also to uphold the EU's supranational regime, especially in its relations with third parties. Enlargement policy is, in this respect, an interesting case, since it gives the Commission the opportunity to promote supranational norms through the conditionality of membership and intensive contact with the candidate countries. In a sense, the candidacy phase is also a trial period for working together as future governance partners: the EU and the candidate state get to know each other by working on accession chapters and through early cooperation on various issues. The Commission is the only body in the EU that engages on a daily basis with the applicant country, through both the country's official/governmental bodies and its civil society institutions.

The member states, through the Council of Ministers and the European Council, are responsible for delivering the ultimate decisions in the accession process of an applicant regarding the acceptance of the country's application, the opening of accession negotiations and (together with the European Parliament) the final decision on accession. Nevertheless, the Commission is often considered a 'central player' that is 'engaged in all stages of the enlargement process' (Diedrichs & Wessels 2006, p. 231). This pivotal position of the Commission in enlargement policy also endows it with a significant role in defining the contours of Europe in discussions about the candidates, due to the requirement that any candidate has to be a European state. Thus, debates and decisions over enlargement also entail discussions about 'Europe' and 'Europeanness'. Hence when the Commission reports and makes recommendations on enlargement, this is not independent from its conceptualisations of Europe and its boundaries.

The case of Turkey in this matter deserves special attention in assessing the boundaries of the supranationalist discourse in the Commission, as it is a contested candidate on grounds of the goodness of fit between its European credentials and the future order of the European project. Analysing the discourses of the Commission on Turkey gives us insights as to how well Turkey fits the supranational model in the eyes of Commission officials, and, if it does not, the reasoning behind such evaluations. Hence, it demonstrates how the boundaries of supranationalism are set and even challenged by the prospects of Turkey's accession, thus questioning the extent to which supranationalist tendencies should be taken for granted in an unqualified fashion in the European Commission. It also sheds light on the ways in which problematic areas in EU–Turkey relations are wrapped up in repertoires of sovereignty and nationalism in the Commission.

We begin the article with a brief theoretical introduction on the central concepts of our study. In this theoretical section, we also refer to existing literature with regard to these issues in the enlargement debate on Turkey and in the analyses of the institutional identity of the Commission. Next, we introduce the data from which the discourse analyses are derived. We follow the analysis of the empirical data with a concluding section where we discuss our main results.

Theoretical Background

Supranationalism is embedded in the institutional identity and discourse of the European Commission at various levels. At the level of EU governance, supranationalism (as opposed to nationalism) is a historical raison d'être of the EU. At the institutional level, the Commission endorses the norm of supranationalism, which is formally defined as being independent from any particular interests (national or other) and mandates through the Treaties and Staff Regulations. Lastly, at the individual level, there is recent empirical evidence that the Commission is a 'hothouse for supranationalism' (Trondal 2007), as it both attracts officials conducive to supranational norms (Suvarierol 2007, 2011) and transforms its officials into adopting supranational norms[1] (Laffan 2004; Risse 2004; Suvarierol 2007, 2011), even officials who join the Commission on temporary contracts such as the seconded national experts (Trondal 2007). This can be explained with the 'logic of appropriateness' (March & Olsen 2004), which posits that (political) actors will act in line with the norms of the organisation they work for. Moreover, as socialisation theory has shown, long and intensive exposure to supranational norms leads to their internalisation (Checkel 2001; Egeberg 2006).

The foregoing theoretical and empirical insights lead us to expect that Commission officials will also adopt a supranational discourse and promote supranationalism in its contacts with third parties. The contacts with candidate countries are an important case in point, as enlargement policy provides the Commission the opportunity to diffuse supranationalism to its prospective members. If one of the fundaments of the Commission's discourse on Europe relates to sovereignty and the related dichotomy of nationalism and supranationalism (Laffan 2004), we can expect these governance issues also to be present in Turkey's accession process, as attitudes with regard to national or shared sovereignty could be seen as indicators of Turkey's compatibility with the EU. Accordingly, we hypothesise that in their encounters with Turkish officials Commission officials will be supportive of supranationalist ideals and wary of nationalistic viewpoints that are protective of national sovereignty.

On the other hand, the EU has also often been criticised for building a 'European fortress' by creating a safe haven for the free mobility of goods, services and persons within the EU while being strict and closed towards third countries, especially in the areas of border security and immigration (Armstrong & Anderson 2007). In such sensitive policy fields where member-states are unwilling to transfer national sovereignty and where there is a lower level of supranationalism, the Commission's role conception might be blurred: Commission officials might either be faithful to their supranational discourse or be protective of European sovereignty in line with the nation-state discourses. If this ambiguity does exist on the part of the Commission, it has consequences for the effectiveness of the principle of conditionality in enlargement (Schimmelfennig & Sedelmeier 2005). If the Commission does not practise what it preaches in terms of adopting supranational norms, then we might speak of a credibility problem, as the signals it is sending to candidate states – in this case Turkey – will not be consistent with its own approach towards national sovereignty. One of the aims of the empirical analysis of the discourses of Commission officials on Turkey is therefore also to address the following question: Are Commission officials convinced supranationalists or 'Euro-nationalists' vis-à-vis Turkey?

The Data

The data analysed in this study cover 19 in-depth qualitative interviews with Commission officials, carried out between April and October 2007. The respondents were all 'AD' (formerly A-level) rank staff of the Commission and consisted of mid-level desk-officers, international relations officers and programme managers working on enlargement in their directorate generals (DGs). Among the 28 DGs, only those DGs (14) that had a specific department/desk dealing with enlargement-related issues including relations with Turkey were approached.[2]

The study makes no claims to having a representative sample of all European Commission officials. While it cannot be dismissed that any such official may have personal opinions on the issue of Turkish accession, the opinions of many would be highly irrelevant to the purposes of this study. First, speaking to 'any' official would make the study little different from any public survey on attitudes towards Turkish accession, since officials working on other matters have little input and influence in the policy-making and debate-formulating process regarding Turkey. Second, such an approach would run the risk of weakening the spoken data and hence delivering 'limited narratives' due to the possibility of 'limited knowledge' that a professionally uninvolved official could deploy in order to construct her/his arguments on the subject. Attention was thus paid to contacting and speaking with officials who were familiar enough with the affairs of Turkey and its relations with the EU, as well as having the means to shape the discursive sphere on Turkey.

These considerations overlap with the research objective, which is to attain lengthy narratives on the 'substantive content of identity' that 'captures variability in meanings' (Checkel & Katzenstein 2009, p. 17). Nevertheless, nonnumeric quantitative expressions such as 'often', 'overwhelmingly' and 'frequently' are used in describing some segments of the discourse. Schegloff (1993, p. 119) argues that this kind of informal quantification helps to deliver 'a characterisation of distribution fully though tacitly informed by the analytic import of what is being characterised', which establishes 'a sense of importance' rather than 'statistical significance' (see also Wood & Kroger 2000, p. 138).

The questions that were posed in the interviews focused on various dimensions of EU–Turkey relations, including democracy and human rights, women's rights, religion, culture, immigration, security and the state of the Turkish economy. For the purposes of this study, only the responses relating to sovereignty, nationalism and supranationalism have been taken into consideration; in other words, the excerpts that are the subject of analysis consist only of those instances where an interviewee invokes any one of these (or other) issue areas in Turkey–EU relations as a matter of Turkish national sovereignty or of the EU's functioning as a political project. From among a larger corpus of data, only a select number of these excerpts are presented in the analysis below. The choice rests on a concern to display an exemplary variety of the argumentation strategies utilised in the discussions on Turkish accession from the viewpoint of sovereignty-related matters. The analysis, thus, not only accounts for the most frequently made arguments, but also covers the less common views encountered on these matters. The goal is to make coherent claims through interpretation, by accounting for exceptions and alternatives.

Turkey as a Sovereign: Turkish Nationalism and EU Accession

Eurobarometer results and previous research on the Commission's top officials have shown that 'Commission officials are more likely to identify with Europe and are more in favour of shifting policy to the European level than national elites or citizens' (Hooghe 2005, p. 875). Our empirical data also confirm that one of the binding elements of 'Europe' in the discourse of the Commission bureaucrats is 'shared/pooled sovereignty', which is crucial in upholding the common European interest in the EU:

> COM 10[3]: We should work together, for common goals that we can no longer achieve individually. Being European for me is also realising our own smallness, in terms of our old borders. European means we should try to work together, to overcome our smallness where it is necessary. What would be the effect of Turkey joining this Community? I do not know whether there is a strong desire in Turkey to build together. It will cause big problems in the preparation stage if the country is not convinced that it will have to give up sovereignty in joining the EU. Joining the EU means giving up sovereignty. You no longer have the rights to define your own trade policy. If the member states together decide to impose sanctions on I don't know which country, you have to follow that. There is no way out.

In combination with the 'we' pronoun that constructs Europeans as a bounded group, the excerpt above utilises predicates such as 'work together for common goals', 'working together', 'build together' and 'overcoming our smallness' that serve to discursively promote a 'consciousness of common belonging' within 'Europe'. As Abélès highlights, such a consciousness that is promoted in Commission discourse via the invocation of a common good/common interest/common European idea can be interpreted as an affirmation 'against what is established as alterity (that of nation-states as opposed to Community) and as particularisms (national histories as opposed to modernity)' in the Commission (Shore & Abélès 2004, p. 11). Hence, the use of such notions in Commission discourse not only aims to serve operational purposes in the sense of fostering efficient policy-making, but, more importantly, helps to define 'Europe/EU' vis-à-vis the member states of the EU (ibid.). In the excerpt above, the reference to 'old borders' designating nation-states of the EU prior to the establishment of the Community, and defining their previous isolated presence as an act of smallness demonstrates how such a definition can be invoked in combination with the notions of common goals and interests.

Within the scope of Turkey-related discussions, this overwhelming emphasis of the Commission officials on 'working together for common goals' is interlinked with the way in which they conceptualise Turkey's outlook on nation-state sovereignty. When probed on their construct of 'Europe' and the positioning of Turkey in this wider discursive construct, the Commission bureaucrats often highlight the issue of 'sovereignty' as one of the key problematic areas in Turkey's accession to the EU. In particular, those respondents working in DGs that are responsible for policy areas that constitute significant segments of the *acquis* infiltrating into national policy-making (i.e. DG Environment, DG Justice and Home Affairs, DG Agriculture, DG Regional Policy, DG Internal Market) highlight 'problems' regarding Turkey's attitude towards 'state sovereignty':

> COM 15: Integration with Turkey will be difficult. I think sovereignty and attitudes play a role. When you discuss with Turkish authorities issues which are not mainly political but to a large extent technical, you feel immediately that this issue of sovereignty is very close to the surface. And of course, when you are a country of 70 million people, you do not have the habit of being told what you have to do and so on. So I understand that there is this sort of a survival instinct, which is still very strong in Turkey and which is necessary given the neighbours. Just to take a comparison: we had in the context of the accession process the screening with Croatia and screening with Turkey, and the nationalist flavour is ten times higher in Turkey, which is not a criticism. I am just saying for historical, size reasons.

> COM 8: First of all, Europeans do not consider themselves to be different from one country to another. Of course they have their specificities, North–South–East–West, but this is a plus. I have the feeling that Turkey stands as Turkey versus Europe. This does not happen with other countries. Of course, they are defending their national interests and principles, but one does have the impression that they have something deep, completely different. Europe is a family and Turkey, for the time being, by its own willingness, considers itself Turkey versus Europe, if you understand. They think that what they are thinking and what they believe in and so on are above criticism. They have the knowledge; they have the right ideas.

Both of the excerpts above predicate Turkey as a 'proud', 'nationalist' and 'arrogant' country unwilling to delegate sovereignty to the EU. In the first excerpt, this 'proud' nature is essentialised further via the biological metaphor of the 'survival instinct', justified through reference to Turkey's neighbours and hence securitising them in a different context. The second excerpt above constructs a clear-cut binary division between Turks and Europeans, homogenising them, positioning them against one another and engaging in stereotypical attributions for both parties. The stereotyped European is defined by similarity rather than difference and bound by natural properties as implied by the 'family' metaphor. While the interviewee constructs Turkey as standing opposed to Europe at its own will, she also essentialises this 'will' by tying it to the innate nature of the country and its people.

It is notable here how the dominant stereotype of 'Turks as proud people' utilised in eighteenth-century European accounts of the Ottoman Empire is still present in the Commission elite's discourse on Turkey.[4] In a majority of interviews, Turkey's attitude towards state sovereignty is tied to the existence of a 'proud' mentality and culture. What further binds the two excerpts above is the way in which both silence alternative narratives that highlight that 'the problem of reconciling the demands of European integration with national "pride" . . . is by no means unique to Turkey' (Diez 2005, pp. 171–172) and concerns even present-day member states (see Checkel 2007). This is not to engage in discussions regarding the 'proudness' of nations and hence to justify such generalising constructs in the first place, but to point to the danger of constructing a flawless homogeneous European identity against a posited Turkish nationalism vis-à-vis the EU.

This issue of 'sovereignty' can also arise in contacts of Commission bureaucrats with their peers working in the relevant Turkish ministries:

> COM 18: People within different ministries that I met are very intelligent, smart and well-educated, so there is no trouble there. But Turks should understand the principles on which the EU is established. The main principle is communication between member states. So for me it is very important that Turkey understands this principle. This, I see, as a bigger problem in Turkey because there is this nationalist feeling that the EU is going to steal their autonomy, that they will lose their sovereignty if they join the EU ... The way they communicate is that they do not want to provide a lot of information; they feel that this is for a later stage, that this is some kind of trade off. I find this a big difference because I come from Central and Eastern Europe and we were more open. We provided a lot of information and we admit our shortcomings. Turks have a tendency to say, 'We are the best', and sometimes I also had the feeling that you have an agreement, and then in one or two days, you find out that the agreement is not in place.

As also demonstrated in the excerpt above, the Commission elite often defines its Turkish interlocutors in a positive manner, underscoring their intelligence, education and, in some cases, modern and European outlook. Nevertheless, the experiences they recount with their Turkish counterparts often take a turn for the negative when the latter's approach to sovereignty enters the picture. The 'pride', 'arrogance' and sometimes 'unreliability' of the Turkish elite, coupled with 'mistrust' towards the EU, are presented as significant problems that prevent a constructive dialogue between the two sides. In the excerpt above, these properties are described as 'national' traits, positioned against those of Eastern Europe, the region from which the interviewee comes.

Hence the positive attributes assigned to their Turkish interlocutors does not preclude the Commission elite from defining their counterparts as comprising culturally determined traits governing the way in which they negotiate with the EU, primarily in reference to their attitude towards sovereignty. This is once again a recurring theme in the interviews of those employed in DGs that deal with 'politically sensitive' issues requiring a great degree of sovereignty delegation from the nation-state level to the EU. For some of these officials, the Europeanness of the Turkish elite is explicitly overshadowed by a culturally inspired stance in their conduct of international relations:

> COM 11: The oriental cultural side of Turkey, of the Turkish elite is that they are very at ease with satisfying the formal requirements without strong commitments behind it, so they deal with formal things with nothing behind it. They do not care; this is not a problem for them. So my preconceived idea about the oriental mentality was not really challenged by the Turks. This was the fashion in public administration, but that was also their duty; they were mandated to be like that.

The excerpt above explicitly utilises the historical concept of the oriental mentality which dates back to the eighteenth century (Said 1995; Çırakman 2005) in stereotyping

Turkish people in general and the elite in particular. The notion of 'ungrounded pride', in particular, seems to have survived to this day in describing the way in which Turks conduct their relations with the EU. It needs to be noted, however, that the concept denoted a much wider range of predicates at the time it was first coined and utilised (i.e. slavish disposition, fanaticism, ignorance) which do not seem to be carried to this day, thus suggesting that caution is required in drawing historical parallels as such.

Perhaps more importantly, what the last two excerpts above suggest is that the narratives on professional/institutional interactions of Commission officials play an important role in assigning to the 'Turks' certain general attributes through discussions on the issue of sovereignty, providing further support to studies that highlight that institutional contacts play a key role in constructing narratives of identity in the European Commission (Laffan 2004; Risse 2004; Suvarierol 2007). Hence, it can be argued that the Commission officials' experiences within the 'epistemic community' (Haas 1992) that they form with their Turkish counterparts provide key nodal points around which certain narratives of identities are constructed in Commission discourse. The stereotypes and generalisations utilised in referring to the Turkish counterparts also show that the new information that has been gained through contact does not seem to have changed the EU officials' existing stereotypes substantively, as they still rely on them to make sense of the behaviour of Turkish officials.

Europe as a Sovereign: Euro-nationalism and Turkish Accession

While the Commission elite often perceive the attitude of Turkey and the Turkish elite towards national sovereignty as problematic, the empirical data suggest that the way in which the Commission bureaucracy conceptualises Europe and the EU is not too distanced from the classic nation-state mode whereby national sovereignty is replaced by the sovereignty of Europe. This is most evident in discussions on two topics: namely the capacity of the EU to integrate new members – also referred to as the absorption/integration capacity of the EU – and security-related matters:

> COM 19: We first need to decide on deepening and strengthening the EU, before we go any further with enlargement policy. We need a strong Europe, with well-functioning institutions and feasible budgetary arrangements. Europe should be capable of decision-making. Clearly, Turkey's size is an issue that needs to be looked at, and even if you project economic trends twenty years into the future, agriculture for example will play an important role in the Turkish economy. There are problems about immigration, again to do with size, and, well, certain politicians have jumped on that for very specific reasons. As long as Turkey continues to boom as it is now, well, hopefully they will create some jobs, because that is the main problem ... Turkey needs to develop, Turkey needs to create jobs, Turkey needs to educate its population. When this happens, I would have no fears on the part of the EU. Otherwise, Turkish accession would be detrimental to the interests of the member states and the Union.

As also demonstrated in the excerpt above, the Commission elite in general are concerned about the current functioning of the EU and argue that an unchanged Turkey in political and economic terms would further undermine the institutional and budgetary capacity of the EU. Thus, while most of them argue that the concept of absorption capacity is being utilised by national politicians as a cover for their hostility to Turkish accession, they believe that there is also some truth to the argument, which, however, could be resolved through a reform of the EU and substantial reform within Turkey.

Nevertheless, in probing the institutional and budgetary effects of the EU, a paradoxical situation arises with respect to their previously mentioned views on the problem of sovereignty in Turkish accession. As seen in the previous discussion, the way in which Turkey guards its national interest is perceived as highly problematic by the Commission elite, against the background argument that national sovereignty should no longer matter in the EU. However, when it comes to the concrete impacts of Turkish accession on the EU and its member states, guarding the national as well as the European interest is acceptable to the Commission elite. This is particularly the case in discussions on the economic impacts of Turkish accession as well as the outlook on Turkish immigration into the EU. It needs to be mentioned that this discourse has already partially been translated into policy by the European Commission. The Negotiating Framework with Turkey[5] already allows for permanent safeguard clauses in areas such as freedom of movement of persons, structural policies and agriculture, and has been applauded by the Enlargement Commissioners in their various speeches both prior to and after the publication of the framework document in June 2005.[6]

The remnant of the nation-state model in the EU also surfaces in debates over immigration, which is almost always portrayed as an issue with a strong security dimension:

> COM 14: If you look at the region at your southern borders, it is clear that a lot of people will be knocking on the Turkish door and their final destination is the EU. I think there is a problem; there is a huge migration pressure. Is it by definition bad? I mean we have a problem in Europe as well. Our population is becoming older and older and we need migrant workers to come here. So I think it is completely wrong to look at it in a very negative manner, saying that the migration problem is by definition bad. We will need people to come to work in Europe, otherwise we will lose our standard of living. But it needs to be done in a way which is not causing additional burden to the societies. So there is an unhealthy tension in society which needs to be addressed. So my position would be a very balanced one ... The border question is a very complex one. You cannot expect that a country bordering regions or countries like Iraq and Iran just applies the same Schengen standards as Poland does with Belarus or Ukraine. The situation is completely different.

The excerpt above, delivered in response to the question on the security dimension of Turkey's accession, hence securitises the issue of 'migration', granting it a sense of urgency whereby it is construed as an 'existential threat' (Buzan, Waever & De Wilde 1998, pp. 21–25). While other works have argued that migration is not always securitised in the discourses and policy practices of the EU, it has also been found that the tendency to securitise increases when the issue concerns Muslim communities already resident in Europe (Boswell 2007). Migration is also predicated as a 'problem' for the EU due to the region that Turkey borders as a 'transit country'. More importantly, the utilisation of container metaphors such as 'door', 'pressure' and 'burden' constructs Europe/EU as a bounded space that needs to be protected from external threats (Charteris Black 2006). Container metaphors utilised as such play a key role in legitimising restrictive policies regarding border controls, since 'the existence of a clearly defined container also implies a conscious controlling entity that fills or empties the container', namely governments (ibid, p. 576). Thus, as commonly seen in the case of the nation-states, discourses on the control of (transit) migration in discussions over Turkish accession in turn help reify the EU as a bounded space and justify centralised policies in this field.

Related to the discussion of the previous excerpt (on p. 476), this interviewee also invokes the 'interests' of EU 'societies' in discussing the implications of migration to Europe/EU from or through Turkey once it becomes a member. Thus, once again, guarding the European interest comes to the fore in debates over Turkish accession, this time more specifically over migration handled as a security matter.

This paradoxical situation in which the Commission elite construct Turkish national interest as problematic while they construct common European/EU interests (as well as national interests in some cases) that need to be upheld, and in which they model Europe/EU on conceptual underpinnings similar to those of the modern nation-state model which they often claim the EU to have surpassed, suggests that the perceptions of the Commission bureaucracy on the cultural dimensions of Turkish accession could provide further important insights regarding their reliance on the model of the nation-state as well as its implications for a multicultural Europe/EU that can govern the EU's relations with its immigrants as well as the other non-European collectivities in its neighbourhood. This, however, would require further research, which would go beyond the scope of this article (see Aydın Düzgit 2012, forthcoming).

Conclusions

This article has aimed to show the extent to which supranationalism as a norm is reflected in the discourses of the European Commission regarding Turkey's membership in the EU. The interview excerpts have shown that Commission officials stress supranationalism and are critical of what they see as manifestations of Turkish nationalism. Yet, when it comes to strategic reflections on Turkey's membership or to sensitive issues where EU member-states are still attached to their national sovereignty, the discourses of Commission officials become 'nationalistic' themselves – what we in this article have termed 'Euro-nationalism'. Whereas the discourses are critical of sovereignty and nationalism when it comes to Turkey, they are protective of European sovereignty and interests in their own discourses on Turkey without framing them as nationalistic.

These findings challenge the image of the Commission as a supranational actor. Besides concluding that the Commission's supranationalism cannot be taken categorically, how can we explain its Euro-nationalism? On the one hand, one might argue that the Commission in this sense merely represents the dominant line set out by member-states themselves. In other words, the outlook of the member-states are nationalistic in policy areas such as security, border control and immigration, and the Commission merely reflects these standpoints. The Commission functions independently from the instructions of national governments, but it is also its task to take the dominant political climate into consideration in order to come up with acceptable policies and to safeguard its legitimacy in the eyes of member-states and eventually of citizens. Moreover, if we conceptualise the Commission as the representative of pooled sovereignty, then the attempt to define and defend the interests of this supranational whole flows from the formal role definition of the Commission. Still, it could be defined as Euro-nationalism to the extent that it is protective of the EU's interests and becomes crystallised in its relations with outsiders, in this case Turkey.

In any case, one could argue that the Commission is acting as a nation-state in the domain of enlargement policy. Whereas its internal governance is marked by supranationalism, it follows the classical rules of international relations when the policy in question extends beyond EU borders. This is reflected in the double discourse on Turkey: whereas Turkey is expected to act as an insider and surpass its nationalism in sovereignty-related issues, the Commission itself frames Turkey as an outsider with regard to issues touching the sovereignty of the EU (or its member states). In fact, this may well be seen as yet another reflection of the problem of credibility in EU–Turkey relations (Aydın Düzgit & Çarkoğlu 2009). Overcoming the insider–outsider distinction as reflected by the discourses on sovereignty could possibly lead to more credibility in socialising candidate countries in general, and Turkey in particular, into supranational norms. We argue in turn that this would increase the transformative power of the Commission in particular and the EU in general, since the candidate country would be given an unequivocal message with regard to complying with the norm of shared sovereignty.

This article has only focused on the Commission as the supranational agent in the governance structure of the EU. Previous research has shown, however, that the discourses of the European Parliament and some member-states on Turkish accession show striking parallels with the Commission on the issue of sovereignty (see Aydın Düzgit 2012, forthcoming). Whilst our data do not allow us to make any concrete statements on temporal change, one may argue that sovereignty-related concerns as such may have even been strengthened further since 2007 with the difficult ratification of the Lisbon Treaty and intensifying debates on the potential destabilising impact of Turkey on the EU, fuelled by Turkey's domestic upheavals and its foreign policy activism in the Middle East. We expect that the normative power and credibility of the EU as a policy actor on the international scene would increase if it could approach candidates as insiders in order to create dialogue as partners in a common European project. Whether the EU's approach will change in the short term is partly dependent on the political climate and attitudes in Europe towards enlargement and Turkey.

Notes

[1] For a counterargument, see Liesbet Hooghe's work (1999; 2001; 2005). She argues that the socialisation capacity of the Commission is limited at best and claims that the supranational norms the officials endorse have been acquired at the national level.

TURKEY AND THE EU: ACCESSION AND REFORM

[2] These DGs are: Trade, Economic and Financial Affairs, Competition, Employment, Social Affairs and Equal Opportunities, Agriculture and Rural Development, Energy and Transport, Environment, Research, Fisheries and Maritime Affairs, Internal Market and Services, Regional Policy, Education and Culture, Justice, Freedom and Security and Enlargement.

[3] The respondents are hereafter referred to as COM (COM standing for the Commission and the digit standing for the number assigned to the interviewee).

[4] For British and French representations of the Turks in the eighteenth century, see Aslı Çırakman (2005).

[5] See Negotiating Framework (Turkey), 3 October 2005, available online at: http://ec.europa.eu/enlargement/pdf/st20002_en05_TR_framedoc.pdf#search=percent22percent22negotiating percent20framework percent22 percent2C percent22turkey percent22 percent22

[6] See, for example, Prodie (2004a, 2004b) and Rehn (2004, 2005).

References

Armstrong, W. & Anderson, J. (eds) (2007) *Geopolitics of European Union Enlargement: The Fortress Empire*, Routledge, London.

Aydın Düzgit, S. (2006) *Seeking Kant in the EU's Relations with Turkey*, Turkish Economic and Social Studies Foundation (TESEV) Foreign Policy Program Report, Istanbul.

Aydın Düzgit, S. (2008) 'Discursive construction of European identity in the EU's relations with Turkey', PhD dissertation, Vrije Universiteit Brussel.

Aydın Düzgit, S. (2012, forthcoming) *Constructing Europe through Turkey: European Discourses on Turkish Accession to the EU*, Palgrave, London.

Aydın Düzgit, S. & Çarkoğlu, A. (2009) 'Turkey: reforms for a consolidated democracy', in *International Actors, Democratisation, and the Rule of Law: Anchoring Democracy?*, eds L. Morlino & A. Magen, Routledge, London, pp. 120–155.

Boswell, C. (2007) 'Migration control in Europe after 9/11: explaining the absence of securitisation', *Journal of Common Market Studies*, vol. 45, no. 3, pp. 589–610.

Buzan, B., Waever, O. & De Wilde, J. (1998) *Security: A New Framework for Analysis*, Lynne Rienner, Boulder, CO.

Charteris Black, J. (2006) 'Britain as a container: immigration metaphors in the 2005 election campaign', *Discourse and Society*, vol. 17, no. 5, pp. 563–581.

Checkel, J. T. (2001) 'Why comply? Social learning and European identity change', *International Organisation*, vol. 55, no. 3, pp. 553–588.

Checkel, J. T. (2007) 'International institutions and socialisation in Europe: introduction and framework', in *International Institutions and Socialisation in Europe*, ed. J. T. Checkel, Cambridge University Press, Cambridge, pp. 3–30.

Checkel, J. T. & Katzenstein, P. J. (2009) 'The politicisation of European identities', in *European Identity*, eds J. T. Checkel & P. J. Katzenstein, Cambridge University Press, New York, pp. 1–25.

Çırakman, A. (2005) *From the 'Terror of the World' to the 'Sick Man of Europe': European Images of Ottoman Empire and Society from the Sixteenth Century to the Nineteenth*, Peter Lang, New York.

Diedrichs, U. & Wessels, W. (2006) 'The Commission and the Council', in *European Commission*, eds D. Spence & G. Edwards, John Harper, London, pp. 209–234.

Diez, T. (2005) 'Turkey, the European Union and security complexes revisited', *Mediterranean Politics*, vol. 10, no. 2, pp. 167–180.

Egeberg, M. (2006) 'Executive politics as usual: role behaviour and conflict dimensions in the College of European Commissioners', *Journal of European Public Policy*, vol. 13, no. 1, pp. 1–15.

Haas, P. M. (1992) 'Introduction: epistemic communities and international policy coordination', *International Organisation*, vol. 46, no. 1, pp. 1–35.

Hooghe, L. (1999) 'Supranational activists or intergovernmental agents? Explaining the orientations of senior Commission officials toward European integration', *Comparative Political Studies*, vol. 32, no. 4, pp. 435–463.

Hooghe, L. (2001) *The European Commission and the Integration of Europe*, Cambridge University Press, Cambridge.

Hooghe, L. (2005) 'Several roads lead to international norms, but few via international socialisation: a case study of the European Commission', *International Organisation*, vol. 59, no. 4, pp. 861–898.

Laffan, B. (2004) 'The European Union and its institutions as "identity builders"', in *Transnational Identities: Becoming European in the EU*, eds R. K. Hermann, T. Risse & M. B. Brewer, Rowman & Littlefield, Lanham, MD, pp. 75–96.

March, G. J. & Olsen, P. J. (2004) 'The logic of appropriateness', ARENA Working Paper 04/09, ARENA, Oslo.

Prodi, R. (2004a) 'Speech delivered at the Turkish Grand National Assembly', in *Turkey in Europe Monitor*, eds S. Aydın & M. Emerson, Centre for European Policy Studies, Brussels, pp. 1–5.

Prodi, R. (2004b) 'The Commission's Report and Recommendation on Turkey's Application', available online at: http://europa.eu/rapid/pressReleasesAction.do?reference=SPEECH/04/440&format=HTML&aged=1&language=EN&guiLanguage=en

Rehn, O. (2004) 'EU and Turkey on the threshold of a new phase', available online at: http://europa.eu/rapid/pressReleasesAction.do?reference=SPEECH/04/538&format=HTML&aged=1&language=EN&guiLanguage=en

Rehn, O. (2005) 'Accession negotiations with Turkey: The Journey Is As Important As The Final Destination', available online at: http://europa.eu/rapid/pressReleasesAction.do?reference=SPEECH/05/556&format=HTML&aged=1&language=EN&guiLanguage=en

Risse, T. (2004) 'European institutions and identity change: what have we learned?', in *Transnational Identities: Becoming European in the EU*, eds R. K. Hermann, T. Risse & M. B. Brewer, Rowman & Littlefield, Lanham, MD, pp. 247–271.

Said, E. W. (1995) *Orientalism. Western Conceptions of the Orient*, Penguin Books, London.

Schlegloff, E. A. (1993) 'Reflections on quantification in the study of conversation', *Research on Language and Social Interaction*, vol. 26, no. 1, pp. 99–128.

Schimmelfennig, F. & Sedelmeier, U. (eds) (2005) *The Europeanisation of Central and Eastern Europe*, Cornell University Press, Ithaca, NY.

Shore, C. & Abélès, M. (2004) 'Debating the European Union: an interview with Cris Shore and Marc Abélès', *Anthropology Today*, vol. 20, no. 2, pp. 10–14.

Suvarierol, S. (2007) *Beyond the Myth of Nationality: A Study on the Networks of European Commission Officials*, Eburon, Delft.

Suvarierol, S. (2011) 'Everyday cosmopolitanism at the European Commission', *Journal of European Public Policy*, vol. 18, no. 2, pp. 181–200.

Trondal, J. (2007) 'Is the European Commission a "hothouse" for supranationalism? Exploring actor-level supranationalism', *Journal of Common Market Studies*, vol. 45, no. 5, pp. 1111–1133.

Urry, J. (2000) 'The global media and cosmopolitanism', Department of Sociology, Lancaster University, available online at: http://www.comp.;ancs.ac.uk/sociology/papers/Urry-Global-Media.pdf

Wood, L. & Kroger, R. O. (2000) *Doing Discourse Analysis: Methods for Studying Action in Talk and Text*, Sage, Thousand Oaks, CA.

Senem Aydın Düzgit (PhD Free University Brussels) is an assistant professor in the Department of International Relations of Istanbul Bilgi University, Istanbul, and an associate research fellow at the Centre for European Policy Studies (CEPS) in Brussels. Her principle research interests are EU enlargement, discourse studies, EU–Turkey relations, politics of identity, and democratisation. Her book *Constructing Europe through Turkey: European Discourses on Turkish Accession to the EU* (London: Palgrave) is forthcoming in 2012.

Semin Suvarierol (PhD Utrecht University) is a post-doctoral researcher in the Sociology Department of Erasmus University Rotterdam. Her current research focuses on national identity constructions through citizenship in France, the Netherlands and the UK. Her research has been published in *Governance* (2008), *West European Politics* (2008), *Journal of Common Market Studies, Journal of European Public Policy* (2011), *International Sociology* (2011) and *Alternatives* (2011).

Turcoscepticism and Threat Perception: European Public and Elite Opinion on Turkey's Protracted EU Membership

Ebru Ş. Canan-Sokullu

This article examines the political debate surrounding Turkey's protracted accession to the European Union (EU) from the viewpoints of mass and elite opinion in Europe, focusing on the impact of Islamophobia and the fears about immigration. It investigates how threat perception reflects itself in the form of Turcoscepticism. It concerns itself with (i) whether Turcoscepticism is based on perceived threats of Islamic extremism or immigration influxes, and (ii) how these perceived threats affect public and elite attitudes towards Turkey's EU membership. Through a quantitative investigation of public and elite polling data (2006–08), the analysis reveals that Islamophobia and fear of immigration contribute to Turcosceptic anxiety in Europe only at the mass level.

This study examines the political debate surrounding Turkey's protracted European Union (EU) accession from the viewpoints of mass and elite opinion in the EU, focusing on the fear of Islamic fundamentalism (the more radical strand of Islam), and the fear of immigration into Europe. It investigates how Islamophobic and anti-immigrationist concerns over Turkish membership reflect themselves in the form of threat-driven Turcoscepticism, and suggests in which contexts Turcophile (or 'Turcoenthusiastic') attitudes might prevail in the EU.

Turcoscepticism is based on a limited perception of Turkey as a poor and populous Islamic country with economic, social, cultural and political problems related to adopting and effectively internalising the values of the European state system. Although Turkey's EU integration project has been a process of political incorporation premised on inclusive notions of rights as well as European political value orientations, debates at both societal and political levels have revolved around perceived differences in collective identities rooted in religion, culture, ethnic and national dynamics (Casanova 2006, p. 74). This debate has contributed to the growth of Turcoscepticism, creating what can be described as doubts or negative feelings and attitudes towards Turkey.

Turcoscepticism has recently been encouraged by fears associated with Islam and Muslim immigration. While Europe has experienced immigration from Muslim countries – in particular from Turkey since the 1970s – in the post-September-11 era, concerns about whether Europe would be Islamised following Turkey's EU membership have made the European vox populi gradually more anxious. Many voices have suggested that the Turkish 'crescent' would endanger the European 'cross', in that the Islamisation of Europe would most likely come about through Turkey's EU membership. The future immigration of Muslim Turks into Europe has, inter alia, heightened popular worries, the prospect of Turkey joining the EU generating unease among Europeans (Casanova 2006, p. 71).

The threat to Europe's cultural and religious identity that has nurtured Turcoscepticism lies at the heart of the problem for European political and bureaucratic elites as well. Former French President d'Estaing, for example, claimed that Turkey is a different culture and that its membership would bring the EU project to an end (Yavuz 2006, p. 251). In Germany, the former chairman of the Christian Social Union, Edmund Stoiber, translated this into rejecting Turkey's accession. Like Huntington (1993, p. 158), who argued that 'the identification of Europe with Western Christendom provides a clear criterion for the admission of new members to the western organisations', Stoiber claimed that the EU's borders of shared values, culture and identity would be breached by Turkish membership (O'Rourke 2002). In contrast to d'Estaing's and Stoiber's Turcoscepticism, former UK prime minister Tony Blair suggested, more constructively, that Turkish membership would add to Europe's multicultural assets, and that the inclusion of a Muslim country would facilitate the rapprochement between Western and Eastern civilisations (Yavuz 2006, p. 251). His Turcophile approach was a clear challenge to alternative Turcosceptic readings of Turkey's membership bid.

Although there is a vast literature on public opinion (Sheperd 1975; Inglehart, Rabier & Reif 1987; Janssen 1991; Eichenberg & Dalton 1993; Gabel & Palmer 1995; Anderson & Kaltenhaler 1996; Anderson 1998; Sánchez-Cueva 2000), elite opinion (Putnam 1976; Hallstrom 2003; O'Connor & Radaelli 2008; Lengyel & Göncz 2009) and comparative research on European integration (Oldendick & Bardes 1981; 1982; Hooghe 2003; Best 2009; Matonyte & Morkevicius 2009 Jerez-Mir, Real-Dato & Vázquez-García 2009),[1] existing comparative research on Turkey's EU membership lacks empirical data focusing on support for a candidate country's bid to join the EU. This study helps fill this gap by bringing together the literature on public opinion and elite preferences in Europe to study the case of Turcoscepticism, with specific reference to the role of threats perceived to arise from this enlargement.[2] It thus aims to contribute to the empirical and conceptual testing of this argument in the EU enlargement literature.

This study adopts a composite definition of the 'EU/European elite'. A number of scholars define 'European elite' as a 'national elite operating together at the European level' (Hveem 1968; Aguilar, Fordham & Lynch 1997; Baehr 1980). However, this seems an overly narrow approach. Identifying reference groups based on elite subcultures and functions, Mills (1956) provides a rationale for distinguishing different clusters of European elites who profoundly shape the EU enlargement agenda, performing different functions at different levels of the administration. Thus, the 'EU elite' as studied in this article includes: the 'political elite', specifically the members of the European Parliament (MEPs) (Andersen & Burns 1996; Schmitter 1995); the 'bureaucratic elite', specifically the Commission officials, or 'Eurocrats' as defined by Spinelli (1966) (Coombes 1970; Andersen & Burns 1996; O'Connor & Radaelli 2008); and the officials at the Council of Ministers (Hayes-Renshaw 1996).[3]

Given this background, this article poses the question of whether concerns, of both masses and elite, originate around religious and cultural fears that construct objections to living in integration with the Muslim population of Turkey. How do Islamophobic sentiments at both a mass public and European elite level affect Turkey–EU relations? It also examines whether Turcoscepticism is founded on the fear of an influx of immigrants into Europe. To investigate these questions, this article focuses on public attitudes in 11 European countries (the 'EU11' of Germany, France, the United Kingdom, the Netherlands, Poland, Slovakia, Portugal, Spain, Italy, Bulgaria and Romania), and the perceptions of the EU elite who are nationals of these countries. The comparative empirical and conceptual framework adopted introduces threat perception as an important determinant of opinion on Turkey–EU relations. The primary sources of data are the Transatlantic Trends and the European Elite Survey series (2006–08).[4] After providing a theoretical discussion on perceived threats that situates the analysis, this article analyses both public and elite perspectives on Turkey's protracted EU accession bid by employing ordinal logistic regression analysis.

Perceived Threats and Turkey–EU Relations

A comprehensive threat-based approach to the problem of Turkey–EU relations has been so far largely neglected in the literature. The realist school of international relations has defined threats 'as the products of some combination of capabilities and intentions ... where a potential adversary has both the capability to do harm and malign intent' (Caldwell & Williams 2006, p. 9) and where the adversary agent can 'inflict a negative consequence on another agent' (Davis 2000, p. 10). Matonyte and Morkevicius (2009, p. 968) argue that historically the EU was created 'to avoid internal and external threats that Europe faced'. As the EU evolved not as a mere political instrument but as a socio-cultural agent, with its supranational institutions and European polity (Cowles, Caporaso & Risse 2001), a social constructivist meaning of threats gained emphasis. From a more constructivist perspective, individuals, societies and identities are referent objects of threats (Buzan 1991). Kirchner and Sperling (2002) claim that there is no satisfactory typology of the threats confronting Europe, or conceptual consensus on the content, form or agents of the threats posed. Their typology of threat combines two dimensions – the target and the agent of the threat.

In the context of Turkey's potential EU membership, this study considers European society and its political system as the target or referent object of the Islamic fundamentalism and immigration threats. The question it poses is to what extent Turkey, with its populous Muslim population, is the perceived agent of these threats.

Islamophobia as Perceived Threat

Since the late 1990s, Turkey's EU membership bid has taken a significant place in the EU's political agenda and has become an issue of public opinion debate in relation to the perceived threat of the rise of Islamic fundamentalism. The post-September-11 era has witnessed an increased tension in the Western world in terms of concerns over Islam and Muslims. The subsequent Madrid (March 2004) and London (July 2005) bombings contributed further to antagonism towards Muslims and the fear of radical Islam. Various incidents have publicly demonstrated European attitudes against Muslims, while at the same time further hindering Turkey's long-drawn-out accession process.[5]

Representations of a global Islamic threat in the post-Cold-War era have created a reservoir of hostility to Islam in the West (Canan-Sokullu 2012, forthcoming). Scholars have tended to position Islam theoretically within studies of religious fundamentalism and terrorism. The literature on radical movements and political Islam has suggested that the projection of Islam as violent and radical creates a cultural and political challenge to Western societies (Akram 2002). Muslim collective identities and their public representation as a further source of anxiety in Europe have given rise to a sense of religious and cultural 'otherness' (Casanova 2006). Inevitably, such representations have encouraged dread, dislike and exclusion of Muslims, as expressed in the term 'Islamophobia' (Runnymede Trust Report 1997, p. 5).

Islamophobia is a result of xenophobic cultural stereotyping of Muslims (De Master & Le Roy 2002; Fetzer & Soper 2005). This increases the temptation to identify Islam with religious fundamentalism and radical movements in the form of jihad (struggle for the faith/God) as a legitimate self-defence of Islamaphobes (Shadid 1991, p. 368). More moderately (Khalid 1982; Wagtendonk & Aarts 1986), the Islamic fundamentalism that encourages Islamophobia is defined as *dawa*, the desire to apply Islamic norms, values and principles in the daily lives of Muslims, by guaranteeing this through changed state constitutions or in the context of re-Islamisation and Islamism (Shadid 1991). Either as an artefact of xenophobia or as a manifestation of re-Islamisation, Islamic fundamentalism is a (perceived) source of threat to the European social and political order.

It is also possible to think of Islam as a 'cultural threat' to Europe, which McLaren (2002) defines as a perceived threat posed by other cultures, or antipathy towards other cultures stemming from nationalist attachments. She argues that antipathy within the EU towards the integration process relates to the fear of, or hostility towards, other cultures. Drawing on these conceptualisations of Islamophobia, and of whether Turkey's EU membership has become the subject of Islamophobic discussion in Europe, this study proposes the 'Islamic fundamentalist threat hypothesis' (H1): 'If Islamic fundamentalism is perceived as an important threat to Europe, then this will cause negative feelings towards Turkey's accession to the EU.'

Immigrants as Threatening Objects

The fear of Islam and Muslim Turkey's EU membership is also intricately related to the issue of an expected immigrant influx of Turkish citizens as workers, settlers and students into Europe (Fetzer 2000; Carey 2002; McLaren 2002; 2003; Canan-Sokullu & Kentmen 2010). Immigration has already brought influxes of Muslims from the Mediterranean basin to Europe's interior since the 1970s (Weiner 1995). While early immigrants were mostly from Christian European countries neighbours who were better integrated with their host societies, the new immigrants are from culturally and socially different countries that have different traditions, religious practices and cultural heritages and where the majority religion is Islam. In particular, during the 1990s, the rise in asylum demands and immigration flow brought the immigration issue to the very top of the European agenda (Santel 1995). For some Europeans, immigrants are a menace 'to regime security and inner stability, to structural security and the security of resources or to concepts of identity' (Jerch, Escribano & Lorca 2002).

In the context of EU enlargement, immigration poses a perceived egocentric threat to an individual's pocket economy. Already, economic integration is tending to move production to member states with cheap unskilled labour, leaving local, more costly workers jobless. Added to this, immigrants are perceived to be stealing jobs from host country citizens (Tsardanidis & Guerra 2000). McLaren (2002, p. 557) describes 'realistic threats' as fears that individuals feel about competing with foreigners for jobs available in the home country. According to her (2003, p. 915), 'members of the dominant group may come to feel that certain resources belong to them, and when those resources are threatened by a minority group, members of the dominant group are likely to react with hostility'.

Studies of social identity suggest that immigration also raises some fears related to identity issues, like the distinction between 'self' and 'other' (Turner 1975; Turner, Brown & Tajfel 1979; Levine et al. 2005). McLaren conceptualises this 'identitarian' (Matonyte & Morkevicius 2008, p. 969) threat as a 'symbolic threat', the fear that others will change the domestic culture. Symbolic threats that stem from prejudices represent a form of resistance to change in the racial status quo based on the majority's moral feelings, and principles and values that they believe the minority group violates (De Master & Le Roy 2000). Carey identifies 'the protection of the in-group and the group identity from the out-group' (2002, p. 394) and argues that individuals who favour in-group protection tend to be less supportive of immigration into Europe. Buzan (1991, p. 447) argues similarly that immigration threatens 'communal identity and culture' by changing the ethnic, cultural, religious and linguistic characteristics of the population. Thus, the out-group is seen as a 'threat' to the 'self' (Ashmore 1970, p. 253).

TURKEY AND THE EU: ACCESSION AND REFORM

Considering EU enlargement, immigrants pose a significant perceived 'symbolic' threat to the collective (national/European) identity and a 'realistic' threat to economic interests. Therefore, this article investigates the extent to which realistic and symbolic threats are likely to be at play in explaining anti-immigrant hostility in Europe as they relate to Turkey's EU membership bid. It proposes the 'immigration threat hypothesis' (H2): 'The attitudes of Europeans towards Turkey's EU membership depend on the fear that out-group Turkish immigrants pose a threat to the in-group European identity.'

Data and Methods

The data for this study come from the Transatlantic Trends Surveys (TTS) and European Elite Surveys (EES) conducted in 2006 2007 and 2008.[6] The dependent variable in this analysis is 'public opinion about Turkey's EU membership'. To operationalise this variable, I use the TTS/EES question: 'Generally speaking, do you think that [Turkey's] membership of the European Union is a bad thing, neither good nor bad or a bad thing?' This is an ordinal categorical variable that is modelled as a true Likert scale, increasing in positivity from 'a bad thing' (1), indicating Turcoscepticism, through 'neither good nor bad' (2), to 'a good thing' (3), indicating Turcoenthusiasm.

The TTS and EES studies incorporate two independent variables that are dummies: 'threat of Islamic fundamentalism' and 'threat of immigration'.[7] These two variables tap two general threat perceptions that we might expect to affect opinion regarding Turkey's EU membership. I include 'age', 'gender', 'ideological self-placement' and 'country of origin' as control variables (Gabel 1998).[8] I choose not to hold the country of origin of respondents constant, as it accounts for the cross-national variance of opinion. Lastly, to investigate whether there is an impact of an elite respondent being an MEP or a Commission or Council official, I include three elite dummy variables. Descriptive statistics for the variables used in the analysis are presented in Table 1.

The analysis was run to gauge the changing impacts of the perceived threat of Islam and immigration on support for Turkey's EU membership, controlling for age, sex, ideology and country of origin. Thus, the model, as shown below, was tested through an ordinal logistic regression technique to detect the ordinal categorical distribution and to calculate the effects of variables (Norušis 2005) between 2006 and 2008.

Ordinal Logistic Regression Model

> Logit (opinion on Turkey's EU membership) = f (perception of threat of Islamic fundamentalism, perception of threat of large number of immigrants, country of origin, gender, age, ideology)

> *Note:* Elite models were run with the inclusion of MEP, Commission and Council official dummy variables, as well.

Empirical Analysis

The association between public and elite opinion on Turkey's EU membership, and the potential impacts of perception of Islamic fundamentalist and immigration threats

Table 1 Descriptive Statistics for Variables in the Analysis

| | 2006 | | | | | | 2007 | | | | | | 2008 | | | | | |
| | Mass | | | Elite | | | Mass | | | Elite | | | Mass | | | Elite | | |
Variable	Mean	SD	Obs	Mean	SD	Obs	Mean	SD	Obs	Mean	SD	Obs	Mean	SD	Obs	Mean	SD	Obs
Turkey's membership 'bad'	0.301	0.458	2709	0.328	0.470	83	0.424	0.494	4252	0.174	0.379	47	0.242	0.428	2668	0.253	0.435	71
Turkey's membership 'neither good nor bad'	0.411	0.492	3703	0.189	0.392	48	0.221	0.415	2782	0.488	0.500	80	0.448	0.497	4939	0.225	0.418	63
Turkey's membership 'good'	0.199	0.399	1801	0.442	0.497	112	0.277	0.447	2220	0.296	0.457	132	0.217	0.412	2395	0.478	0.500	134
Threat of Immigration 'important'	0.753	0.431	6786	0.620	0.486	157	0.662	0.472	6644	0.637	0.481	172						
Threat of Islamic fundamentalism 'important'	0.866	0.340	7805	0.917	0.276	232	0.519	0.499	5211	0.637	0.481	172	0.825	0.379	9096	0.750	0.433	210
Male	0.449	0.497	4054	0.802	0.399	203	0.442	0.496	4436	0.803	0.397	217	0.456	0.498	5033	0.771	0.420	216
Left	0.307	0.461	2769	0.387	0.488	98	0.267	0.442	2684	0.329	0.470	89	0.281	0.449	3102	0.396	0.490	111
Centre	0.287	0.452	2593	0.276	0.448	70	0.246	0.430	2468	0.374	0.484	101	0.265	0.441	2925	0.246	0.431	69
Age	46.181	16.670	8989	3.43	0.631	253	47.210	16.976	9982	4.27	1.023	262	47.922	16.966	11009	4.24	1.03	280
MEPs				0.802	0.399	203				0.629	0.483	170				0.642	0.480	180
Commission officials				0.197	0.399	50				0.185	0.389	50				0.178	0.383	50
Council officials										0.185	0.389	50				0.178	0.383	50

Note: SD: Standard Deviation; Obs: number of observations.

were examined through ordinal logistic regression analysis. The dependent variable was treated as an ordinal and polychotomous variable under the assumption that opinion on Turkey's membership has a natural ordering (bad to good), but that the distances between adjacent levels are not evenly spaced. Therefore, ordinal logistic regression is the most appropriate statistical technique (Gelpi, Feaver & Reifler 2005/2006, p. 32).[9] To predict the value associated with the negative and positive opinion categories, I reconceptualised the problem of Turkey's EU membership in an attempt to predict the probability that an individual is either Turcosceptic or Turcophile.

Before proceeding with the analysis, I checked for collinearity, to test how much the independent variables are linearly related to each other. Menard (2001) suggests that a tolerance value less than 0.1 indicates a serious collinearity problem. On the other hand, Myers (1990) suggests that a variance inflation factor (VIF) greater than 10 is a cause for concern. In this study, VIF and tolerance values in all models were below these criteria. This indicates that in estimating the models in this study, collinearity between the independent variables is not a problem.

Table 2 presents the results of the ordinal logistic regression models for three consecutive years. The parameter estimates can be interpreted as representing the impact of independent variables on the likelihood that an individual falls into a higher category of opinion on Turkey's EU membership, all else being equal. Thus, negative coefficients are associated with lower scores regarding Turkey's EU membership (Norušis 2005, p. 73), whereas positive coefficients are associated with higher scores.[10]

Regarding mass opinion in 2006, Table 2 shows that the perceived threats of both immigration and Islamic fundamentalism contribute significantly to public opinion on Turkey's EU membership. A one-unit increase in the perceived threat of immigration from unimportant to important moved opinion from Turcoenthusiasm to Turcoscepticism. The perceived threat of Islamic fundamentalism changed opinion in the same way. Regarding elite opinion in 2006, Table 2 shows that the perceived threat of immigration had no significant effect. However, in direct contrast to the mass model, a one-unit increase in the perceived threat of Islamic fundamentalism *increased* the ordered log-odds of the EU elite becoming Turcophile.

In 2007, the threat perception questions asked how likely an individual was to be 'personally affected' by these threats in the next ten years. Regarding mass opinion in 2007, a one-unit increase in the perceived threat of immigration resulted in a decrease in the ordered log-odds of being Turcophile. However, compared with 2006, it had a lower impact. On the other hand, the likelihood of personal exposure to the threat of Islamic fundamentalism had no significant impact on individuals being either Turcophile or Turcosceptic. Regarding elite opinion in 2007, the results showed that neither threat significantly changed opinions on Turkey's membership of the EU.

The TTS and EES surveys in 2008 incorporated only the indicator of the perceived threat of personal exposure to Islamic fundamentalism. Regarding mass opinion in 2008, an increase in the perceived likelihood of personal exposure to radical Islam decreased the likelihood of evaluating Turkey's EU membership positively. Regarding elite opinion, in contrast, an increase in the perceived likelihood of personal exposure

Table 2 Ordinal Logistic Regression of European Mass and Elite Opinion on Turkey's EU Membership

Predictors		Coefficient (standard errors)					
		2006		2007		2008	
		Mass	Elite	Mass	Elite	Mass	Elite
Threat of immigration 'important'		−0.785 ***	−0.416	−0.238***	−0.075	−	−
		(0.056)	(0.468)	(0.051)	(0.294)		
Threat of Islamic fundamentalism 'important'		−0.326 ***	1.476**	0.073	0.388	−0.196***	0.913**
		(0.081)	(0.665)	(0.048)	(0.293)	(0.060)	(0.333)
Control variables							
Gender	Male	−0.015	−0.111	0.147**	0.940**	0.097*	−0.494
		(0.046)	(0.368)	(0.045)	(0.364)	(0.042)	(0.341)
Ideology	Left	0.480***	2,426***	0.163**	0.554	0.491***	1.315***
		(0.058)	(0.408)	(0.055)	(0.772)	(0.050)	(0.321)
	Centre	0.297***	0.434	0.136*	0.273	0.201***	0.165
		(0.058)	(0.373)	(0.057)	(0.336)	(0.052)	(0.332)
Age	Young	0.244 ***	0.644	0.182**	0.554	0.208**	−0.070
		(0.073)	(0.541)	(0.072)	(0.772)	(0.068)	(0.827)
	Middle-aged	0.093	0.018	0.87	−0.307	0.054	−0.232
		(0.098)	(0.307)	(0.064)	(0.448)	(0.060)	(480)
Actor	MEPs	−	−0.300	−	−0.245	−	0.550
			(0.600)		(0.514)		(0.556)
	Commission officials	−	−	−	1.069**	−	0.493
					(0.471)		(0.428)
N		6912	231	6971	241	8326	260
Model χ^2 [a]		649,589	96,741	133,521	34,297	742,258	58,603
Degrees of freedom		15	16	15	17	16	18
Nagelkerke R^2		0.102	0.391	0.022	0.152	0.097	0.231

Note: The dependent variable is 'opinion about Turkey's EU membership: bad / neither good nor bad / good'. Dummies for the country of origin are not reported in Table 2 to make the interpretation of the table easier. Results are available from the author upon request. Estimates of cut points are available from the author upon request. In the 2006 elite model, the reference category for the elite groups is the Commission, and it is the Council officials in the 2007 and 2008 elite models.

* $p < 0.001$, ** $p < 0.01$, *** $p < 0.05$.

[a] All model χ^2 statistically significant at $p < 0.001$.

to radical Islam significantly *increased* the ordered log-odds of being Turcophile. This resembled the result of the 2006 elite model, suggesting that the influence of Islamophobia on Turcoscepticism for the European elite was weakening. However, we should note that respondents were asked about a different indicator of threat perception: the likelihood of personal exposure to the threat of Islamic fundamentalism.

Briefly examining the control variables reveals some additional interesting findings. Relative to right-wing respondents, individuals from the centre towards the left are more likely to become Turcophile in all three years. From the coefficients, left-wing ideological self-placement by elite respondents had the largest impact on the log-odds of a positive opinion on Turkey's EU membership. The 'young age' coefficient exerted a statistically significant positive effect on opinions about Turkey's EU membership in all models, indicating that younger Europeans are also more likely to be Turcophile than older respondents. Regarding any effect of the institutional status of elite respondents, the results showed that, all other variables being held constant, being a commissioner or an MEP had no significant impact, relative to being a Council official, on variance in anti- or pro-Turkish attitudes. The only exception to this pattern was in 2007, with an increase of 1.069 in logit (opinion on Turkey's EU membership) for the Commission officials.

Overall, regarding mass public opinion on Turkey's EU membership, the results provide strong support for both the 'Islamic fundamentalist threat hypothesis' (H1) and the 'immigration threat hypothesis' (H2). In other words, when either Islamic fundamentalism or immigration was perceived as an important threat to Europe and individuals, public opinion towards Turkey's accession to the EU became more negative. In contrast, regarding the EU elite's perception of these threats, both hypotheses were rejected.

Conclusion

This study tested whether perceived threats regarding large waves of immigrants and Islamic fundamentalism affect public and elite opinions in the EU on Turkish EU membership, using survey data from 2006, 2007 and 2008. This analysis contributes to the existing literature on support for EU enlargement in at least two ways. First, it offers a comparative insight into the analysis of mass and elite attitudes towards enlargement with Turkey. Second, it introduces the analysis of the impact of the fears of radical Islam and influx of immigrants into the literature. Individual citizens with higher threat perceptions are more likely to be Turcosceptics when either Europe, as a whole, or individuals themselves are the referent objects of these threats. Turcoscepticism thus seems to be rooted in the perception of an Islamic fundamentalist threat. While this finding supports the findings of the existing literature, it also adds an important new result: an Islamophobic reading of Turkey's EU membership is only true for ordinary citizens, not for the elites. Elite opinion about Turkey's EU membership was not only unaffected by perceived fears of immigation, but, in direct contrast to mass opinion, actually made *more* supportive by an increase in the perceived threat of Islamic fundamentalism. Possibly, the impact of uncontrolled factors comes into play here, such as levels of political awareness and education. These may make the EU elite better informed about Turkey being a predominantly Muslim country yet having a secular state structure with long-standing aspirations to European values of liberalism, rights and democracy. In support of this, when other factors are controlled for, ideology has a clear positive effect on Turcoenthusiasm. Both left-wing and centrist respondents are more likely to support Turkey's membership. It could also be the case that elites believe that, especially in the face of Islamic fundamentalism, it will be important to integrate Turkey into Europe, as Turcophile leaders such as Tony Blair have argued. The results challenge the tendency to view Europeans – citizens, politicians and bureaucrats – as a monolithic entity. The findings provide strong confirmation that there is a clear divide between European public and elite opinion on EU enlargement to include Turkey.

This study shows that Turkey's EU membership has become subject to Islamophobic tensions and anti-immigrationist sentiments that arouse Turcoscepticism among EU citizens. Fears about immigration create a negative climate towards Turkey, because once Turkey joins the EU, Turks would not be 'Euro-immigrants' but Euro-citizens. Such perceptions contribute to a sceptical and a phobic public opinion climate. I conclude by characterising the European public opinion climate as a confluence of 'Islamophobic and immigrant-hostile Turcoscepticism'. However, more optimistically, there appears to have been a gradually declining trend of such opinion between 2006 and 2008. Even more optimistically, the EU elite reads Turkey's membership bid more positively, even though perceived threats are at stake. Future research may explore other approaches that can help explain the differences in public and elite opinions, such as utilitarian, rights-based or identity-based calculations. It would be interesting to examine the role of attitudes towards EU integration and enlargement, as a whole, to map whether opinion towards Turkey's EU membership has been driven by threat perceptions, or whether it is due to anti-integrationist sentiments present in Europe.

Acknowledgements

I am indebted to Gamze Avçi and Ali Çarkoğlu, the editors of this special issue, and two anonymous reviewers for comments and useful hints on the data.

Notes

[1] See Foyle (1997) for the role of elites' complex influence on public opinion. See Russett (1990) and Holsti (1996) for an extensive debate on the influence of public opinion on decision-making.

[2] This is an important question, since after the European Council approves of, and the European Parliament gives assent to, an accession treaty, it is sent to member states for ratification. Member states either ratify the accession treaty in their parliament or submit it to referendum. Either way, a candidate country's accession is subject to the consent of a member state's citizens.

[3] In the remainder of the article, the political and bureaucratic elites will be called the 'elite' or 'EU elite' interchangeably.

[4] The data utilised in this article were made available through http://www.icpsr.umich.edu/icpsrweb/ICPSR.

[5] These include the controversy in France over the incompatibility of the Islamic headscarf with French *laïcité*, the assassination of Theo Van Gogh, the Dutch filmmaker, by a Dutch-Moroccan Muslim man, the controversy about cartoons in a Danish newspaper depicting the Prophet Mohammed, and the controversial Regensburg lecture of Pope Benedetto in Germany reflecting the Vatican's struggle over how to confront Islam (2006).

[6] The TTS and EES 2006 and 2007 studies included public opinion in France, Germany, Italy, the Netherlands, Poland, Portugal, Slovakia, Spain and the United Kingdom. Bulgaria and Romania are included in 2008. To compare the data from the EES with that gathered by TTS, results from the public were weighted according to the size of each member state. The results of the survey of MEPs were weighted according to the size of the MEPs' national delegation and of each European parliamentary group. 'Don't know' and 'refusals' are excluded from the analysis. Neither the original collectors of the data nor the sponsor of the studies bears any responsibility for the analysis or interpretations presented here.

[7] The survey question read: '[To Europe]: I am going to read you a list of possible international threats to Europe in the next 10 years. Please tell me if you think each one on the list is an extremely important threat, an important threat, or not an important threat at all: (a) Islamic fundamentalism (the more radical stream of Islam) [TTS and EES 2006]; (b) large number of immigrants and refugees coming into Europe [TTS and EES 2006].' (I created a dummy measuring 'important' [1] and 'not important' [0].) '[Personal exposure]: In the next 10 years, how likely are you to be personally affected by the following threat? (a) Islamic fundamentalism [TTS and EES 2007 and 2008]; (b) Large number of immigrants and refugees coming into Europe [TTS and EES 2008].' (I recoded them as a dummy 'likely' [1] and 'not likely' [0].'

[8] Age is recoded as (1) 'young' (18–34), (2) 'middle-aged' (35–54) and (3) 'old' (55+). Ideology is recoded as (1) 'left', (2) 'centre' and (3) 'right'. Each country origin was computed as dummy variable (1) against Slovakia (0). Gender is created as a dummy with (1) 'male' and (0) 'female'. General opinions on EU enlargement and integration are important control variables that might have an impact on attitudes towards Turkey-specific enlargement of the EU; since datasets do not include them, this study omits their analysis.

[9] Ordinal logistic regression is the most appropriate technique for ordinal categorical response data when there are more than two events. For a categorical dependent variable Y and an explanatory variable X, the regression model is

$$\ln\left(\frac{\text{prob(event)}}{1 - \text{prob(event)}}\right) = \beta_0 + \beta_1 X_1 + \beta_2 X_2 + \ldots + \beta_k X_k$$

(Norušis 2005, p. 70).

[10] Since it is the logit, we interpreted the coefficients instead of the odds ratio in the results (Gelpi, Feaver & Reifler 2005, p. 32).

References

Aguilar, E. E., Fordham, B. O. & Lynch, G. P. (1997) 'Research note: the foreign policy beliefs of political campaign contributors', *International Studies Quarterly*, vol. 41, pp. 355–366.

Akram, S. M. (2002) 'The aftermath of September 11, 2001: the targeting of Arabs and Muslims in America', *Arab Studies Quarterly*, vol. 23, no. 2–3, pp. 61–118.

Andersen, S. S. & Burns, T. R. (1996) 'The European Union and the erosion of parliamentary democracy: a study of post-parliamentary governance', in *The European Union: How Democratic Is It?* eds S. S. Andersen & K. A. Eliassen, Sage, London, pp. 227–253.

Anderson, C. J. (1998) 'When in doubt use proxies: attitudes toward domestic politics and support for European integration', *Comparative Political Studies*, vol. 31, no. 5, pp. 569–601.

Anderson, C. J. & Kaltenhaler, K. C. (1996) 'The dynamic of public opinion toward European integration, 1973–93', *European Journal of International Relations*, vol. 2, no. 2, pp. 175–199.

Ashmore, R. D. (1970) 'Prejudice: causes and cures', in *Social Psychology: Social Influence, Attitude Change, Group Processes, and Prejudice*, ed. B. E. Collins, Addison-Wesley, Boston.

Baehr, P. R. (1980) 'The Dutch foreign policy elite: a descriptive study of perceptions and attitudes', *International Studies Quarterly*, vol. 24, no. 2, pp. 223–261.

Best, H. (2009) 'History matters: dimensions and determinants of national identities among European populations and elites', *Europe–Asia Studies*, vol. 61, no. 6, pp. 921–941.

Buzan, B. (1991) *People, States and Fear: An Agenda for International Security Studies in the Post-Cold War Era*, Harvester Wheatsheaf, London.

Caldwell, D. & Williams, R. E. (2006) *Seeking Security in an Insecure World*, Rowman & Littlefield, Lanham, MD.

Canan-Sokullu, E. Ş. (2012, forthcoming) 'Perceptions of Islam, Turkey and the European Union – Islamophobia and Turcosceptism in Europe? A four nation study', in *Islam in the Plural: Identities, (Self-) Perceptions and Politics*, eds C. Flood, S. Hutchings, G. Miazhevich & H. Nickels, Brill, Amsterdam.

Canan-Sokullu, E. Ş. & Kentmen, Ç. (2010) 'Turkey in the EU?: an empirical analysis of European public opinion on Turkey's protracted candidacy', in *A Sisyphean Story: Fifty Years of EU–Turkey Relations (1959–2009)*, ed. A. E. Çakır, Routledge, London, pp. 105–134.

Carey, S. (2002) 'Undivided loyalties: is national identity an obstacle to European integration?', *European Union Politics*, vol. 3, no. 4, pp. 387–413.

Casanova, J. (2006) 'Religion, European secular identities and European integration', in *Religion in an Expanding Europe*, eds T. A. Byrnes & P. J. Katzenstein, Cambridge University Press, Cambridge, pp. 65–93.

Coombes, D. (1970) *Politics and Bureaucracy in the European Community: A Portrait of the Commission of the E.E.C.*, George Allen & Unwin, London.

Cowles, M. G., Caporaso, J. & Risse, T. (eds) (2001) *Transforming Europe. Europeanisation and Domestic Change*, Cornell University Press, Ithaca, NY.

Davis, J. W. (2000) *Threats and Promises: The Pursuit of International Influence*, Johns Hopkins University Press, Baltimore.

De Master, S. & Le Roy, M. K. (2000) 'Xenophobia and the European Union', *Comparative Politics*, vol. 32, no. 4, pp. 419–436.

Eichenberg, R. E. & Dalton, R. J. (1993) 'Europeans and the European Community: the dynamics of public support for European integration', *International Organisation*, vol. 47, no. 4, pp. 507–534.

Fetzer, J. S. (2000) *Public Attitudes towards Immigration in the United States, France and Germany*, Cambridge University Press, Cambridge.

Fetzer, J. S. & Soper, C. S. (2005) *Muslims and the State in Britain, France and Germany*, Cambridge University Press, Cambridge.

Foyle, D. C. (1997) 'Public opinion and foreign policy: elite beliefs as a mediating variable', *International Studies Quarterly*, vol. 41, no. 1, pp. 141–169.

Gabel, M. J. (1998) 'Public support for European integration: an empirical test of five theories', *Journal of Politics*, vol. 60, no. 2, pp. 333–354.

Gabel, M. J. & Palmer, H. (1995) 'Understanding variation in public support for European integration', *European Journal of Political Research*, vol. 27, pp. 3–19.

Gelpi, C., Feaver, P. D. & Reifler, J. (2005/2006) 'Success matters: casualty sensitivity and the war in Iraq', *International Security*, vol. 30, no. 3, pp. 7–46.

Hallstrom, L. (2003) 'Support for European federalism? An elite view', *Journal of European Integration*, vol. 25, no. 1, pp. 51–72.

Hayes-Renshaw, F. (1996) 'The role of the Council', in *The European Union: How Democratic Is It?* eds S. S. Andersen & K. A. Eliassen, Sage, London, pp. 143–165.

Holsti, O. R. (1996) *Public Opinion and American Foreign Policy*, University of Michigan Press, Ann Arbour.

Hooghe, L. (2003) 'Europe divided? Elites vs. public opinion on European integration', *European Union Politics*, vol. 4, no. 3, pp. 281–304.

Huntington, S. P. (1993) 'The clash of civilisations?', *Foreign Affairs*, vol. 72, no. 3, pp. 22–50.

Hveem, H. (1968) 'Foreign policy thinking in the elite and the general population: a Norwegian case study', *Journal of Peace Research*, vol. 5, no. 2, pp. 146–170.

Inglehart, R., Rabier, J. R. & Reif, K. (1987) 'The evolution of public attitudes toward European integration 1970–86', *Journal of European Integration*, vol. 10, pp. 135–155.

Janssen, J. H. (1991) 'Postmaterialism, cognitive mobilisation, and support for European integration', *British Journal of Political Science*, vol. 21, pp. 443–468.

Jerch, M., Escribano, G. & Lorca, A. (2002) *The Impact of Migration from the Mediterranean on European Security*, IEEI, Lisbon.

Jerez-Mir, M., Real-Dato, J. & Vázquez-García, R. (2009) 'Identity and representation in the perceptions of political elites and public opinion: a comparison between Southern and post-communist Central-Eastern Europe', *Europe–Asia Studies*, vol. 61, no. 6, pp. 913–919.

Khalid, D. (1982) *Re-Islamisierung und Entwicklungspolitik*, Weltforum Verlag, Munich.

Kirchner, E. J. & Sperling, J. (2002) 'The new security threats in Europe: theory and evidence', *European Foreign Affairs Review*, vol. 7, no. 4, pp. 423–452.

Lengyel, G. & Göncz, B. (2009) 'Elites' pragmatic and symbolic views about European integration', *Europe–Asia Studies*, vol. 61, no. 6, pp. 1059–1077.

Levine, M., Prosser, A., Evans, D. & Reicher, S. (2005) 'Identity and emergency intervention: how social group membership and inclusiveness of group boundaries shape helping behavior', *Personality and Social Psychology Bulletin*, vol. 31, no. 4, pp. 443–453.

Matonyte, I. & Morkevicius, V. (2008) 'Threat perception and European identity building: the case of elites in Belgium, Germany, Lithuania and Poland', *Europe–Asia Studies*, vol. 61, no. 6, pp. 967–985.

McLaren, L. M. (2002) 'Public support for the European Union: cost/benefit analysis or perceived cultural threat?', *Journal of Politics*, vol. 64, pp. 551–566.

McLaren, L. M. (2003) 'Anti-immigrant prejudice in Europe: contact, threat perception, and preferences for the exclusion of migrants', *Social Forces*, vol. 81, no. 3, pp. 909–936.

Menard, S. (2001) *Applied Logistic Regression Analysis*, Sage, Thousand Oaks, CA.

Mills, C. W. (1956) *The Power Elite*, Oxford University Press, New York.

Myers, R. (1990) *Classical and Modern Regression with Applications*, PWS-Kent Publishing Company, Boston, MA.

Norušis, M. J. (2005) *SPSS 14.0 Advanced Statistical Procedures Companion*, Prentice Hall, Englewood Cliffs, NJ.

O'Connor, K. & Radaelli, C. (2008) 'How bureaucratic elites imagine Europe: towards convergence of governance beliefs?', *Journal of European Public Policy*, vol. 16, no. 7, pp. 971–989.

Oldendick, R. W. & Bardes, B. A. (1981) 'Belief structures and foreign policy: comparing the dimensions of elite and mass opinions', *Social Science Quarterly*, vol. 61, pp. 434–441.

Oldendick, R. W. & Bardes, B. A. (1982) 'Mass and elite foreign policy opinions', *Public Opinion Quarterly*, vol. 46, no. 3, pp. 368–382.

O'Rourke, B. (2002) EU: Stoiber's remarks on limits to Europe touch sensitive nerve. Radio Free Europe/Radio Liberty, available online at: http://www.rferl.org/nca/features/2002/05/2105200 2082330.asp

Putnam, R. (1976) *The Comparative Study of Political Elites*, Prentice-Hall, Englewood Cliffs, NJ.

Runnymede Trust Report (1997) *Islamophobia: A Challenge for Us All*, Runnymede, London.

Russett, B. (1990) *Controlling the Sword: The Democratic Governance of National Security*, Harvard University Press, Cambridge, MA.

Sánchez-Cueva, I. (2000) 'The political basis of support for European integration', *European Union Politics*, vol. 1, no. 2, pp. 147–172.

Santel, B. (1995) 'Loss of control: the build up of a European migration and asylum regime', in *Migration and European Integration: The Dynamics of Inclusion and Exclusion*, eds R. Miles & D. Thranhardt, Pinter, London, pp. 75–91.

Schmitter, P. C. (1995) 'Democracy in the emerging Euro-polity: temporary or permanent deficit?', manuscript, Center for European Studies Stanford University, Stanford, CA.

Shadid, W. A. (1991) 'The integration of Muslim minorities in the Netherlands', *International Migration Review*, vol. 25, no. 2, pp. 355–374.

Sheperd, R. J. (1975) *Public Opinion and European Integration*, Lexington Books, Lanham, MD.

Spinelli, A. (1966) *The Eurocrats: Conflict and Crisis in the European Community*, Johns Hopkins University Press, Baltimore.

Tsardanidis, C. & Guerra, S. (2000) 'The EU Mediterranean state, the migration and the "threat" from the South', in *Eldorado or Fortress? Migration in Southern Europe*, eds R. King, G. Lazaridis & C. Tsardanidis, Macmillan Press, Basingstoke, pp. 321–344.

Turner, J. C., Brown, R. J. & Tajfel, H. (1979) 'Social comparison and group interest in intergroup favoritism', *European Journal of Social Psychology*, vol. 9, pp. 187–204.

Turner, J. C. (1975) 'Social comparison and social identity: some prospects for intergroup behavior', *European Journal of Social Psychology*, vol. 5, no. 1, pp. 5–34.

Wagtendonk, K. & Aarts, P. (eds) (1986) *Islamitisch Fundamentalisme*, Coutinho, Muiderberg.

Weiner, M. (1995) *The Global Migration Crisis: Challenge to States and to Human Rights*, HarperCollins, New York.

Yavuz, M. H. (2006) 'Islam and Europeanisation in Turkish-Muslim socio-political movements', in *Religion in an Expanding Europe*, eds T. A. Byrnes & P. J. Katzenstein, Cambridge University Press, Cambridge, pp. 225–256.

Ebru Ş. Canan-Sokullu (PhD University of Siena) is an assistant professor in the Department of Political Science and International Relations, Bahçeşehir University, Istanbul. She was a visiting scholar at the University of Cambridge (2006) and Ohio State University (2005). In the past, she worked for Transatlantic Trends and European Elite Surveys. Her research focuses on security and defence politics, public and elite opinion on foreign policy, military operations, immigration and the EU. Most recently she has been editing *Debating Security: Changes and Challenges for Turkey in the 21st Century* (Lexington, 2011, forthcoming).

Euro-Turks as a Force in EU–Turkey Relations

Ayhan Kaya

This study focuses on the ways in which Euro-Turks affiliate themselves both with their countries of destination in the European Union and with their country of origin, Turkey. Using the institutional channelling theory, this study claims that Euro-Turks are more likely to comply with the political, economic, legal and cultural structure of their countries of settlement. The study also claims that Euro-Turks have recently become actively engaged in political participation processes at a time defined by rising Islamophobia. However, official lobbying activities of the Turkish state among Euro-Turks are likely to be more destructive than constructive in the way in which they make the Euro-Turks compete with each other on ideological grounds.

Turkish-origin migrants residing in Western Europe have so far been overwhelmingly perceived by the autochthonous populations as well as by the Turkish public to be conservative, nationalist, religious and unwilling to integrate socially, politically, economically and culturally in their countries of settlement (inter alia, Landman 1992; Heitmeyer, Müller & Schröder 1997; Kelek 2005; Berlin-Institut für Bevölkerung und Entwicklung [BIBE] 2009). To put it bluntly, the European public, by and large, believe that Turkish migrants do not integrate, and the Turkish public assume that they are still *gurbetcis*[1] who have always longed for their homeland. Both perceptions are still very strong despite the fact that social, political, economic and cultural conditions of Euro-Turks have radically changed in comparison to the earlier days of the migratory process. These stereotypes have also recently been coupled with the stereotypical image of Islam in the West. Furthermore, it is often stated by various groups in Western European countries that negative perceptions of Turkey spring from those Turkish migrant workers who are not willing to comply with European norms and values (Kemming & Sandikci 2006; Barysch 2007). This study will argue the other way around: I shall claim that Euro-Turks have constructed various *hyphenated identities* in a way that successfully incorporates them into multiple identities of Europeanness defined on the basis of universal values such as democracy, human rights, civil and civic participation, and equality. I will also claim that Euro-Turks have created a bridge between Turkey and the European Union (EU). I will draw my arguments from qualitative and quantitative research carried out in 2003 and 2007 in Germany, France and Belgium among Turkish origin migrants and their descendants (Table 1), whom I call 'Euro-Turks' irrespective of their ethno-cultural and religious backgrounds in Turkey.[2]

This study focuses on the ways in which Euro-Turks affiliate themselves both with their countries of destination in the EU and with their country of origin, Turkey. There are approximately 4.5 million Euro-Turks dwelling in Western European countries. The nature of the transnational space constructed by the Euro-Turks between/beyond the geographical, political and even cultural boundaries of Turkey and the EU makes it apparent that Euro-Turks have already established a bridge between Turkey and the EU.

Transnational Space: Dwelling in a Space of Their Own!

The perspectives of the Euro-Turks on Europeanness, the EU, Turkey, religiosity, integration and political participation should be contemplated within the contemporary European context defined by neoliberalism, prudentialism, 'clash of civilisations', 'culture wars', unemployment, poverty, Islamophobia and securitisation of migration (O'Malley 2000; Doty 2000; Huysmans 2006; Inda 2006; Kaya 2009a). The Euro-Turks research conducted in 2003 and 2007 highlights the question of whether the Euro-Turks living in Germany, France and Belgium can be a driving force for Turkey in the accession process. It maps out the social, political, and cultural discourses on Turkey–EU relations among the Turkish diaspora – a diaspora that constitutes a rather heterogeneous group with respect to recent economic, political, cultural, ethnic and religious dispositions (Kaya & Kentel 2005; 2007). As a result, their views on the prospects of Turkey's EU membership point in several, sometimes conflicting, directions. The research also reveals that migrants of Turkish origin and their descendants can no longer be simply considered to constitute temporary migrant communities, living with the 'myth of return', and that nor are they passive victims of global capitalism, alienated by the system and swept up in a destiny dominated by the capitalist West. Rather, they have become permanent settlers, active-reflexive social agents and decision-makers dwelling in a transnational space between/beyond the boundaries of the countries of origin and of residence, a space that needs further inquiry (Kastoryano 2003; Kaya 2009a).

Alejandro Portes and colleagues (2001, p. 3) define 'transnational space' as a term coined in the migration studies literature to refer to 'the web of contacts created by immigrants and their home country counterparts who engage in a pattern of repeated back-and-forth movements across national borders in search of economic advantage and political voice'. Transnational spaces are not an entirely new phenomenon, since similar patterns can be traced back to the trading diasporas of the Middle Ages (Cohen 1997) and to the European immigration to the United States at the turn of the twentieth century (Foner 1997); however, certain features differentiate the present form of transnational spaces from their historical counterparts. First, the overwhelming speed of transportation technology and electronic communications facilitate easy, cheap, and expeditive contact across national borders. Secondly, a growing number of immigrants and their counterparts in their homeland generate intensive contact made through these technologies. Thirdly, there is a tendency for an increasing number of sending country governments to guide the transnational initiatives of their diasporas (Portes, Haller & Guarnizo 2001).

In the age of transnationalism, many migrants are no longer physically detached from their countries of origin due to poverty or lack of access to means of transportation and communication. For instance, today's German-Turks have little in common with the old 'guest-worker' stereotypes of the past; more than 60,000 Turkish businesses in Germany currently employ approximately 420,000 workers in 100 different fields of activity. Only 23 per cent of Germany's Turkish businesses are in the traditional strongholds of the restaurant and catering industries; 35 per cent are involved in retail/trade and 23 per cent in the services sector.[3]

There is, however, also the parallel phenomenon of the rising numbers of unemployed people who cannot be affiliated with any formal occupation, as an inevitable outcome of the global recession. Many of these people have the right to obtain unemployment benefit from the welfare system, but an increasing number cannot avail themselves of state aid because they have not been in a position to contribute to the welfare system due to their chronic unemployment status.[4] Those unemployed Euro-Turks, easily encountered in places like Kreuzberg (Berlin), Keupstrasse (Cologne), Villier le Bel (Paris), Schaerbeek (Brussels), Bos en Lommer (Amsterdam), are in general against Turkey's candidature for the EU (Kaya & Kentel 2005; 2007; Kaya 2009a). Despite the fact that the poverty and political/social exclusion of a group of Turkish-origin migrants and their descendants is still a common phenomenon in various urban settings, generally speaking, it is erroneous to view the Euro-Turks as passive, obedient, powerless and incompetent. Furthermore, the boundaries between Turkey and the Euro-Turks can no longer be strictly demarcated. Networks of cultural, political, economic and social transactions taking place between Euro-Turks and Turks have brought homeland and hostland together in a way that has mutually shaped the cultural political economy of both places. For instance, the ways in which German-Turks form civil society organisations have a strong impact in Turkey. Alevi organisations, some other religious organisations like the European Association of National Vision (Avrupa Milli Görüş Teşkilatı, AMGT), and some gay–lesbian organisations (Petzen 2004) have generated counterparts in Turkey, having a visible impact on the social and political life of the homeland.

Becoming Politically Engaged: Making an Impact

Why do migrants withdraw from 'host-society' political life? By what means do they politically mobilise themselves? Why do they mobilise themselves along ethno-cultural and religious lines? Patrick Ireland (1994; 2000) has drawn attention to the legal conditions and political institutions of receiving countries in mapping out the nature of immigrant mobilisation. He argues that 'certain immigrant communities have withdrawn voluntarily from host-society political life in the face of institutional indifference and hostility' (1994, p. 8). Ireland has formulated the 'institutional channelling theory' as an alternative to class and race/ethnicity theories, in order to understand immigrant political strategies. While class analysis claims that immigrants' class identity ultimately determines the nature of their political participation (Castles & Kosack 1985; Miles 1984), race/ethnicity theory argues that the immigrants' ethnic identity is of fundamental importance and that ethnic politics will endure, at least for the foreseeable future (Rex & Tomlinson 1979). However, institutional channelling theory maintains that legal and political institutions shape and limit migrants' choice possibilities. These include institutions such as political parties, parliament, religious organisations, citizenship, judicial bodies and humanitarian institutions that can weaken or strengthen the effects of differences in resources. They have a tendency to act as institutional gatekeepers, controlling access to the venues of political participation available to immigrants or other similar marginal groups. Accordingly, Ireland claims that the reason why migrant groups organise themselves politically along ethno-cultural and/or religious lines is primarily because 'host-society' institutions have nurtured ethnicity, culture and religion through their policies and practices.

In recent years, Euro-Turks have begun to raise their voices in complaint against the paternalistic approach of the Turkish state. They no longer want to be perceived as passive, obedient and in urgent need of support from the Turkish government, or, for that matter, as cash machines minting foreign currency for the homeland. As part of a constituency of 4.5 million Turks in the West, Euro-Turks, in general, wish to become more active in developing Turkish–EU relations and in helping Turkey adapt to the new EU regimes. In the meantime, they are also becoming politically engaged in their countries of residence. Many German-Turks (59 per cent) and even more French-Turks (74 per cent) and Belgian-Turks (90 per cent) either already have or are planning to apply for citizenship in their country of residence (Kaya & Kentel 2005; 2007). These high numbers indicate that Euro-Turks are seeking integration and political participation. The rise in such numbers may be explained by both structural and conjunctural changes in the countries of residence. On the one hand, the liberalisation of citizenship regimes, as in Germany since 2000 (Kaya 2009a), and granting migrant origin residents the right to vote in local elections, as in Belgium after 2000, seem to have had an impact on the political mobilisation of Euro-Turks (De Raedt 2004, p. 16). On the other hand, the conjunctural rise of Islamophobic tendencies in the countries of destination seems to have prompted Muslim origin migrants and their descendants to raise their oppositional voices in the legitimate political arena at local, national and European levels. For instance, the Belgian local elections of 8 October 2006 proved to be rather successful for Turkish origin migrants and their descendants, Belgian-Turkish candidates making their mark across the country. With an estimated 7,700,000 Belgian citizens going to the ballot boxes (the vote is obligatory in Belgium),

42 ethnically Turkish candidates were elected to local municipality and county councils. By comparison, in the 2000 elections, only 28 Belgian-Turks were voted into various positions (Kaya & Kentel 2007; Kaya 2009a).

When the members of excluded or marginalised groups are oppressed because of their membership and ethno-cultural difference, their standing in the world becomes a collective, not an individual, issue. Germany, the Netherlands and some parts of Belgium have lately become fertile grounds for migrants to become politically active at domestic, national and even European levels. One should not underestimate the fact that European Muslims have become even more politically mobile after the rise of Islamophobic tendencies in the West in the aftermath of 9/11. Local elections in both Belgium and the Netherlands in 2006 resulted in the political participation of thousands of Euro-Turks, both as candidates and as voters.

On the other hand, contrary to common belief, research on Euro-Turks (Kaya & Kentel 2005; 2007) reveals that there is a positive correlation between their membership to migrant associations and their political participation. The denser the network of associations of a particular ethnic group, the more political trust they have and the more they participate politically. Voluntary associations in Germany, Belgium and the Netherlands create social trust, leading to more political trust and higher political participation (Jacobs & Tillie 2004, p. 421); furthermore, the ethnic media also contribute to the political activities of the communities of migrant origin in the wider society.

Many Euro-Turks who are not EU citizens remain disenfranchised, particularly in Germany and France, where they do not have the right to vote in local elections (even though many are long-term residents). Young Euro-Turks, with a higher level of education and familiarity with political institutions, have greater confidence in their ability to effect change than the older generations. Euro-Turks are active in mainstream political parties. Parties based on ethnic and religious identity are not in a position to gain their support. Increasing numbers of Euro-Turks are standing for political office, but face additional scrutiny and questions because of their ethnic or religious background. Political parties are developing initiatives that aim to increase their appeal to and communication with voters from different minority groups. In Hamburg,

Table 1 Sampling Distribution

Germany	Number of respondents	France	Number of respondents	Belgium	Number of respondents
Niedersachsen–Bremen	82	Ille De France	222	Brussels	112
Nordrhein–Westfalen	381	Centre	41	Antwerp	58
Hessen	121	Rhone Alpes	150	East Flanders	66
Baden–Württemberg	233	Franche Comté	32	Limburg	76
Bayern	184	Alsace	109	Liege	48
Berlin	64	Loraine	46	Hainaut	40
Total	1065	Total	600	Total	400

for example, a German-Turkish forum was established by the Social Democratic Party of Germany (SPD) more than five years ago. Following this example, the Christian Democratic Union (CDU) set up a similar forum (DTF, Deutsch-Türkische Forum) prior to the 2008 Hamburg election to make the party more attractive to voters with a Turkish background. One of the striking examples of the increasing power of the Euro-Turks in political elections is the 2002 general election in Germany. In September 2002, the Turkish daily *Hürriyet* hailed German Chancellor Gerhard Schröder as the 'Chancellor of Kreuzberg', as a way of emphasising the importance of Turkish votes for Schröder's extraordinarily slim victory; indeed, the Chancellor won the 2002 election with a margin of 6,027 votes. There are around three million Turkish-origin inhabitants in Germany, around 700,000 of whom can vote in elections.

In the early stages of the migratory process, Euro-Turks used to be more oriented towards the conservative parties due to their scepticism towards the left-wing parties in Turkey (Kaya 2001). Table 2, however, shows that German-Turks have recently become more affiliated with left-wing political parties such as the SPD (27 per cent) and the Greens (8.5 per cent). The same trend is also visible among the French-Turks and Belgian-Turks. The swing to the left suggests that Euro-Turks are becoming more reflexive in the daily politics of their countries of settlement, rather than derivative of earlier political affiliations back home, in a way that may indicate that they are actually very well integrated. Some German-Turks are disillusioned by recent manoeuvres of parties like the CDU to use Turkey's candidature of the EU as a campaign instrument to attract right-wing nationalist votes.

Meanwhile, the official attempts of the Turkish government to form a Turkish lobby in EU countries have given rise to competition among groups with various political and ideological standpoints within the respective Turkish communities for the claim of being their sole representative. To illustrate, one could recall the rivalry between Türkische Gemeinde zu Berlin (TGB, Turkish Community of Berlin) and Türkische Bund in Berlin–Brandenburg (TBB, Turkish Association of Berlin–Brandenburg) in conducting lobbying activities in the 1990s (Kaya 2001). These ethnic organisations and/or persons that are in search of recognition by the countries of both destination and origin also tend to exhibit a more positive attitude to the homeland state, and to

Table 2 'Which political view are you affiliated with in your country of settlement?'

	Germany, per cent	France, per cent	Belgium, per cent
Liberal parties	3.3	1.5	8
Conservative parties	2.6	0.7	8
Social democratic parties	27.0	28.2	42
Green and environmentalist parties	8.5	5.2	5
Radical-right and nationalist parties	.8	1.7	0.5
Radical-left and communist parties	1.2	3.8	1
In equal distance to all	4.1	5.3	5
None of those above	52.3	53.7	31

work for the political and economic interests of the homeland. At the same time, such a transnational political network leads the Turkish minority organisations to play more on the axis of Turkishness as a result of the hegemonic ideology of the Turkish nation-state. For instance, Ergün Top – an advisor to Yves Leterme, the leader of the Belgian Christian-Democrats and Belgium's Prime Minister in 2008 and 2010 – considers himself to have had an impact on Leterme's position on the Armenian 'genocide' debate. According to Top, the 1915 killings of Armenians in Anatolia do not constitute a 'genocide', and both Leterme, and Johan Vande Lanotte, the leader of the Socialist Party, refused to call the massacre of the 1.5 million Armenians a 'genocide'. Leterme said that 'international experts disagree on the historical facts' while Vande Lanotte said that the Armenian issue is 'extremely sensitive'.[5] Here, it should be stated that, while the official lobbying activities attempt to contribute to the creation of a Turkish lobby, on the one hand, they deepen the ideological cleavages between the extremely heterogeneous Turkish communities, on the other.

Hyphenated Identities and European Citizenship: Underlining Democratic Elements

The interviewees were asked what the EU meant to them, and were given various items to comment on concerning the future of the EU, Turkey–EU relations, and the quality of the EU (Table 3). Belgian-Turks gave rather ambiguous answers due to the recent debates within the EU countries concerning the future of the EU as well as the Eurosceptic, nationalist and parochial tendencies in Turkey, which went through a tense electoral cycle in 2007 (Kaya 2009b). The research on Euro-Turks held among German-Turks and French-Turks in 2004 displayed a rather different picture concerning their positive perception of Turkey's membership of the EU. One could also draw a different lesson from here regarding the source of Euroscepticism among Euro-Turks: Turkish-origin migrants and their descendants are likely to generate a sceptical discourse about the EU when various politicians of the EU countries deploy negative discourse about Turkey's EU entry. Hence, the European perspective of Euro-Turks is substantially constrained by the views of European politicians.

Table 3 'What does the EU membership of Turkey mean to you?'

	Germany, per cent	France, per cent	Belgium, per cent
More human rights	69.3	78.8	53
More democracy	62.7	66.7	46
More job opportunities	61.4	83.0	57
Breakdown in moral and familial values	52.0	36.3	35
Exploitation	37.2	34.2	34
End of independence	23.9	24.0	29
Division of the country	23.8	22.5	24

On the other hand, there is a big discrepancy among the Euro-Turks in arguing that membership will cause moral breakdown in Turkey (52 per cent German-Turks, 36 per cent French-Turks and 35 per cent Belgian-Turks). Cross-tabulations show that those groups, who are concerned about the moral breakdown, are mainly those with lower socio-economic status. It is also remarkable that Euro-Turks have a rather clear perception of the EU. While around 48 per cent of German-Turks, 64 per cent of French-Turks and 42 per cent of Belgian-Turks regard the EU as an economic integration project, 21 per cent of German-Turks, 11 per cent of French-Turks and 22 per cent of Belgian-Turks regard it as a 'Christian club' (Table 4). These numbers may be put into better perspective when compared with those of Turks in Turkey, 40% of whom were inclined to regard the EU as a Christian club in 2003 (Yılmaz 2004). Similarly, according to the Transatlantic Trends 2005 survey held by the German Marshall Funds of the United States (2005), 42 per cent stated that the EU was a Christian club, where no place for Turkey could be found.

In their own eyes, Euro-Turks have gained strong merits in terms of developing a democratic political culture that highlights human rights, democratisation, participation and reflexivity, rule of law, rights, equality and trust, and they have adopted a *rights-specific* political culture rather than a *duty-specific* one, as exists in Turkey. The answers given to the individual questions comparing Germany, France and Belgium with Turkey indicate that these countries are considered by respondents to be much more democratic, liberal, egalitarian and disciplined than Turkey. Interestingly, Turkey was considered more favourable than the host nations when the interviewees were asked about mutual tolerance and moral values.

Germany seems to be a very good test case in order to understand the importance of a liberal citizenship regime in integrating migrant origin individuals who are ethno-culturally and religiously different from the majority society. It seems that German-Turks are less inclined than the others to want to be 'naturalised'. However, the new citizenship law that came into force in 2000 revealed that they are more receptive to German citizenship when the citizenship law is reasonably liberal and inclusionary; the latest statistics indicate that the number of naturalised German-Turks has tripled since

Table 4 'What does "European Union" mean to you?' (multi-response)

	Germany, per cent	France, per cent	Belgium, per cent
EU is an economic cooperation	48.2	63.7	42
EU is a common cultural policy	5.7	5.7	7
EU is a democracy project	6.5	6.3	6.5
EU is a political and military superpower	4.8	7.3	5.5
EU is a bureaucratic community detached from public	6.6	1.8	4
EU is a Christian club	21.3	11.2	22
EU is exploitation and imperialism	6.9	4.0	10

the year 2000. With the introduction of a more moderate citizenship law vis-à-vis migrants and their descendants, the total number of German-Turks opting for naturalisation went up to almost 1 million from 300,000 in the last ten years. These legal reforms allow descendants of Turkish migrants to acquire dual citizenship for a period of time and they offer German-born 'foreigners' the opportunity to go beyond their 'denizen' status[6] and enjoy political as well as civic, social, cultural and environmental rights. In other words, the new laws partially distance receiving societies from the hegemony of the once essentialised ethnic identities such as 'German', 'Turkish', 'Kurdish', 'Iranian'. They hold the potential to open the way for the construction of hyphenated civic identities and bridges such as 'German-Turk' 'German-Kurdish' and 'German-Iranian'. On the other hand, the fact that sizeable minorities are apparently unwilling to apply for German, French or Belgian citizenship does not necessarily mean that they are against integration, or that they are nationalist, conservative or Islamist. It is probable that some of them are satisfied with denizenship status, defined as giving migrants civil, social and cultural, but not political rights (Hammar 1990).

One should, however, also question whether EU citizenship provides the Euro-Turks with further advantages. The introduction of EU citizenship is a remarkable example where citizenship and nation have in some way been disentangled, but one of the most important challenges here is that a cardinal tie of citizenship to a predefined national identity is under dispute. Article 8e of the Maastricht Treaty refers to the 'dynamic' and 'evolutionary' nature of citizenship rights. The Maastricht Treaty inserted into the amended Treaty of Rome a new section ('Citizenship of the Union'), Article 8, which declares that 'every person holding the nationality of a Member State shall be a citizen of the Union'. Furthermore, it adds that 'Citizens of the Union shall also enjoy the rights conferred by this Treaty and shall be subject to the duties imposed thereby'. The term 'Community citizenship' actually became a debated issue after a letter from Felipe Gonzales, the former Spanish premier, to the Office of the European Council, proposing that citizenship should be made one of the three pillars of European political union (the other two being the European Monetary Union and a common foreign and security policy). Although the Maastricht Treaty's notion of European citizenship originates from the understanding of 'dynamic' and 'evolutionary' rights, which are not prescribed, and thus are subject to change, some of the earlier problems remain unresolved. These criticisms concentrate on the debates around the political inclusion of *extracommunitari* from non-EU countries, such as Turkish migrants in Germany.

Table 5 shows that Euro-Turks themselves confirm these hyphenated identities, with majorities in Germany, France and Belgium accepting *both* Turkish and European identities. Even so, sizeable minorities still define themselves solely as 'Turkish'. However, cross-tabulations reveal that young generations of Euro-Turks identify themselves more with hyphenated identities like 'Turkish-European' and/or 'European-Turkish'. For instance, compared with eight per cent of people born in Turkey identifying themselves as 'European-Turkish', 14 per cent, 23 per cent and 22 per cent of those born in Germany, France and Belgium, respectively, identify themselves as such (Table 6).

Table 5 'Which identification suits you most?'

	Germany, per cent	France, per cent	Belgium, per cent
Only Turkish	36.6	24.2	23
First Turkish and then European	49.9	58.5	55
First European and then Turkish	9.2	11.3	15
Only European	3.8	3.5	4
Others	0.5	2.5	3

Table 6 'Which identification suits you most?' (by birthplace)

	Turkey, per cent	Germany, per cent	France, per cent	Belgium, per cent
Only Turkish	39.9	24.3	13.8	17
First Turkish and then European	48.2	57.5	60.6	50
First European and then Turkish	7.7	13.5	22.9	22
Only European	3.5	4.5	0.9	6

However, one could have a better picture of the ways in which Euro-Turks identify themselves if they were compared with the autochthonous populations. It is often publicly stated in Germany, France and Belgium that 'Turkish migrants do not integrate, and they are very nationalist'. The figures in Table 7 display a very different picture of the ways in which autochthonous populations and Euro-Turks identify themselves. Euro-Turks have very similar inclinations to the autochthonous populations with respect to identifying themselves primarily with their nationality, or with Europeanness, or with both. It seems that French-Turks are less nationalist than the French, German-Turks are as nationalist as the Germans, and Euro-Turks are as European as the autochthonous populations (Table 7).

Table 7 European and National Identity

European and national identity	Only nationality	First nationality and then European	First European and then nationality	Only European
Germans*	38	45	10	4
German-Turks**	37	50	9	4
Turks in Turkey ***	54	30	5	4
French*	35	50	9	3
French-Turks**	24	59	11	4
Belgian-Turks*[a]	17	50	22	6

Sources: * Eurobarometer 2003; ** Euro-Turks research, 2004–07; *** Yılmaz (2004).
[a]Figures for Belgians do not exist, as the Eurobarometer surveys no longer include the particular question regarding the preference of European citizens to identify themselves with nationality or Europeanness.

Conclusion

Against this background, one could explicitly argue that Euro-Turks clearly constitute a bridge between Turkey and the EU. Euro-Turks no longer fit into the category of 'migrant'. They should be called 'transmigrants', able to travel very easily across national borders, in both real and symbolic terms, through the channels of global transportation and communication. Being simultaneously exposed to social, political, economic and cultural developments in the countries of origin and of residence, they have generated a rather different set of identities from the Turks residing in Turkey. Hence, their perspectives about the EU and Europeanness should be taken into consideration by the Turkish public. The way they perceive the EU, the way they have internalised certain values such as democracy, human rights, equality, welfare state, political participation and open society, irrespective of their class and ideological differences, indicates that they have acquired a more realist perception of the EU than that of the majority of Turks in Turkey. Euro-Turks have also generated a multicultural competence in transnational space, bringing together different cultural heritages deriving from their countries of origin and of settlement. Their experience in the European space has led them to attach a European element to their multiple identities in a way that contributes to the formation of hyphenated identities. They are now, for instance, identifying themselves as European-French-Muslim-Turk, combining different flavours of universalist, political, religious and ethnic affiliations. The number of Euro-Turks who are inclined to use a European element in their self-identification is rapidly increasing, especially among young generations born and raised in the European space. Educated and qualified younger generations also make it clear that they strongly support Turkey's membership of the EU. However, they are also very sensitive to the rise of Islamophobia and Turkophobia in the EU. This is why there has been a trend since the early 2000s among well-qualified young Euro-Turks to come to the major cities of Turkey, such as Istanbul, Izmir, Antalya and Ankara, to work. This is a new trend that needs further enquiry.

The relatively long span of time they have spent in their countries of residence seems to have made Euro-Turks more engaged in everyday politics in a way that leads them to use legitimate political grounds more than ever. The increasing number of elected representatives of Turkish origin at local, national and European level is a sign of this development. This is a relatively new phenomenon, which has also partly resulted from the escalation of Islamophobic and racist tendencies in the EU countries in the aftermath of the September 11 attacks. In response to these exclusionary political and social manoeuvres, Euro-Turks have become politically more reflexive than before. The rising political mobilisation of Euro-Turks has also made an impact on the ways in which domestic political figures of their countries of residence have perceived political, social, cultural and economic developments in Turkey. However, there is also evidential data indicating that official lobbying activities of the Turkish state among the Euro-Turks are likely to be more destructive than constructive in the way in which they make the Euro-Turks compete with each other on ideological grounds (Kaya and Kentel 2007).

Notes

[1] *Gurbetçi* refers to someone who lives in *gurbet* (diaspora). *Gurbet* is an Arabic word which derives from *garaba*, to go away, to depart, to be absent, to go to a foreign country, to emigrate, to be away from one's homeland, to live as a foreigner in another country.

[2] For detailed information on the research, see Kaya and Kentel (2005; 2007). The first part of the research was conducted with the financial assistance of the Open Society Institute in Istanbul, Istanbul Bilgi University Research Fund, Heinrich Böll Foundation in Istanbul and the Turkey Promotion Fund. The selection of the two countries, Germany and France, was chiefly because these countries were the driving forces of the EU, and that public opinion in these countries about Turkish origin migrants and their descendants was very much based on negative stereotypes. The second part was carried out with the financial assistance of the King Baudouin Foundation in Brussels. The research included in-depth interviews and focus-group discussions, as well as 1,065 structured interviews with 90 questions in German, and 600 hundred interviews in France. Structured interviews were followed by in-depth interviews and focus group discussions held by Ayhan Kaya and Ferhat Kentel in Germany, France and Belgium, and were conducted face to face in December 2003 and January 2004 by two local public-poll companies in Germany and France, with the involvement of Turkish-speaking university students who were fluent in either German or French. The interviews were conducted in one of the three languages (Turkish, German and French) depending upon the choice of the interviewees. The research team set up a quota-sampling system in both countries, paying particular attention to the density of the Turkish-origin population in the urban space and the rural space. The quota-sampling covered the variables of age, gender, occupation and region in order to get a representative picture of the Euro-Turks. The same research is now being undertaken in Belgium with a sample of 400 structured interviews as well as in-depth interviews and focus-group discussions (Kaya & Kentel 2007).

[3] For a detailed analysis of the economic potential of Turkish immigrant entrepreneurs in Germany, see 'The Economic Potential of Turks: Migrant Entrepreneurs in Germany', 2003, available online at: http://www.zft-online.de/english.phd (accessed 2 February 2010).

[4] The rate of unemployment was 24 per cent among the Belgian-Turks in 2007, 22 per cent among the German-Turks in 2004, 18 per cent among the Dutch-Turks in 2004 and seven per cent among the French-Turks in 2004. The figures for Germany, France and Belgium were derived from Kaya and Kentel (2005; 2007); and the unemployment figure for the Netherlands was taken from Centraal Bureau voor de Statistiek, Den Haag, 2005.

[5] See http://www.canadafreepress.com/2007/brussels070507.htm.

[6] 'Denizenship' status refers to all the layers of citizenship rights except political rights (Hammar 1990).

References

Barysch, K. (2007) 'What Europeans think about Turkey and why?', *Centre for European Reform Essays*, 25 September, available online at: http://www.cer.org.uk/pdf/essay_turkey_barysch_25sept07.pdf

BIBE (2009) *Ungenutzte Potenziale: Zur Lage der Integration in Deutschland* [Unused Potential: On the Situation of Integration in Germany], Berlin-Institut für Bevölkerung und Entwicklung, Berlin, available online at: http://www.berlin-institut.org/fileadmin/user_upload/Zuwander-ung/ Integration_RZ_online.pdf

Castles, S. & Kosack, G. (1985) *Immigrant Workers and Class Structure in Western Europe*, Oxford University Press, Oxford.

Cohen, R. (1997) *Global Diasporas: An Introduction*, University College London Press, London.

De Raedt, T. (2004) 'Muslims in Belgium: A case study of emerging identities', *Journal of Muslim Affairs*, vol. 24, no. 1, pp. 9–30.

Doty, R. L. (2000) 'Immigration and the politics of security', *Security Studies*, vol. 8, nos 2–3, pp. 71–93.

Foner, N. (1997) 'What's new about transnationalism? New York immigrants today and at the turn of the century', *Diaspora*, vol. 6, pp. 355–375.

German Marshall Funds of the United States (2005) 'Transatlantic trends—topline data 2005', available online at: www.transatlantictrends.org

Hammar, T. (1990) *Democracy and the Nation State*, Avebury, Aldershot.

Heitmeyer, W., Müller, J. & Schröder, H. (1997) *Verlockender Fundamentalismus* [Enticing Fundamentalism], Suhrkamp Verlag, Frankfurt am Main.

Huysmans, J. (2006) *The Politics of Insecurity*, Routledge, London.

Inda, J. X. (2006) *Targeting Immigrants: Government, Technology and Ethics*, Blackwell, Oxford.

Ireland, P. R. (1994) *The Policy Challenge of Ethnic Diversity: Immigrant Politics in France and Switzerland*, Harvard University Press, Cambridge, MA.

Ireland, P. R. (2000) 'Reaping what they sow: institutions and immigrant political participation in Western Europe', in *Challenging Immigration and Ethnic Relations Politics*, eds R. Koopmans & P. Statham, Oxford University Press, Oxford, pp. 233–282.

Jacobs, D & Tillie, J (2004) 'Introduction: social capital and political integration of migrants', *Journal of Ethnic and Migration Studies*, vol. 30, no. 3, pp. 419–427.

Kastoryano, R. (2003) 'Transnational participation and citizenship: immigrants in the European Union', National Europe Centre Paper, no. 64, University of Sydney, February.

Kaya, A. (2001) *Sicher in Kreuzberg: Constructing Diasporas, Turkish Hip-Hop Youth in Berlin*, Transcript Verlag, Bielefeld.

Kaya, A. (2009a) *Islam, Migration and Integration: The Age of Securitization*, Palgrave, London.

Kaya, A. (2009b) 'Turkey–EU relations: the impact of Islam on Europe', in *Yearbook of Muslims in Europe*, eds J. S. Nielsen, S. Akgönül, A. Alibašić, B. Maréchal & C. Moe, Brill, Leiden, pp. 377–402.

Kaya, A. & Kentel, F. (2005) *Euro-Turks. A Bridge or a Breach between Turkey and the European Union*, CEPS, Brussels.

Kaya, A. & Kentel, F. (2007) *Belgian-Turks. A Bridge or a Breach between Turkey and the European Union*, King Baudouin Foundation, Brussels.

Kelek, N. (2005) *Die fremde Braut* [The Foreign Bride], Kiepenheuer & Witsch, Cologne.

Kemming, J. K. & Sandikci, Ö. (2006) 'Turkey's EU accession as a question of nation brand image', *Place Branding and Public Diplomacy*, vol. 3, no. 1, pp. 31–41.

Landman, N. (1992) *Van mat tot minaret. De institutionalizering van de islam in de Nederland* [From Mat to Minaret: The Institutionalization of Islam in the Netherlands], VU Uitgeverij, Amsterdam.

Miles, R. (1984) *White Man's Country*, Pluto Press, London.

O'Malley, P. (2000) 'Risk, crime and prudentialism revisited', in *Crime, Risk and Justice: The Politics of Crime Control in Liberal Democracies*, eds K. Stenson & R. Sullivan, Willan, London, pp. 89–103.

Petzen, J. (2004) 'Home or homelike? Turkish queers manage space in Berlin', *Space and Culture*, vol. 7, no. 1, pp. 20–32.

Portes, A., Haller, W. & Guarnizo, L. E. (2001) 'Transnational entrepreneurs: the emergence and determinants of an alternative form of immigrant economic adaptation', Working Paper WPTC-01-05, Transnational Communities, available online at: http://www.transcomm.ox.ac.uk/workingpercent20papers/WPTC-01-05per cent20Portes.pdf

Rex, J. & Tomlinson, S. (1979) *Colonial Immigrants in a British City: A Class Analysis*, Routledge & Kegan Paul, London.

Yılmaz, H. (2004) *Euroscepticism in Turkey*, Open Society Institute, Istanbul.

Ayhan Kaya (PhD University of Warwick) is a professor in the Department of International Relations, Istanbul Bilgi University, and Director of the European Institute at the same university. He specialises in European modernities and identities, Euro-Turks in Germany, France, Belgium and the Netherlands, Circassian diaspora in Turkey, the construction and articulation of modern diasporic identities, and tolerance and multiculturalism. Among his books are *Islam, Migration and Integration: The Age of Securitization* (Palgrave, London, 2009), *Belgian-Turks* (King Baudouin Foundation, Brussels, 2008, co-written with F. Kentel) and *Euro-Turks: A Bridge or a Breach between Turkey and the EU* (CEPS, Brussels, 2005, co-written with F. Kentel). His forthcoming book is *Europeanization and Tolerance in Turkey* (Palgrave, London).

Index

Page numbers in **Bold** represent figures.
Page numbers in *Italics* represent tables.

Accession 15–19, 22–3, 43–53, 115–24; pre-accession process 184
Accession Partnership 18, 232, 234
Accession study 261–71; interviewee COM (8) 266; interviewee COM (10) 265; interviewee COM (11) 267; interviewee COM (14) 269; interviewee COM (15) 266; interviewee COM (18) 267; interviewee COM (19) 268; limited knowledge 264; limited narratives 264; logic of appropriateness 263
acquis communautaire 119, 178; National Programme for the Adoption of the *Acquis* (NPAA) 132, 231
Adalet ve Kalkınma Partisi *see* Justice and Development Party (AKP)
Adaman, F. 5, 101–11
adultery: AKP agenda 220–2
Akşit, S.: Şenyuva, Ö. and Gürleyen, I. 7, 187–97
Al-Omar, B. 72
Albert, M.: and Walter, J. 243
Alevi minority 143–53; complaints and demands 147–52; history 145–7; lifestyle and cultural divide 144; and the Republican regime 144, 145–7; settlement areas 145
Alliance of Civilizations 75
Amsterdam Treaty 17–18
Ankara Agreement: Ankara Protocol 205
Ankara State Security Court 232
Annan, K. 52
Annan Plan (2004) 205, 235
Antalya 149
Armenia 74
Association Agreement (1963) 161
Atalay, Interior Minister B. 136
Atatürk, M.K. 215
automotive industry 33
Avcı, G. 7, 201–11, 227–37; and Çarkoğlu, A. 1–9
Aydin-Düzgit, S.: and Süvarierol, S. 8, 261–71

Babacan, A. 67
Baç, M.M. 5
Bağiş, Minister E. 67
Bahçeli, D. 229–30, 232
Başer, General E. 135
Bayar, A.: *et al* 35, 37
Baykal, D. 78, 221
Berejikian, J.: and Dryzek, J.S. 244–5
Bilgili, N.Ç.: and Çarkoğlu, A. 143–53
Blair, Prime Minister T. 276
Brewin, C. 60–2
Brussels Bureau 179
Bruszt, L.: and Stark, D. 16
Bureau of European and Eurasian Affairs 48
bureaucracy (public) 58
B"yükant, Y. 131
Buzan, B. 279

Can, O. 58
Canan-Sokullu, E.☒. 8, 275–85
Carey, S. 279
Çarkoğlu, A. 164; and Avcı, G. 1–9; and Bilgili, N.Ç. 143–53; and Kentmen, Ç. 6, 157–258
Caucasus Stability and Cooperation Platform 75
Celep, Ö. 215–23
cem houses 149
Central and Eastern Europe (CEE) 4, 13, 203; democratisation 17
China 30, 32
Christian Democrats (CDU, Germany) 118
Christianisation (Turkish society) 219
Cichowski, R.A. 166
Civil Code 178–9
civil society 110, 173–85; EU affairs 176–84
Civil Society Development Programme (CSDP) 182–3
civil society organization (CSO) 175–6, 180; structures 182
civil-military relations 85–6, 87–92; reforms 97
civilian institutions 87

INDEX

Clinton, President W. 44
Cold War 45, 59, 78, 117
post-Cold War: activism 76; era 48
collective-action 105
post-communist transformations 15–19
conditionality 21–2, 134
Constitutional Amendments *61–2*, **62**
Constitutional Code 120
Constitutional Court 206, 209
Copenhagen Criteria 18, 57, 68, 89, 115
Copenhagen Summit (2002) 17, 49–51
corruption 101–11, 104–7, 105; Ethics for the
    Prevention of Corruption in Turkey 102;
    Group of States against Corruption
    (GRECO) 101–2; manifestations 107–9
Corruption Perceptions Index (2010) 102
Council of Europe 65
Council of the European Union 21, 50, 262;
    Council Regulations 21
Council of State (CoS) 151
Court of Auditors 88
credibility 5–6
Criminal and Civil Codes 117
Criminal Code 65, 119, 178–9
cultural fears 277
cultural incompatibility 246
Customs Union (CU) 4, 27–39, 49, 159; non-
    tariff barriers (NTBs) 29; preferential trade
    agreements (PTAs) 28; problems 34; tariff
    rates 28; and Turkish economy 29–38;
    welfare effects 34–8, *see also* exports;
    imports
Cyprus 52, 204–5, 235

Davutoğlu, A. 73, 123
De Santis, R. 35, 37
Defence Industry Support Fund (DISF) 95
democracy 90, 116–17
democracy criterion 23
democratic evolution 184
Democratic Left Party 122, 231
Democratic Society Party (DTP) 135, 190
democratisation 78; Europeanisation strategy
    202; issues 181–2; reforms 162
d'Estaing, President V.G. 276
Dimitrova, A. 4, 13–23
Directorate of Religious Affairs (DRA) 147–
    52
disability rights: UN convention 209
discourses: domestic 242; EU-Turkey
    relationship *252–6*; EU-Turkey relationship
    (in Germany) *247–51*; European
    Commission 261–71; human rights 116;
    multiculturalism 257; Q methodology 242,
    244–56
Diyarbakir Chamber of Commerce (DTO)
    137

Doğan Media Group 103, 207
domestic politics 76–80
donations: forced 108–9
Dryzek, J.S.: and Berejikian, J. 244–5

Ecevit, B. 129
economic crisis (2001) 32
Economic Development Foundation (IKV)
    177–8
economic integration 279
economy (Turkey) 28
electronics industry 33
elite 267; Turkish Elite Survey (2009) 188,
    190–6, **193**
elite perception 189
Enterprise Survey (2008) (World Bank) 103
epistemic community 268
Erdoğan, Prime Minister R.T. 77, 147, 201–
    11; Europe 208; normalisation 208
Ergenekon case135
Ethics for the Prevention of Corruption in
    Turkey 102
ethno-cultural difference 295
European Union (EU): conditionality 22;
    democracy 16; institutions 181; institutions
    (trust in) *192*; integration 6, 16, 177, 183,
    189, 228; negotiation process 178; opinions
    on *298*; progress reports 150; standards 3;
    studies 2; trade with (TurkStat) **31**;
    transformative power 135, *see also*
    Accession; Council of the European Union
EU membership 51–2, 188–90; discourse and
    P-Set 245–6; discourse and Q methodology
    244–56; discourses 241–58; elite opinion
    283; enlargement *256*; Eurobarometer
    survey **159**, 265; logit results *165*; mass
    preferences 161–4; opinions on *297*;
    referendum setting (1996–2010) **160**;
    statistics (descriptive) *281*; support 157–258
EU reform 5, 87, 236; demands 14; process
    86
EU-Turkey relations 3, 4, 38, 47, 47–8, 48–
    51, 123; Turkish parliamentarians 194–6;
    US policy 44–7
Euro-Asianism 201
Euro-Mediterranean Partnership 117
Euro-optimism 256
Euro-scepticism 163, 211, 228; Hard Euro-
    scepticism 217; parties 231
Euro-Turks 291–301, 294; research 292
Eurobarometer survey 158; EU membership
    159, 265
Europe 8, 268–70; bureaucracy 230; domestic
    adaption 14; economy 195; identity *300*;
    radical-right parties 220; sovereignty 263
European Commission 8, 20, 34, 118;
    Agenda (2000) 17, 20; discourses 261–71;

306

INDEX

enlargement 262; Negotiating Framework for Turkey 118, 132, 204, 269; *Progress Report on Turkey (2010)* 102; Regular Progress Reports 20, 21, 150; supranationalism 270; Turkey report 130
European Convention on Human Rights 122
European Council 262
European Court of Human Rights (ECHR) 129, 150, 206
European Elite Surveys (EES) 280
European enlargement 19–21, *256*, 279; Enlargement Commissioners 269
European fortress 263
European market 33
European Parliament (EP) 162; Women's Report 180
European Security and Defence Identity (ESDI) 233
European Women's Lobby 179
Europeanisation 72, 179; East 14, 19; literature 18; studies 202
Europeanness: cognitive-evaluative dimension 191; emotive dimension 191; projective dimension 191
Euroscepticism *see* Euro-scepticism
exports 31, 74; trade with EU (TurkStat) **31**, *see also* Customs Union (CU)
extremist parties 228

Fontaine, N. 50
foreign direct investment (FDI) 35
foreign policy 71–81, 73–6
France 118
Frankfurter Allgemeine Zeitung (newspaper) 243
free trade agreements (FTAs) 28

G20 74–5
Gençkaya, Ö.F.: and Özbudun, E. 63
Gendarmerie Intelligence and Counter-Terrorism Organisation (JİTEM) 92
gender policies 179
German-Turkish forum 296
German-Turks 294
Germany 8, 242–3, 276; Christian Democrats (CDU) 118; cultural incompatibility 246; EU-Turkey relationship discourse *247–51*; media 243, 244; multiculturalism 246; Social Democratic Party of Germany (SPD) 296
Global Integrity 103
globalisation 175
governance: hierarchical 19; internal 271
government: donations (forced) 108–9; interim military 1; parliamentary attitudes 187–97; Turkish Grand National Assembly (TGNA) 58, 187, 233

Grabbe, H. 19
Greece 89
Greek-Turkish tensions 52
Grossman, M. 46
Group of States against Corruption (GRECO) 101–2
Growth and Jobs Strategy 34
Guarnizo, L.E.: Haller, W.and Portes, A. 292
Gül, Foreign Minister A. 88, 135, 205–6
Gürleyen, I.: Akşit, S. and Şenyuva, Ö 7, 187–97
Gürsoy, Y. 5

Haller, W.: Guarnizo, L.E. and Portes, A. 292
Harrison, G.W.: *et al* 38
headscarf ban 206
Helsinki Summit 49, 60–2, 87, 177
High Council of Judges and Prosecutors 67, 121
High Election Commission 67
High Military Council (HMC) 90–1
Holbrooke, R. 46
human rights 5–6, 51, 115–24; discourse 116; European Convention on Human Rights 122; European Court of Human Rights (ECHR) 122, 129, 150, 206; UN disability convention 209; women's rights 119
Hürriyet (newspaper) 296

İçduygu, A. 173–85
ID card: religion section 152
identity 162, 264, 299; hyphenated identities 291–2, 297–300; opinion poll *300*; opinion poll (by birthplace) *300*; Turkish Elite Survey (2009) **193**
ideology: National View (Milli Görüş) 219
illiberal regimes 22
immigration 279
import control: non-tariff barriers (NTBs) 29
import liberalisation 32
import penetration (IP) 30
imports 30–1; preferential trade agreements (PTAs) 28; tariff rates 28; trade with EU (TurkStat) **31**, *see also* Customs Union (CU)
industry: automotive 33; large-scale enterprises (LSEs) 37; machinery and equipment 33; manufacturing 33; manufacturing exports **32**
informal sector 106
informality 108
İnönü, Prime Minister (later President) İ. 216
intergovernmental conferences 204
interim military government 1
internal governance 271
Internal Service Act 96
Internal Service Regulations 96

307

INDEX

international organizations 74–5
international relations literature 188
International Religious Freedom Report
  (2008) (US Department of State) 151
international security 77
International Social Survey Programme
  (ISSP) survey 158
Iran: Islamic Revolution (1979) 79
Iraq 74, 121
Ireland, P. 294
Islam 150; interpretations 151; values 219
Islam-Turkish synthesis 146
Islamic fundamentalism 284
Islamic Revolution (1979) Iran 79
Islamic threat 278
Islamist Welfare Party (RP) 63, 230–1
Islamophobic sentiments 277
Israel 73, 80
Israeli-Turkish relations 80
Istanbul Greater Metropolitan Municipality
  103

Justice and Development Party (AKP) 1–2,
  36, 72–3, 115, 201–11; adultery agenda
  220; EU agenda 220–2; EU commitment
  207–8; EU related reform 208–10; pro-
  Western identity 216; reform package 221–
  2

KADER 179
KAGİDER 179
Kalaycioğlu, E. 5, 57–69
Kantian conception 261
Kaya, A. 8, 291–301
Kemalist policies 163
Kemalist Republic 145
Kentmen, Ç.: and Çarkoğlu, A. 6, 157–258
Kirchner, E.J.: and Sperling, J. 277–8
Kirişci, K. 6, 127–39
Koenig, T.: et al 257
kulturkampf (cultural struggle) 59–67
Kurdish autonomy 121
Kurdish issue 127–39
Kurdish problem 130
Kurdish question 128–9, 129–32
Kurdistan Regional Government (KRG) 121,
  136
Kurdistan Workers' Party (PKK) 51, 127,
  205, 229
Kuşadasi municipal council 149

Landaburu, E. 20
languages: mother-tongue 131
Lanotte, J.V. 297
large-scale enterprises (LSEs) 37
Lausanne Treaty 234
Law of Associations 117

Law on the Court of Auditors 95
Law on Political Parties 120
liberal commentators 138
liberal regimes 22
liberalisation 206
Lipset, S.M.: and Rokkan, S. 218
Lisbon Treaty 194
Logoglu, Turkish Ambassador F. 50

Maastricht Treaty 217, 299
machinery and equipment industry 33
McLaren, L. 194; and Müftüler-Baç, M. 188,
  189
McLaren, L.M. 278, 279
manufacturing industry 33; exports
  (TurkStat) **32**
Mardin, ş. 218
Matonyte, I.: and Morkevicius, V. 277
Mayhew, A. 16
media: Doğan Media Group 103, 207;
  Frankfurter Allgemeine Zeitung
  (newspaper) 243; *Hürriyet* (newspaper) 296;
  Radio and Television Supreme Council
  (RTUK) 132; *Süddeutsche Zeitung*
  (newspaper) 243; Turkish Radio and
  Television Broadcasting Corporation
  (TRT) 132
Menard, S. 282
Merkel, Chancellor of Germany A. 118, 241
Middle East 79
migration 269, 269–70; immigration 279;
  transmigrants 301
the military 85–98; autonomous power 86;
  budget 95; General Staff 89; High Military
  Council (HMC) 90–1; interim government
  1; political autonomy indicators 93;
  political autonomy and reforms 92–6, *see
  also* civil-military relations
military junta 146
military takeover 146
military tribunals 67
Milliyetçi Hareket Partisi (MHP) *see*
  Nationalist Movement Party (MHP)
Mills, C.W. 277
Ministry of Defence 95
Ministry of Foreign Affairs 209
minorities 133
modernisation 207
modernity: Westernisation-based 174
Morkevicius, V.: and Matonyte, I. 277
Motherland Party 231
Movement for Europe 177
Müftüler-Baç, M. 71–81; and McLaren, L.
  188, 189
multiculturalism 246; discourse 257
Muslim identities 278, *see also* Sunni Islam
Muslim minority *see* Alevi minority

308

INDEX

Myers, R. 282

National Assembly 64
national discourses *see* discourses
national experts 263
national identity *see* identity
National Intelligence Organisation (MİT) 94
National Outlook 147
National Programme for the Adoption of the *Acquis* (NPAA) 132, 231
National Security Council (NSC) 87, 220
National Security Policy Document (NSPD) 91
national sovereignty 269
National View (Milli Görüş) ideology 219
nationalism 134, 265–8
nationalist ideology 162–3
Nationalist Movement Party (MHP) 118, 129, 166, 227–37; coalition government 231–4
Negotiating Framework for Turkey (European Commission) 118, 132, 204, 269
New World Order 175
The Nine Lights and Turkey (Türkeş) 229–31
Ninth Ordinary General Congress 235
non-tariff barriers (NTBs): import control 29
North Atlantic Treaty Organisation (NATO) 45, 75

Obama, President B. 44
Offe, C. 15
opinion polls *see* identity; public opinion
optimism 246
organisations: primordial 180; religion-based 180; Western-type 180
oriental mentality 267–8
otherness 243–4
Ottoman Empire 174–6, 266
Özal, Prime Minister T. 91
Özbudun, E. 120; and Gençkaya, Ö.F. 63
Özkök, Chief of Staff H. 89

Pamuk, O. 210
parliamentary attitudes 187–97
Partiya Karkeren Kurdistan (PKK) 92
Peace and Democracy (BDP) 137
Penal Code 210
Peres, S. 80
Petek, S.: Rüth, C. and Steunenberg, B. 8, 241–58
polarisation 134
political autonomy 85–98, 92, 92–6
political change 57–69
political clientelism 106
political elite 64, 188–90
political pragmatism 201–11
political reform 77

political violence 205
politics: domestic 76–80; shift 204–5
Population Registry 136
Portes, A.: Haller, W. and Guarnizo, L.E. 292
power: asymmetry 203; shift 79; soft 132–8; transformative 2
preferential trade agreements (PTAs) 28
Presidency Conclusions (2004) 177
pride 246, 268
primordial organisations 180
productivity 31–4; and growth 32, 37
Progress Report on Turkey (2010) (European Commission) 102
Protocol on Cooperation for Security and Public Order (EMASYA) 90
public bureaucracy 58
public opinion 160, 276, 284; identity *300*; identity (by birthplace) *300*, *see also* identity

Radio and Television Supreme Council (RTUK) 132
Rasmussen, A.F. 50
reciprocity 105, 108
referendum: EU Membership support (1996–2010) **160**
reforms: and political autonomy of the military 92–6
regimes: illiberal 22
Regular Progress Reports: European Commission 20–1
religion: *cem* houses 149; Directorate of Religious Affairs (DRA) 147–52; ID cards 152
religion-based organisations 180
religious education 150
religious foundations: non-Muslim 233
religious identity 163
Republican Farmers Nation Party 229
Republican People's Party (CHP) 117–18, 135; *Ergenekon* case 206; EU membership 215–23
Rokkan, S.: and Lipset, S.M. 218
Roux, C.: and Verzichelli, L. 193–4
Russia: USSR 76
Rustow, D. 116
Rüth, C.: Steunenberg, B. and Petek, S. 8, 241–58

Sarkozy, President N. 48, 119, 134
Sayarı, S. 4, 43–53
Schegloff, E.A. 264
Schimmelfennig, F. 17
Schoen, H.: *et al* 257
Schröder, Chancellor of Germany G. 129, 296

INDEX

Secretariat General for EU Affairs (EUSG) 209
secularist state 146
security: international 77
Şenyuva, Ö.: Gürleyen, I. and Akşit, S. 7, 187–97
September 11th attacks 301
Sezer, President A.N. 88, 209
Single European Act (1986) 217
Sixth Administrative Court 148
Slovakia 17
social class: analysis 294
social conservatism 219
Social Democratic Party of Germany (SPD) 296
sociotropic models 161
soft power 132–8
Southeastern Anatolia Project (GAP) 128
sovereignty: national 269
Sperling, J.: and Kirchner, E.J. 277–8
Stark, D.: and Bruszt, L. 16
State Security Courts 220
state sovereignty 266
state-society relationship 110
Steunenberg, B.: Petek, S.: and Rüth, C. 8, 241–58
Stoiber, E. 276
Süddeutsche Zeitung (newspaper) 243
Sunni Islam 148; electoral tradition 152; traditions 145
supranational norms 263, 271
supranationalism 262–3
Supreme Board of Prosecutors and Judges 210
Süvarierol, S.: and Aydin-Düzgit, S. 8, 261–71
symbolic threats 279
Szczerbiak, A.: and Taggart, P. 217

Taggart, P.: and Szczerbiak, A. 217
tariff rates 28, see also Customs Union (CU); imports
Taşdelen municipality 148
tax 29–30
Taymaz, E.: et al 37; and Yılmaz, K. 32
terrorism: anti-terrorism 235; September 11th attacks 301
threat perception 275–85, 277–80; immigrants 279–80; Islamophobia 278–9
threats (symbolic) 279
Top, E. 297
trade: with EU (TurkStat) 31; free trade agreements (FTAs) 28
trade agreements: North-South 30; preferential trade agreements (PTAs) 28
Transatlantic Trends Surveys (TTS) 280
transformative power 2

transmigrants 301
transnational space 292–3
transnationalism 293
True Path Party 216
Turcoenthusiasm 282
Turcoscepticism 275–85, 282
Türkeş, A.: The Nine Lights and Turkey 229–31
Turkish diaspora 8, 292
Turkish Economic and Social Studies Foundation (TEPAV) 102
Turkish Elite Survey (2009) 188, 190–6; identity **193**
Turkish Grand National Assembly (TGNA) 58, 187, 233
Turkish lira (TL) 29
Turkish Radio and Television Broadcasting Corporation (TRT) 132
Turkish Straits 44–5

Uğur, M. 36, 202–3
Unions of Soviet Socialist Republics (USSR) 76
United Nations (UN): Conventions on the Rights of Persons with Disabilities 209; Interim Force in Lebanon (UNIFIL) 75; Security Council 53, 75
United States of America (USA) 43–53, 298; foreign policy 46; policy-makers 50; US-Turkish alliance 45
United States Congress 45
universal values 183
US Department of State: International Religious Freedom Report (2008) 151
utilitarian expectations hypothesis 161

Vachudová, M.A. 22
velvet triangles 179
Venice Commission 120
Venice Criteria 122
Verzichelli, L.: and Roux, C. 193–4

Walter, J.: and Albert, M. 243
welfare effects: Customs Union (CU) 34–8
Western alliance 77
anti-Western attitude 235
Western world 278
Westernisation 163, 219
Westernisation-based modernity 174
Women's Centre (KAMER) 138
women's movement 178
women's rights 119, see also human rights
World Bank: Enterprise Survey (2008) 103
World Economic Forum 75

Yılmaz, K. 4, 27–39; and Taymaz, E. 32

Zahariadis, Y. 35–6